A Bri

Diego Olstein

A Brief History of Now

The Past and Present of Global Power

Diego Olstein
Department of History
University of Pittsburgh
Pittsburgh, PA, USA

ISBN 978-3-030-82419-8   ISBN 978-3-030-82420-4   (eBook)
https://doi.org/10.1007/978-3-030-82420-4

This Palgrave Macmillan imprint is published by the registered company Springer Nature Switzerland AG
The registered company address is: Gewerbestrasse 11, 6330 Cham, Switzerland

Para Irit, con amor y gratitud por las décadas pasadas y venideras

לעירית, באהבה ובתודה על העשורים שמאחורינו ולפנינו

ACKNOWLEDGMENTS

To Perry Anderson, William McNeill, Charles Tilly, and Immanuel Wallerstein who I never met but from whom I tried to learn to think big and to Yuval Harari who unintendedly showed me how to try to write (more) accessible.

To my colleagues and students at the University of Pittsburgh and around the world for their intellectual stimulation.

Heartfelt thanks to Raja Adal, Shigeru Akita, Reid Andrews, Yoshiko Ashiwa, Michel Gobat, Mariko Iijima, Miyuki Kobayashi, Jonathan Lewis, Malgorzata Markoff, Scott Morgenstein, Bo Young Park, Stanley Payne, James Pickett, Marcus Rediker, Boram Shin, Tornike Sreseli, John Tortorice, David Wank, Elise Yoder, and Moshe Zimmerman for their dedication and assistance.

Special thanks to Benjamin Kedar, Ezequiel Lein, John Markoff, and Gregor Thum for their friendship and engagement with my work.

Loving thanks to my Ejdem, Olstein, Zaselsky, and Lerner families for their warmth and support and to my beloved family—Irit Lerner-Olstein, Racheli, Ariel, and Maya Holstein—for the joy of our life together.

Praise for *A Brief History of Now*

"This fast-paced book identifies five large themes to guide our thinking about 200 years of human history: world hegemony, economic globalization, political regimes, socioeconomic inequality and technological breakthroughs. Only a master juggler like Diego Olstein can keep these five balls in the air simultaneously, and he does so by dexterously recognizing large patterns, examining their interactions and embedding his analysis in a dynamic account of systemic historical change. In taking us to remote times and to the far-flung corners of the world, this capacious historical sociology helps us come to terms with how we got to where we are—and to find ways to productively think about our future. If you want to understand why history is essential to mastering the present—and the future—read this book."

—Sven Beckert, *Laird Bell Professor of History, Harvard University, USA, and author of* Empire of Cotton

"Instead of the repeated wolf-cries of minatory futurologists, Diego Olstein gives us a forward-looking history of globalization: evidence from the past with which to contemplate a post-American century, poised between unpromising "global regimes," and threatened by what the author calls "demotarianism." The narrative lines are sweeping, the analysis bold, the writing intimate, and the message challenging. Diego

Olstein is the sort of historian – increasingly rare nowadays – who can recapture the attention of a wider public."

—Felipe Fernández Armesto, *William P. Reynolds Professor of History, University of Notre Dame, USA, and author of* The World: A History

"We are living in a time of mounting political instabilities, environmental disasters, economic uncertainties and other deep crises, so this book comes exactly at the right moment. Written with deep concern for our current world and its future contours, it offers fascinating global historical perspectives of various important problems including the rise and fall of hegemonic powers, the trajectories of international trade, or the underpinnings of democracy. Diego Olstein's masterpiece is based on deep historical reflections, daring global interpretations, and a profound knowledge of various academic fields. Written in an engaging, lucid style, this work is not only relevant to academic experts but also of great interest to a general audience. In fact, it is a must-read for anyone concerned about our current global condition and the historical forces shaping it."

—Dominic Sachsenmaier, *Georg-August-Universität Göttingen, Germany, and author of* Global Perspectives on Global History

"Diego Olstein's *A Brief History of Now* encapsulates a comprehensive timeline of historical phenomena within a space without borders, by situating *Now* against the backdrop of the pandemic. The author interweaves and converges the synergy of global economies, hegemonies or the lack of it, democracy in chaos, and technology that impacts climate change; It is basically about the 'power of now' that teases out newer and crucial questions in global history."

—Meeta Deka, *Professor and Former Head, Department of History, Gauhati University, India, and author of* Women's Agency and Social Change: Assam and Beyond

"This is a really challenging history of the rise and oscillation of globalization in modern world history, with a persuasive chronology and imaginative take on causation. One of the many assets is a reinterpretation of the early 20th century in ways that go beyond conventional narratives. The book's final segment places current developments in context both of the larger periodization and of analogies with the past, in ways that will stimulate productive if anxious debate."

—Peter N. Stearns, *George Mason University, USA, and author of* The Industrial Revolution in World History

"Olstein's *A Brief History of Now* is an invaluable and timely book that provides a sweeping reinterpretation of our present in an accessible narrative for a broad audience and historians alike. While the proliferation of fragmented accounts on the human recent past have reminded us of our cultural diversity, Olstein's book offers us a possible framework to put all the pieces together in a vivid explanation on the origins of the world around us. The book displays the evolution of ideas on society originated in the North Atlantic and the conditions and agencies that forge their permanency and transformation as essential parts of the historical process."

—Alexandre Moreli, *Universidade de São Paulo, Brazil, and editor of* Rethinking Power in Global and Transnational History

"Given the multitude of events that make up the past 150 years, and the avalanche of books that historians have produced to explain them, it's easy to miss the forest for the trees. But not here: in this witty, sometimes idiosyncratic, fast-paced account, the contours of the major changes of the pre-history of the present become very visible. Diego Olstein draws clear lines into the confusing sand of developments that will help orient students and sometimes surprise experts: a stimulating guide to the history of our globalized age!"

—Sebastian Conrad, *Freie Universität Berlin, Germany, and author of* What is Global History?

"This book clearly illuminates the 'hegemonic-globalization paradox' and change of world hegemony from the Pax Britannica to the Pax Americana, not only in political-economy but also in popular culture and sports. It also covers the impacts of the current ICT Revolution and environmental issues for our daily life. The author gives us a stimulating 'road map' for identifying NOW from a longer historical perspective, and presents a fascinating dialogue between the Past, the Present and the Future."

—Shigeru Akita, *Professor of Global History, Department of World History, Graduate School of Letters, Osaka University, Japan, and editor of* American Empire in Global History

"Olstein's narrative is witty, compelling, and thought-provoking. It is global history at its best and appeals to readers interested in history, IR, and current affairs. It is a must-read for all of us who seek to make sense of an ever more complex world. This is a provocative, innovative, and rich history with profound theoretical implications."

—Marc Frey, *Universität der Bundeswehr München, Germany, and editor of* International Organizations and Development 1945–1990

"The present meets its last 170 years of history in this innovative and timely global history by Olstein. Succinctly untangled into recurrent patterns and clearly visualized in waves, *A Brief History of Now* provides sophisticated yet easily comprehensible frameworks to discern the past and its connections to the seemingly unconnected developments of today. This is likely to become an essential text in the classrooms, enriching courses on global history and history of globalization, as well as adding value for anyone interested in understanding the historical roots and developments that brought us to the global now."

—Taejin Hwang, *Kyungpook National University, South Korea, and author of* Cold War Brotherhood Contested

"In a tour de force of macrohistory and historical sociology, *A Brief History of Now* offers an inspiring new account of post-1850 global history. Combining the big picture with careful attention to specific historical trajectories and the numerous feedback loops between them, the book suggests a new chronology of modernity and a novel conceptual toolbox. This book helps to make sense of our present world—a world beyond neoliberalism."

—Jürgen Osterhammel, *Professor Emeritus, Universität Konstanz, Germany, and author of* The Transformation of the World: A Global History of the Nineteenth Century

"Diego Olstein's insightful study draws out the most important threads in the long-term economic, political, and technological processes that have made our world what it is today, and then weaves these together in a clearly written analysis. *A Brief History of Now* explores both patterns and bobbles in the fabric of world history from the Industrial Revolution to the COVID pandemic, with a truly global scope that takes readers from soccer stadiums in Argentina to the streets of Cairo during the Arab Spring."

—Merry Wisner-Hanks, *Distinguished Professor Emerita, University of Wisconsin-Milwaukee, USA, and Editor-in-Chief*, Cambridge History of the World

CONTENTS

LIST OF ILLUSTRATIONS

List of Tables

CHAPTER 1

Introduction: Setting the Frame

Now

In December 2019, the coronavirus (COVID-19) disease was identified in the Chinese city of Wuhan. Soon, the World Health Organization (WHO) declared this outbreak to be a public health emergency of international concern. On March 11, 2020, the concern was officially declared by the WHO to be a pandemic. Within a year, there were around 126 million global cases and 2,762,000 global deaths. This open-ended outbreak continues to trigger multiple and varied consequences in all spheres of social life seemingly dwarfing, sidelining, freezing, or postponing the most pressing issues on the global agenda.

It was merely a few days after the outbreak of COVID-19 in Wuhan, on January 22, 2020, that Antonio Guterres, United Nations Secretary-General, listed the most urgent problems that humankind is facing. His list includes global geostrategic tensions, global warming, social and political tensions resulting from economic globalization's inequalities, and technological disruptions. Now, as we seem to start reemerging from the global pandemic crisis, these problematic conditions are regaining prominence. These major concerns are the result of six major global trends that have been with us for the last few years or decades. They are the growing challenges to the interconnected global economy; the uncertain prospects of the U.S. world hegemony; the displacement of liberal democracy by authoritarianism and illiberal democracy; the widening of socioeconomic

D. Olstein, *A Brief History of Now*, https://doi.org/10.1007/978-3-030-82420-4_1

1

inequality; the transformative powers unleashed by major technological breakthroughs; and climate change. Each one of these processes and the synergies between them are rapidly creating a very different world in front of our very eyes as we struggle to grapple with these fast, radical, and multifaceted transformations on top of which a pandemic outbreak was added.

Since mid-2018 and before the coronavirus pandemic, the global economy was significantly damaged by the trade war between the two largest economies, the United States and China. The economic clashes between these two giants took a toll not only on them but also on their trade partners. One of those affected economies was that of Japan, the third-largest economy, while it was simultaneously facing a trade dispute with South Korea, the eleventh-largest economy. When South Korea's Supreme Court ruled, in October 2018, that Korean victims of forced labor can demand compensation from Japanese companies, the Japanese government revoked South Korea's status as preferred trade partner. A trade war between these two largest East Asian economies ensued. In Europe, many countries—including those whose economies globally rank fourth (Germany), sixth (United Kingdom), seventh (France), and eighth (Italy), are embattled in their own economic conflicts in the context of the Brexit, as the United Kingdom has since 2017 been gearing up to extricate itself from the European Union, a move finally materialized in 2021.

These multiple conflicts have been undermining economic global-ization as it has been crystallizing since the end of the Cold War (1991). As in any crisis there are, of course, some specific beneficiaries from these multiple conflicts in economic relations, such as the Viet-namese, Taiwanese, Mexican, and Chilean economies. However, overall, the mounting economic disputes have detrimental effects for global economic growth, investment, consumption, and stability as the markets became more volatile. More fundamentally, these simultaneous economic disputes, which result in barriers, tariffs, retaliatory measures, tit for tat downward spirals, and revisions of or withdrawals from existing trading partnerships, are calling into question the prospects of economic global-ization. Is it possible for our global economy to become dis-integrated?

With a quarter of global wealth, close to a third of the 2,000 most profitable companies and world innovation, and half of the top 100 universities in the world, among many other strengths, attributes, and advantages, the United States continues to be the leading world power as it has been since, at least, the end of the Second World War. And yet, the prospects of U.S. world hegemony right now appear uncertain. A decline in American world power is widely perceived in multiple regions and scenarios around the world. Russia has reasserted its presence first in contiguous territories of Georgia and the Ukraine, and then beyond, in the Middle East. The meddling in the U.S. presidential election in 2016 has further threatened the ensuing of a new Cold War era.

And Russia is not charging alone. China has become bolder in its immediate geographies, tensing its military muscles offshore in the South China Sea, enhancing its grasp over Hong Kong, and subduing Muslim minorities in its Western end. Moreover, China's outreach beyond its perimeter is far more ambitious than that of Russia, as it expands its presence throughout Eurasia, Africa, and Latin America via investments and entrepreneurship. At the same time, Chinese firms are developing and marketing cutting-edge technologies able to outcompete U.S. firms even within the markets of U.S. strategic allies, as shown by Huawei's temporary success in deploying the 5G network in Great Britain.

For their part, the Western European allies have been cold-shouldering the United States not only in economic but also in geopolitical and strategic matters. Since the American invasion of Iraq in 2003, the relationship between the United States and its continental European allies has been growing more distant and continued distancing around disputes on the funding of and vision for North Atlantic Treaty Organization (NATO). Similar disputes on military funding and strategy are occurring between the United States and its closest East Asian partners, Japan and South Korea. With disagreements mounting among close allies, it is hardly surprising that there are multiple individual states, such as Venezuela, Iran, Pakistan, and North Korea, that do not abide by the desires of the United States while others that try, such as Afghanistan, Mali, and Nigeria, cannot.

As the stance of the United States in global affairs deteriorates, is it possible that it will end up losing its world hegemony? And to whom—China? To a coalition of China and Russia followed by many states around the globe that follow their lead? Or, rather, is the type of world order in which a single world hegemon sits atop of the international system about to be replaced altogether by an alternative model?

These recent ongoing challenges to the international system have been evolving in tandem with prominent domestic political transformations.

During the last decade liberal democracy has been widely displaced as the leading type of political regime by authoritarianism, illiberal democracy, and populism in a growing number of states around the world. Russia and China, the two most powerful challengers to the U.S. world hegemony, are ruled by authoritarian regimes. And so are other challengers of a lower caliber such as Venezuela, North Korea, and Iran. However, even long-time U.S. allies still formally ruled by democratic regimes foster nationalistic and authoritarian values and agendas rather than liberal ones. Such illiberal democracies, exemplified by the leaderships of Matteo Salvini in Italy, Victor Orbán in Hungary, Recep Tayyip Erdoğan in Turkey, Narendra Modi in India, Rodrigo Duterte in the Philippines, and Jair Bolsenaro in Brazil, to name just a visible few, have changed the course of the lasting global trend of transition toward democratic regimes that began during the 1970s and was accelerated by the end of the Cold War. Now, even in the most deeply rooted democratic regimes of Western Europe, xenophobic and authoritarian movements and parties are making ever-larger inroads into the public sphere and governing institutions. Democracy clearly has been in a fast retreat since 2011. At this pace, will democratic regimes become a rarity in the global political landscape?

Grassroots support for such nationalist, xenophobic, and authoritarian movements, parties, and governments can be partially understood as a reaction to the ways in which economic globalization impinges on large parts of each nation's society. The opening of world markets and ensuing exposure to foreign competition has triggered the closing, outsourcing, or offshoring of both manufacturing and services local companies and manufacturing as well as the arrival of the competing workforce of immigrants and refugees at home. The resulting unemployment, underemployment, or fragile employment has been compounded by the shrinking of welfare state support. As a result, the economic and social standing of working classes in most advanced economies, such as those of the OECD members, has been declining. Conversely, the beneficiaries of globalization in the developed world have seen their revenues increased and their consumption costs reduced as a result of these very same steps: the opening of the world markets and the shrinking of welfare state support. The first allowed for work and investment opportunities abroad as well as the flow of cheaper goods and commodities; the second came in tandem with tax cuts. At the same time, the suppliers for that consumption in the developing world, into which companies were offshored and investments made—countries such as China, India, Indonesia, and Vietnam—have benefited too, boosting the emergence of a growing middle class there. This simultaneous occurrence of downward socioeconomic mobility for some and upward socioeconomic mobility for others has generated a wider gap of socioeconomic inequalities *within* societies while at the same time reducing socioeconomic gaps *between* some societies. Even so, the nominal per capita gross domestic product (GDP) gap between the first and second largest global economies of the United States and China, despite the tremendous economic growth of China for four decades in a row, is still almost 700%! Is it possible, then, to bridge the inequality gap between societies? And what about the socioeconomic inequalities within societies that have been soaring during this same time? The gap between the highest 1% bracket of household income in the United States is also almost 700% the median household income![1]

While the impact of globalization accounts to some extent for the growth of socioeconomic inequalities within societies, this is not the entire story. Job losses and job precariousness is due not only to offshoring but also to automation, i.e., the automatic operation of equipment made by control systems. The technologies that displace or reduce human intervention from work processes are rooted in the artificial intelligence revolution. Although research and development in this direction have been underway for some 70 years, it is in the last two decades that the growth of computing power, the huge amounts of ever-growing collected data, and a better theoretical understanding of computer and brain sciences have increasingly provided computers with the core human cognitive functions of problem-solving and learning. These functions are deployed by carefully programming sets of very precise instructions known as algorithms. Algorithms are capable not only of performing assigned tasks but also of learning from data, developing new strategies to respond to processed data, and even writing other algorithms. As algorithms are now rapidly permeating all fields of human activity, what economic, social, and political repercussions can be expected? How will globalization, hegemony, democracy, and inequality be impacted? And what about climate change?

Scientists alert, governments discuss, social movements demonstrate, and the younger go on strikes. Still, global warming, extreme climate events, and environmental biodegradation continue soaring without much of a response. And this despite the fact that scientists tell us we have entered a new geological era, an era in which human activity is transforming the face of the planet and its atmosphere. This is the Human Epoch or Anthropocene. As the very ecosystem in which we live—that sustains globalization, hegemony, democracy, inequality, and artificial intelligence—is at risk from the polluting emissions made by human activities, this concern is the most pressing and fundamental. But can it be tackled amidst the undermining of economic globalization and the collaborations that go with it? Can it be done despite the lack of leadership by a declining world hegemon that has walked out from the major international agreement on the matter? Can it be done by illiberal regimes? And while the widening of domestic inequality and the narrowing of international inequality continue to boost consumerism?

All these six current major concerns have long trajectories. Fluctuations in economic globalization, the rise and fall of world hegemons, the upswelling and residing waves of democracy, the broadening and narrowing of socioeconomic gaps, increasingly fast-paced technological innovation, and human-made climate change have been with us in ways directly traceable to the present at least since the global industrial economy coalesced around the mid-nineteenth century. *A Brief History of Now* harnesses a global history vantage point bringing economic globalization, world hegemony, and political regimes into the perspective and proportions provided by the wider temporal context while tangentially referring to socioeconomic inequality, technological innovation, and climate change. Long-lasting patterns in the evolution of each of these processes and their interactions can be visualized in the sweep of almost two centuries. We will start by defining each of the six processes and providing a bird's-eye view before delving in the trajectories that have been making our world.

ECONOMIC GLOBALIZATION

Economic globalization is the process that creates an economy working on a global scale through flows of trade, capital, and labor. These flows are enabled by a combination of policies and technologies. For globalization to happen the polities in command of the largest centers of production, services, and consumption around the world need to enact liberal policies that allow the free crossing of borders. At the same time, information, communication, and transportation infrastructures and networks with global reach are necessary in order to bring these centers into constant and lasting interaction. As economic globalization unfolds, transnational and transregional economic interactions grow larger relative to the share of domestic, national, and regional interactions. Concomitantly, this shift transforms domestic economies by scaling up the production of goods and services for export and scaling down those goods and services that can be obtained more cheaply via import. The funding and labor for these shifts of scale can also be obtained through these same transnational and transregional economic interactions. In this way, economic globalization raises the share of all world production, finance, and labor that crosses international boundaries.[2]

The adoption of neoliberal policies by most nation-states worldwide, since the 1990s, combined with the unprecedented speed and volume of information, communication, and transportation enabled by new technologies in telecommunications, computing and internet, air travel, and containerization have been fostering economic globalization as never before. Yet our contemporary economic globalization, prominent since the last decade of the twentieth century, has its precedent during the nineteenth century, even though if with a different pace and volume. Back then, too, the technological breakthroughs made by the telegraph, the steamship, and the railroads, as well as infrastructure projects such as the Suez and Panama Canals, facilitated the flow of information, communication, and transportation in unprecedented ways. Combined with liberal policies, these innovations resulted in flows of trade, capital, and labor on a global scale. So much so, that the share of foreign assets as a percentage of the world GDP reached close to 20% by 1910, while the ratio of exports to world GDP reached approximately 10% by 1913, on the eve of the outbreak of the First World War (1914–1918) that signaled the beginning of the withdrawal from that nineteenth-century economic globalization.

Such proportions of foreign investment and global trade were to be reached again by the 1990s, when globalization became a leading buzzword in mass media and public awareness as if we had landed in an entirely new phenomenon: globalization! Rather, a new wave of an existing phenomenon has been rising once again after a very long hiatus running throughout the catastrophes of the twentieth century: The First, Second, and Cold Wars. So long and deep was the valley of global economic disintegration amidst two peaks of economic globalization—the first rising around 1850, the second around 1990—that by the time the second peak was emerging, memories from the first peak seemed to be entirely forgotten. The historical landscape of globalization, then, looks like a U-shape with highs rising from the 1850s to 1914 and from the 1990s onward. It carries a cautionary tale: globalization comes, globalization can go. What additional insights can the first wave shed on the second?[3]

World Hegemony

World hegemony is the privileged position enjoyed by the most powerful state in the world that allows it to influence or force other polities and set the rules, norms, and values for the international system. That supreme power is achieved by combining economic affluence with political leadership and military might as well as ideological inspiration and cultural appeal. The world hegemon represents for most of the other polities the desirable horizon to move toward, a glimpse into what the future will look like. As such, the world hegemon becomes the aspirational goal, even the dream for states and societies around world. Based on the entwinement of these attributes, the world hegemon becomes the leading role model that other states try to imitate and feel compelled to collaborate with. Alternatively, for those states and societies unwilling or reluctant to yield to the spell of the world hegemon, the choice is confrontation, be it overt or connived; be it economic, political, military, ideological, and/or cultural; or a combination thereof.

Since the mid-nineteenth century there have been two times in which one state achieved world hegemony and multiple occurrences of hegemonic contestation. Beginning in 1815, Great Britain was consolidating its world hegemony after defeating Napoleonic France. By 1851, when London overwhelmed its visitors with the Great Exhibition of the Works of Industry of All Nations, the British world hegemony was full-fledged. Still, this world hegemony was contested by Britain's former principal ally in the anti-Napoleonic coalition: the Russian Empire. Since 1830, the mightiest maritime empire and the largest continental empire were at odds in a protracted conflict known as the "Great Game;" at stake was nothing less than the control of Asia. In 1907, in view of the rise and empowerment of the German Empire, the former allies moved back into collaboration mode, aiming to outflank the newer threatening power in the heart of Europe. By then, however, a new and decisive hegemonic contestation was in the making. In the sequence of the First and Second World Wars, the defeated Kaiser Reich and Third Reich, respectively, brought the British world hegemony to a close.

The end of the Second World War also marks the consolidation of the United States as the new world hegemon. As before, the former allies, the mightiest maritime power and the largest continental empire—now the United States and the Soviet Union, respectively—entered a protracted conflict known as "The Cold War" (1947–1989). The stakes in Asia were again very high and resulted in three devastating wars in China, Korea, and Vietnam. This time around there were stakes for the entire world, and the highest of them all was the risk of mutually assured destruction (MAD). Yet, for the many formidable challenges that this conflict entailed, the United States sustained its world hegemony throughout this conflict and was seemingly geared toward new heights with the decline and subsequent collapse of the Soviet Union (1991). However, in a matter of slightly over a decade, the United States embroiled itself in the Second Gulf War, undermining its position as the leading role model that other states try to imitate and feel compelled to collaborate with.

Interestingly, the rise and consolidation of the British and U.S. world hegemonies coincide with the strengthening of economic globalization during the two peaks of its U-shape trajectory. Similarly, the challenge of these world hegemons brought the prospects for economic globalization into question. The demise of the British world hegemony resulted in the de-globalization of the world economy. Clearly, the leading role of the world hegemon in providing an inspirational horizon, influencing or coercing other states, and setting rules, norms, and values for the international system has been crucial for the advancement of economic globalization. What turn will contemporary globalization take in the wake of "America First"?

DEMOCRACY

Democracy is a political regime based on the rule of law in which citizens are involved in processes of public decision-making, typically by voting in free elections between multiple political parties. This regime represents the embodiment of liberalism, the ideology that fosters separation of power into independent branches of government, private property rights and market economy, and an open society with political and civil freedoms and human and civil rights for all.

This type of political regime was a marginal exception for most of human history until the mid-nineteenth century. States had started emerging some 5,000 years ago. The standard type of regime that ruled them was some form of dictatorship. One authority—a king, an emperor, a general, or a dictator—and a very limited group of minions oversaw all decision-making on public affairs without much restraint and accountability to their fellow humans. Accountability was only for the eyes of metaphysical entities such as gods or heaven, whereas the population at large was convinced or suppressed into acquiescence. Athenian democracy (from the fifth century until the Macedonian conquest in 322 BCE) is the best-known exception to five millennia of authoritarian rule. The Roman Republic (509–27 BCE) and a multiplicity of representative legislative institutions started by the Cortes of León in 1188 and up to the Parliament of England (1215–1707) and the French Estates-General of 1789 represented additional limited democratic bubbles floating in an authoritarian sea.

It was only with the American (1776) and French (1789) revolutions that public decision-making started to devolve toward growing constituencies. The American Revolution resulted in the adoption of The United States Constitution (1787) which established the rules to elect a government while protecting civil rights and liberties for non-slaves and voting rights for white male property owners. The French Revolution led to the Declaration of the Rights of Man and of the Citizen by the National Constituent Assembly and the election, by all males, of a short-lived (1792–1795) legislative body: The National Convention.

Aside from these revolutions, there was also a gradualist path toward democracy. Back in 1214 John King of England had lost most of his ancestral lands in France to the French king Phillipe Auguste and earned the nickname "Lackland." By then, King John had drained for a decade his barons' wealth through taxes. In 1215, with his popularity and strength at its lowest, the king's barons imposed on him the Magna Carta, a charter that committed the king to stop taxation without their consent. This principle not only found its way into the revolutionary path, as the demand of the Thirteen Colonies for "no taxation without representation" indicates. Rather, it also took root in the gradual growth of the English parliamentary power. More broadly, throughout the centuries, parliamentary forces found in the Magna Carta an anchor and pillar for curtailing the absolute claims to power by the monarchs. By the time that revolutions brought incipient democratic alternatives to monarchic dictatorship in the United States and France, the gradualist road had led in England to the replacement of monarchy by constitutional monarchy. The Glorious Revolution (1688) was the pivotal steppingstone for the parliament, constituted of elected representatives, to progressively limit the role of the monarchs to mere figureheads. The Act of Union (1707) and the Acts of Union (1800) extended the parliamentary reach.

These revolutionary and gradualist departing points enabled the take-off of the "First Wave of Democracy" during the nineteenth century. In its framework, the American Revolution entered a new democratic phase, known as Jacksonian democracy. The Democratic Party, led by Andrew Jackson, prevailed in the national elections of 1828. His election represented the end of the monopoly of the American socioeconomic-educated elite over the Presidential office. In addition, the right to vote was extended to most white males. In the meantime, three new iterations of French revolutions in 1830, 1848, and 1871 replaced the principle of hereditary monarchy with popular sovereignty and established a Second and Third Republic, respectively. Male universal suffrage was granted in 1848. Also, in the gradualist United Kingdom the Representation of the People Act of 1832 almost doubled the number of voters to about a fifth of the male population.

More importantly, besides the social broadening of enfranchisement in democratic countries, the "First Wave" also widened the democratic geographical scope. At its zenith this First Wave brought about the emergence of some 26 new democratic regimes in Europe, the Americas, New Zealand, Japan, and Ethiopia. However, in the wake of the First World War and till the end of the Second one (1918–1945), democracy was on retreat, bringing the First Wave to a close. Only in the 1950s did democracy again start to spread, peaking at 36 democratic countries in the world by 1962. This mild democratic recovery represents the "Second Wave of Democracy."

The fundamental yet limited reach of the first two waves of democracy helps us appreciate the magnitude of the "Third Wave of Democracy," in which more than 60 countries throughout the world replaced their authoritarian regimes with democratic ones. Starting in Southern Europe in the mid-1970s, the wave continued to expand during the 1980s throughout Latin America, Asian Pacific, Eastern Europe, and since 1989 in sub-Saharan Africa. The strength of this third wave combined with the heritage of the first two invites us to view the story of the twentieth century as a relentless advance of democracy over dictatorship. At the outskirts of that century the victory of democracy was declared to be nothing less than the end of history!

The outbreak of the Arab Spring in 2011 seemed to announce a new link in this Third Wave chain in a region of the world, the Middle East, previously almost untouched by democracy. However, pro-democracy mass protest reverted into the return of dictatorships. Coincidentally, by that time liberal democracy had started its current withdrawal around the world. As in the past, every ebbing of a democratic wave corresponded with the re-emergence of illiberal regimes. When First Wave Democracy subsided, dictatorships in inter-war Europe and Latin America consolidated (1920–1945). As the Second Wave Democracy was reaching its limits, dictatorships throughout Eastern Europe, Latin America, Africa, and Asia after the Second World War proliferated (1945–1989). Currently, the withdrawal of democracy is not only paired with the rise of dictatorships but also with a divorce between democratic procedures and liberal values. Since the first democratic wave, democracy and liberalism worked hand in hand; they were one and the same thing. Not any longer. At present (2021), democratic electoral and governmental procedures operating within constitutional frameworks allow for the enactment of illiberal policies, practices, and rhetoric that favor illiberal ideologies such as conservatism, nationalism, ethnocentrism, xenophobia, economic protectionism, and isolationism, compounded by attacks on the media, the freedom of expression, minorities, opposition, and pluralism. This current trend has gone far beyond countries with troublesome democratic records to make inroads into the very hegemonic pillars that had harbored democracy, sustained world orders for two centuries, and forged U-Shape globalization: Brexit Great Britain and Trump's United States The growing electoral success of the far right in Europe, exemplified by Marine Le Pen's National Front, even threatens the birthplace of the democratic revolution. Under what conditions were democracies and dictatorships on the rise or in decline during the past three democratic waves?

Socioeconomic Inequality Within and Between Societies

Socioeconomic inequality refers to the disparities in the distribution of wealth, income, or both within a society and between different societies. Within a single society bounded by its national boundaries, socioeconomic inequality is commonly measured by a metric known as the Gini coefficient which runs from 1 to 0. Number 1 represents maximum inequality (all the wealth or income in that country goes to one single person); number 0 represents maximum equality (every member in that society owns the same amount of wealth or receives the same amount of income). In equitable societies the Gini coefficient is as low as 0.3 or lower. Such societies can be graphically visualized as diamond shapes: the bulk of the population is concentrated in the middle of the distribution of wealth, income, or both, with small groups both above and below the majority of the population. As the value of the Gini coefficient rises above 0.3 and more particularly after it crosses the 0.5 threshold, the coefficient indicates large disparities in the distribution of wealth, income, or both. The structure of such a society is best graphically depicted as a pyramid in which the bulk of the population is on the lower ladders of wealth and/or income distribution, a tiny minority is far afield at the very top, and a more or less thin layer in between these two represents a third group of middle wealth and/or income. The overall trajectory of world societies in regard to socioeconomic inequality during the last two centuries consists of one transition from pyramidal social structures into diamond shape structures followed by another in the opposite direction. Pyramids began morphing into diamonds beginning in the 1920s through the mid-1970s, when a reversion back toward pyramids began. It is clear and uncontested that socioeconomic inequality within societies has been globally on the rise since the mid-1970s. For example, in 1920 in the most developed economies, the wealthiest top 1% earned, depending on the country, between 12 and 28% of the total national income. By 1980, their share had dropped by 4–11%. By 2014, the share of the top 1% had risen again by 7–21%[4] (Diagram 1.1).

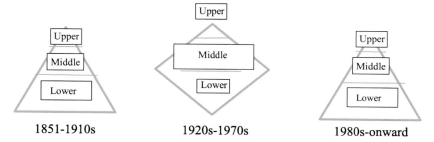

Diagram 1.1   The changing shapes of social structures

Socioeconomic inequality between societies is commonly measured by the per capita GDP at purchasing power parity (PPP) in every society around the world. The GDP is the value of all final goods and services produced within a country each year. Per capita, or per person, means dividing the GDP value by the average number of people living in that country in that same year (people are born and people die, people come and people go). PPP measures the cost of buying the same things in different places, a sort of exchange rate for the price of the same basket of goods and services in multiple locations. For example, Egypt's per capita GDP stands at $2,573 whereas Switzerland's is $82,950. However, once the prices of some 3,000 goods and services in each country are factored in, the actual gap between these two per capita GDPs at PPP stands at $13,366 versus $64,449.[5]

As with single societies within the confines of national boundaries, also the global society composed of all world states can be visualized as a pyramid, when there are huge disparities between most states' per capita GDPs at the bottom compared to a few states with much higher per capita GDPs at the top. As with socioeconomic inequality within societies, the departing point for socioeconomic inequality between societies is best envisioned by a pyramidal arrangement of all world societies. Yet, in contrast with socioeconomic inequality within societies, the pyramid of inequality between nations did not experience any transition into an alternative diamond like shape.

Instead, the pyramidal structure remained in place, solidified by its durable building blocks: a few economies at the top relying on huge amounts of accumulated capital and cutting-edge technology; numerous economies at the bottom with little capital and dated technologies; and a changing number of economies in the middle ground with some accumulated capital and technological capabilities. Economies at the top can offer the world goods and services that only a few other economies can offer, if at all. This situation makes for little or no competition and hence for large profits that keep nurturing the upward spiral of capital accumulation and technological development. Conversely, economies at the bottom of the pyramid rely on exporting raw materials and/or goods and services that are being offered by many other similar economies. Intense competition makes for a narrow margin of gain that perpetuates the downward spiral of little accumulation of capital and technological advancement. Economies in the middle ground fall somewhere within the spectrum.

Economies at the top of this pyramid sustain societies with larger proportions of their populations enjoying higher wages, higher consumption, lower exploitation, and lower coercion. By contrast, economies at the bottom can only afford societies in which most of their members are low-skilled workers suffering from lower income, lower consumption, higher exploitation, and higher coercion. Societies ranking in the middle of the pyramid combine, in different proportions, both social scenarios side by side. Institutionally speaking, economies at the top of the global pyramid rely on a broad tax basis on which a powerful state can effectively run its domestic public sphere and simultaneously pursue its interests abroad while projecting its power. By contrast, societies at the bottom of the pyramid with their limited resources allow for a weak and usually corrupt state whose armies' main function is to police domestic social unrest. That is particularly true for small states. Large states can consolidate a wide fiscal basis by the sheer number of their population, even if the per capita income is relatively low. The strength of states ranking in the middle of the global pyramid varies along the economic spectrum and by their size (Map 1.1 and Table 1.1).

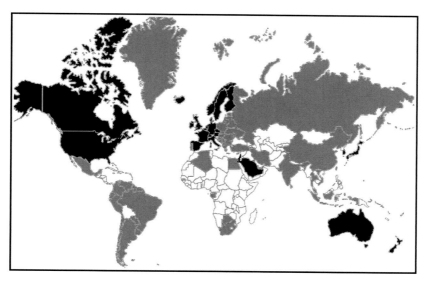

Map 1.1   Socioeconomic inequality between societies

Table 1.1   Socioeconomic inequality between societies

	■ *Per capita GDP at PPP above Int$ 35 k*	▦ *Per capita GDP at PPP ranging Int$ 10–35 k*	▢ *Per capita GDP at PPP ranging Int$ <2–10 k*
Economy	Quasi-monopoly products, high accumulation of capital, high technological development, dominate the world economy	Combines characteristics of the other two groups to different extents	Based either on raw materials and/or on products that face intense competition. Narrower margin than that of quasi-monopoly products. Low capital accumulation, low technological production
Society	High wages, high consumption, low exploitation, and low coercion. Formulate the discourse that interprets the world	Societies vary along the spectrum created by the other two patterns	Most of the members of the societies are low-skill workers suffering from low income, low consumption, high exploitation, and high coercion
Politics	Wide fiscal basis, efficient bureaucracy, powerful armies, and strong states aim to perpetuate and foster the well-being of their societies. Establish the rules of the interstate system	States vary along the spectrum created by the other two patterns	Weak and usually corrupt states. The main aim of the weak peripheral states is to repress their pauperized societies, unless they are large states

Although no transition toward a diamond shape structure had occurred in terms of socioeconomic inequality between societies, there were noticeable movements of upward and downward mobility for many societies within the pyramid structure. For example, downward mobility occurred in Western Europe during the first half of the 1940s, in India and China until the mid-1970s, in Latin America since the mid-1970s, and in Africa all the way through. North Atlantic nations experienced sharp upward mobility during the second half of the twentieth century, Latin America experienced a moderate upward mobility between the 1940s and 1960s, and China has experienced a sharp upward mobility since the 2000s.

Given these trends of mobility, is the global society moving toward more or less socioeconomic inequality? In short, it depends on whether you adopt a relative or absolute yardstick. For example, in the United States the per capita GDP PPP amounted in 1975 to US$25,956; in China it was US$1,425. In 2016, the U.S. per capita GDP PPP topped at US$53,015; in China it had risen to US$12,320. In 1975 the per capita GDP PPP of China represented 5.5% of that of the United States, whereas in 2016 it represented 23.2%. That is a significant relative reduction of socioeconomic inequality between the two. However, the US$24,531 gap of 1975 had grown by 2016 into a US$40,695 gap. That is an absolute growth (in terms of dollars) of the socioeconomic inequality between the two.

Finally, as useful as the per capita GDP PPP is to visualize the pyramid of global socioeconomic inequality, this measurement is based on the division of the GDP evenly among the members of society. If that would be the case in reality, societies would measure zero on their Gini coefficient for socioeconomic inequality within. However, the Gini numbers have continued to rise for more than four decades in most societies (see above, p. 13). So, given worldwide mounting domestic inequality for the last four decades and shrinking inequality between countries for the last two decades, at least in relative terms, what is the state of global inequality now? How and why have we arrived there?

Technological Innovations

The current wave of innovations in robotics, artificial intelligence, nanotechnology, quantum computing, biotechnology, genetic editing, Internet of things (IoT), 3D printing, fifth-generation wireless technologies (5G), fully autonomous vehicles, exploration into alternative fuel and energy systems, and more, are the current link in the long chain of the permanent technological revolution launched by the Industrial Revolution.[6] Since the fundamental technological breakthrough made by the steam engine in the beginning of the eighteenth century, that of being able to digest energy and transform it into movement, the drive to mechanize ever more human activities, as well as to replace older technologies with more effective ones, kept accelerating. This is what the process of technological innovation has been about since the dawn of the Industrial Revolution. It has yielded an immense list of new technologies that coalesced into four major waves of transformative proportions for social life on a global scale.

The point of departure is the momentous transformation in which steam engines attached to an ever-growing number of machines, such as pumps, looms, ships, and locomotives, started displacing the force of animal and human muscles, wind, and water currents. The production of coal, iron, and textiles as well as the laying of railroads and establishment of navigation lines are among the major outcomes. By the mid-nineteenth century, a century and a half since inception, these new technologies had completely transformed the first industrializing societies in the North Atlantic and became prominent worldwide. This original Industrial Revolution laid the foundations for technological innovations to come—not just as the point of departure that set the precedent but more fundamentally by nurturing a mindset eager for continuous research and development.

Next, a succession of additional technological breakthroughs starting in the 1870s, including the production of steel, the synthesis of chemicals, electrification, telecommunication, and transportation (the car, airplane, and the adoption of petrol as fuel of the internal combustion engine) opened a new phase in the history of the Industrial Revolution. Combined with new methods of management designed to reduce time, expertise, and effort in the productive work sequence, this second Industrial Revolution enabled mass production and mass consumption. The subsequent incorporation of further technological innovations for an entire century into the 1970s, such as the harnessing of nuclear energy and the early phases of computation, enhanced the outreach, deepening, and diversification of this second Industrial Revolution into further corners of the planet, larger segments of the world societies, and additional aspects of daily life. In a matter of a century, the second Industrial Revolution brought the promises of the original Industrial Revolution to fruition.

Moreover, by making the first inroads into computation, the second Industrial Revolution also planted the seeds for the growing of the third wave: The Information Revolution. The development of computers, which started to enhance manufacturing processes through information processing and automation, also enabled a new economy of services based on information and communication relying on personal computers, satellite communications, cellular phones, and the internet. In a matter of two decades, by the 1990s a new knowledge-based high-tech economy, also known as the post-industrial economy, was born. Twenty more years of growing amounts of data accumulation, the development of algorithms, and further research and development triggered the Industrial Revolution 4.0 we are experiencing now. What were the social consequences of the previous three waves of technological innovations? What can be learned from that as we confront the fourth?

CLIMATE CHANGE

The coalescence of the Industrial Revolution around 1850 coincided with the waning of the Little Ice Age. Starting around the year 1300, several regions of the planet experienced, at different times, periods of cooling temperatures at some point during these six centuries. Arguably, the decrease of human populations due to conquest and epidemics may account for that. The mass devastation brought by the Mongol conquests and the Black Death in Eurasia during the thirteenth and fourteenth centuries and the collapse of most of the Americas' population in the wake of the European conquests after 1492 brought a sharp decline in agricultural activity. Reforestation ensued, resulting in growing sequestration of carbon dioxide from the atmosphere that contributed to cooling temperatures. Such explanations compete with or complement other hypotheses pointing to non-human causes, such as decreased solar radiation, heightened volcanic activity, changes in the circulation of oceanic current flows, and variations in the planet's orbit and axial tilt.

Interestingly, the human-caused explanation for the Little Ice Age mirrors the understanding of contemporary global warming: more people, emitting more greenhouse gases (carbon dioxide and methane), with less forest to sequester the carbon. However, we know for sure that human activity is causing the contemporary warming. Human activity in the industrial age has been causing the rise of global surface temperatures. The effects of global warming include the retreat of glaciers that affect many species and result in the rising of sea levels that threaten coastal cities where the largest share of the world population lives; regional changes in precipitation responsible for floods and draughts; more frequent extreme weather events such as heat waves, prolonged monsoon periods, and more potent hurricanes and typhoons; heat and pest-related effects on agriculture, desertification, and species extinction.

Climate change has been a constant feature of Planet Earth. Current global warming has displaced the Little Ice Age, which displaced the

Medieval Warm Period (ca. 950–1250), which replaced the Late Antique Little Ice Age (ca. 536–660), which did the same to the Roman Warm Period (ca. 250 BCE–400 CE), and so on. What is new about contemporary climate change is its simultaneity across the globe and its indisputable origin in human activities. Those activities are directly related to the technological innovations brought by the Industrial Revolution in its four iterations, which at the same time corresponds with the expansion and contraction of socioeconomic inequalities, the political regimes that steered those processes, the consolidation of and contestations against the world hegemons, and the fluctuations in economic globalization. Such correspondences become visible once the trends of each of these six dimensions are superimposed on the trends of the other five.

Now and then: Trajectories in Global History

In a nutshell, the entwinement of the trends for all six dimensions shows that world societies underwent two waves of economic globalization (1851–1929 and 1973–onward) coincidental with two hegemonic world orders (based on British and American world hegemonies, respectively), relying on two fundamental technological breakthroughs (the Industrial Revolution and the Information Revolution). Both these waves coincided with the proliferation of democratic regimes (the so-called First and Third Waves of Democracy) and growing socioeconomic inequalities. By contrast, the time period sandwiched in between (1929–1973) has experienced economic de-globalization, lack of an undisputed world hegemon, technological breakthroughs less fundamentally revolutionizing for the economy, growing numbers of nondemocratic regimes as well as a reduction in socioeconomic inequalities (Diagram 1.2).

With such panoramic clarity it is worthwhile asking what underlies the correspondences of these patterned trajectories? What links are there between economic globalization and world hegemony? Are there particular types of political regimes conducive to economic globalization and economic de-globalization? What role has economic globalization to play in the unfolding of socioeconomic inequalities? And how does economic globalization synergize with technological innovations? Is there a particular type of political regime that the world hegemon aims to disseminate? Is there a particular type of political regime that aims to confront world hegemons? Why has the global expansion of democratic regimes corresponded with growing socioeconomic inequalities? What role have

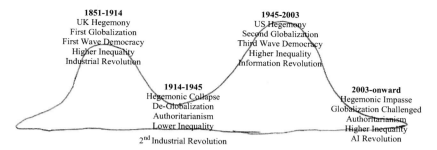

1851-1914
UK Hegemony
First Globalization
First Wave Democracy
Higher Inequality
Industrial Revolution

1945-2003
US Hegemony
Second Globalization
Third Wave Democracy
Higher Inequality
Information Revolution

1914-1945
Hegemonic Collapse
De-Globalization
Authoritarianism
Lower Inequality
2nd Industrial Revolution

2003-onward
Hegemonic Impasse
Globalization Challenged
Authoritarianism
Higher Inequality
AI Revolution

Diagram 1.2   A brief history of now

technological innovations played in the fate of the world hegemon? Are technological innovations reducing or enlarging socioeconomic inequalities? Are there particular types of political regime that allow technological innovations to bloom and socioeconomic inequalities to narrow?

By visualizing this patterned periodization these questions can be formulated and engaged and our present stops being a huge pile of seemingly unconnected developments. It becomes, instead, an intelligible series of processes that fit well in this long-lasting chronological sequence: Our present represents a new backlash against globalization, hegemony, and democracy. However, in our present day, the combination of trends is unique compared to the previous three phases. Now, the declines in economic globalization, world hegemony, and democracy are atypically matched by the widening of some socioeconomic gaps and the breakthroughs of multiple transformative technologies. That uniqueness stresses that patterns have their limits. *A Brief History of Now* deploys both recurrent patterns and their limits to comprehend the past and guide the understanding of the present.

Patterns have an additional and more fundamental limitation too. Although the above zooming-out exercise has allowed us to visualize, organize, and make sense of the huge amount of seemingly unconnected developments around the globe for the last 170 years, there is a reason for the chaotic impression created by today's fast-paced daily news. Namely, developments, initiatives, decisions, and speech acts are occurring all the time, moving in multiple directions, and triggering additional intended and unintended developments, initiatives, decisions, and speech acts that scale up in an exponential feedback cycle. For all the clarity and convenience of the retrospective sequencing that lets us identify recurrent patterns, in real time developments are convoluted, contradictory, surprising, perplexing, and unexpected. Hence, side by side with the reconstruction of the broad strokes that describe the major trends and processes throughout the period, *A Brief History of Now* also presents some of the convoluted, contradictory, surprising, perplexing, and unexpected developments, initiatives, decisions, and speech acts that unfolded in real time in their raw and chaotic fashion. Also in these regards, and even more so, there is a plethora of questions to explore. Just as a starter, how was Great Britain able to attain world hegemony? How was its path similar to and different from that of the United States? What brought about the demise of Great Britain's world hegemony and what does that say about the prospects of U.S. world hegemony? What is unique and common about the two waves of economic globalization? What were the global impacts of the Communist revolution in Russia despite its multiple failed attempts to propagate Communism? What are the crucial commonalities and differences between the two largest Communist states—the Soviet Union and the People's Republic of China? Are socialism and nationalism opposed ideologies? Where did the libertarian demonstrations of the youth worldwide in 1968 lead in the longer run? How did localized regional wars, such as those in the Middle East and the South Atlantic, change the course of global history? What is neoliberalism and what were its multiple effects? What has been replacing it for more than a decade?

A Brief History of Now tackles these questions and aims to provide a global history vantage perspective to better contextualize contemporary processes. But in order to do that, first and foremost, a coherent, cogent, and compelling global aerial view of the trajectory of the world since the coalescence of the Industrial Revolution needs to be presented. Welcome on board and fasten your seat belt!

NOTES

1. Howard R. Gold, "Never Mind the 1 Percent. Let's Talk About the 0.01 Percent," *Chicago Booth Review*, Winter 2017/2018, https://review.chicagobooth.edu/economics/2017/article/never-mind-1-percent-lets-talk-about-001-percent.
2. K. O'Rourke and J. Williamson, "When Did Gobalisation Begin?" *European Review of Economic History* 6 (2002): 23–50. C. Chase-Dunn, "Globalization: A World-System Perspective," *Journal of*

World-Systems Research 5, no. 2 (1999): 194–197. C. Chase-Dunn, Y. Kawano, and B. Brewer, "Trade Globalization since 1795: Waves of Integration in the World System," *American Sociological Review* 65, no. 1 (2002): 77–95.

3. O'Rourke and Williamson, "When Did Globalisation Begin?" 26. Michael Bordo, "Globalization in Historical Perspective," *Business Economics* 72 (2002): 20–29. R. Baldwin and P. Martin, *Two Waves of Globalization: Superficial Similarities, Fundamental Differences*, NBER Working Paper 6904 (Cambridge, 1999). J. A. Scholte, *Globalization: A Critical Introduction* (New York: Palgrave Macmillan, 2005), 117–19. R. Feenstra, "Integration of Trade and Disintegration of Production in the Global Economy," *Journal of Economic Perspectives* 12, no. 4 (1998): 31–50. J. Sachs and A. Warner, *Economic Reform and the Process of Global Integration*, Brookings Papers on Economic Activity 1 (1995): 1–118. J. Williamson, *Globalization and Inequality Then and Now: The Late 19th and Late 20th Centuries Compared*, NBER Working Paper 5491 (Cambridge, 1996). K. O'Rourke and J. Williamson, *Globalization and History: The Evolution of a Nineteenth-Century Atlantic Economy* (Cambridge: MIT Press, 1999).

4. Max Roser, "Global Economic Inequality," *OurWorldInData.org*, 2020, https://ourworldindata.org/global-economic-inequality. "Average Gross Domestic Product," World Inequality Database, *wid.world*, https://wid.world/world/#agdpro_p0p100_z/US;FR;DE;CN;ZA;GB;WO/last/eu/k/p/yearly/a/false/0/75000/curve/false/country.

5. "The Big Mac Index," *The Economist*, July 11, 2018. "World Economic Outlook," International Monetary Fund, April 2019, https://www.imf.org/external/pubs/ft/weo/2019/01/weodata/.

6. Klaus Schwab, "The Fourth Industrial Revolution: What It Means, How to Respond," webforum.org, January 14, 2016, https://www.weforum.org/agenda/2016/01/the-fourth-industrial-revolution-what-it-means-and-how-to-respond/.

CHAPTER 2

We Were All Brits (1851–1914)

Hegemony, What Is It?

On July 13, 2014, the sunshine was hitting the lawn of the Maracanã Stadium in Rio de Janeiro. 113 nerve-racking minutes had already passed for the 75,000 viewers in the stadium and for billions of people around the world. Suddenly, André Schürrle crossed a center pass from the left side. Mario Götze absorbed the ball on his chest before volleying it into the net. Argentina did it again! It lost a FIFA World Cup final to Germany. For most of the fans that was it: the best world team had beaten the team of the world's best player (Lionel Messi). For a history-minded viewer, however, a bigger question loomed: how did a nineteenth-century English public school pastime come to captivate the hearts and minds of 3.2 billion, almost half the world population, in 2014?[1] That is hegemony.

Every standard introduction to the British Empire states that at its territorial peak, in the wake of the First World War, it encompassed more than one-fifth of the planet's surface and ruled over more than one-fifth of the world population. It was not the first empire on which the sun never set—the Spanish was—but it was the largest empire ever. It was even more than that: a world hegemon with military might, economic power, and cultural appeal well beyond its imperial boundaries, leaving no corner untouched. This is what happened with the adoption of soccer: Britain ruled the oceans' waves, its companies laid the railways in all continents, and British workers challenged the locals with their game. Relying

© The Author(s), under exclusive license to Springer Nature Switzerland AG 2021
D. Olstein, *A Brief History of Now*,
https://doi.org/10.1007/978-3-030-82420-4_2

on a braid of political might, economic power, and cultural appeal, hegemony equates to becoming the leading role model. Its success awakens the desire to collaborate, to imitate, or both. Britain's success secret was unleashing twin revolutions: industrial and democratic (Map 2.1).

The Industrial Revolution was a major technological, economic, and social revolution. The radical transformations it produced made fast changes in these areas a permanent feature of the modern world. Politically, the democratic revolution brought about the enfranchisement of ever-broadening sectors of society through incremental steps, while socially it narrowed the gap between the privileged and unprivileged by slowly expanding access to better housing, nutrition, health care, education, and technology for ever-larger segments of society. Both "revolutions" actually consisted of gradual processes that permanently unfolded at an accelerating pace. A powerful synergy appeared between these two "gradual revolutions." Industrialization's rise in productivity enabled social democratization. In turn, social democratization, reflected in rising wages, stimulated technological innovation, which by cutting labor costs further accelerated industrialization.

By the mid-nineteenth century, this synergy was nowhere else as powerful as in Great Britain. The synergy, combined with the favorable geopolitical conditions after defeating Napoleon, was what catapulted

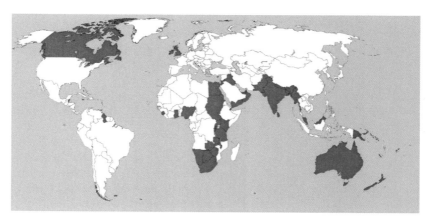

Map 2.1   The British Empire in 1918

this society toward world hegemony. Additionally, the worldwide ideological appeal of emerging beliefs in the principles of "free trade" and "comparative advantage" (or the British determination to impose them by force), was on the rise. With this set of principles and the most powerful navy in world history, Great Britain opened up all world regions and polity types: constitutional regimes in Western Europe, gunpowder empires throughout Eurasia, African and Asian colonies, and Latin American oligarchic republics. In so doing, this first world hegemon also transformed the world economy into the first industrial globalization.

British world hegemony, economic globalization under its stewardship, and cultural Britannization—that is, the dissemination of British culture worldwide, as exemplified by the adoption of soccer around the globe—bloomed for the most part during the second half of the nineteenth century. Three spoilers stood in Great Britain's way, however: a newly (1871) unified Germany; its rebellious former colony, the United States; and the defiant ideology of communism. Germany and the United States did not abide by the ideologies of free trade and comparative advantage. Instead, they protected their industries to catch up with the leader. By the end of the nineteenth century they were fulfilling that goal. As for the defiant Communist ideology, it did not seem a serious threat at the time, which accounts for how striking the surprise would be in a matter of two decades.

INDUSTRIAL REVOLUTION

The Industrial Revolution was a major technological transformation that reshaped economy and society. Technologically, the Industrial Revolution equates to the invention, improvements, and applications of water mills and the steam engine. The trick of the steam engine consists of transforming heat into movement. Since ancient times, wind and water currents were harnessed for propelling ships and mills. However, most of the work was conducted by human and animal muscles. The steam engine brought the drastic shift from muscle to steam power. All that was needed, aside from creative ingenuity, was a source of energy to generate the steam that pushed the piston that transformed the steam power into the desired motion.

In deforested England that source of energy was coal, of which there was plenty in its subsoil. Its extraction, though, required pumping subterranean water. This task was accomplished by a pump propelled by a steam engine (the Newcomen Atmospheric Engine). A virtuous circle was established: a better pump required a better steam engine, and both combined allowed for the extraction of more coal to feed more pumps or steam engines. The pistons of those exponentially growing number of engines moved other machines while applications multiplied as well. Textile looms and trains were just the first and most prominent ones. The trajectory of the steam engine in its invention and branching-out applications also set the precedent for centuries to come in terms of research and development for further technological breakthroughs.[2]

This technological revolution brought about an economic revolution that equates to the sustained growth of work productivity. The same workers' muscles that once moved tools were then operating machines that progressively digested growing amounts of energy and delivered growing amounts of ever-diversifying outputs: more cloth, textiles, hats, shoes, bikes, chinaware, and a long etcetera that was soon to encompass almost all manufactured goods. And all of them were transported by larger and more powerful trains and steamships.

The byproduct of sustained productivity growth was sustained economic growth. Until then, more production depended mostly on more producers. And so more output (economic growth) was shared by more people, equating to no *per capita* economic growth. Economic growth went hand in hand with demographic growth, leaving the population at the very same level of income and wealth. The economic breakthrough that the Industrial Revolution brought about was the sustained per capita economic growth. The growth of wealth outpaced demographic growth. And gradually, after the devastating blows of early industrialization on the working class and for all of the extremely uneven concentration of wealth, there was more income and wealth for most. In this regard, the Industrial Revolution, in the mid- and long run, is the incarnation of the "trickle-down effect." The compounded gains in income and wealth since then make the difference between our current standards of living and those of the first decades of industrialization or the pre-industrial era.

WHICH PYRAMID?

This "trickle-down effect," in its turn, is one of the ways in which the Industrial Revolution revolutionized society. Over time, the cumulative effect of industrial wealth percolating throughout a society will generate a better-off stratum of workers that, together with professionals, admin-istrators, shopkeepers, and employees will steadily enlarge an emerging middle class. The sustained growth of such a middle class will transform the perennial pyramidal structure of society into a diamond shape.

However, the first social revolutionary effect of the Industrial Revolu-tion was the emergence of a new type of polarized social pyramid, side by side with the old perennial one. In this new pyramidal society, a minority of industrial capitalists rested on the broad base provided by industrial workers without too much of a middle-ground cushioning stratum to ease the social frictions. This social pyramid was formally similar to the traditional one in which a small landed aristocracy rested on the broad base of rural workers. The meteoric duplication of Great Britain's popu-lation from 13 to 27 million people between 1780 and 1851 sufficed to sustain two instead of typically one social pyramid.[3]

Having now two parallel societies, the perennial agricultural pyramid and the incipient industrial one, which society is preferable? The tradi-tional one in which wealth grew from muscles plowing the land of the aristocracy? Or the modern industrial one in which wealth grows by oper-ating the machinery of the capitalists' factories? These are quintessential *cui bono?* or "to whose profit?" questions. And given that the opinion of rural and industrial workers did not count much, the titanic battle of interests pitted landed aristocrats against industrial capitalists, beginning in England.

One concrete way to put such confrontation is this: do we want to grow rich by selling crops or manufactures? Well, why not sell both? That seems possible and perhaps desirable, enjoying both sources of income. However, the more we will earn on crops the less we will earn on manu-factures. But why should there be such a zero-sum game between the goals of landed aristocrats and those of industrial capitalists? That is because the more expensive the bread is, the richer the aristocrat becomes. However, more expensive bread means higher salaries for workers to be able to feed themselves and their families. And higher salaries mean reduced profits for the industrial capitalist. A similar logic applies the other way around. Cheap bread allows for lower salaries, which enlarges the capitalists' margin of profit that they will re-invest in their ever-growing enterprises.

In stark contrast to many societies, this furious conflict was peace-fully solved in the United Kingdom in the parliament. In 1846 both the House of Commons and more surprisingly the House of Lords voted to repeal the Corn Laws that since 1815 imposed restrictions and tariffs on imported grain.[4] The effect of this nullification combined with the sharp decline in transportation costs—resulting from the industrialization of shipping—was the ruin of British agriculture and the blooming of its industry. Staples began arriving from all over the world, and British manufactures traveled back. With that, Great Britain made its hegemonic leap forward in the economic sphere as it did in 1815 in the military sphere. By 1851 Great Britain celebrated itself by showing its prowess to the world in the Great Exhibition of the Works of Industry of all Nations in Hyde Park, London, attaining cultural hegemony too. By then and for almost the next hundred years … we were all Brits, or we wanted to be.

The Industrial "Gradualution"

The new pyramidal society made of capitalists and workers had prevailed over the agricultural old one in Britain first, and then throughout the world. Concomitantly, the new pyramidal society also changed its locus from the fields to the factories and from the village to the city, once again in Britain first, in the world next. That shift constitutes a geographical revolution that entailed a mass migration, the emergence of a new type of human settlement—the industrial city—and the decline of the perennial human settlement, the village.

During five millennia of perennial traditional pyramidal society there were cities in which about five percent of the total population lived. Those millenary cities accommodated the aristocratic landowners, with their rulers and priests at the top and their multiple servants—administrators, merchants, artisans, and slaves—at the bottom. The bulk of the wealth, though, was produced in the fields. With the Industrial Revolution the bulk of production shifted toward the industrial cities. The city stopped being the dissociated beneficiary of rural production and became the very center of industrial production. A new type of city, indeed a new type of human settlement was born: the industrial city.

The Industrial Revolution, then, entails at least four interrelated revolutions: technological, economic, social, and geographical. These were revolutionary in their scope, which is why it is also known as "The Great Transformation."[5] But the Industrial Revolution was not revolutionary in its pace; it unfolded over a century of gradual transformations in Great Britain starting around 1760 and up to about 1870. Revolutionary in its transformative powers, gradual in its pace: such was the "Industrial Gradualution."

Since then, we have been living in a permanent Industrial Revolution that has brought about, among other things, the internal combustion engine, electrification, atomic energy, alternative energies, and its own post-industrial alternatives. To this expansion throughout time another one throughout space should be added. We were all Brits, or we wanted to be: Western Europe, North America, Eastern Europe, Latin America, East Asia, Africa … each region in turn did its part to make the Industrial Revolution global.[6]

By doing so, technologies and economies changed worldwide, perennial pyramidal societies entered into competition with new industrial pyramidal societies around the world. Sometimes this paved the way for diamond-shaped societies, sometimes not. And yes, the globally predominant type of human settlement became the industrial and post-industrial city at the expense of the village in exactly the same timeframe. In that sense, we are still living in the industrial gradualution, this set of gradual processes that brought about revolutionary changes.

Unsurprisingly, as perennial technological, economic, social, and geographical patterns were being displaced by new ones, a similar dynamic of displacement of the perennial for the revolutionary unfolded in the political sphere. Perennial authoritarianism was to lose ground to broadening democratization along time and across space.

DEMOCRATIC REVOLUTION

The upcoming of democratic regime and society entailed another gradualution. Around the time of the launching of the industrial gradualution Britain was neither ruled by a democratic regime nor contained a democratic society. True, monarchic authoritarianism as such had been displaced since the days of the Glorious Revolution (1688) and the parliament had grown through the Act of Union (1707) and the Acts of Union (1800) into the Parliament of Great Britain and the Parliament of the United Kingdom, respectively. The growth of this parliamentarian constitutional monarchy and the gradualist road that led to it made Britain a beacon for liberals. In this regard, the liberals of the world were Brits or wanted to be. But hegemonic modeling aside, Britain was anything but democratic. Politically, only 3–5% of the English could vote and that proportion was even lower for the Scots and Irish. Socially, the British society was remarkably hierarchical, based on assumptions of entitlement at the top of the pyramid and deference flowing from the bottom up.

The democratic gradualution consists of the overcoming of these two situations: a say in politics restricted to a miniscule group only and the entitlement-deference complex. Politically, the democratic gradualution incrementally brought about the enfranchisement of broadening male constituencies between 1832 and 1918. By the end of the First World War all men aged 21 and older were given the right to vote. The same Representation of the People Act of 1918 conceded voting rights to property-owning women over 30 years old. Ten years later equal voting rights were granted for women and men at 21 or older without property ownership restrictions. 128 years after the Acts of Union (1800) all British citizens enjoyed the right to vote. In 1969 the right was extended to the 18–21 years old bracket.[7]

Socially, the democratic gradualution narrowed the gap between privileged and unprivileged by gradually opening the access to better housing, nutrition, health care, education, and technology for larger and larger segments of society. As social democratization advanced, social deference declined, paving the way to growing self-assertion and even open defiance.

THE SYNERGIC REVOLUTIONS

The encompassing of both political and social transformations by the democratic gradualution perfectly matches the dual character of the industrial gradualution with its technological and economic side pairing with its social and geographical transformations. For these reasons, in addition to their simultaneity and gradual nature, the industrial and democratic revolutions are considered to be the "twin revolutions."[8] And indeed, further similarities come to mind. As with the industrial gradualution, the democratic one has been proving so far to have a lasting expanding character both in time and space. In time, larger and larger constituencies have been embraced by it. In space, more and more states embraced it to end up by the dawn of the twentieth century as the leading type of political regime and social way of life globally.

Besides being regarded as twins, the industrial and democratic revolutions deserve also to be also viewed as the "synergic revolutions" because their relationship contains a feedback loop. The rise in productivity that industrialization brought about enabled social democratization.

With prices going down and wages going up as a result of the rise in productivity, better housing, nutrition, health care, education, and technology for larger and larger segments of society were enabled. Moreover, as is well known, the customers are always right and hence with consumption rising, consumers started becoming powerful social actors through their purchase power. Consumers' demands will be addressed if businesses are looking for their goods and services to be in demand. Conversely, the social democratization resulting from rising wages stimulated constant technological innovation aiming to further reduce labor costs, thus accelerating industrialization.

At the same time, the emergence of the new pyramidal society of urban dwellers generated by the Industrial Revolution stimulated the association of people sharing the same existential concerns. They organized in professional associations, unions, and political parties. The resulting agendas and demands gradually made inroads into the public sphere—hitherto a domain of a privileged few—demanding a say in public decision making. Conversely, enfranchised citizens were a more engaged and educated working force; improved human capital matched the physical and financial capital accumulated by industrialization. Synergy stroked back, then, bringing a more productive working force to the ever-growing cycle of industrial productivity.

Hence, by virtue of the "synergic revolutions" the former subjects of authoritarian regimes were being upgraded into consumers and citizens of gradually democratizing societies and polities. Industrialization launched political and social democratization. Democratization, in turn, fostered industrialization. This is the spiraling synergy that empowered British economy, army, society, and cultural appeal to catapult toward world hegemony. Next time you watch a football/soccer match you should realize that you are doing that because of the "synergic revolutions" that made Great Britain the world hegemon.

Non-Identical Twins

The "twin revolutions" have differences as well as similarities. The steady progression of industrialization was not matched by steady democratization. In multiple cases, democratic progression was impeded in the face of an authoritarian reaction. Each of the three subsequent industrial revolutions (the second Industrial Revolution, the Information Revolution, the Artificial Intelligence Revolution) superseded the former technologies, methods of organization, output, and overall social outlook. Also, the First Wave of Democracy was innovative in establishing a new type of political regime. However, the other two waves of democracy, aside from superseding other political regimes or broadening democratization, in multiple cases just restored democracy where it had faltered. There was no such restorative property to the industrialization waves. The second wave of industrialization never was about bringing steam power back after its obsolescence.

Another major difference between the twins has to do with location. Whereas the Industrial Revolution was exclusively British at first, the democratic revolution erupted at several locations almost at once. As the British democratic gradualution was underway, genuine revolutions—democratic ones—exploded in British North American (1776) and France (1789). The American Revolution (1776–1783) got rid of the authoritarian British monarchy at its earliest stage in gradual democratization. Colonists in the thirteen colonies did not enjoy even the marginal representation that the landed aristocracy achieved in England at the outset of the English Civil War (1642–1649) and Glorious Revolution (1688).

That was the original demand raised by the American patriots: "no taxation without representation." Once the British parliamentary monarchy versus patriots conflict escalated, the demands escalated, too. The American Revolution ended up establishing a new political entity—the United States—under a new political regime—a republic—with a new constitution based on the division of executive, legislative, and judiciary powers as well as the principle of representation. Resting on this solid basis, the American democratic revolution continued expanding politically and socially throughout the democratic waves in a similar fashion to the British trajectory.

Politically, enfranchisement reached all male citizens by 1870 (Fifteenth Amendment), all citizens by 1920 (Nineteenth Amendment), and younger citizens (18 years young and older) by 1971 (26th Amendment). In 1965, though, it was necessary to sign the Voting Rights Act to prevent racial discrimination of voters, highlighting the American singularity as a post-apartheid society. Along the social dimension, broadening constituencies gradually gained access to better housing, nutrition, health care, education, and technology. The growing self-assertion that comes with social democratization is well reflected in American history by the emergence of the Democratic Party and its electoral victory in

1828. With it the young republic stopped being the exclusive domain of the socioeconomic-educated elite. Since, broadening segments of society have continued asserting themselves at the center stages of public life and markets.

The other genuinely revolutionary crucial instance for the Democratic Revolution was the French Revolution (1789). Once again, this revolution was triggered by monarchical demands for taxation. These demands were directly connected to the French expenditures in decisive support for the patriots in the American Revolutionary War. Those demands ultimately ended, inspired by the precedent of the English Civil War, with the decapitation of the monarch. And as with the Democratic Revolutions in Britain and the United States, this was followed by a gradual expansion along the political and social dimensions—expanding enfranchisement and betterment of life conditions. What singles out the French case as the apotheosis of the Democratic Revolution is the thorough mobilization of society as a whole and its harnessing to foster a political project.

The project was a French empire: a European one, perhaps a global one, maybe even the very enthronement of France as the world hegemon. What sport would have half of the world population be watching by 2014, then? Pétanque? The thorough mobilization was achieved through military universal recruitment, the *levée en masse*. Remember, the Democratic Revolution made subjects into citizens. Citizens acquire rights, but they have also obligations including this new one: to defend what the revolution has achieved for them and to prevent the landed aristocracy, sitting atop of the social pyramid either at home or abroad, from taking their recently obtained rights. In sharp contrast, what sane autocratic ruler throughout Europe (or beyond for that matter) would grant weaponry and military training to these multitudes of subjects, at the bottom of the social pyramid, that he was supposed to keep at bay for the benefit of his fellow landed aristocrats?

It is this sharp contrast that lies at the core of the French exceptional success during the Revolutionary and Napoleonic Wars. Through its democratization—namely, opening access to the masses—the French army, the Grande Armée, amounted to some half million soldiers strong, perhaps even as many as 680,000. Their army's foes, made up of landed aristocrats and professionals, all combined could not even begin to match these numbers. The Austrian and Prussian forces combined, for instance, amounted only to 81,000 men at the beginning of the conflict. All other things (military technology, logistics, tactics, strategy, and motivation levels) being roughly equal, the difference in numbers resulted in a long series of French victories until "General Winter," the crude Russian winter, turned the tide in 1812 by decimating the massive French army in the prairies of Russia, reducing it to a mere 100,000 members.[9]

More importantly, this sharp contrast also marks the upcoming of mass politics. Five thousand years of a perennial arrangement that granted near-monopolies in landowning, military command, and public decision-making to the landed aristocracy atop of the social pyramid reached the beginning of its end. First the French Revolution and then the French Empire, by inspiring admirers, imposing rule over the conquered, or by making their enemies adopt some of their innovations, triggered the involvement of ever-growing constituencies into the public sphere.

AN EXPERIMENT WITH SYNERGY

The unfolding of the Democratic Revolution in France and in the United States also highlights the synergic powers of the "synergic revolutions" in catapulting Great Britain to world hegemony. Since the end of the Thirty Years War (1630–1648) France had been the would-be world hegemon striving to fill the hegemonic vacuum left by the defeat of the Iberian Union, the global empires of Spain and Portugal combined under one king (1580–1640). France was never closer to fulfilling this 150-year goal as it was in the Revolutionary and Napoleonic wars. The Democratic Revolution with its advent of mass politics, citizenship, and universal conscription gave France a powerful edge in finally breaking through the standoff with its long-lasting foes.

However, for all of the leverage that this most daring case of democratization brought, it was no match not only for General Winter but more fundamentally for the synergy of industrialization and democratization, even in its milder extent, in Britain. It was only after the two and a half decades long Revolutionary and Napoleonic wars (1792–1815) that France entered its Industrial Revolution. By then, the abolition of serfdom, legal equality under the new legal regime framed by the Code Napoléon, and the creation of a national market by erasing internal tariffs—all stimulated by the French Revolution—easily synergized with upcoming industrialization. For world hegemony, however, it came too late.

Nevertheless, France became a major partner in the British hegemonic world order, particularly after the unification of Germany in 1871. As such, despite being left behind in politico-military might and economic/financial power, French culture enjoyed a hegemonic status in multiple domains such as urban planning, architecture, literature, fashion, and gastronomy. The 1855 Exposition Universelle in Paris—second only to the Great Exhibition in Hyde Park, London—asserted that. Indeed, about half of the world population does actually follow the Tour de France nowadays, with many more viewers if we were to include additional cycle races, a French invention dated to 1868.[10] When it comes to soccer, the FIFA World Cup and the UEFA Euro Cup were both instituted by Frenchmen Jules Rimet and Henri Delaunay, respectively. As for performance, that's another matter. Neither the English nor the French national teams hold the most impressive records. Those honors go to Brazil, Italy, and Germany. Even world hegemony has its limits.

A similar lack in synergy is observed in "the hegemon in the making." The American Democratic Revolution transformed the fate of the thirteen colonies, but it did not propel them to the hegemonic stage. True, it made the United States a model for the future of the Western Hemisphere. In conjunction with the French Revolution and Napoleonic Wars, the American Revolution inspired the Latin American patriots who between 1810 and 1820 vanquished colonial rule, established republics, and drafted constitutions following in the footsteps of the American model.[11] But for truly world hegemonic position, the democratic revolution needed to be paired with industrialization. The United States had to wait until 1813 for that synergy to be launched. That is when Francis Cabot Lowell came back from Britain with the design for power looms stored in his memory for the firm purpose of replicating them in Massachusetts. The Industrial Revolution was fully launched following this successful experience.[12] Synergy was not late in this case. World hegemony loomed on the horizon for the United States.

ANOTHER SET OF TWINS: FREE TRADE AND COMPARATIVE ADVANTAGE

One of the multiple outcomes of the "Synergic Revolutions" is the rise of free trade. As an economic approach, free trade simply states that everybody should enjoy the freedom to trade with everybody else without restrictions, barriers, tariffs, subsidies, taxes, or any other impediment or distorting imposition. That prospect, enthusiastically formulated by the British economists Adam Smith and David Ricardo, was as far from reality as it could possibly have been before the spinning-up of the "Synergic Revolutions." Back then, near-monopoly was the name of the game. World trade was dominated by the European maritime empires. They religiously stuck to the principles of mercantilism geared to seal the trade with the colonies for the benefit of their metropoles only. Contraband was the only way to circumvent these barriers, but for as much contraband that there was (and there was much), still it represented a sideshow.

All of that started drastically changing with the outbreak of the American Revolution that ended up ejecting the British out of the near-monopoly game by 1783. At that juncture, the British attitude was: if we can't play monopoly any longer, why should we allow others to do? The mercantilist arrangement for trade was tough enough. It assumed a zero-sum game between the metropoles, in which anybody's gain in trade access with the colonies was everybody else's loss. As rough as this game was, though, far worse was to be left out of it altogether as happened to Great Britain with the loss of the thirteen colonies. The British conclusion did not take long to come: if we lost our monopoly there, why shouldn't others lose their monopolies to their colonies too? "Free trade!" became the British outcry.

But the British outcry for free trade was not just a matter of equalizing conditions. It wasn't just an attitude of, "We all played monopoly before, but given that we can't play monopoly any longer let's all play free trade now." Much more than that, the British outcry for free trade was an opportunistic move looking to capitalize on their crucial advantage: industrialization! The mercantilist arrangement of world trade was based on each metropole taking advantage of its colonies. Arranging world trade according to the principle of free trade while being exclusively equipped with industrialization meant that Great Britain could take advantage of all of the colonies, not just their own. In fact, not just all of the colonies, but the colonies' respective metropoles as well. And not only the global maritime empires but also those parts of the world thus far out of the reach of the European metropoles: The Gunpowder Empires of Eurasia and most of the African continent. The British loss of its mercantilist quasi-monopoly vis-à-vis its colonies was transformed into a British gain of a free trade quasi-monopoly globally. With Great Britain in a position geared to take commercial advantage of all, thanks to industrialization, what was left for all the others? In two words: comparative advantage.

The principle of comparative advantage states that a society is better off by producing and exporting the products it is best positioned to produce accordingly to its factor endowments—land and environment, labor, and capital—while importing all other products. Moreover, the combined production of societies engaged in free trade and practicing the principle of comparative advantage will always be larger than their combined production if these same societies are self-sufficient or autarkic. Unconvinced? The English economist David Ricardo (1772–1823) has mathematically demonstrated that for you.

In his famous example, Ricardo considers a world economy consisting of two countries, Portugal and England, which produce two goods of identical quality. In Portugal it is possible to produce wine and cloth with less labor than it would take to produce the same quantities in England. However, the relative costs of producing those two goods differ between the countries. In Portugal, 90 hours of work are necessary to produce one unit of cloth and 80 hours for one unit of wine. In England it is 100 and 120 hours, respectively. Hence, England could commit 100 hours of labor to produce one unit of cloth or instead produce 5/6 units of wine. By comparison, Portugal could commit 90 hours of labor to produce one unit of cloth or instead produce 9/8 units of wine. Portugal, then, possesses an absolute advantage in producing both cloth and wine due to higher productivity. England, in this extreme hypothetical example, is in absolute disadvantage. It takes them 220 hours of work to produce one unit of cloth and one of wine, whereas in Portugal these same quantities are produced in 170 hours of work. However, England's comparative advantage resides in the production of cloth in which its disadvantage with respect to Portugal is lower: 100 hours per unit versus Portugal's 90 hours, compared to 120 hours per unit of wine versus Portugal's 80 hours.

If both countries produce both cloth and wine, it will take England 220 hours of work to produce one unit of each product and Portugal 170 hours to do the same. After 390 hours of works there will be two new units of cloth and two new units of wine in the world. By contrast, if these two countries abide by the mathematically proven principle of comparative advantage, England can spend its 220 labor hours to produce 2.2 units of cloth while Portugal can spend its 170 hours to produce 2.125 units of wine. A net gain of 0.2 units of cloth and 0.125 units of wine was achieved by this world division of labor and specialization according to the principle of comparative advantage! Both countries are better-off![13]

Both of these statements may be true. However, the prosperity advertised by this principle comes at a huge price. The truth is that the application of this principle perpetuates and justifies the world division of labor and, hence, the world division of capital and power. In short, this principle, solidly based in mathematical equations, justifies and freezes the hierarchical status quo in which world societies are positioned. Concretely put, a society specialized in the production of wine given its land availability, suitable climate, cheap labor, and low availability of capital is warmly welcomed by the principle of comparative advantage to continue producing wine indefinitely. A society manufacturing textiles manually, without looms operated by steam engines, is warmly encouraged to stop doing that and concentrate instead on an activity that better suits its factor endowments, say, cultivating cotton. It will make sense for this cotton, then, to be woven into textiles where the looms are situated. So, an industrialized society should concentrate on manufacturing these textiles, not in cultivating cotton. Sounds familiar? Of course! This sounds exactly like the Corn Laws Repeal Act! (Britain, 1846; see above, pp. 29–30)

There are two sides to the results of applying the comparative advantage principle. On one hand, and following the above example, agricultural workers were trapped in a cycle of working in the vineyards with low capital investment, low technology, low productivity, low salaries, and low consumption. The textile handicraft workers, hitherto earning medium salaries, were demoted to the level of agricultural workers as specialization sent them to produce cotton instead. And finally, the rising productivity of industry combined with the expanding outlets for free trade enhanced capital accumulation, technological development, further increase in productivity, rising salaries, and growing consumption. On the other hand, each of these different dynamics became entrenched by virtue of believing and practicing the principle of comparative advantage that assigned specific tasks to different societies. In this way, a world division of labor was created. Portugal underwent the first option, India the second, and Great Britain the prosperous one. And that was not just in theory or mathematical demonstrations; that is what actually happened in practice. This is how the three-tiered global society (see above, pp. 14–17) came into being.

This additional set of twins, free trade and comparative advantage, provided philosophical and scientific support to the lead already gained by the wealth and power accumulated by the unleashing of the synergic revolutions. This support consisted in the framing of a world view or ideology as well as a set of concrete policies. The ideology prescribed a world division of labor that allocated specializations to different world locations. The policies strove to eradicate any barriers obstructing the free flow of trade. Together, these ideologies and policies helped organize the world into a hierarchical ladder of wealth and power with a range of inequality that had never before existed in world history.

Two Sets of Twins on a World Tour: At Home in Western Europe

And off they went! By the mid-nineteenth century, the world hegemon, equipped with its two sets of twins—democratic and industrial revolutions; free trade and comparative advantage doctrines—rallied a world tour that transformed the world and made us all Brits. In the shores across the English Channel, conditions were ripe to assure an expeditious imitation and accommodation to the horizon that Great Britain had opened, showing the direction toward the future. As in Britain, Western Europe had been engaged with scientific exploration and technological innovations for a couple of centuries already. As in Britain, workers' salaries were high enough to provide a decisive incentive to mechanize production. And as in Britain, large quantities of coal were available in the subsoil to provide affordable energy. These three proved to be sufficient conditions for replicating industrialization on the continent.

Economic growth surged: railroads and trains, steamships and ports, factories and banks expanded frenetically between 1850 and 1870. Profound social transformations followed from economic growth: the rise of cities and the emergence of the new social pyramid. Great Britain became the desired model for Western Europe in an additional regard. In an act indicative of the subtle might of soft power, France, homeland of the mercantilist doctrine, dropped its tariffs. British ideological leadership resulted in the establishment of free-trade agreements between Great Britain, France, Belgium, and the Netherlands. Hand in hand with British hegemony, industrialization and free trade had arrived in Western Europe to stay[14] (Map 2.2).

Map 2.2   Two sets of twins on a world tour

TWO SETS OF TWINS ON A WORLD TOUR: PLAYING "CATCH-22" WITH GUNPOWDER EMPIRES

The results of the twins' tour were completely different in the rest of Eurasia. Between the Baltic Sea and the Pacific Ocean five gunpowder empires—Russian, Ottoman, Safavid, Mogul, and Chinese—responded to the innovations fostered by the twins with utmost conservatism[15] (Map 2.3).

That was the case because gunpowder empires were at the very antipodes of the twin revolutions and their synergic spiral. Gunpowder empires relied on surplus-taking from the large body of their peasant subjects submerged at the bottom of their pyramidal society. An authoritarian regime with a tsar, sultan, shah, or emperor at its head protected the interests of the landed aristocracy specialized in the military skills. Conquest of more land and people was its way to keep expanding its economic and military power. This arrangement was fully in line with the perennial socioeconomic-political arrangement that crystallized with the emergence of states, kingdoms, and empires starting around 5,000 years ago. It was modified, though, mostly by fostering a military revolution resulting from the adoption of gunpowder weaponry to which these empires owe their generic name.

It was this military revolution that allowed the Ottoman Empire to pose a threat over Europe, e.g., by bringing Vienna under siege in

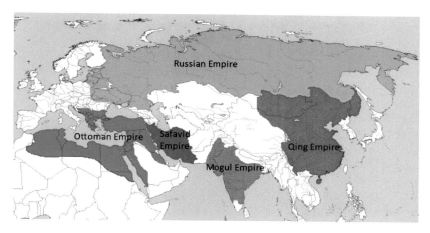

Map 2.3   The five Eurasian gunpowder empires

1529 and 1683. It also enabled the Chinese Empire to subdue, in the 1520s, the Portuguese Caravels and to dismiss, in 1586, Spanish attempts of takeover such as that of Tenochtitlan (the capital city of the Aztec Empire conquered by the Spaniards in 1521). Unmolested by the European global ambitions that their military revolutions managed to curtail, gunpowder empires continued their perennial cycle of imperial development by taking surplus from the agricultural economy and by expanding through conquest. But that seemingly everlasting pattern was destined to change in the wake of the synergic revolutions that drastically upset the balance of power. Once new sources of energy were harnessed and productivity and innovation were unleashed by the Industrial Revolution, gunpowder alone could no longer stand in the way of European global expansionism and of its hegemonic leader in particular.[16]

This revolutionary transformation in the balance of power posed a "Catch-22" type of dilemma—i.e., a situation in which either solution results in bad outcomes—for all the gunpowder empires. If they were to keep European global expansionism at bay, they must industrialize. But if they were to industrialize, they would awaken the democratization twin. Their perennial agricultural-aristocratic-authoritarian economic-socio-political arrangement would be at risk. Eventually the arrangement would be ended, defeated by the powerful synergy of the twins known for erecting a new economy and social pyramid of progressively enfranchised citizens engaged in mass politics. That was too high a risk for any tsar, sultan, shah, or emperor. The alternative was straightforward: play your game, do what you know best, keep the perennial model as is. Inner stability would be guaranteed as long as the old ways remained in place. But that stability would come at the heavy price of a high risk, namely, the overtaking of each gunpowder empire by an industrialized and democratized European power, most probably its hegemon (Diagram 2.1).

And this is what actually happened: each of the five gunpowder empires gambled on the inner stability route. In doing so they necessarily made themselves vulnerable to European expansionist designs due to the technological, economic, and social gaps generated by the synergic revolutions. Between 1853 and 1856, British and French combined forces coming to the self-serving rescue of the Ottoman Empire knocked out the Russian army in the Crimean War. The Russian inroads into the Balkans were brought to a halt and the Russian imperial aspirations to access the Mediterranean Sea were put to a definitive rest. For its part, the Ottoman Empire witnessed how its fate was in the hands of the European powers, not its own.

Less timely was the British campaign to rescue the Iranian empire under the Qajars, a successor dynasty to the Safavids. In this case, by the time of their arrival the Russian empire had already swallowed the entire Caucasus region (Dagestan, Georgia, Armenia, and much of Azerbaijan). However, once again the British presence brought Russia's expansion to a halt and contained its influence to the northern strip of the country. Once again, another gunpowder empire witnessed its fate overtaken by the intervention of the world hegemon. For Great Britain, asserting its

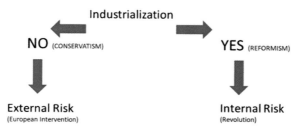

Diagram 2.1 Playing "Catch-22" with gunpowder empires

presence in southern Iran was crucially important, because across the border lay the hoped-for Jewel of the Crown.

Clearly the most decisive instance of British intervention was in South Asia. The East India Company started penetrating the lands of the Mogul Empire as early as 1608 and progressively encroached on much of it. Its successor state, the Maratha Empire (1674–1818), was swiftly defeated by the East India Company beginning in 1775 and in a definitive way in 1818. In all instances of military confrontation, the revolutionary twins carried the day while confronting enormously larger states and societies that opted to continue their perennial ways. The last major confrontation occurred between 1857 and 1859 during a major local uprising against the East India Company. Considered to be the First War of Independence in contemporary India, this massive rebellion challenged and, in fact, effectively ended the rule of the East India Company in South Asia. The British Crown dissolved that company and established the British Raj or direct rule in 1858. British India ended up encompassing contemporary Pakistan, India, Bangladesh, Myanmar, and Sri Lanka.

But the revolutionary twins were not alone in establishing a global heyday for Britain. The other set of twins—free trade and comparative advantage doctrines—was as powerful as the synergic revolutions. A fictitious scenario will make the point while illustrating the fortunes of another gunpowder empire that gambled on conservatism: Qing China. Imagine. On June 3, 2039 the USS Rentz, a guided missile frigate of the U.S. Navy, intercepts a vessel smuggling more than 300 kilograms of cocaine. Fire sends the vessel and its $10 million cargo to the Pacific Ocean's depths; the drug dealers are released. Back home, the Colombian drug cartels appeal to their government demanding compensation from the United States and succeed in their demand. The U.S. government, however, is unyielding in claiming its rights to sovereignty, trade control, and a war on drugs. In response, the Colombian government sends a sixteen-warship expeditionary force. The Cocaine Wars break out in the spring of 2040. Technological superiority allows a small Colombian force to prevail over the much larger U.S. army. In 2042, the Treaty of San Francisco not only grants indemnity to the drug cartels but also opens five ports for free trade and extraterritoriality to Colombia as well as ceding Alameda Island.

Sounds completely implausible, right? Well, that is almost exactly what happened two centuries earlier in China. The Qing attempt to bring the British opium trade to a halt triggered a similar chain of responses that culminated in The Opium War (1839–1842). The Middle Kingdom, hitherto only willing to accept tribute from other countries, was forcefully opened to free trade as a result of it.

With the Russian and Ottoman Empires astonished by the Crimean War, Iran and China at Britain's mercy, and India under direct rule, the lessons of the "Catch-22" poor gamble seemed to emerge crystal-clear: imitate or perish! The gunpowder empires realized the price of their unfortunate gamble and attempted corrective measures soon after. If they were to contain European expansion and avert additional military defeat at their hands, modernizing along the lines of the synergic revolutions was mandatory. Yet again, no easy solutions were available. In this "Catch-22" dilemma in which the gunpowder empires were caught, every solution was the source of another major problem.

Are you a gunpowder empire wishing to become a proper military match to the industrial powers? Go industrialize! And in the process, succumb to the great transformations unleashed by it! In the aftermath of every major military defeat, the intrinsically authoritarian regimes of the gunpowder empires started modernizing by means of top-down reforms. As the dilemma informs us, though, these attempts to address the external threats by inner reforms led to the final collapse of gunpowder empires with their authoritarian regimes taken by storm from within, from the bottom-up. Once the floodgates of reform were slightly opened, the revolutionary stream became unstoppable.

In the aftermath of the Crimean War, Tsar Alexander II "the Liberator" in 1861 freed the serfs, who had been ascribed to the land they worked; launched industrialization projects in the major cities financed through foreign direct investment; allowed a degree of local self-government through the establishment of local councils (*zemstvo*); and sanctioned universal education and prohibited conscription. Such a mild package of reforms set in motion the synergic powers of industrialization and democratization even at this low dose. The ultimate results would be revolutionary indeed, as the Tsarist authoritarian regime was displaced first by a liberal revolution (March 1917) and then by a communist one (November 1917) roughly half a century down the road.[17]

The Crimean War also accelerated the reorganization or *Tanzimat* of the Ottoman Empire launched in 1839. A series of reforms, including reassurances on imperial subjects' lives, well-being, and property rights; the reorganization of the financial, judicial, military, and educational systems; and the establishment of a Central Bank, Stock Exchange, health care, academic and school systems as well as post offices, telegraphs, railways, and ferries networks were all geared toward the modernization of the Empire. In the aftermath of the war in 1856 an imperial reform edict granted the constitution of Provincial Councils, in which decisions could be made by voting.

This wave of reforms peaked in 1876 when the Empire transitioned into a constitutional monarchy with a functioning parliament, the General Assembly of the Ottoman Empire. Sultan Abdul Hamid II suspended both constitution and parliament in 1878. This attempt to close the floodgates resulted in the Young Turk Revolution (July 1908) that restored the constitution and launched multi-party politics. As in the case of the Russian Empire, so also for the Ottoman Empire the First World War nailed the last nail into the coffin. In November 1922 the Grand Assembly of Turkey abolished the Ottoman Empire. A year later the Republic of Turkey was formally declared.[18]

Taking comfort in the balance of power between Great Britain and the Russian Empire that neutralized the risk of foreign invasion, the Qajar dynasty in Iran persisted in its conservative policies. In that regard, the Iranian case sharply contrasts with the reformatory shifts observed in the Russian and Ottoman gunpowder empires in the aftermath of military defeat and facing the prospect of future ones. However, not all in Teheran were ready to see foreign powers taking ownership of the Empire with the consent of a puppet dynasty. In 1905, disaffection with the subservient Qajar dynasty lead to the Iranian Constitutional Revolution. Mass demonstrations demanded the creation of a Majles, a parliament. Elections were first held in 1906. The 156 members primarily represented the merchant class from Teheran. The Majles functioned as a constitutional assembly that transformed Iran into a constitutional monarchy. The Shah was meant from then on to be bound by the rule of law and crowned by the people.

But the British and Russian responses arrived swiftly. In 1907, they formalized their partitioning of the country in the Anglo-Russian Entente and backed the bombardment of the parliament and suppression of the revolution in 1908. The discovery of petroleum that same year enhanced British interest in the country. The Anglo-Iranian Oil Company, known today as BP (British Petroleum), was immediately founded. The authoritarian regime was sustained by its tutelage under a new dynasty starting in 1925, the Pahlavi. This was the dynasty to execute the modernizing reforms—technological, economic, financial, socio-cultural, military, and administrative. Politically, though, the regime remained authoritarian. After a failed attempt to topple it in 1953, this authoritarian regime was removed in 1979 by the Islamic Revolution that established the Islamic Republic.[19]

The constitution of the British Raj in South Asia liquidated any local gunpowder empire willing and able to take the reformist road in the aftermath of conservative failure. At most some 565 princely states were left out of British direct rule but were subject to British tutelage. As a result, the reformatory modernizing steps were directly carried out by the British, not by a local dynasty as in the gunpowder empires. An educational system in English was established, judicial codes and procedures based on English law were introduced, and the fourth largest railway system in the world was built. Massive construction of roads, ports, and telegraph lines enhanced transportation and communication.

All the same, the British Raj did not escape the consistent pattern of the Catch-22 paradox, "conservatism = military defeat from the outside; reformism = regime collapse from within." In 1885, politicized members of the newly emerging educated middle class founded the Indian National Congress. Reforms and repression, carrots and sticks, floodgates up and floodgates down, all were tried. In August 1947 the British Raj was replaced by the Dominion of India, the Dominion of Pakistan, and (in 1948) the Republic of the Union of Burma. The two dominions later became the Republic of India (1950), the Islamic Republic of Pakistan (1956), and the People's Republic of Bangladesh (1971).

But South Asia is also indicative of an additional pattern. Clearly it was worse to be another country's colony than to be a surviving reformist gunpowder empire. Entirely vulnerable to the designs of an imperialist power, South Asia became one of the poorest societies in our contemporary world. This same equation, namely, "no surviving\existing gunpowder empire = colonial status = left entirely at the mercy of imperialist power designs = poorest world society" also ruled the fate of sub-Saharan Africa (see below, pp. 60–64). Left to the mercy of the British imperial enterprise, South Asia was the ultimate laboratory for the free trade-comparative advantage twins. As industrialization brought dramatic growth in productivity, textile prices fell. As the number and efficiency of steamships and the mileage of railways rose drastically, transportation costs dropped. The combined effect of these two trends was to force textile manufacturers in South Asia into the agro-exporting business: the workforce was sent out from the looms and into the cotton fields.

Deindustrialization in South Asia was the flip side of industrialization in Britain.[20]

China escaped colonial status, being forced to concede a few protectorates only, but it succumbed to the free trade-comparative advantage twins. Before the twins' global tour, India and China combined produced 80% of the world's manufacturing output. As the tour unfolded this share was progressively taken over by the industrialized economies of the Atlantic North led by Great Britain. And yet, as observed in all previous cases, military defeat brought about not only losses, humiliation, and grievances but also, as should be expected at this point … reforms! The successive defeats in the Opium Wars (1839–1842 and 1856–1860) triggered the emergence of the Self-Strengthening Movement in Qing China. This series of reforms, unfolding between 1861 and 1895, aimed to achieve economic and military modernization without social and political reform. It attempted, in short, to separate the revolutionary twins. European firearms, machines, scientific and technical knowledge and training were adopted. Military industries, arsenals, and shipbuilding dockyards were constructed. Merchant undertakings in industries and mills, mines exploitation, steam navigation, and telegraph communication were allowed under imperial supervision.

Defeat at the hands of the Japanese during 1894–1895 highlighted the limitations in the effectiveness of these reforms. An attempt to accelerate the pace ensued during the Hundred Days' Reform (1898) only to awaken a reactionary backlash lead by Empress Dowager Cixi. But once again, the floodgates failed to seal the torrent of economic and social changes and concomitant political demands. In October 1911 the Chinese Revolution entered its decisive phase. In February 1912 the Last Emperor abdicated. The perennial socioeconomic-political order came to an end in its most perennial locus, and the Republic of China was born[21] (Table 2.1).

For all of its prominent singularities, Japan provides a final example of the consistent pattern of conservative gunpowder empires between the Black Sea and the Pacific Ocean that was revolutionized by the global tour of the two sets of twins. Although ruled by an emperor, Japan was not a territorial empire. Although firearms were introduced in 1543 their use drastically declined during the mostly peaceful Tokugawa Shogunate (1603–1867). Hence, Japan was not a gunpowder empire. Nevertheless, even in Japan conservatism reached its end due to foreign threat, although

Table 2.1 Gunpowder empires—Conservatism to defeat; defeat to reformism; reformism to revolution

	CONSERVATISM	CONQUEST or CAPITULATION	REFORMISM	REVOLUTION
MOGUL INDIA	YES	BRITISH EMPIRE 1773/1858		
QING CHINA	YES	OPIUM WARS 1839-1842 1856-1860	SELF-STRENGTHENING MOVEMENT 1861-1895	1911
SAFAVID PERSIA	YES	AFGHAN CONQUEST 1722 BRITISH-RUSSIAN CONTROL	PAHLAVI DYNASTY 1925	1979
OTTOMAN	YES	CAPITULATIONS 1838-1856	TANZIMAT 1839-1876	1908
RUSSIA	YES	CRIMEAN WAR DEFEAT 1853-1856	NICOLAS I 1861	1917

not that of the contemporaneous world hegemon but rather the future one.

Almost a decade and a half after witnessing the First Opium War across the East China Sea, the Japanese government, like all gunpowder empires, continued living by its conservative policies. However, when the American East India Squadron showed up at Edo (Tokyo) Bay in 1853 and fired blank shots, the Japanese government was better positioned to respond than the Chinese government was back in 1839. In a quite straightforward way Japan simply surrendered. Unequal treaties were signed with the United States and Great Britain in 1854 and later with several Western powers to ensure "free trade." These external impositions brought isolationist and conservative policies to an end. Forcefully opened from the outside, Japan underwent a thorough reformation from within under a new regime known as the Meiji Restoration (1868–1914).

By giving in pacifically, Japan managed not only to avoid confrontation but actually to provide a fascinating counterpoint to the overall pattern. Domestically, Japan proceeded with a highly expeditious and effective industrialization. Externally, Japan aligned with Great Britain in effectively policing East Asia, in consonance with British goals in the region. This dual move was captured by the regime's slogan "rich country, strong army." The rich economy was propelled directly by the state. Regional tariffs were abolished. Railway and telegraph systems were built and run by Japanese engineers. These two moves combined resulted in the creation of a large domestic market. To supply the development and maintenance of these infrastructures, Japanese industries were established and nurtured by the state. The ministries of Interior and Industry crafted an industrial policy geared to import modern technology from the industrialized West. In Western Europe technology was cost-effective due to high wages: a one-time investment in a machine can save so much in salaries. In South Asia, by contrast, low wages prevented technology from being cost-effective. Why invest so much capital in technology if it is cheaper to have workers doing that same work manually? Japan shared with South Asia low wages. But Japan also shared with the West the firm aspiration to industrialize. And unlike South Asia it was not a British colony.

So, the Japanese government imported Western technology only to re-engineer it to fit its low-wage economy. In order to lower the costs, the machines were made of wood instead of metal and they were powered by human muscles to take advantage of low wages and save on coal. These adaptations allowed Japan to become the world's lowest-cost spinner of cotton by the early twentieth century, out-competing India, China, and Britain. The proceedings of this advantageous trade were invested in the importation of machinery and raw materials. With these two, Japan launched a full-fledged Industrial Revolution favored by the decline in imports from the industrialized economies belligerent during the First World War years. The strong army developed in tandem with industrialization. By 1895 Japan defeated China, making clear that the regional balance of power had shifted. Ten years later Japan asserted its domination of Korea and furthered its ambitions in Manchuria by thoroughly defeating Russia.

Reforms shortcomings in tandem with military defeats brought about the demise of gunpowder empires elsewhere. By contrast, success in the adoption and adaptation of the synergic revolutions, combined with military triumphs, made of Japan an industrialized maritime empire. Ironically, it was success rather than failure that doomed the Japanese Empire. The British (and more broadly Western) rejection of Japan as a member of the exclusive club of industrialized maritime empires by the end of the First World War brought Japan into collision with the same powers it capitulated to back in 1853. At this later stage (1941–1945) Japan did join, in its singular way, the trajectory opened by the two sets of twins' global tour for all Eurasian regimes: revolutionize or perish, or revolutionize and perish.[22]

Few historical questions have attracted so much attention as the ascent of Western European societies on the global stage and particularly vis-à-vis the societies with which they share the Eurasian landmass. The notion of a "Great Divergence," specifically between England and China, and more broadly between Western Europe and the rest of Eurasia, became a major explanatory narrative. As a shorthand, the Great Divergence explains the Western European take-off ahead of the rest of Eurasia as being based on a large series of intertwined factors that includes the legacies of the feudal past, the richness of subsoil in coal, the combination of maritime trade with naval power, the collaboration between entrepreneurs and states, and, last but not least, the exploitation of African slaves and American resources.[23]

The idea of a global tour by two sets of twins adds to this interpretation that the Great Divergence was not only an economic story but a socio-political one as well. The economic and social advantages generated by the synergic revolutions and the ideologies and policies associated with them were immediately leveraged by the industrialized powers under British hegemony against the gunpowder empires. These empires were, for the most part and with the important exception of the Mogul Empire, impenetrable for Western European powers before the industrial era. In contrast, by around mid-nineteenth century virtually all of Eurasia was submerged into a network of "free trade" where the principle of comparative advantage ruled. Except, that is, that these large gunpowder empires entered this network un-freely, constrained by military might, and under disadvantageous conditions. The idea of a global tour by two sets of twins comes also highlights that the divergence was "great" not only in its depth but also in its global scope, as it affected the fate of the Americas and Africa.

Two Sets of Twins on a World Tour and the American Divergence

Throughout Eurasia the two sets of twins encountered in their tour gunpowder empires, which they challenged to revolutionize or perish, only to cause them to revolutionize *and* perish. In the Western Hemisphere, by contrast, these two sets of twins encountered republics. This discrepancy in political regimes is indicative of an even larger divergence than the Great Divergence. This discrepancy reflects the Greatest Divergence, namely, the divergent trajectories of the Eastern and Western hemispheres. Detached since the end of the last Ice Age, around 11,600 years before the present, the histories of the two hemispheres unfolded separately, as two worlds apart. Interestingly, however, these worlds apart underwent remarkably similar socioeconomic and political processes.

Original hunter and gatherer societies were replaced by agricultural societies in the wake of the domestication of plants and animals, known as the Agricultural Revolution. The growing settlements of this sedentary communities resulted in the advent of cities. Cities carving a hinterland and subduing other cities with their hinterlands established kingdoms. Kingdoms swallowing others erected empires. A multiplicity of empires stabilizing huge tracts of territory protected and exploited long-distance trade networks. Huge empires and long-distance trade networks encompassed hemispheres fully. Such "hemispherization," a sort of globalization on a hemispheric scale, occurred in Eurasia around the beginning of the Common Era. Such hemispherization was probably on the brink of materializing in the Americas when the Europeans arrived and conquered beginning in the early sixteenth century, disrupting that integration, and hijacking this world apart into their own. This brought about a different process of integration, one on a global scale, namely, globalization.

It was also during the sixteenth century that in most of Eurasia gunpowder empires emerged. These were centralized state machines propelled by commanding fire power. In Western Europe they are called Absolutist Monarchies. Singling them out with a different name can be justified by the significant differences between these authoritarian regimes and their Eurasian counterparts. In Eurasia, gunpowder empires were erected principally on the revenues proceeding from taxing agriculture. The pyramidal chasm between a landed aristocracy and exploited peasantry was paramount. By widening such a fiscal base, territorial expansion was the road to economic growth and political empowerment as well as a way to reassert claims on universal sovereignty relying on traditional core beliefs and sacred texts. By contrast, in Western Europe a capitalist middle class, positioned between the top (landed aristocrats) and the bottom (peasants) of the social pyramid, was prominent. Through its commercial and financial activities, it was able to concentrate capital and finance the Absolutist Monarchies with its taxes and credit. Jointly, capitalists and Absolutist Monarchies established and enlarged maritime empires that reached genuinely global proportions. These global empires were also facilitated by, and facilitated, scientific research and technological development.

The Americas happened to be the first receiving end of this European global expansion. The establishment of colonies was the modus operandi. But colonies were not made of one cloth. The Spaniards took possession of the most densely populated, wealthy, urbanized, and politically articulated areas where the Aztec and Inca empires and Mayan civilization resided. Such locations with their wealth, particularly huge quantities of silver in contemporary Bolivia and Mexico, and manpower generated the ambition and provided the resources for tight imperial control. The encounters between settlers and locals gave birth to ethnically mixed societies, known in the literature as "mixed colonies."

By contrast, the sparsely populated area that became British North America, which lacked clearly identifiable valuable resources, kept motivations and profits low for evolving a centralized imperial administration. This last circumstance, known as the "benign neglect" attitude of the British Crown toward its colonies, paved the way for the blooming of local and autonomous initiatives of the European settlers. Living by their own in a sparsely populated area these colonies formed a type of colony known as "pure settlements."

Settlers were far less inclined to establish themselves in the tropical American strip along the Caribbean Basin with southern North America (contemporary U.S. south) to its north and northern South America to its south (contemporary Brazil). In this stretch of the Americas, the European Atlantic powers established plantation economies, taking advantage of climate conditions and some ten million of slaves transported from Africa as well as the multiple generations of their enslaved offspring up to some point (depending on the location) during the nineteenth century. This type of settlements constituted the so-called "plantation colonies"[24] (Map 2.4).

Hence, by the time that the twin synergic revolutions were incipient an American Divergence was well underway, resulting in the clear threefold differentiation listed above. As one of the epicenters of the Democratic Revolution was in British North America, the differentiation deepened further. The thirteen colonies gained their independence by detaching themselves from the emerging world hegemon, the British Empire, by relying upon the support of the declining powers of France and Spain. The first independent republic in the Western Hemisphere was established. It was a republic of small landowners and city dwellers, with a

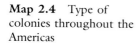

Map 2.4 Type of colonies throughout the Americas

landed aristocracy concentrated in the southern states. Its independence was reasserted by fighting Great Britain for a second time in 1812. Its democratization deepened beginning in the 1820s during the Jacksonian era.

In Latin America the road to decolonization inverted the Northern American equation. The declining Spanish Empire was ejected from the hemisphere with the support of the emerging global hegemon. In so doing, Latin America entered the British hegemonic sphere of influence or "informal empire." As the new republics remained entangled for as long as that hegemony was lasted, their independence was nominal. Domestically, most of these republics were torn apart by constant infighting. Nothing of the characteristics of the First Wave of democratization can be found there. To the contrary, these were polarized societies in which the ruling elite was in full command of the economic resources, land, mines, and work. These were oligarchic republics. It is under these circumstances that the Americas were about to meet the two sets of twins in their world tour.

Gunpowder empires in Eurasia, republics in the Americas. For all of the differences that the Greatest Divergence made, the Western Hemisphere, as much as Eurasia, was confronted with the same crucial questions as the two sets of twins toured the globe: to industrialize and revolutionize, or not? To open up for free trade and exploit a comparative advantage, or not? The ways in which this question was differently tackled and solved in North America as opposed to Latin America was the last definitive moment in the long-lasting process of the American Divergence.

What are the odds that a former colony-new republic (or part of one) would like to industrialize, to democratize, to open up for free trade, and/or to single out a comparative advantage? Back to basics: The major incentives for industrializing are high salaries and high capital concentration. If the labor force is too expensive, costs can be reduced by replacing workers with machines or raising worker productivity (output per hour) by making the machines extensions of the workers. Having machines requires upfront investment from accumulated capital or affordable credit. Then, to build the machine and operate it, iron and coal deposits, respectively, must be affordably available.

For democratization, the two most conducive conditions are urbanization and the existence of a middle class. Democratic institutions, based on either direct decision-making or representation, develop in tight networks of interaction. For large groups of people, urban settings are far more conducive than rural ones in this regard. 15,000 or 15,000,000 people concentrated within the boundaries of a city are far more interconnected than the same number of people dispersed through huge rural areas. A robust middle class amidst the social poles of elites at the top and commoners at the bottom smooths the resulting tensions of stark social contrasts. The repression or contention of the commoners as well as the attack and ejection of the elite can be replaced by a more balanced sociopolitical configuration when a mediating middle class serves as a buffer. The historical instances of democratic regimes support these abstractions: Athens and Rome, Venice and Antwerp, London and Paris.

The willingness to open up to free trade depends on how convenient opening is to the ruling class. Let's take the short version of the free trade test: Is there anything better and cheaper you can and want to buy from abroad? Is there anything you have to offer abroad—especially if your prospective partner will reciprocate you by relinquishing any impending obstacles? If both answers are "yes," then it's a win–win! You are all for free trade. Any negative response to the above questions? Free trade might not be for you. The test for willingness to specialize in a comparative advantage is even shorter: Do you have any self-evident presumably special asset to offer? If yes, you might be willing to make hay out of it. Welcome to comparative advantage! Not so sure? You might need to work harder to procure whatever you need because you have nothing to provide your suppliers in exchange.

Having in mind the trajectory of the American Divergence as it developed so far, before the world tour of the couple twins, let's assess where each type of former colony (later a republic) stands vis-à-vis these questions. In taking these tests,

"Plantation colonies" are a clear-cut case: Is manpower expensive? No; slave purchase and their bare-bones subsistence are the major expenses of this low-cost working force. Is capital concentration high? Not much capital is needed when labor cost is so low. Capital gains are better invested in extensive expansion (development of more plantations in new ground), in other channels, or in conspicuous consumption. A slave plantation owner-based society is as polarized a society as it can be. With the plantations being the gravitational points of such societies, urban development is secondary. Whatever grows in these plantations (e.g., sugar, cotton, tobacco, rice, or indigo) is the presumable comparative advantage commodity that plantation owners want to sell without any restrictions while purchasing from abroad most of the rest. When plantation colonies met the couple twins they said: synergic revolutions? No! Free trade and comparative advantage? Yes!

"Pure settlement colonies" are at the other end of the spectrum. With abundant free land and much demand for workers, the wages of the non-coerced workforce were relatively high. In order to curtail that expense, capital accumulated in the colonies rather than being sent to the metropole and was invested in mechanization efforts aiming to increase worker productivity. Without clear leading commodities for export, pure settlement colonies specialized in manufacturing goods and trade. Urban centers such as Boston, Philadelphia, and New York were the loci of such activities where a middle class flourished. Hence, when pure settlement colonies met the couple twins they said: synergic revolutions? Yes! Free trade and comparative advantage? No!

By contrast, "mixed colonies" depended heavily on a coerced workforce. Coercion of the local and mixed (mestizo) populations kept wages low. Without a strong incentive to raise worker productivity and with accumulated capital exported to the metropoles and thrown into conspicuous consumption, industrialization was not a priority. Although urbanization was important in administrative centers like Mexico, port cities like Lima, and mine centers such as Potosi, social polarization was as extreme in them as it was in the rural domain. These colonies were the closest to making the El Dorado legend come true. Their leading export commodity was silver, followed by gold and emeralds. Politically, after emancipation mixed colonies produced mixed results. They became republics, but authoritarian ones. Economically, the new republics continued their commodity exporting trajectory. So, not too much of synergic revolutions but all for free trade and comparative advantage.

Hence, the threefold colonial trajectories deeply conditioned the ways in which the two sets of twins were received in the Americas. In turn, these different receptions further deepened the American Divergence. British North America gravitated toward the "democratization-industrialization-protectionism-economic diversification" scheme. Whereas Latin America and the Caribbean leaned toward the "authoritarianism-mineral or agro-export-free trade-comparative advantage" scheme. These divergent trajectories were sealed in two of the largest wars the American Hemisphere ever knew: The American Civil War (1861–1865) and the Triple Alliance War in South America (1864–1870).

Given their socioeconomic and political structures, 11 states in the North American South—the Confederacy—would have preferred the "authoritarianism-mineral/agro export-free trade-comparative advantage" scheme. These economies rested on agro-exports produced by enslaved workers. Cotton was the leading export commodity following the adoption of the cotton gin in 1794, a machine that quickly separates cotton fibers from seeds. The importation of all other goods, mainly from Great Britain, would preferably be made without any tariffs. An authoritarian regime can keep such polarized arrangement of economy and society in order. So strong were these motivations that the 11 southern states opted to secede from the Union at even at the cost of what remains up to this day the most dramatic war in U.S. history. However, the agro-exporting economy of the Confederacy was, in the mid-run, no match for the industrializing economy of the Union. The "democratization-industrialization-protectionism-economic diversification" scheme prevailed in the United States. The defeated states of the South as well as the newly emerging states of the Midwest and West either became entangled in this scheme or became their backwaters.

Conversely, given its socioeconomic and political structures, Paraguay would have preferred the "democratization-industrialization-protectionism-economic diversification" scheme. Such a prospect was challenging for the giant agro-exporting nations to its boundaries,

Brazil and Argentina. Such a prospect was also detrimental to the world hegemon, Great Britain, the largest consumer of agricultural commodities as well as largest supplier of manufactures in the region. Between 1864 and 1870 Brazil, Argentina, and Uruguay, backed by Great Britain, smashed Paraguay. Industrializing Paraguay was able to hold off its hegemonic-backed giant neighbors for more than five years only to succumb in a war from which it has not recovered to this day. In North American terms it would be as if Connecticut were left alone to fight the Confederacy and Great Britain would have acted on its latent inclination to back the agro-exporting client. The "authoritarianism-mineral/agro export-free trade-comparative advantage" scheme definitively prevailed in Latin America.

The collision between the industrializing North and the agro-exporting South ended with the North prevailing in the American Civil War (1861–1865). The result was the exact opposite in the War of Paraguay (1864–1870), in which agro-exporting Argentina, Brazil, and Uruguay devastated industrializing Paraguay. The long-lasting unfolding American Divergence was sealed to stay (Table 2.2).

Table 2.2 The stages of the American divergence

	Pre-Columbian	Colonial	Independence War	Post-Colonial
Anglo-America	Lower population density of hunter-gatherers, horticulturalists, and agriculturalists societies	No local valuable resources; no local manpower; no local administrative structures; No centralization at home; **Result: Marginal and autonomous**	Against rising hegemon backed by defeated powers	Core vs. periphery model struggle won by core model (1861-1865)
Latin America	Higher population density of agriculturalists societies that evolved empires	Local valuable resources; Local manpower; Local administrative structures; centralization at home; **Result: Valuable and under tight control**	Against defeated power backed by rising hegemon	Core vs. periphery model struggle won by periphery model (1864-70)

Two Sets of Twins on a World Tour: The Scramble for Africa

The arrival of the couple twins in Sub-Saharan Africa occurred in the aftermath of Western Europe catching up with Great Britain. Accordingly, the tour was not led by Great Britain alone but also by France and Germany with Belgium, Portugal, Italy and Spain participating as well. Around 1880 only about 10% of the African continent was under European rule. By 1914 this share had risen to 90%. The development of quinine was for Africa what gunboats and gun machines had been for gunpowder empires: the means to breach a previously impregnable frontier. Only Ethiopia, the first non-Western state to defeat a Western state (Italy, in 1895–1896) relying on its partial industrialization, escaped the Scramble for Africa.

By diplomatic means between European states and by military might deployed against African societies, the continent was carved into colonies. In all, a cluster of British colonies ran throughout the eastern half of Africa, from Egypt in the north to Cape Colony in the south, interrupted only by the German colony of Tanganyika (contemporary Rwanda, Burundi, and Tanzania). Another German colony, Namibia, outflanked the British stretch from the west. Similarly, the Portuguese colonies of Angola and Mozambique outflanked the British cluster from west and east, respectively. The Western half of the continent became mostly the French cluster, arranged in two colonial federations: French West Africa and French Equatorial Africa. As with the British cluster, in the French one there were two German colonies inserted: Kamerun (contemporary Cameroon and part of Nigeria) and Togoland (contemporary Togo and east Ghana).

Four British colonies along the Gulf of Africa (Gambia, Sierra Leone, Nigeria, and Gold Coast, i.e., contemporary Ghana) as well as three Portuguese (Portuguese Guinea, São Tomé and Príncipe, and Cape Verde) and two Spanish (Spanish Sahara and Equatorial Guinea) were also inserted in the otherwise French cluster in west Africa. Conversely, the French had some holds on the eastern half of the continent in what are now Djibouti, Madagascar, Comoros, and additional Indian Ocean islands. Last but not least, at the very heart of Africa and surrounded by colonies from all of the above powers but Spain, the colony of Congo was granted to the Belgian king Leopold II as his private possession at the Berlin Conference in 1884 (Map 2.5).

Map 2.5 The scramble for Africa

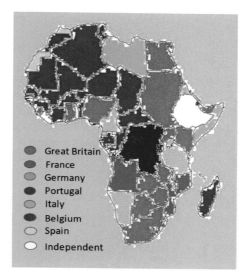

Great Britain
France
Germany
Portugal
Italy
Belgium
Spain
Independent

This conference was the cornerstone of the European diplomatic effort to carve up Africa without military confrontation. And military confrontation was indeed averted at all cost, even when a collision seemed imminent. Such was most crucially the case when the French design of a west–east axis (blue area in the map), running from the Atlantic Ocean to the Red Sea and Indian Ocean, necessarily collided with the British north–south axis (pink area in the map), running from the Cape of Good Hope where the waters of the Atlantic and Indian Oceans merge and up to the Mediterranean Sea.

On September 18, 1898, Field Marshal Sir Herbert Kitchener and Major Jean-Baptiste Marchand ran into one another on Fashoda on the banks of the White Nile in contemporary South Sudan. They agreed on gentlemanly terms to wait for a diplomatic decision to be made in London and Paris. As expected, the world hegemon showed the way out to its major associate. In a British world hegemonic order, the north–south African axis was fulfilled. The French west–east axis was not meant to be. In the aftermath of brinkmanship, the strategic alliance between these two powers, the *Entente Cordiale*, was sealed in 1904. Interestingly, this British-French end game in the scramble for Africa is comparable to the above described British-Russian end game in the scramble for Asia known as the Great Game. That dispute running west to east throughout Asia from the Ottoman Empire, through Persia, and up to Afghanistan also ended up in an Entente established in 1907 once the zones of influence to the north and south of this axis were agreed upon.

Once this key strategic resolution between the mightier colonizers was accomplished, control of the mounting tensions with the third power, Germany, exemplified yet again the prevalence of diplomacy. Germany challenged French control over Morocco and presumably also aimed to counteract British naval supremacy by establishing a presence on the Moroccan coast. Brinkmanship peaked in 1905 and again in 1911, respectively. However, in both cases the situations were handled and settled through international conferences. Germany agreed to a French protectorate in Morocco in exchange for a portion of French Equatorial Africa (contemporary Republic of the Congo) added to German Kamerun (contemporary Republic of Cameroon). European powers found their way out of conflict at the expense of African societies that had no say in their own fates.

Except, of course, when they stood firmly for their rights. In such cases the road to solution was not diplomacy but military might. Such was the case when the High Commissioner for the British Empire in South Africa, Sir Henry Bartle Frere, delivered a surrender ultimatum to the Zulu king in 1874. In the wake of King Cetshwayo's declination, a military campaign was launched in the area of the contemporary South African province KwaZulu-Natal. Five months later the Zulu kingdom lost its independence. Almost 25 five years later at the opposite end of the British north–south African axis, the same Field Marshal Sir Herbert Kitchener, en route to the Fashoda incident above described, confronted the Mahdiyah (the regime of the Mahdi or messianic redeemer in contemporary Sudan) in 1898. The Anglo-Egyptian force annihilated a 30,000-army strong relying on Maxim machine guns. Sudan was subsequently brought under British rule.

By 1899, though, such piecemeal asymmetrical military campaigns were over for the British. That year the South African Republic (or Transvaal) and the Orange Free State, the states of the Boers, i.e., the descendants of Dutch settlers, declared war against Great Britain. After two rounds of conventional warfare, with the Boers having an upper hand at first and the British next, the Boers resorted to guerrilla tactics. Once again, it was Field Marshal Sir Herbert Kitchener who took the lead conducting a scorched earth tactic. This tactic included the confinement of the civil population in concentration camps, where about 50,000 of the 115,000 inmates died. The Boers surrendered in 1902, obtaining in exchange a promise of future self-government—a promise that materialized in 1910 with the creation of the Union of South Africa. For Great Britain, this was the longest, most expensive, and bloodiest conflict since its ascent to world hegemony in 1815. The world hegemon, the supposed champion of liberalism, was discredited as never before.

The Boer War was not the only one in which the civil population was deliberately targeted in South Africa. The Herero people were a society of cattle herders in contemporary Namibia. After German colonists occupied grazing lands, the Herero revolted in 1903, killing about 60 German settlers. The revolt was suppressed through a genocidal campaign of massacres, starvation, water well poisoning (and resulting dead by thirst), and work to death in concentration camps. By 1908 the majority of the Herero population, estimated between 24,000 and 100,000, was eliminated.

These were some of the instances of confrontation that resulted from the scramble of Africa and the campaigns of thorough repression sustained by the European colonial powers against the local societies. The Maji Maji War in Tanganyika (1905–1907), the Bambatha rebellion in Natal (South Africa, 1906), the Chilembwe uprising in contemporary Malawi (1915), and the Anglo-Somali War in the Horn of Africa (1900–1920), are additional examples of early resistance before the outburst of independentist movements after the Second World War.[25]

Hence, the recurrent pattern in the scramble for Africa consisted of European powers managing to avert military confrontations between themselves while sustaining asymmetrical military campaigns against the local societies, imparting devastating blows. The singularity of this pattern is highlighted once brought into the larger context of the two sets of twins' world tour. Confronted with these two sets of twins, Eurasian gunpowder empires were left to maneuver within the limits of a "Catch 22" irresoluble paradox: "revolutionize or perish; revolutionize and perish." American republics, constrained by their colonial trajectories and emancipation struggle, were left to maneuver within the boundaries of the American Divergence: either "democratization-industrialization-protectionism-economic diversification" or "authoritarianism-mineral/agro export-free trade-comparative advantage." Africa, by contrast, had no maneuverability at

all. It was swallowed by the imperialist power of the leading industrializing states. As the case of South Asia already shown, colonies
subordinated to the decisions made by the metropoles were worse off
than gunpowder empires and former colonies-new republics. The equation "no surviving\existing gunpowder empire $=$ colonial status $=$ left
entirely at the mercy of imperialist power designs $=$ poorest world society" is as true for sub-Saharan Africa as it was for South Asia. Except that
sub-Saharan Africa already entered the world tour as the poorest region
of the globe. By the end of the tour it was the poorest still. But now
it was also subordinated to the decisions made by the metropoles and
subject to their exploitation. The work of the population was harnessed
to an agro/mining-exporting economy that provided European colonial
powers with, for instance, palm oil, cocoa, rubber, diamonds, and gold.

First Globalization and Britannization

Off they went, off they arrived! Around the world in 80 years or so, the
two sets of twins changed the face of the globe beyond recognition. They
brought about the first industrial globalization. True, very valid argu-
ments can be made for previous beginnings of globalization. Ferdinand
Magellan and Juan Sebastian Elcano circumnavigated the globe between
1519 and 1522. Sir Francis Drake found an even more accessible passage
for this same enterprise in 1578. Since 1566, the Spanish Treasure Fleet
connected the metropole with its colonies across the Atlantic. A full-
fledged triangular trade connecting Atlantic Europe, Western Africa, and
the Americas crystallized soon after. In 1571 the Spaniards established an
entrepôt in Manila and launched soon after the Manila Galleon, a trade
route between China and Mexico. The conjunction of these two oceanic
circuits made trans-global connections possible for the first time!

True, also, the cargo transported through these trade routes during
the colonial sixteenth to eighteenth centuries can fit in a few of
today's Chinamax cargo ships (with some 400,000-deadweight tonnage).
However, that should not call into question the validity of the early beginning of globalization, sometime around 1571. Such an early beginning is
not to be measured quantitatively, but qualitatively. A quick test of your
imagination will clearly make this point: can you imagine the Far West
without cowboys riding horses and herding cattle? Can you imagine the
Argentine Pampas without the gauchos doing the same and dining *asado*
at the end? Can you imagine California and Chile without wineries? Costa

Rica and Colombia without coffee? Switzerland and Belgium without chocolate? Italy without salsa pomodoro? Ireland, Germany, Russia … without potatoes? Europe at large without tobacco? You most probably cannot because 1571 early globalization relocated so many plants, animals, and germs. And it brought about new human encounters too: Europeans and Africans met Americans for the first time.

And yet, with all due respect to this early round of globalization, if we were to recognize globalization as we know it today, by hard quantitative measures, then yes, this is the accomplishment of the two sets of twins. Because it was only through the works of industrialized manufactures; democratized consumption; steamships and railroads; telegraph lines and the Postal Universal Union; news agencies; and free trade globally and comparative advantage tailored locally that the world economy and society became integrated into a unit working close to real time. The flow of information and communication combined with affordable transportation allowed for prices to converge worldwide. That means that the price of a given commodity, say bananas, became roughly the same worldwide regardless of the fact that it naturally existed in abundance in one location, say Costa Rica, and in scarcity in another, say Canada.

Such a synchronization of prices occurred because of the drastic fall in the costs of transportation thanks to industrialization, the removal of tariffs according to the precepts of the free market, the reshuffling of local economies to advance their competitive advantages based on information on the world market, and the growth of consumption stemming from social democratization. Under these circumstances the volume of global trade as a share of world GDP was by 1913 almost 10%, a level it would not reach again until the 1970s. And the share of foreign investment as a percentage of world GDP reached almost 20% by 1913, not again replicated until the 1990s![26]

By the end of the couple twins' world tour the world became as globalized as it is today but, of course, for lower quantities in the flows of everything and the absence of the late twentieth-century technological breakthroughs in communication, information, and transportation. As of now, globalization was also back then entwined with an astonishing sociocultural homogenization. Today, you can ride your car to a mall, purchase your choice of brands for yourself and as gifts, and get back into the car on the highway leading to the airport. After a transcontinental flight you will collect your luggage in an airport similar to the one you left only ten hours ago. You will ride a car again through a similar highway. Any intended purchase slipped out of your memory? Stop briefly at the closest suburban mall. Then, reach your destination. The trip is over. The only question is, did you leave home, or have you arrived at home? It's hard to tell with such a firm baseline of commonalities across huge spaces and regardless of distances. These are the sort of socio-cultural homogenizations advanced by the current globalization.

Historians refer to every major trend of socio-cultural homogenization across vast spaces since antiquity by adding the suffix–ization to the name of the hegemonic power promoting it. So, when a traveler moved from Londinium in Roman Britain through cobblestone roads and navigated across the Mediterranean waters to Leptis Magna in present-day Libya only to leave one city forum (with its cardo or main street, hippodrome, theater, gymnasium, and baths) and arrive in another while all the time making himself clear in Latin, well, that was Romanization. Urbi et orbi: the Roman cities of the Roman world shared indeed a firm baseline of commonalities across huge spaces and regardless of distances. And if today socio-cultural homogenization is referred as Americanization, can we not say that the first industrial globalization lead to a Britannization?

Three of the leading twins that took the world by storm were decidedly British: industrialization, free trade, comparative advantage. The fourth one, democratization, was British but also—and even more so—French and American. As with Romanization and Americanization, Britannization changed human geography worldwide, albeit at different paces, following the British model of mass migration from rural settlements to industrial and/or port cities. These cities, connected by railways to the centers of raw material extraction, have similar train stations, often designed by British engineers and built by British workers who played soccer in their leisure time. And through port cities, commodities from around the world arrived in Britain while manufactures were dispatched the other way around from the world's factory. In the process of exchange, English was emerging as the leading global language.[27]

With trade and communication also came technological transfers, material culture items, and lifestyle options both in regard to attitudes toward politics, law, philosophy, and economics, as well as daily life practices in clothing, leisure, and diet. We were all Brits, or we wanted to be. True, there was nothing comparable to the global ubiquity of McDonald's, KFC, or Burger King during the days of the first globalization and British hegemony. Gastronomy was not, seemingly, one of the most prominent British strengths. And yet, think of the Cornish pasty filled with beef and onion, sliced vegetables, and seasoned with salt and pepper. How different is that from a samosa you can have anywhere between the Horn of Africa and Burma? And from an Argentinean *empanada de carne* and its varieties throughout Latin America? And is the shepherd's pie any different from the *pastel de papa* enjoyed from Nicaragua to Chile?

Even as today you drive the highway to the airport, instead of riding the train to the seaport, be alert if the car driving far too slowly just ahead of you is using a L-plate. If that is the case your tacit Britannization should alert you that that car is being steered by a learner driver. That would be the case from Tel Aviv to Guwahati to Singapore. This additional example portrays Britannization in action through another daily practice within the former British Empire, in its former mandates as well as its former colonies and protectorates. And such daily practices of global scope bring us back to the point of departure—to the moment our eyes, and those of half the planet, were glued to the screen waiting to learn who the new world football champion is. Now you see how much more was behind the scenes of the FIFA World Cup Final!

And yet, for all of the success of the global tour of the couple of twins, the spanning of economic globalization, and the reach of cultural Britannization, the world hegemon did not remain unchallenged. For once, the Boer War (see above, pp. 62–63) was a bad war for the British not only militarily and economically, but more fundamentally in undermining its position as a world hegemon that presumably led all nations toward the highest standards of progress and freedom. Moreover, the integrated world economy that Britain was leading started, in 1873, to experience a global recession that would last or recur, depending on the part of the world, until 1896. Over-optimism in the nascent world industrial economy and several of its key components, such as the fast-growing network of railways and ports with their docks and warehouses, ended with the deflation of the stock exchanges in Europe and the United States. Financial panic divested production in the industrialized economies and recession ensued. As a result, the demand for commodities around the world as well as their prices declined. Hence, the suppliers of raw materials suffered too. But nowhere were the effects as detrimental as in Great Britain, whose free trade and comparative advantage global architecture was confronted by protectionist policies as a result of the recession, known at the time as the "Great Depression." The British world hegemony resiliently overcame the damages of a bad war and a bad recession. Its economic leadership, though, started faltering and there were yet more challenges lying ahead.[28]

Spoiling the Hegemonic Party: The Exceptional Outliers

Throughout their world tour the two sets of twins harvested nothing but success. With carrot or stick, by consent or coercion, in partnership or by brutal force, by hook or by crook, the entire world was opened up for free trade. Because in a free trade world, who would have the better comparative advantage than the leading industrialized economy? But for every rule there are exceptions, and the global success of the two sets of twins' world tour was not any different. The silver and bronze medalists of industrialization's Olympics were convinced that they could do better if only they refused to yield to free trade ideology and escaped the comparative advantage siren's song.

These exceptional outliers were Germany and the United States. By 1850 industrialization in the German states lagged behind that of Britain and the earliest adopters of the two sets of twins: France, Belgium, and the Netherlands. Yet by 1900 Germany had become a leading industrial economy in Europe. Such meteoric transition was the work of a differential treatment that the German states at first and the German Empire after unification in 1871 dispensed to the touring sets of twins. The synergic revolutions were allowed in; the ideologies and policies twins were firmly kept out! Instead, a firm protectionist policy was put in place to ensure that incipient domestic industrial production was not swept out by cheaper imports. According to the protectionist approach the only real advantage is to become industrialized. And the way to make it happen is by protecting the national baby industries with trade barriers. These barriers will allow the baby industries to grow into full-fledged robust ones before any economic showdown with the earlier-established foreign industries would suffocate them.

As had happened earlier in Britain, a dual rural–urban pyramidal society was rising in the German states starting around the 1830s. Agricultural improvements resulted in the rise of food production that released rural workers to the emerging textile and metallurgical industries in the cities. The perennial aristocracy-peasantry pyramid was now paired with the new emerging one made of capitalists at top and proletarians at the bottom. There was an important contrast with Britain, however. In Britain, the aristocracy-capitalist zero-sum game was solved in favor of the latter by the repeal of the Corn Laws (see above, pp. 20–29, 40). In the German states, however, a win–win situation was achieved by the "rye and iron" formula. That formula consisted of a concerted effort of both social leading classes based on a regional division of labor. The landowning aristocracy from north to east, particularly Prussia, provided the staples. The industrialized core in the west, particularly the Ruhr region where the coal mines were and that was subsequently incorporated by Prussia, moved industrialization forward. The exploitation of coal mines in Upper Silesia brought industrialization to the east of the country as well.

This collaboration was paired with the establishment of an economic union, known as the Zollverein, established in 1834. This union removed trade barriers between its member states. Enabled by a growingly vast railroad network, a large domestic market was created for nurturing the baby industries with a consumer outlet. Industrialization unfolded, then, protected from without and nurtured from within. By 1866 the Zollverein included most of the German states. By 1871, and after militarily defeating Denmark, Austria, and France, this economic union also became a political one, resulting in the emergence of the German Empire.

At that point of economic and political accomplishments, Germany started matching Britain as a leader of the Second Industrial Revolution. This new phase of industrialization is signified by the development of the internal combustion engine and the use of petroleum as its energy source as well as the production of new materials chemically synthesized, electrification, and innovation in communication technologies (i.e., telegraph, telephone, and radio). These developments were geared toward the harnessing of new sources of energy relying on scientific-based innovations accomplished by scientists and engineers. With lesser coal resources than the other Western European industrializing economies and with the best scientific research institutions, Germany had the highest incentive and the best positioning to take the lead in this second wave.

The advantage of backwardness, a well-known dynamic, also played into Germany's hand. According to this principle, a latecomer to whatever sort of innovatory process has the possibility of leapfrogging directly to the very cutting-edge frontier of that process precisely because of joining in late. That clearly was the case of industrialization in Germany, where multiple British trial and errors, cul de sacs, and less effective practices could be avoided all together. In addition, industrialization in Germany was notorious for being fostered through high concentration of capital achieved by the concern (Konzerne) system. This system was based on the merging of multiple companies under a unified management. Its logic is not too different from that of the Zollverein. What the Zollverein did for the integration of markets, the Konzerne did for the concentration of capital. And, indeed, concerns such as Daimler, BASF, Siemens, Bayerische Motoren Werke (BMW), and so many others heavily invested capital in the new leading sectors: chemistry, motors, and electricity.

As it turns out, Germany raised its own sets of twins: "rye and iron," bringing landed aristocracy and capitalists into close collaboration; and "protectionism and Zollverein," shielding baby industries from outside and providing them a market from within. "Lesser coal and more research" provided the right incentive and the best positioning to innovate. "Backwardness and Konzerne" streamlined the industrialization process and provided concentrated capital to foster it. But if Germany was becoming the leading industrial economy then, what did that mean for world hegemony? Where was the world hegemon? Well, it was still ruling a quarter of the world's landmass and a fifth of its population. That made for a remarkable imbalance between economic trajectories moving toward virtual parity between the British and German Empires and the huge disparity of their respective grips on the globe. That imbalance was to spoil the world hegemonic party.[29]

The economic history of the United States for this period is highly comparable to that of Germany in these same regards. The United States gave a similar welcome to the touring sets of twins: industrialization and democratization were "in," and free trade and comparative advantage were "out." A "wheat and iron" formula was the backbone of a regional division of labor between the industrial East Coast and the agricultural Midwest. Protectionism coupled with the articulation of a large domestic market shielded and nurtured the baby industries. The advantage of backwardness combined with the pursuit of technological innovation and the concentration of capital streamlined industrialization. In all of that Germany and the United States, were twins.

However, they weren't identical twins. Most prominently, the United States was conducting a continental-scale territorial expansion. The opening of huge frontier lands starting with the Louisiana Purchase in 1803 allowed for cheap available land that caused a large demographic increase. Population roughly doubled in just 20 years (from 9.6 million people in 1820 to 17 million by 1840). Interestingly, most of the immigrants came from the German states.[30] And yet, land availability kept its price low and the numbers of farmers grew from 10 to 22 to 31 million between 1860, 1880, and 1905, respectively.[31] This crucial difference between these non-identical twins, Germany and the United States, explains the sharp contrast between the "rye and iron" formula and the "wheat and iron" formula. It is not just a matter of cereal preference. Rather, it underscores the powerful role that the landed aristocracy, the Prussian Junkers, as the main landowners and agricultural producers played in the German case as opposed to the preeminence of the American capitalists' over the small farm owners in their "wheat and iron" formula. Hence, although the agricultural-industrial integration and regional division of labor are similar, the leading social forces steering the processes are different: landed aristocracy in Germany, capitalists in the United States, a difference resulting from land availability.

The centrality of land availability and its impact in the American historical trajectory inspired historian Frederick Jackson Turner to write his famous 1893 essay "The Significance of the Frontier in American History." In this essay Turner provided an encompassing interpretation of American history not as an unfulfilled imitation or continuation of the European path, but as a genuinely groundbreaking experience. Turner argued that the most prominent features of American politics, economics, and culture such as freedom, democracy, entrepreneurship, and inventiveness, stem out of the presence of an open-ended frontier. When the government was too oppressive, the economy too stagnant, people could simply move westward in search of better opportunities. In order to prevent depletion by westward migration, the eastern sections ought to match the promising conditions of the frontier. Such a mechanism ensured an evenly dynamic, prosperous, and egalitarian society. For all of his optimistic view, however, Turner posed in this essay a highly pressing concern: the frontier is now over. The United States had already exhausted the continent. Its settlements ran now all the way westward up to the Pacific shores.[32]

Turner's concern was addressed without further delay. In July 1898, the United States annexed Hawaii. In August 1898, the United States finalized its invasion campaigns in Cuba, Puerto Rico, Guam, and the Philippines. In the process it confronted and defeated the moribund Spanish Empire. In this regard—picking foes for imperial confrontation in the service of global expansion—the German and American non-identical twins could not be more different. In the very days of April 1898 that President McKinley launched his attacks on the last Spanish imperial possessions, Emperor Wilhelm II signed the first Naval Law. By this act Germany committed itself to build up a navy capable of challenging the British Royal Navy. The goal of this strategic design, known as the Tirpitz Plan, was to deter Great Britain from blocking Germany ascendency as a world power. The result, however, was an arms race. A global powder keg resulted, and the clock was ticking.[33]

Finally, there was another spoiler of the British world hegemonic party—not a tangible opponent with its own sets of twins, but rather a specter. A specter growing back home, in Britain and in its industrializing followers. This was the specter of Communism. In London 1848, in preparation for the second congress of the Communist League, the existence of such a specter was unveiled in the opening lines of The Communist Manifesto. Famously, that Manifesto opens by asserting that "the history of all hitherto existing society is the history of class struggles." That, the argument goes, was the case since antiquity and up to the present. The major change in the contemporary period, though, was the substitution of the perennial pyramid of landed aristocracy and rural workers in its different variants (freeman and slave, patrician and plebeian, lord and serf) with the new pyramid involving capitalists and industrial workers, or "bourgeoisie and proletariat." This new dichotomy, the Manifesto maintains, had simplified class antagonism and sharpened hostilities. Moreover, given the constant technological innovation brought by the Industrial Revolution—the "constant revolutionizing of production"—"uncertainty and agitation" characterizes and singles out this period: "All that is solid melts into air."

To this intrinsic turbulence of the new historical phase created by the two sets of twins the creation of "enormous cities" must be added. There were the cities that had "rescued a considerable part of the population from the idiocy of rural life." The concentration of urban industrial workers helped galvanize them into permanent associations and ultimately into a revolutionary political party. And it is at that moment when the specter becomes real—a real threat to the hegemonic order whose open goal is the "forcible overthrow of all existing social conditions."

Karl Marx and Friedrich Engels, the authors of the Manifesto, emphasized the pivotal role of industrialization. However, they were perfectly aware of the synergic twins. In their view, the modern state, the creation of the democratic revolution, was "a committee for managing the common affairs of the whole bourgeoisie." Moreover, they were similarly aware of the ideologies and policies twins: free trade, the "single unconscionable freedom," was depicted as the tool to unleash "naked, shameless, direct, brutal exploitation," veiled by "religious and political illusions," one of which could certainly be comparative advantage. Consequently, they did not lose sight of the global tour of these two sets of twins and the global scale of the new emerging socio-political economy: "The need of a constantly expanding market for its products chases the bourgeoisie over the entire surface of the globe. It must nestle everywhere, settle everywhere, establish connections everywhere."[34]

The clear vision of the global scope of this future global hegemonic order had already been articulated by Engels in his *Principles of Communism* (1847): "... big industry has brought all the people of the Earth into contact with each other, has merged all local markets into one world market ... whatever happens in civilized countries will have repercussions in all other countries... It follows that if the workers in England or France now liberate themselves, this must set off revolution in all other countries—revolution which, sooner or later, must accomplish the liberation of their respective working class." The course of such revolution would bring the political regime under the direct dominance of the working class in England, where this class already constituted the majority of the population. But given that "big industry has already brought all the people ... into such close relation with one another that none is independent of what happens to the others" it would not be possible for this revolution to take place in one country alone. The Communist revolution was understood to be "a universal revolution and ... have a universal range." "It must take place simultaneously ... in England, America, France, and Germany ... it will have a powerful impact on the other countries of the world."[35]

Would the specter conquer the minds and hearts of the English majority, the working class? With the British empire in control of a quarter of the landmass and a fifth of the world's population and with its global hegemonic order reaching beyond, would a Communist revolution hitting at this very epicenter mean a Global Communist revolution?

ALL ABOARD! WELCOME TO THE GLOBAL TRAIN

While summing up his view on the Great Divergence between Western European and Asian societies, historian Andre Gunter Frank used a train metaphor. In it, Europe used its American money to buy itself a ticket on a third-class seat on the Asian economic train, then leased a whole railway carriage, and only in the nineteenth century managed to displace Asians from the locomotive. Indeed, with industrialization being the key component of the divergence, few metaphors could be as appropriate as one based on a train. Another train metaphor, this time for the two sets of twins' global tour, cannot be as parsimonious but is, nevertheless, illustrative.

The synergic revolutions and the ideologies and policies toured the world pulled by a locomotive named Britain. First-, second-, and third-class carriages represented by industrializing allies in Western Europe, independent states (gunpowder empires in Eurasia, oligarchic republics in Latin America), and colonies in South Asia and Africa, respectively, were in a hierarchical relationship. All that time, some of the train passengers—Communist workers and intellectuals—dreamt of overtaking the train engineer and capturing the pilot seat. The engineer confidently and effortlessly kept them out of the cab. However, he was dismayed to realize that some 50 miles (years) after departure there were parallel rails, east and west, to his own. A quick glance back revealed that two locomotives, Germany and the United States, at least as powerful as his own, were rapidly approaching and threatening to catch up … at any moment!

NOTES

1. "2014 FIFA World Cup Reached 3.2 Billion Viewers, One Billion Watched Final," fifa.com, December 16, 2015, http://www.fifa.com/worldcup/news/y=2015/m=12/news=2014-fifa-world-cuptm-reached-3-2-billion-viewers-one-billion-watched--2745519.html.
2. Robert C. Allen, *The British Industrial Revolution in Global Perspective* (Cambridge University Press, 2009), 80–105.
3. Christopher Harvie and H. C. G. Matthew, *Nineteenth Century Britain: A Very Short Introduction* (Oxford: Oxford University Press, 2005), 10–12.
4. C. Schonhardt-Bailey, *From the Corn Laws to Free Trade: Interests, Ideas, and Institutions in Historical Perspective* (Cambridge, MA: MIT Press, 2006), 239.
5. K. Polanyi, *The Great Transformation: The Political and Economic Origins of Our Time*, 2nd ed. Foreword by Joseph E. Stiglitz; introduction by Fred Block (Boston: Beacon Press, 2001).

6. Kaoru Sugihara, "Global Industrialization: A Multipolar Perspective," in *The Cambridge World History*, eds. J. R. McNeill and Kenneth Pomeranz (Cambridge University Press, 2015), 106–135.
7. Derek Heater, *Citizenship in Britain: A History* (Edinburgh: Edinburgh University Press, 2006), 107–136.
8. Eric J. Hobsbawm, *The Age of Revolution (1789–1848)* (New York: New American Library, 1962).
9. Howard G. Brown, *War, Revolution, and the Bureaucratic State* (Oxford: Clarendon Press, 1995), 35. Timothy C. W. Blanning, *The French Revolutionary Wars: 1787–1802* (London: St. Martin's Press, 1996), 120–121.
10. Small Data: Are there four billion Tour de France viewers?—BBC News.
11. Richard Graham, *Independence in Latin America: A Comparative Approach* (New York: McGraw-Hill, 1994).
12. Chaim Rosenberg, *The Life and Times of Francis Cabot Lowell* (Blue Ridge Summit, PA: Lexington Books, 2011).
13. David Ricardo, "On Foreign Trade," in *On the Principles of Political Economy, and Taxation*, ed. with an introduction by R. M. Hartwell (Harmondsworth: Penguin, 1971), 115–124.
14. David S. Landes, *The Unbound Prometheus: Technological Change and Industrial Development in Western Europe from 1750 to Present*, 2nd ed. (Cambridge and New York: Cambridge University Press, 2003).
15. Marshall G. S. Hodgson, *The Venture of Islam: Conscience and History in a World Civilization*, Vol. 3 (Chicago: University of Chicago Press, 1974), 1–133. Douglas E. Streusand, *Islamic Gunpowder Empires: Ottomans, Safavids, and Mughals* (Taylor & Francis, 2010). ProQuest Ebook Central, https://ebookcentral.proquest.com/lib/pitt-ebooks/detail.action?docID=625184.
16. K. Roy, "Horses, Guns and Governments: A Comparative Study of the Military Transition in the Manchu, Mughal, Ottoman and Safavid Empires, Circa 1400 to Circa 1750," *International Area Studies Review* 15, no. 2 (2012), 99–121. https://doi.org/10.1177/2233865912447087. Gábor Ágoston, "Military Transformation in the Ottoman Empire and Russia, 1500–1800," *Kritika: Explorations in Russian and Eurasian History* 12, no. 2 (2011): 281–319. https://doi.org/10.1353/kri.2011.0018.

17. Robert Service, *A History of Modern Russia: From Tsarism to the Twenty-first Century* (Cambridge, MA: Harvard University Press, 2009).

18. Sina Akşin, *Turkey From Empire to Revolutionary Republic: The Emergence of the Turkish Nation from 1789 to the Present* (Washington Square, NY: New York University Press, 2007).

19. Ervand Abrahamian, *A History of Modern Iran* (Cambridge University Press, 2008). ProQuest Ebook Central, https://ebookcentral.proquest.com/lib/pitt-ebooks/detail.action?docID=352961, 66–97.

20. Barbara D. Metcalf and Thomas R. Metcalf, *A Concise History of Modern India* (Cambridge University Press, 2006). ProQuest Ebook Central, https://ebookcentral.proquest.com/lib/pitt-ebooks/detail.action?docID=274880, 81–91, 124–130, 217–222.

21. Michael Dillon, *China: A Modern History* (London and New York: I.B. Tauris, 2010), 29–64, 145–196.

22. Andrew Gordon, *A Modern History of Japan: From Tokugawa Times to the Present* (New York: Oxford University Press, 2020), 47–55.

23. K. Pomeranz, *The Great Divergence: China, Europe, and the Making of the Modern World Economy* (Princeton: Princeton University Press, 2001).

24. D. Abernethy, *The Dynamics of Global Dominance: European Overseas Empires, 1415–1980* (New Haven, CT: Yale University Press, 2002), 45–63.

25. IAbernethy, *Dynamics of Global Dominance*, 1–103.

26. D. Flynn and A. Giráldez, "Path Dependence, Time Lags and the Birth of Globalisation: A Critique of O'Rourke and Williamson," *European Review of Economic History* 8 no. 1 (2004), 85–108. K. O'Rourke and J. Williamson, "When Did Globalisation Begin?" *European Review of Economic History* 6 (2002), 23–50.

27. Douglas Northrup, *How English Became the Global Language* (Palgrave Macmillan, 2013).

28. Eric Hobsbawm, *The Age of Empire (1875–1914)* (New York: Vintage Books, 1989), 35–37.

29. Dietrich Orlow, *A History of Modern Germany: 1871 to Present* (Taylor & Francis, 2018). ProQuest Ebook Central, https://ebookcentral.proquest.com/lib/pitt-ebooks/detail.action?docID=5453468, 13–23, 59–62.

30. U.S. Bureau of the Census, *Historical Statistics of the United States: Colonial Times to 1970 (1976)* series A-1 and A-2, (U.S. Bureau of the Census, 1976), 8.
31. U.S. Bureau of the Census, *Historical Statistics of the United States: Colonial Times to 1970 (1975)* series K-1—K-16 (U.S. Bureau of the Census, 1975), 437.
32. Frederick Jackson Turner, *The Frontier in American History* (New York: H. Holt and Company, 1920).
33. Jonathan Steinberg, "The Tirpitz Plan," *Historical Journal* 16, no. 1 (1973), 196–204.
34. Karl Marx and Friedrich Engels, *The Communist Manifesto*, trans. from the German by Samuel Moore (Harmondsworth: Penguin, 1967).
35. Friedrich Engels, *Principles of Communism*, trans. Paul Marlor (New York: Monthly Review, 1952).

CHAPTER 3

Until the "Big Brexit" (1914–1945)

A Globally Convoluted Interplay

Two years had passed since Mario Götze's defining goal and on July 13, 2016, the sunshine was still hitting the lawn of the Maracanã Stadium in Rio de Janeiro. But world attention was on partially clouded London. There, at the Palace of Westminster, Queen Elizabeth II had appointed Theresa May the incoming prime minister of the United Kingdom. Only four weeks earlier the British had cast their votes on the United Kingdom European Union membership referendum. Almost half (48.1%) of the voters were dismayed to learn in the early morning that the "leave" campaign had carried the day. In a matter of hours Prime Minister David Cameron announced his resignation. The United Kingdom began making its way out of the European Union. This Brexit sent shockwaves throughout the European Union, the North Atlantic, and around the globe. Its results remain a matter of much discussion and speculation: will the United Kingdom be better or worse off as a result of this break? What impact will this break have on the European Union? How will the global economy be affected? With the Brexit having materialized in early 2021, all of that still looms in uncertainty.

Much better known were the results of another Brexit. A major Brexit. The "Big Brexit." That is, the process by which Great Britain faded from the hegemonic stage in a world that it had done so much to create. Great Britain had brought industrialization into this world. But then,

© The Author(s), under exclusive license to Springer Nature Switzerland AG 2021
D. Olstein, *A Brief History of Now*,
https://doi.org/10.1007/978-3-030-82420-4_3

its hegemonic leadership was so inspiring that in time most world societies wanted industrialization for themselves too. Great Britain also led in bringing about democratization, the emergence of mass politics, and mass society. Suddenly, a world for some 166 generations accustomed to perennial authoritarian regimes moved to embrace mass politics, if not necessarily democracy. The synergic revolutions that made Great Britain the world hegemon increasingly generalized and globally spread. With that, the nineteenth-century world of great divergences was primed for multiple attempts at convergence.

Convergence of rights and living conditions for the passengers of the second- and third-class carriages of the "Global Train" and convergence of hegemonic stances for the locomotives sprinting east and west of the main railway produced a change in the Global Train's course. It was quickly moving away from British hegemony and toward the Big Brexit caused by the three-party spoilers. In an intricate and convoluted series of developments the deeds of Germany, the global Communist revolution, and the United States brought British hegemony and the first industrial globalization that it had created to an end.

To begin with, and as if following Chekhov's dramatic principle to the letter, the guns loaded during the Anglo-German arms race initiated in 1898 were shot by 1914. Then, the unprecedented level of mobilization demanded by the First World War resulted in an unprecedented degree of state intervention in society and economy. Germany's successes on the Eastern Front facilitated the outbreak of a communist revolution in Russia, which gave birth to a new type of political regime inspired precisely by the First World War mobilizational state. In this way, the mobilizational state that emerged in response to the total war conditions came to be the prototype of the anti-hegemonic party state, a type of political strategy that went beyond the democratic-nondemocratic dichotomy. The first such anti-hegemonic party state, Bolshevik Russia, followed at first Engel's "Principles of Communism" (1847) and aimed to bring about a global communist revolution—aimed and failed. Notwithstanding, this failed attempt ended up making anti-hegemonic party states a type of political strategy with global reach. In reaction, new authoritarian regimes mushroomed starting in the early 1920s in an attempt to contain political and social democratization. As a result, First Wave Democracy, which had reached its zenith around 1922 with some 29 democratic regimes in Europe, the Americas, New Zealand, and Japan came to a dramatic close.

Germany's failure on the Western Front was as decisive for the unfolding of the Big Brexit as was its temporary successes in the East. True, Germany's attempt to confront British hegemony head-on resulted in defeat and by November 1918 Germany surrendered to the Allies. And yet, Germany's blows seriously weakened Britain's grip on its formal and informal empire. Moreover, this European self-inflicted devastation allowed the United States to emerge as a new prospective hegemon bringing with it new rules for a world order. The Wilsonian moment, the brief years of American global engagement between 1917 and 1919, had offered the world a new vision based on the principle of self-determination, necessarily contrarian to an imperial order. For the time being the United States declined its prospective hegemonic position for the sake of its cherished tradition of isolationism. It was not ready, however, to give up its new role as the global financial powerhouse. The First World War had transformed the United States from a debtor nation into the largest world creditor and, as such, the world's economic leader. Hence, when the American economy crashed in 1929 the global economy, gradually created by the British hegemony in the course of eight decades, instantly collapsed too. Moreover, the depression triggered in Wall Street was decisive in paving Hitler's rise to power. Germany was ready for a second anti-hegemonic round, this time galvanized as an anti-hegemonic party state. The Second World War brought the Big Brexit process close to its end. In the course of 30 years (1914–1945) the "Global Train" had been insistently and progressively derailed by the three spoilers. A new carriage arrangement was in order thereafter.

Contested Hegemony, Head-On

The standard place of departure for any narration of the First World War is Sarajevo. It was there that Archduke Franz Ferdinand, the heir to the Austro-Hungarian throne, and his wife Sophie, Duchess of Hohenberg, were assassinated by a Serbian nationalist. The much quieter cities of Hamburg, Bremen, or Kiel are more unlikely places of departure for the War and yet they are not less suitable ones. Indeed, it was in these ports that the newly constructed Imperial German High Seas Fleet was stationed. Ultimately, that was the fleet that sent Britain to join the Triple Entente that combined its forces with those of its long-lasting enemies, France and Russia. It was only the construction of that German navy that ejected the British from its historical alliance with Prussia. And for good reason. Great Britain probably could not afford to have Germany gain continental hegemony based on its most powerful economy and army. But Great Britain certainly could not afford to have a Germany with a powerful navy capable of challenging its maritime supremacy. That would risk allowing Germany to become a new global hegemon. Britain stepped into the *Entente Cordiale* and later into the war because the seas through which the first globalization flowed were otherwise at risk.

The dual assassination on June 28, 1914 sent two sets of aligned states into motion toward an unprecedented military collision. On one side there was the Triple Entente—Britain, France, and Russia—joined by Italy, Romania, Greece, Japan, and most crucially the United States. In the opposite camp, Germany and Austria-Hungary—known as the Central Powers—were joined by the Ottoman Empire and Bulgaria. Given the global reach of European empires the war spread beyond Europe and throughout Africa, Asia, the Pacific Rim, and the Indian and Atlantic oceans. Given the harnessing of the mighty powers of the synergic revolutions now mastered by both camps, exemplified by indus-trialized production of armaments and national military drafts, the war resulted in a death toll of about ten million combatants.

On July 28, exactly one month after the assassination, Austria-Hungary declared war on Serbia. By July 29, Russia had mobilized troops along its frontiers with Germany and Austria-Hungary. Germany declared war on Russia on August first. Less than 48 hours later, Germany declared war on France, invading Belgium immediately after. On August 7, Russia invaded East Prussia. Within a three-day period and 11 days since war was first declared, two fronts were open to the east and west of the Central Powers. The Eastern Front ran from the Baltic to the Black Sea covering a distance of more than 1600 kilometers. German, Austro-Hungarian, Bulgarian, and Ottoman forces were to the west of this line, Russians and Romanians to its east. The Western Front ranged from the North Sea to the French border with Switzerland, a line totaling around 700 kilometers. French, British, and later U.S. forces were to the west of this line, Germans to its east (Map 3.1).

These two fronts represented the materialization of the deliberate strategy of the Franco-Russian Alliance, established back in 1891—namely, sandwiching Germany between two simultaneous fronts. The chief of the German General Staff, General Count von Schlieffen, reasoned back in 1905 that this would indeed be the scenario of a future

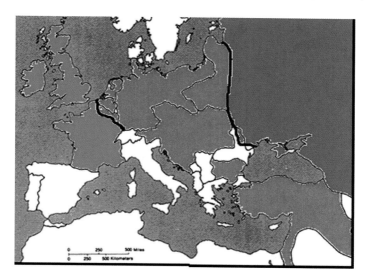

Map 3.1   Two fronts, east and west of the central powers

war with France. Accordingly, the German army planned on a defensive stand on the eastern border while employing the bulk of its power in a swift capture of Paris by outflanking French defenses via Holland, Belgium, and Luxemburg. Indeed, that was how the German army approached the war in August 1914, except that Holland was spared.

The Schlieffen Plan went wrong on several counts: on the east, the Russian army was able to mobilize far faster and with greater strength than expected, thus demanding more resources for the defense of Berlin. On the west, the Belgian resistance was more resilient than anticipated, the British Expeditionary Force very effective, and the French railway system proved to be decisive in bringing reserves and supplies to the theaters of battle. As a result of all this, the German advance was brought to a halt by September 15, 1914 in the wake of the Battle of the Marne and soon after the first trenches started appearing on the Western Front.

Following the halt and retreat of the German month-long penetration up to the outskirts of Paris, the Western Front became one of trench warfare. That is, the fighting lines became a complex of rather fixed trenches sheltering the troops from enemy fire and artillery by defensive devices such as mines, machine guns, and barbed wire regularly supplied by railway. By 1915 its inability to achieve a breakthrough in the west led the German army to strengthen its efforts to make conquests in the east. The Eastern Front originally envisioned by Germany as a defensive one became offensive and very dynamic. Offensives and counter-offensives resulted beginning in mid-1916 in an ongoing sustained advance of the Central Powers at the expense of Russia and Romania. By the end of that year the Central Powers pushed the Russian Army to a line running from Riga through Jakobstadt, Dünaburg, Baranovichi, Pinsk, Dubno and up to Ternopil.

Trench warfare in the West and fast advances eastward represent the continental track of a confrontation that ultimately was resolved at sea. The upgrading of the Franco-Russian Alliance into the Triple Entente by incorporating Great Britain in 1907 meant that in case of war Germany would need to confront not only the continental sandwiching by France and Russia but also strangulation by British maritime siege. This second scenario also materialized with the outbreak of the war. During the first year of the war, British naval forces and their allies captured many of the isolated German colonies, including Samoa, Micronesia, Qingdao, German New Guinea, Togo, and Kamerun. Conversely, the German navy raided the Indian Ocean, sinking or capturing 30 merchant ships and warships, bombarding Madras and Penang, and destroying a radio relay on the Cocos Islands. The German East Asia Squadron stormed the port of Tahiti, engaged the Royal Navy off the coast of central Chile, and was finally defeated near the Malvinas (Falkland) Islands in the South Atlantic.

The inner circle of this impressive global range of naval engagement, though, was in the seas around the European continent: the Black Sea, where the Ottoman and Russian fleets continuously engaged in naval battles and coastal bombardment; the Mediterranean Sea, where, most crucially, the Triple Entente attempted to topple the Ottoman Empire by taking Istanbul via Gallipoli; the Baltic Sea defended by the Russian fleet till the collapse of the Tsarists regime that led to the transformation of this sea into a German lake; and most significantly, the North Atlantic and the English Channel on the one hand and the North Sea on the other hand. In both locations German and British forces, respectively, enforced naval blockades on their enemies. The British blockade on the North Sea was highly effective, cutting Germany off from overseas trade and resources. This blockade remained in place until the end of the war, despite a series of German attempts to break it, most notably in the Battle of Jutland (1916). Failure to do that led Germany to concentrate on its own blockade of the British Islands already in place since 1915. By early 1917 this blockade reverted into unrestricted submarine warfare, including attacks without warning and attacks on neutral vessels. In an attempt to slow down American support to the Allies and tie down the American army, Germany tried to incite Mexico to declare war on the United States and recover with German help the lost territories of Texas, New Mexico, and Arizona. This attempt made by telegram, the Zimmerman Telegram, was intercepted by the British and helped to precipitate the American declaration of war on Germany.

While stalemate was the feature of ground battles on the Western Front, these mutual sea blockades played a pivotal role in deciding the outcome of the war. On the one hand, the British blockade on the North Sea deprived Germany of basic supplies. On the other hand, the German blockade on the North Atlantic and British Channel based on submarine indiscriminate attacks ended up bringing the United States into the war, tipping the balance between the rival coalitions. On November 11, by 11:00 a.m. (11/11/11:00) 1918, an armistice went into effect bringing the war to a close. For more than four years it had been a Total War—a Total War that reshaped the functioning of states.[1]

A Bigger Brother

Britannization was crucially brought about by a set of twins: industrialization and democratization. The Big Brexit, prompted by the First World War, gave birth to a new sibling: Total War State. This bigger brother came under warfare circumstances to impose himself upon his twin siblings. Following the First Battle of the Marne (1914) the Schlieffen Plan had failed. Germany would not win the war quickly. The protracted war ahead became a Total War that demanded each major belligerent to fully mobilize its economy and society. The engine of this thoroughly sustained mobilization for more than four years was the state. In so doing the state became a Total War State—namely, a state defined by "political centralization, economic regimentation, and thought control." This bigger brother took the two sets of twins under its wings. Industry was brought under state control. Democratization as the advent of mass politics expressed itself in universal recruitment compensated by social welfare.

Governments in charge of Total War States accumulated and centralized power to an unprecedented degree. They were able to recruit virtually every member of society for the war effort they directed. They harnessed the economy for their needs and goals. They nurtured a nationalist mindset to justify all of the above, achieved by combining propaganda, manipulation of information, and censorship. Political discordant voices were silenced. Party politics were marginalized. In short, Total War States governments attempted to mobilize everyone and everything while being checked or contested by nobody. To the best of their capabilities Total War States tried to balance this uneven equation by taking task also with social welfare. To differing extents across belligerent states the relationships between state, economy, and society were transformed beyond recognition.

The population at large was mobilized by the state. Military conscription resulted in calling up nearly every fit man into the lines of the army. Women were also mobilized to take up the production tasks left behind by the recruits. The economy at large was mobilized by the state too. Strategic resources such as coal and iron mines; infrastructures such as railways, roads, and ports; and transportation and communication systems such as merchant fleets and telegraph lines were all brought under state control. Agricultural and industrial production became subordinated to state rather than market demands.

The political leaderships joined the industrialists in the belligerent states to articulate plans for future production. Aiming to bring these planes to fruition, workers' strikes were forbidden. At the same time, however, the same leadership reached agreements with trade unions granting improved conditions for the workers and their families. Moreover, in a compensatory attempt to a society fully vested in the war effort, Total War States also became more prominent in social welfare. Proactive policies of housing, schooling, and public health were vigorously fostered. These material rewards were supplemented by ideological means. Total War States promulgated much propaganda supporting the war effort. A collectivist ideology, nationalism, was front and center in this regard. Nationalism took the lead also in trade policy, burying the other set of twins of the Britannization days: free trade and comparative advantage. Instead, an autarkic effort to sustain the nation by the exploitation of domestic resources through the concerted efforts of its members developed and continued to survive after the end of the First World War.[2]

A STRANGE COUPLE

Not all belligerent states were equally ready to transition into Total War States. As a bigger brother of the two sets of twins, it is unsurprising that Total War States gained a firmer grip in Britain, France, and Germany where industrialization and mass politics had come to fruition to a larger extent. In Russia, a Catch-22 gunpowder empire, late modernization reforms proved insufficient to sustain a Total War State. In February 1917 a revolution toppled Tsar Nicholas II and replaced the Tsarist regime with a provisional government. However, this new government, led by Alexander Kerensky, was determined to continue waging war despite its unpopularity. In the failed Russian Total War State, it was possible for an opposition to get organized. In growing numbers, the Bolsheviks increasingly demonstrated under the banner "down with the war."

Vladimir Lenin seized the opportunity to return to Russia from his exile in Switzerland. The German government seized the opportunity to infiltrate him and 31 more activists into Russia to steer events there. Lenin's goal was for the Bolsheviks to take power in Russia. The German government's goal was to make good the Bolshevik "out of the war" promise. The partnership paid off for both sides. On April 16, 1917 Lenin and his exiled Communist comrades arrived back in Russia after crossing Germany in a "sealed train" from Zürich to Sassnitz on the shore of the Baltic Sea. A ferry to Helsinki and a train to Finland Station in Petrograd culminated the journey. By November 7 (October 25 by the Julian calendar), the Bolsheviks had taken power. Soon after, Germany rushed its offensive in the East where huge territories in the Ukraine, Finland, and the Caucasus were added to its previous territorial gains in Poland and the Baltic provinces. On March 3, 1918, almost a year after the departure of the "sealed train," the German and Bolshevik governments signed a peace treaty at Brest Litovsk.

Despite their antagonism, two of the party spoilers of British hegemony—Imperial Germany and the Global Communist Revolution –had successfully collaborated, bringing a short-lived payoff to the German army on both fronts and a long-lasting achievement for Communism. The treaty of Brest Litovsk released the German army from the Russo-French sandwiching by knocking Russia out of the war and allowing it to concentrate its efforts exclusively on the Western Front. By March 21, Germany renovated its offensives there. Four months later, though, the Allies, now with American support, started launching their undecisive counter-offensives on the ground. By the eleventh hour of the eleventh day of the eleventh month of 1918 the war was over. Germany had been strangled from the sea, rather than crushed on the battlefields, making room for many to believe in the myth of a "stab in the back," that is, pointing to a domestic treason as the culprit for the defeat. The armistice signed that day between Germany and the Allies on the Western Front also invalidated the treaty of Brest Litovsk signed nine months before. This same armistice, however, could not invalidate the Bolshevik Revolution that the Eastern Front helped to bring about.[3]

A Global Communist Revolution

Karl Marx and Frederich Engels, the founding fathers of self-proclaimed "Scientific Communism," viewed the Global Communist Revolution as the never-ending frontier of the synergic twins. In their view, the Industrial Revolution was so successful in addressing the material needs of humankind that the only pending task was a Communist Revolution that would lead to a genuine democratization. That is, that the fruits of the unleashed powers of industrialization would be shared by society at large. This, they believed, was the necessary rational remedy to the irrational destruction of overproduction and partial destruction of productive forces every time that the bourgeoisie ran into a commercial crisis. There are only so many new markets that can be conquered. There is only so much intensification that can be exercised in previously conquered markets. It is for that long that society will tolerate the destruction of overproduction to overcome commercial crises. However, ultimately the limiting conditions resulting from the consolidated ownership of the factories by a few families will be dismantled once society claims these means of production their own.

This trajectory was considered by Marx and Engels to be inescapable, scientifically predictable, and historically demonstrable. It represented an additional step in the fulfillment of the optimistic idea of progress and betterment of humankind. This scientific prognosis expected the Communist Revolution to explode where the synergic twins were at the heights of their powers in Great Britain, France, and Germany. This scientific analysis determined one additional necessary condition: for the Communist Revolution to succeed it must also be global, just as the capitalist economy is global. These two prerequisites could presumably have been met if a revolution were to break out in Great Britain. A Communist Revolution in the home front of the world hegemon would rest on a strong industrial basis and, with one-quarter of the planet being under its direct rule and much more constituting its informal empire, it would instantly become global. But nothing of the sort happened. The prediction of a Communist Revolution in the cradle of the synergic revolutions never materialized. And Britannization reverted into the Big Brexit forced by the First World War that in turn did indeed trigger the outbreak of a Communist Revolution, but in Russia.

With not too much of the synergic twin revolutions at his disposal, Vladimir Lenin, leader of the Bolshevik Party in Russia, turned to the Bigger Brother instead. This outgrowth of the First World War, the Total War State, was fine-tuned by Lenin as the tool that would make the Global Communist Revolution happen. His Germany-backed arrival in Russia in April 1917 was short-lived. The Provisional Government accused him of being a German agent provocateur. But Germany was not only instrumental in having Lenin delivered back to Russia. Germany, particularly the German Total War State, was inspirational for envisioning how a state is able to command economy and society. From his renewed exile, now in Helsinki, Lenin wrote *The State and Revolution*. In it he distinguished between two phases of Communism. Stateless Communism was defined as a final stage sometime in the future. But immediately after the planned revolution, a Dictatorship of the Proletariat was in order. By this Lenin meant a political regime in which one social class, the industrial workers, holds state power to suppress another social class, the bourgeoisie. The old bureaucracy would be replaced by a new one that would bring the whole economy under its control.[4]

These preliminary ideas become War Communism, the Communist version of the Total War State. As with Total War States, a fateful war was underway when War Communism was established in the 1918. That was the Russian Civil War confronting the Communist Red Army against the White Army, which was a loose coalition of anti-Communists backed by the First World War allies. This war lasted till mid-1923, consumed more than a million lives,[5] and added to the overwhelming devastation of Russia initiated by the First World War. At the very outset of this conflagration the state was renamed the Russian Soviet Federated Socialist Republic and was constitutionally proclaimed to be a one-party regime. The Communist Party, a 600,000-strong centralized and disciplined body, became the new bureaucracy to run the state. And the state ran all industries, agricultural surpluses, finances, infrastructures, and foreign trade in a centralized way. This arrangement was legitimized by the party control over the news, the educational and scientific institutions, publishing houses, literature, and the arts.[6]

This new political regime owes much more to Lenin's voluntarism, opportunism, and determination to ride on the crest of the First World War than to Marx and Engels ideology. It does not represent the fulfillment of Marx's "scientific" prognosis but rather the combination of the Catch-22 effects on a gunpowder empire aggravated by the First World War combined with the Total War State model that the war had produced. In fact, Lenin knowingly discarded the first Marxist requirement for a Communist revolution to take place, namely, a full-fledged industrialized economy. But, precisely because of that, he stuck very firmly to the second condition: the global scope of the Revolution. If the Communist Revolution were to take hold in Russia that would be only possible by reaching out to additional societies, particularly industrialized ones. So, the omnipresent party had one more crucial mission to fulfill, this one abroad: to create an international Soviet republic!

SURPRISING SUCCESS

The success of the Bolshevik revolution had a global impact. The new Soviet state stimulated, encouraged, and attracted revolutionary forces everywhere as a powerful magnet. Without delay, in early March 1919 the Comintern or Third Communist International was founded in Moscow. A First International, trying to bring together all revolutionary forces and in which Marx and Engels had a decisive role, had already been founded in 1864 but it disbanded in 1876 due to irreconcilable disagreements between Communists and Anarchists. A Second International was established in 1889 yet similarly dissolved in 1916 due to inner divisions, in this case the clashes between anti-war socialists and pro-war patriotic socialists amidst the First World War.

In 1919, by contrast, the Comintern was anchored by the success of a first Communist Revolution that aimed to become global. For Lenin, having the Communist Revolution expanded was not only a doctrinaire precept. It was an urgent need to survive the crushing attempts by the domestic and international anti-Communist coalition. For international communists, the Soviet Union was the springboard to launch revolutionary attempts. This convergence of motives and the shared ideological views resulted in a multiplicity of such attempts in Finland (1918), Bavaria (1918–1919) and Berlin (January and March 1919), Hungary (March–July 1919), northern Italy (1919–1920), Saxony and Hamburg (1923), and Bulgaria (1923). All of them, though, ended in failure.

Mongolia was the only exception. There, in 1921, amidst the Russian Civil War, the Red Army assisted by Mongolian units prevailed over the ruling Baron Ungern von Sternberg, a White lieutenant general. The one and only Communist success in Mongolia in 1921 resulted in the emergence of an anti-hegemonic party state there following Bogd Khan's death in 1924. The Mongolian People's Republic was proclaimed by the People's Party and under the Soviet auspices. The consolidation of the new regime was followed in 1928 by the expropriation of the nobility and the monasteries, the establishment of state farms for crop growing, and the collectivization of herds and herding. The state also started a modest industrialization of animal husbandry products. Transportation, communications, domestic and foreign trade, and banking and finance were nationalized.[7]

By 1937, however, Soviet assistance became a full-fledged occupation. In facing Japanese expansionism, the Soviet Union deployed troops in Mongolia. By then, the anti-hegemonic state in Mongolia was transformed into an authoritarian Soviet satellite that purged and demobilized the People's Party, adopted the Red Army as its new backbone, and readjusted its economy according to the Soviet Union's guidance and needs. In this way, the Mongolian People's Republic ended up anticipating and prefiguring the Soviet satellite states that constituted the Soviet Bloc after the end of the Second World War.

Global Communist Revolution failure aside, the Soviet Union unintentionally succeeded in exporting not its revolution, but its political regime inspired by the Total War State. The duplicity and overlap of party and state; the mobilization of some social groups to suppress others; the guidance of a collectivist ideology that defines the collective (e.g. the class, the nation, or the race) and its goals; the aim to substantially transform the economy, the society, and the positioning of the state in the world order—all of the above are the prominent features of this emerging political strategy, the Anti-Hegemonic Party State.

Neither authoritarian nor democratic but cognizant of the democratic revolution as the advent of mass politics, eager to engage with the Industrial Revolution, informed by Total War States, and either in reaction against, directly guided by, or imitating the Soviet Union, anti-hegemonic party states spread globally during the rest of the twentieth century. This new type of global tour was already underway during the 1920s and 1930s, with stations in one Western European state, one gunpowder empire, and one of the oligarchic republics in the Americas.

By Reaction Against

In the Russian Empire the First World War brought the Catch-22 dilemma to the limit. The attempt to sustain a Total War State without the firm basis of the synergic revolutions resulted in the outbreak of a more radical revolution that aimed to bring about industrialization and democratization in a faster and more drastic fashion. A War Communist State was created to accomplish these goals. Among other belligerents, the sequence consisting of the First World War, the resulting Total War State, and the inspiration of the Communist revolution in Russia had profoundly shaken their economies and societies.

Italy was one of these scenarios. There, the withdrawal of the Total War State meant the immediate shrinking of the economic activity and the layoff of industrial workers. For those still in the workforce, mounting inflation eroded their wages. The unions responded with strikes and the occupation of factories. In the rural areas, peasants organized by trade unions seized land for themselves. The Socialist Party shifted from its prewar reformist stand toward a revolutionary one. That is how the years 1919–1920 became known as the *biennio rosso*, the two red years. The outcry was "Fare come in Russia!" (to do as in Russia).[8]

The prospect of a coalition of workers and peasants bringing about another Communist revolution loomed prominently in the Italian horizon. Under these circumstances a preemptive strike was made by the mobilization of an alternative broad social coalition. This coalition made of industrialists, landlords, lower middle class, and small state owners was mobilized by the Fascist Party founded in 1921. Its primary and most urgent goal was the suppression of workers and peasants.

In 1922 King Victor Emmanuel III handed over power to the fascist leader Benito Mussolini. The Fascist Party then underwent a process of centralization through the establishment of the Fascist Grand Council (1922) and the purge of Party bosses at the local level (1924). By 1924, opposition parties were effectively eliminated. The dictatorship of a one-party state was formalized by law in 1928. Party membership became a mandatory requirement for accessing public office. With that an overlap was established between state institutions and the ruling party. Moreover, as party organizations executed state policy a duplication of state and party institutions became evident. For example, the fascist youth movement performed educational and cultural functions; a counseling organ of the party—the Chamber of Fasci and Corporations—functioned since 1939 as the lower house of the legislature.

This regime empowered by the duplicity of state and party progressively intervened more and more in the economy. The result was the emergence of a "corporate state." Such political economy consisted of attempting to settle the conflict between capital and work by means of state intervention and control. At the same time an autarkic policy was applied regarding trade, finances, and the development of heavy industry. These features reminiscent of Total War States were indeed geared toward war.

Dissatisfied with the results of the First World War, the Fascist anti-hegemonic party state fostered a militant foreign policy that aimed to expand in the Mediterranean basin and in Africa. Guided by this vision, Ethiopia was conquered during 1935–1936, Franco's National Movement was supported during the Spanish Civil War during 1936–1939, and Albania was attacked in 1939. By then, Fascist Italy became embroiled in the Second World War that brought about its demise in 1943.

Arising as a reaction to the threat of a Communist revolution in Italy, the fascist regime represented the emergence of the second anti-hegemonic party state as early as 1922. For the second time state and party mechanisms overlapped to mobilize a broad coalition guided by a collectivist ideology aiming to transform economy, society, and the positioning of that state in the world order.[9]

DIRECTLY GUIDED

Even before the outbreak of the First World War the Catch-22 dilemma reached its limits in the Chinese Empire. Defeats in the Opium Wars (1839–1842 and 1856–1860) triggered reforms that led to revolution. In 1911 the Xinhai Revolution overthrew the Qing dynasty (in power since 1644) and established the Republic of China in 1912. As happened in Russia five years later, the revolution led to the establishment of a Provisional Government. Sun Yat-Sen, the revolutionary leader "Father of the Nation," was elected provisional President by the representatives of the provinces united in an assembly in Nanking. Without the First World War trigger no Communist revolution came to topple the provisional government as in Russia. However, a civil war between the incipient regime and the remnants of the old one was in the making. A political compromise prevented it momentarily. Yuan Shikai, the Premier of the Qing dynasty, was enthroned as the second provisional President, displacing the revolutionary leader Sun Yat-Sen. The compromise, though, was doomed to failure as the parties were headed in opposite directions. Yuan Shikai aimed to restore the Empire, which he briefly did between December 1915 and March 1916. In contrast, Sun Yat-Sen intended to affirm the republic as a springboard for modernization. The collision was brief (July to September 1913) and ended with Yuan Shikai's upper hand and Sun Yat-Sen's exile.

With Yuan Shikai's death in 1916, the Republic of China plunged into the Warlord era. This period, characterized by the fragmentation of the country and the control of its multiple regions by different military groups, lasted until 1928. It was in this context that Sun Yat-Sen made his political comeback directly guided by the proven best teachers in mass mobilization. In 1923 the Soviet Union pledged assistance for China's national unification. Soviet advisers began to arrive in China soon after to aid in the reorganization and consolidation of Sun Yat-Sen's party, the Kuomintang, along the lines of the Communist Party of the Soviet Union. The advisers also helped the Kuomintang set up a political institute to train propagandists in mass mobilization techniques. One of Sun Yat-Sen's lieutenants, Chiang Kai-shek, was sent for several months of military and political training in Moscow. In 1924 Chiang Kai-shek became Sun Yat-Sen's successor as the leader of the Kuomintang, in 1927 he suppressed the Chinese Communist Party, and by 1928 he became the unifier of all China.

Between 1923 and 1928 the Soviet Union helped establish a right-wing Nationalist government in China. Regardless of ideological fundamental discrepancies, once they came to power in 1928 the Kuomintang turned to articulating an anti-hegemonic party state in China. The regime relied on a series of both state and party institutions that aimed to achieve centralization. In this fashion the state's Central Legislative Council, the Central Organization Department, and the Central Planning Board were overseen by the party's Central Party Office managed by the Central Executive Committee. The Kuomintang anti-hegemonic party state relied on a social coalition supported by the urban middle class and perhaps, even more support so, by wealthy overseas Chinese. This concentration of power was articulated to reassert China's sovereignty and to transform China into a powerful industrial country. These goals were intertwined and complementary in their quest to modify China's place in the world division of labor and power.

Chiang Kai-shek's Industrial Plan was the first attempt to envisage an integrated developmental economic plan based on recruiting foreign capital for industrializing a rural China. However, due to the economic depression of the 1930s, very little foreign investment entered China, thwarting the developmental strategy conceived. Economic development, therefore, proceeded without any single or coherent strategy but was still centralized by the National Economic Council. This institution, counting on the collaboration with the League of Nations, promoted a series of reforms of sericulture that improved the silk industry, one of the most important exporting industries; initiated projects for flood control and water conservancy; built roads, railroad networks, and introduced civil aviation; began the development of oil fields and mines as well as the planning of an hydroelectric power station and an electrification program; and fostered public education in order to enable economic development. These economic developments were disrupted in July 1937 by the outbreak of war with Japan.[10]

By Imitation

Like China, Mexico was for centuries a rural society polarized between landlords and landless peasants. Also as with China, an authoritarian regime, albeit ruled by a dictator not an emperor, kept the masses at bay for the benefit of a landed aristocracy. As with China, Mexico was swirled in the nineteenth century by the two sets of twins' global tour that opened it widely to free trade and unequal exchange. In contrast to China, however, rather than being forced into that arrangement, the ruling elite was pleased with it, willingly collaborated, and profited from it. However, as these profits grew and new opportunities for enrichment were at stake for the Mexican elite, discontent grew in tandem with rising expectations. After three decades of *Porfiriato*, the dictatorship of Porfirio Díaz, the Mexican elite increasingly resented its nepotism and corruption.

In 1910 at the outset of yet another rigged election a revolution toppled the dictator. As in 1911 China, defeating the regime was a fairly easy task as both regimes lacked any broad support. However, establishing a new stable regime proved far more difficult to attain. In Mexico as in China it occurred only after a protracted civil war that lasted from 1913 to 1920. The war fragmented the country in ways comparable to the Chinese Warlord Era with different regional factions fighting to achieve either a centralized rule over the entire country or at least to preserve regional autonomy. The Mexican civil war, usually known as the Mexican Revolution, was the most devastating war ever fought in the Western hemisphere, leaving around a million and a half people dead. It unfolded simultaneously and with connections to the First World War, the Bolshevik Revolution, the Civil War in the Soviet Union, and the development of the Soviet anti-hegemonic party state.

By 1917 violence subsided and a problematic compromise came to the fore. On one hand, a Constitutional Congress approved the remarkably progressive *Political Constitution of the United Mexican States* that paved the way for land reform, protection of organized workers, expropriation of foreign investors, and displacement of the Catholic Church from public education. On the other hand, the President elected, Venustiano Carranza, did not actually intend to implement any of these reforms. The stalemate lasted for almost two decades.

In 1934 Lázaro Cárdenas won the official nomination for the presidency within the ruling party, Partido de la Revolución Mexicana. The unfulfilled promises of the Mexican Revolution combined with Soviet inspiration to enable the emergence of the first anti-hegemonic party state in Latin America. Even before assuming the presidency in December of that year, Cárdenas consolidated a broad social coalition composed of peasants associations, organized workers, army officers, and soldiers. Relying on this wide support, he was able to dismantle the centers of power on which the Partido de la Revolución Mexicana had relied so far. Plutarco Elias Calles, President during 1924–1928 and the governing figure behind the scene (Jefe Máximo) until Cárdenas' election, was forced into exile. Hundreds of ranks from the government and the army associated with the former leader were fired, and the local *caciques* were put under check by arming the peasantry.

Subsequently, the hacienda system in the hands of the traditional landowning class was partially dismantled by a land reform that distributed 50 million acres of land to some 800,000 peasant families. Later, a process of collectivization took place through the formation of 226 community farms (*ejidos*), in which some 35,000 people raised cotton, cereals, and other crops. These internal undertakings were closely related to foreign economic policy as governmental support of *ejidos*

aimed also to relieve the need to import staple products. More prominent in this respect was the nationalization of the British and U.S. oil
companies in 1938, whose refusal to comply with the decision of the
Supreme Court on a labor conflict was regarded as a defiance of national
sovereignty. Petróleos Mexicanos (PEMEX), a national company, was
established. In a similar vein, a centralized six-year-plan (Plan Sexenal),
of Soviet inspiration, launched land, labor, education and health reforms,
as well as electrification projects.[11]

Failure, the Mother of Improvisation

Understanding the Soviet inspiration of the Mexican *ejidos* and six-year
plans requires following the tracks of both Global and War Communism.
The Global Communist Revolution could not possibly have taken place
based on the one and only success of the Comintern in Mongolia. The
Soviet Union could not be saved, then, by the expected and attempted
Communist Revolutions in advanced industrialized economies. Meanwhile, domestically, by 1921 War Communism was reaching its limits.
Since 1918 the Red Army has been successfully supplied and deployed
throughout the Russian Civil War. In October 1922 the Red Army
emerged victorious out of this war. However, the heavy burden that it
placed on the Russian society resulted by 1921 in peasants' uprisings,
urban workers' strikes, and even mutiny by soldiers and sailors against the
Communist regime. The fate of War Communism started looking danger-
ously similar to that of the Total War State that ended in the collapses of
the Tsar regime and the Provisional government in March and November
1917, respectively.

Back then, Lenin managed to channel wide discontent by offering
peace to soldiers and sailors, bread to urban workers, and land to the
peasants: "peace, bread, land!" was the Bolshevik war cry back in the
day. More than three years down the road, none of these were at hand
for their intended beneficiaries. Russia was indeed pulled out of the First
World War, but only to plunge into its own civil war. Starvation, not
bread, drove urban workers out of cities and although land was granted
immediately after the Bolshevik Revolution, its production was soon after
requisitioned for provisioning the troops.[12]

And so, striving to prevent the fate of the two previous regimes, in
1921 the Bolshevik government drastically changed the course of its
regime as it started emerging under War Communism by launching a

New Economic Policy (NEP). At the heart of this metamorphosis was the downsizing of state control over the economy, allowing for a mixed economic model to take over. In this new model private ownership from within and foreign investment from outside were welcomed in order to reactivate the nascent Soviet industry. In the fields, compulsory grain requisitions were brought to an end and replaced with a taxation system that allowed farmers to freely trade with the rest of their production. In the wake of such liberalization markets awoke and production soared, quickly achieving a 40% increase.[13]

The NEP, almost coincidental with the end of the Russian Civil War, managed to stabilize the Soviet economy and to bring productivity back to pre-First World War levels. Now, however, the land was in the hands of the producers and the industries were owned by the state and run by the Soviets. The "peace, bread, land" promise was finally made good. The workers' and peasants' revolution seemed to be reaching its goals. The fears of disruptive domestic threat were left behind by the Bolshevik Revolution and its stabilization under the NEP. It seemed as if the time had come to declare victory under the auspices of the NEP. And yet, in 1928 the new Soviet leader, Joseph Stalin, took the "Great Turn," displacing the NEP by a centralized planned economy. To this we could say, if it ain't broke, don't fix it! Why disrupt a successfully working economy?

The answer is that the NEP achievements were addressing only one side of the Catch-22 dilemma that the Soviet Union inherited from the Russian Empire (see above, pp. 42–44). The fears of disruptive domestic change were left behind by the Bolshevik Revolution and its stabilization under the NEP. However, the other horn of that dilemma, the risk of being overtaken by the industrial nations, was not. The Soviet Union, as the Russian Empire before, still remained vulnerable to the potential threats coming from the industrialized nations. It was to address this risk inherited from the Russian Empire that the Soviet Union followed the lead of the declining but then pathbreaking hegemon, Great Britain, and industrialized. Such industrialization would also solve a fundamental ideological dissonance: A Communist regime should be grounded on an advanced industrial society, not on a backward rural one. And so it was that although the NEP had not broken, it was, nevertheless, fixed by fostering a fast industrialization. In order to enable that, urban workers needed to be properly supplied. To guarantee such supply, rural productivity needed to increase and dared not be compromised. To fulfill this intermediate goal, private farms were expropriated by the state which replotted them into larger collective farms named *kolkhozy*. This collectivization was pursued in tandem with fast industrialization and all was orchestrated by a centralized five-year plan.

These are the farms and plan that inspired the Mexican *ejidos* and Sexennial Plans. These are the farms, plan, and model for a centralized economy that would inspire many anti-hegemonic party states all around the globe. In contrast with this global reach and in staggering contradiction with the founding Principles of Communism, the Global Communist Revolution was openly demoted by Joseph Stalin to a National Communist Revolution circumscribed to the Soviet Union alone under the new banner of "Socialism in One Country."

The Carousel of Revolution

The First World War was a major factor in derailing the "Global Train" and initiating the Big Brexit. The Global Communist Revolution was not as much of a force in this regard. It was a derailing force only indirectly, to the extent that it generated a mobilizational type of regime with a revisionist attitude toward the hegemonic world order. The anti-hegemonic party state that emerged out of the Communist Revolution in Russia (1917–1922) became a point of arrival for the other two major revolutions that opened up the twentieth century: the Mexican (1910–1940) and Chinese (1911–1937) revolutions.

These three huge societies, largely based on agrarian economies and ruled by authoritarian regimes, were shocked by the transformations brought from the outside by the synergic revolutions. These shocks triggered major revolutions that, for all of their singularities, had significant underlying commonalities. These commonalities constitute an entire shared sequence. First came a departure from the challenge posed by the synergic twins and the reforms made to confront or adjust to them. This was followed by the toppling of the ruling authoritarian regime by a moderate political force in the wake of the unsatisfactory reforms. Then, the attempt of political forces associated with the old regime to roll the situation back, on the one hand, and the emboldening of radical political forces by the revolutionary volatility to foster a social revolution, instead of just a political one, resulted in devastating civil wars that tore each of the involved countries apart. Foreign intervention against the radical forces ensued. Each of the major forces in the conflagration attempted to re-unify the entire country under its rule while minor forces strived to hold onto their circumscribed sections. Finally, the protracted and devastating civil wars ended in military victory and reunification of the state under an anti-hegemonic party state. These sequential commonalities amount to an overall shared pattern: The Carousel of Revolution.

Russia and China, two gunpowder empires caught in the Catch-22 dilemma, entered a phase of modernizing reforms in the wake of military defeats by the industrialized powers (Britain and France). Mexico, an oligarchic republic that willingly gave in to free trade and comparative advantage, also introduced similar reforms. By implementing modernizing reforms these three authoritarian regimes opened the floodgates for several constituencies to act upon their grievances. The political elites resented the monopolistic grip on power by a ruling autocrat; the economic elites resented their displacement by domestic nepotism and foreign investors; workers and peasants resented their long-lasting exploitation. Such accumulated multiplicity of grievances exploded in revolutions. At first political revolutions toppled and replaced the authoritarian regimes: tsar, emperor, dictator. Radical forces were emboldened by the unleashed volatility to pursue social revolutions while reactionary forces organized to roll these changes back. Full-scale civil wars ensued tearing each of these large countries apart into fractioned enclaves. Leading forces aimed to have their countries reunified under their rule; lesser forces tried to hold onto their sectionalism.

Ultimately, in Russia the leading radical force, the Bolsheviks, prevailed. Their victory relied on a War Communism anti-hegemonic party state inspired by the Total War State that emerged out of the First World War. In China the politically revolutionary force, the Kuomintang, was able to prevail following the Soviet Union guidance and formed its own anti-hegemonic party state. Meanwhile, the more radical force there, the Chinese Communist Party, acquiesced to Soviet demand. On the one hand, this demand reflects the Soviet Union transition from its failed intention to become the epicenter of Global Communist Revolution into its surprising success as an anti-hegemonic party state. On the other hand, this acquiescence by the Chinese Communist Party postponed one crucial dimension of the Chinese Civil War: the confrontation between the moderate and radical camps, the Kuomintang and the Chinese Communist Party. When the Japanese occupation ended (1945), China plunged into this pending face of its civil war during 1945–1949.

In Mexico as in China the moderate camp prevailed in the civil war and reunified the country, suppressing some of the factionalist radical

Table 3.1 From smooth revolutions to protracted Civil Wars

	Mexico	China	Russia
Revolution	1910	1911	1917
Civil War	1913–1920	Averted at first 1926–1937 1945–1949	1917–1923

forces and reaching agreements with others. Such agreements reflected by the ratification of a radical constitution and the appointment of moderate presidents resulted in a deadlocked compromise. The deadlock was broken by the establishment of an anti-hegemonic party state in Mexico under President Lázaro Cárdenas (1934–1938). The radical provisions of the constitution were finally addressed with radical executive measures. With this, the Carousel of Revolution had reached its anti-hegemonic party state station across the ocean (Table 3.1).

THE OTHER CAROUSEL: REACTION

But the Carousel of Revolution was not the only game in town. Any attempt to suppress this carousel set in motion another one, the Carousel of Reaction. A successful Carousel of Reaction needed to calibrate its speed and strength in order to preempt or surpass the spinning of the Carousel of Revolution. Public discontent and unrest leading to popular demands was contained by reactionary responses in which the army became the primary arbiter of law and order by deploying its naked force. In the wake of military interventions, authoritarian regimes were established aiming to eliminate any risk of riding the Carousel of Revolution. As a matter of fact, the Carousel of Reaction outpowered and outpaced the Carousel of Revolution in most societies most of the time and ended up globally with the upper hand.

A quick global tour portrays the full swing of the Carousel of Reaction during the 1920s and 1930s. Aside from the North Atlantic core made of early adopters of the synergic revolutions and First World War undefeated states (Great Britain, Ireland, Belgium, France, Switzerland, Netherlands, Denmark, Norway, Sweden, and Finland) the rest of the European continent spiraled down into the Carousel of Reaction. Coups d'état undertaken by the military established authoritarian regimes in the Iberian Peninsula (Spain and Portugal), the Balkan Peninsula (Albania,

Yugoslavia, Bulgaria, Greece, and Romania), and the newly established states in the aftermath of the First World War (Poland, Lithuania, Hungary, Austria, Estonia, and Latvia).[14]

Gunpowder empires that had been caught in the shared "Catch-22 modernize and perish" dynamic underwent diverse trajectories. Russia and China represent extraordinary cases in which the collision of the Carousels of Revolution and Reaction resulted in protracted civil wars that ended up with the triumph of revolution. The other gunpowder empires did not take the Carousel of Revolution but in synchronicity with the global trend jumped into the Carousel of Reaction instead. Iran is a clear case in point as a military coup d'état there in 1921 paved the way to 54 years of the authoritarian Pahlavi dynasty regime. Russia to the north and Great Britain from the south had partitioned their Iranian zones of influence back in 1907 after suppressing the Iranian Constitutional Revolution. All was good and sound for them, in this regard, during the happy days of the Anglo-Russian Entente. But as in so many other regards the Communist Revolution disrupted this arrangement too.

In the aftermath of the Communist Revolution and the outbreak of the Russian Civil War British forces made inroads into Russia from Iran. Conversely, the Red Army entered northern Iran and helped establish a Soviet Republic in the Gilan province. By late 1920, this Persian Soviet Socialist Republic was preparing to overtake Teheran. Under these circumstances, the Commander-in-Chief of the Persian Army, Reza Shah Pahlavi, launched a military coup d'état with support from Great Britain, replaced the ineffective Qajar monarchy, and marched north to suppress the Soviet Republic in Gilan. Upon his return in 1923, Reza Shah Pahlavi became Prime Minister and in 1925 he was crowned emperor—Shah— of Persia. The Carousel of Reaction had prevailed over the Carousel of Revolution.[15]

The emergence of authoritarianism in the former Ottoman Empire is more intricate. In the wake of the disadvantageous treaties imposed by the Allies on the Sublime Porte at the end of the First World War the Turkish War of Independence broke out in 1919 and the Republic of Turkey emerged in 1922. By 1923 the field marshal that commanded the Turkish army to victory, Mustafa Kemal Atatürk, the father of the Turks, became the first President of the Republic, inaugurating two decades and a half of an authoritarian regime. As Reza Shah Pahlavi did for Iran, Mustafa Kemal Atatürk launched in Turkey a top-down program of reforms aiming to catch up with Western European countries under authoritarian rule.

Industries were fostered, infrastructures constructed, educational systems established, and old mores—such as the veiling of women—abolished. While that happened in the Anatolian portion of the former Ottoman Empire, its former possessions in the Levant were submerged under the colonial variety of authoritarianism as Britain and France carved out the Middle East under the euphemism of mandates—legitimately sanctioned by the League of Nations—establishing the Mandates of Palestine, Syria, and Mesopotamia. The colonial variety of authoritarianism continued to rule the fates of South Asia, South East Asia, and Africa.

Japan continued its counterpoint trajectory among gunpowder empires. The First World War represented an additional opportunity to display the Japanese industrial and military success. However, despite its contribution to the Allies' military efforts and its imperial gains on the Pacific Ocean and costal China at the expense of Germany and China respectively, Japan was denied the rank of equal among equals by the Western powers. Its racial equality clause proposal at the Paris Peace Conference as well as its demands for the control of China were rejected. The resulting alienation from these rejections by both the declining and rising hegemons internationally coincided domestically with the turbulent postwar years. Public demonstrations sustained during 1919 and 1920 demanded universal male suffrage, finally granted in 1925. The emerging labor movement insisted on economic and social demands while the newly established socialist and communist parties aimed for reform and revolution, respectively.

Under these international and domestic circumstances, a reactionary anti-hegemonic party state started to emerge in Japan. As with the other new authoritarian regimes, it was the army that took the lead in the political scene, while the left-wing opposition and labor unions were forcefully suppressed. Yet, unlike the other new authoritarian regimes, the Japanese society at large was fully mobilized rather than suppressed. It was not mobilized by a mass party as in Fascist Italy but by the army. Yet as in Fascist Italy this mobilization was supported by industrialists and landowners and it was channeled into conquest campaigns starting with the invasion of Manchuria (1931) and China (1937). And then, conquest abroad enhanced further mobilization at home. The National Mobilization Law of 1938 nationalized strategic industries and the media, allowed for the drafting of civilians to supply work force for strategic industries, and established the National Spiritual Mobilization Movement under the

Ministries of Interior and Education with the goal of ideological indoctrination and rallying the nation at war. The Imperial Rule Assistance
Association was established in 1940 by Prime Minister Fumimaro Konoe
as the only allowed political party; all other political parties were dissolved.
By then Japan had become a fully-fledged reactionary anti-hegemonic
party state.

As with Russia in Europe and China in Asia, Mexico was an exceptional Carousel of Revolution case in Latin America. Apart from Mexico,
the Latin American oligarchic republics that ruled at the top of polarized societies followed the global authoritarian trend. During the 1920s
significant political and social reforms aiming to broaden the participatory
basis in the elections and the social welfare of the working classes through
legislation were pursued in many Latin American oligarchic republics.[16]
As the floodgates were seemingly opening far too much and far too fast
for the ruling oligarchies, the Carousel of Reaction spun throughout Latin
America during the 1930s in perfect synchronicity with the global authoritarian trend. Military coups deposed one reformist government after the
other. This inaugurated for the region a modus operandi that would
remain in place for most of the rest of the century to come: reformist
governments deposed by military force.[17]

Authoritarianism is perennial. The few ruling all for the sake of the few
goes back to the advent of state formation some 5,000 years ago. And
yet, the authoritarianism emerging during the 1920s and 1930s was of a
brand-new type. It followed the global tour of the synergic revolutions,
which meant that the genie of democratization was already out of the
bottle. For millennia humankind had lived in pyramidal rural societies. For
millennia the "Great Chain of Being," a worldview portraying a natural
hierarchical world order from god to king to nobles to subjects had been
framing people's mindsets and living conditions.[18] But not any longer
after the couple of twins' global tour.

The incipient urban pyramidal societies were not as inclined to acquiesce to social hierarchies and disparities. On the contrary, they were
furnished with a repertoire of new worldviews ranging from liberalism
and nationalism to communism and anarchism. Operating under these
new circumstances is what makes this wave of authoritarianism novel. This
was indeed the first wave of new authoritarian regimes. Its task was not
simply ruling all for the sake of the few by the few any longer. From then
on, authoritarianism's primary task was to neutralize mass politics and
demobilize society such that everyone minds his and her own business

Map 3.2 Political regimes during the 1930s—Democracies (black); none-democracies (grey); colonies (white)

while deserting the public sphere. Such political paralysis of society represented the closest act to putting back the genie of mass politics inside the bottle. Only then the rule of all by the few for the few can unfold, but not without proclaiming its legitimacy by blending in different combinations of "Great Chain of Being" and modern ideological worldviews. In the aftermath of the First World War, the first wave of this new type of authoritarianism combined with the pre-existing and expanding colonial authoritarianism that ruled over most world societies (Map 3.2).

A World Safe for Democracy

And so it was that soon after Woodrow Wilson was idealistically claiming, from isolationist and isolated United States, to wage war against Germany in order to make the world "safe for democracy," the states of the world were spinning around in one of the two Carousels. Most of them ended up under the rule of either authoritarian or anti-hegemonic party states. As severe as this Wilsonian misperception was, that was not the way in which the United States played its role in spoiling the British hegemonic party. The Wilsonian principle of self-determination, instead, definitely was. As the First World War was approaching its end the American President promoted a new world order based on his "fourteen points." Seven of them referred to specific peoples entitled to the right to have their own country or decide on their type of government. The general principle underlying these seven clauses was self-determination: the right of peoples to determine their fate by claiming the formation of states within which boundaries they live.[19]

The idealism represented by the principle of self-determination was deeply rooted in the American experience in which the very point of departure was exactly that: the Patriots' resolve to determine their fate by claiming the formation of the United States. Both in 1776 and in 1918 the American taste for self-determination turned very unfavorable for Great Britain. This time around, in the First World War, is happened on a global scale. The principle of self-determination promoted by the American President not only challenged the British hegemony in the most fundamental way but indeed represented a watershed of world historical proportions.

During 5,000 years the history of state formation went overall in one direction: the big fish ate the small fish. The first states to emerge starting around 4,000 BCE were the Mesopotamian city-states: rulers in command of walled settlements and their rural hinterland. Trade networks were woven between city-states, but no ruler managed to grab a full network until an Egyptian Pharaoh accomplished that along the Nile River banks around 3100 BCE. A kingdom was born. Then city-states and kingdoms became entangled in webs of trade, diplomacy, and warfare, paving the way for an even larger scope of political command: the empire. Sargon the Great had entered the history books as the founder of the first empire, the Akkadian Empire, in 2250 BCE encompassing Ancient Mesopotamia at large and pushing to the shores of the Mediterranean Sea. A long succession of empires followed in this region; a long list of empires emerged globally following a similar sequence. New empires succeeded older ones. Even if throughout the process there was some devolution back to kingdoms, city-states, or local warlords, in the longer run the empires struck back.

Overall, the above-mentioned rule of thumb works: larger empires kept emerging in the wake of smaller ones. This way, the political history of the world was the history of an ever-shrinking number of empires swallowing ever-larger chunks of continents. By the time immediately before the First

World War, most of the planet was under the rule of a handful of empires, with the British Empire dominant in possessing one-fifth of the globe's landmass. Had that dynamic continued past the five millennia, we would have to expect an even smaller number of empires ruling even larger territories or even perhaps the long-lasting ideal of a single universal empire to come true!

But what we got instead in the wake of the First World War was the launching of an entirely new dynamic in the political history of the world, namely, political fragmentation under the auspices of the self-determination principle. In just one century the world transitioned from a handful of empires in command of the majority of the planet landmass (except for most of the western hemisphere that gained independence from imperial rule by 1820 and a few exceptions such as Liberia, Ethiopia, Afghanistan, and Thailand) into a world carved out by almost 200 states! What the democratic revolution did for the world history of domestic politics—bringing perennial authoritarianism to an end—Wilsonian self-determination did for the world history of international politics, bringing the perennial history of ever fewer and bigger empires to an end!

For a while after the end of the First World War the defeated empires paid the self-determination bill. The territory amassed by the three Central Power empires devolved into seven nation-states (Germany, Austria, Hungary, Yugoslavia, Czechoslovakia, Poland, and Turkey) and three mandates (Palestine, Syria, Mesopotamia). Four states (Finland, Estonia, Latvia, and Lithuania) were also carved out of the defeated Russian Empire. The triumphant Allied Empires, Great Britain and France, did nothing but grow further, for now. But the writing was on the wall. Next time around, in the wake of the Second World War, it would be for them to pay the price of self-determination globally just as the defeated empires did at the outset of the First World War on the European continent.

The writing on the wall went even further: in the 1918 context self-determination as an expression of American idealism was also meant to be an alluring alternative to the idealism embedded in the principles of Communism and the prospects of a Global Communist Revolution. Whereas the latter claimed to offer social equality for all, the principle of self-determination promised to grant freedom from imperial domination and statehood on an equal foothold for all national communities. The principle of self-determination became a global success. For the rest of the twentieth century the world witnessed the emergence of 139 new states, transitioning from 57 in 1914 to 196 by 2017. That speaks volumes for the emergence of a new hegemon for whom self-determination was near the top of its agenda's priorities. And yet, in nurturing the expectations of peoples suppressed by colonial authoritarianism throughout the world without delivering self-determination promptly enough, these same peoples ended up embracing the principles of communism. In fact, for many people in the world these two idealistic competing agendas became synergic rather than mutually exclusive, generating a new pair of synergic twins that in manifold combinations fostered the emergence of anti-hegemonic party states globally. For the rest of the short twentieth century many of these new states were ruled by anti-hegemonic party states that fused idealisms formerly conceived as competitors.

IT'S THE ECONOMY, STUPID!

Infringing a 5,000-year principle of world politics and imprinting a new one instead was the first decisive act of the incoming, even if hesitant, emerging hegemon. And yet, there was a more mundane way in which the nascent hegemon inadvertently derailed the British hegemony: by blowing up the foundations of the first industrial globalization. The post-First World War years are widely known as the "Roaring Twenties," the "Crazy Years," the "Golden Twenties" and are closely associated with rapid economic growth and prosperity (e.g., yearly GDP growth above 4%), technological innovation (e.g., radio, automobile, aviation, telephone, and the power grid) and cultural effervescence (e.g., jazz, cinema, Art Deco, and fashion). Yet, all of that was resting on the very shaky grounds of a loose system of credit.

All started back during the war years. Back then, the United States had been providing loans to the Allies, loans with which they were able to sustain the Total War effort. At the end of the war the time came to start repaying those loans. For that purpose, Great Britain and France relied on the reparation payments that Germany owed them based on the Versailles Peace Treaty. In order to meet this demand, it was now Germany's turn to obtain loans coming from the United States.

The resulting post-First World War financial cycle consisted, then, of the U.S. banking system providing loans to the German government that used these funds to pay reparations to Great Britain and France, for these two countries in their own turn to pay back their war generated debt to the U.S. banking system. In the meantime, this financial cycle solidified by the nascent prospective hegemon allowed global levels of production and trade in a decade time to reach or even surpass pre-First World War levels. The globally integrated economy of the first industrial globalization, the one created by the British couple of twins, seemed to be back and in full swing. Except that this time around the global bonanza was heavily resting on the credit provided by the U.S. banks.

And then Black Tuesday hit and hit hard. On October 29, 1929 the stock market crashed in New York. The highly speculative investment in shares carried over the Roaring Twenties had multiplied the Dow Jones Industrial Average by more than six times For despite the stock market's growth, the real economy had not grown by more than 600% in a decade's time. By mid-1932 when the Dow Jones Industrial Average reached rock bottom it held a mere 11% of its pre-Black Tuesday value. A financial meltdown ensued. Some 5,000 U.S. banks went bankrupt. Investments evaporated. Production shrank almost by half. Unemployment soared. The consumer market shrank in tandem. And all of these spiraled down together. The U.S. economy had entered its toughest depression.

The nascent hegemon did not enter economic depression alone. Stock exchanges and financial markets collapsed globally and instantly. Great Britain was not any different. On September 20, the London Stock Exchange crashed, and the downward spiral of finance, production, unemployment, and consumption followed suit. The result was the dismantling of the global economy that the global tour of the two sets of twins had brought about gradually in the course of some 80 years. As transnational investments and trade came to an abrupt halt, national and colonial economies confronted a fundamental reshuffling of their structures. The guiding principles of free trade and comparative advantage were not helpful any longer as the global demand even for comparatively advantageous commodities had drastically dropped. Under these circumstances, the agricultural and mining-exporting economies around the world started shifting into industrializing ones out of necessity in order to replace their shrinking imports from the industrialized nations. These economic shifts and the rise of alternative economic models pushing for industrialization entailed major social and political transformations. Landed oligarchies in charge of the agro/mining-exporting model lost political terrain and new leaderships supportive of industrialization started gaining significant prominence supported by growing cohorts of industrialized workers. With such domestic transformation evolving rather simultaneously worldwide it is not surprising that there were major consequences to the global economy. A world of more and more self-relying economies made for a world of economic globalization decline.

Last but not least, the "Global Depression" launched by the Wall Street crash damaged British hegemony in an additional way by nurturing the rise of the fifth anti-hegemonic party state of the first wave. With it, the outbreak of the Second World War further dug the grave of British hegemony to its final dimensions.[20]

A GAME CHANGER

As in Russia, military defeat sparked social revolution in Germany. By 1917 the ongoing defeat of Russia in the First World War brought about the collapse of the Tsarist regime, the formation of a provisional government, and the outbreak of a Communist revolution. A similar sequence evolved in Germany immediately after its defeat in November 1918. The Kaiser abdicated, a republic was declared and governed by a provisional government, and a Communist revolution started in multiple locations throughout the country from Kiel in the north to Munich in the south, where a Bavarian Soviet Republic was established in April 1919. Yet, in sharp contrast with the Russian trajectory, by May 1919 the German Communist revolution was over. The provisional government there led by the Social Democratic Party (SPD) reacted by unleashing not only the army in order to suppress the revolution but also the Freikorps. The Freikorps were reactionary paramilitary units made of war veterans driven by anti-revolutionary, nationalist, and racist motivations.

By August 1919 the German Republic was consolidated with the adoption of the Weimar Constitution. The time seemed right to dissolve the thus-far instrumental Freikorps. In February 1920, the government ordered the disbandment of two of the most powerful of them. As a result, in one month's time a putsch set the government on the run. Berlin had fallen to a military coup. In response, a general strike that had paralyzed the country for six days brought the coup to an end and gave the government back to Berlin. The Freikorps, however, were there to stay and its spirit was to significantly contribute to the rise of the Nazi movement.

As in Italy during the *biennio rosso*, in Germany postwar conditions sparked workers' organized protests and plans for seizing power, even after the forceful suppression of the Communist revolution in 1919.

In the immediate aftermath of the military coup in 1920 and up to 1923, revolutionary uprisings broke out throughout Germany from west to east. Across the Ruhr area local soviets took power in several major cities backed by the Red Ruhr Army during March 1920. A month later they were defeated and suppressed by the army and, yes, the Freikorps. In October 1923 failed Communist uprisings took place in Saxony, Thuringia, and Hamburg. By then, the Freikorps had grown to become a political force, the National Socialist German Worker's Party (NSDAP) lead by Adolf Hitler. Inspired by Mussolini's March on Rome a year before, Hitler attempted a putsch in Munich to overtake power in Berlin. The attempt was suppressed, Hitler incarcerated, and the NSDAP marginalized for as long as Germany's economy kept recovering through American loans provided since 1924. This financial support took Germany out of the fast spinning Carousels of Revolution and Reaction, while it lasted. By Black Tuesday (November 1929) it was over. The Carousels spun fast again for three more years until, as was typical, the reactionary one prevailed. By 1933, Germany became a reactionary anti-hegemonic party state.

As in Italy, in Germany the anti-hegemonic party state relied on a coalition composed of the middle class, landowners, including small ones, and industrialists, with some support from the working class, which as an organized class was thoroughly repressed. However, in the case of Germany, there were no constraints to the centralization of power. By July 1933 all political parties other than the NSDAP were banned, and the elections held in November 1933 resulted in a one-party state. At the top, by adopting the title of Führer, Hitler incorporated presidential authority to his prerogatives as chancellor after Hindenburg's death in 1934. At the bottom, special state governors were installed by the Nazis at the local level. Finally, the army was also Nazified. This centralization of power by the party combined with the continuity of institutions and civil service resulted in the development of parallel institutions that by competing and overlapping, as in the case of the Youth Leader of the Reich vis-à-vis the Minister of Education, or the Reich SS leader with the Minister of Defense and Minister of Economy, or the *Waffen Schutz Staffel* and the army, maximized the monopoly of the state on violence executed by the SS-Gestapo-SD complex.

The economic policy until 1936 was reminiscent of the "corporate state" in Italy: elimination of trade unions, unemployment reduction, and control of wages. Except that the autarkic policy implemented there was replaced in Germany by a policy of convening favorable trade agreements with nation-states in the Balkans and South America as providers of raw materials and recipients of credit for purchasing German industrial products. In 1936 the Four-Year Plan was launched aiming at a self-sufficient agriculture, industry, and improved infrastructures. The centralized planned economy further consolidated once the Second World War began. Germany was the only Western state that succeeded in eliminating unemployment between 1933 and 1938. During these same years, the Nazi regime developed an aggressive expansionist policy that became a war policy by 1939. Starting from the destruction of the hegemonic world order as re-arranged by the Versailles Treaty, this policy continued by incorporating the nation-states and territories inhabited by German speakers and ended in a further expansionist policy which aimed to take over either the European continent or the entire globe[21] (Map 3.3).

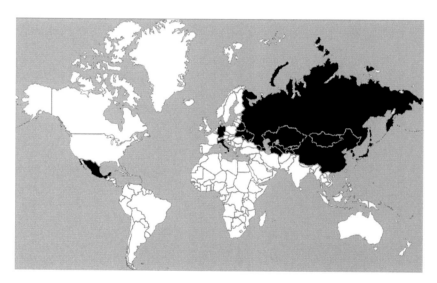

Map 3.3   Anti-hegemonic party states 1930s–1940s—By reaction, by guidance, by imitation

Second Round

The Second World War was so different from the first one and yet so similar. The First World War was outstanding for being static and defensive, the Second World War for being a set of fast-moving conquering campaigns. The First World War mainly engaged the rival armies; in the Second World War civil populations and infrastructures were deliberately targeted. So, means and targets were remarkably different, yet some of the goals and settings remained strikingly alike. For the second time Germany tried to assert its place in the world order and that meant either partnering with or confronting Great Britain. As the world hegemon agreed to appease but not collaborate, the two powers collided head-on again after a hiatus of 25 years. And for the second time Germany remained sandwiched by France and Russia on the continent and contained by Great Britain at sea as it was in 1914. Several similarities evolved out of these shared points of departure.

By the outbreak of the Second World War, on September 1, 1939 Germany had already annexed Austria and occupied the Sudetenland, Bohemia, and Moravia (the contemporary Czech Republic) and with most of the remaining parts of the former Austro-Hungarian Empire— Hungary, Romania, Croatia, and Bosnia— Slovakia and Bulgaria joining Germany's military efforts between 1940 and 1941. In this way, the First World War Central Powers geopolitical formation was almost entirely replicated with the major exception of the neutrality of the Republic of Turkey that emerged out of the collapse of the Ottoman Empire. Once again this formation, now under Nazi rule, confronted the prospects of an Eastern Front running from the Baltic to the Black Sea spanning a front of more than 1600 kilometers and a Western Front ranging from the North Sea to the French border with Switzerland, a line totaling around 700 kilometers. A Schlieffen Plan of sorts was in order once again aiming for a standoff on the eastern border while employing the bulk of Germany's military power in a swift capture of Paris.

Acquiescence of Soviet Russia was indeed achieved by diplomatic means this time, setting this even stranger couple into collaboration once again (see above, pp. 87–88). On August 23, 1939 the Ribbentrop-Molotov Pact was signed between the Nazi and Soviet ministers of foreign affairs granting mutual non-aggression and dividing out the territories running from the Baltic to the Black Sea. Accordingly, the Soviet Union occupied Estonia, Latvia, south Finland, the eastern half of Poland, portions of Romania, and by a later amendment also Lithuania. Germany conquered in a month's time the western half of Poland, triggering France and Great Britain to declare war. This was an almost inconsequential declaration as no major action took place until the time came for Germany to take the initiative once again. Starting in May 1940 the German army quickly pocketed the French and British armies in Belgium after having surprisingly accessed northern France across the Ardennes Mountains. The swift capture of Paris ensued in June 14. Albeit with variations, the Schlieffen mindset had proved correct 35 years after its conception and 26 years after it was first attempted.

Addressing the naval threat posed by Great Britain came next. Also in this regard, the Second World War was a mixture of new and old in comparison to the First one. Novelty stands out during the Battle of Britain by the leading role of the air forces, the Luftwaffe and the Royal. The German submarine attacks that sank some 14.5 million gross tons to the Atlantic Ocean depths represented a recurrence of the First World War. Once again Great Britain stood up to the German assault. This time, however, for all of the losses they sustained, submarine warfare was not enough to mobilize the United States into the World War. That step was only taken after the attack on Pearl Harbor on December 7, 1941. Having been excluded from the Western imperial club, Showa Japan became an anti-hegemonic party state and accordingly had changed sides in the global alliances. This time around Japan launched its imperial ambitions in Asia under the banner of the "Asian Co-Prosperity Zone" and aligned with the Axis Powers.[22]

Germany supported the Japanese attack by immediately declaring war on the United States in expectation for Japan to open an eastern front against the Soviet Union that Nazi Germany had successfully invaded in June 1941 up to the outskirts of Leningrad, Moscow, Stalingrad, and Baku. With Paris under Nazi rule and Japan as part of the Axis, this time it was the Soviet Union that was sandwiched, not Germany. Yet deterred by previous defeats sustained against the Soviets in 1939 and focused on its march south, Japan never opened this eastern front against the Soviet Union. Neither did the deeds of the third Axis Power turned favorable for the positioning of Germany.

Italy, which had signed the "Pact of Steel" with Germany in 1939, aimed for the East Mediterranean basin, conquering Albania in 1939, failing to conquer Greece in 1940, and suffering a major setback in North Africa by 1941. A failed attempt to defeat the British in Egypt ended up with the Italian army rolled back to its stronghold in Libya. To pursue the Mediterranean front, Germany came to Italy's rescue. By spring 1941, on the eve of the invasion of the Soviet Union, Greece was conquered and the attack on British Egypt was resumed. For the next two years the Axis Powers continued pushing forward along all three fronts, the Soviet Union, the Mediterranean basin, and South East Asia encroaching the entire Eastern Hemisphere albeit progressively losing steam.

The spring of 1943 brought the reversal of direction rather simultaneously in all three theaters of war with the American victory on the Guadalcanal campaign in the Pacific, the Allied annihilation of the Axis presence in North Africa, and most crucially the Soviet victory in Stalingrad. During the next two years the Allies advanced gradually but steadily. Italy surrendered in September 1943 except that the Nazis held onto the occupied north of the Italian Peninsula till the end of the war. Germany, in contrast with the early successes of the Schlieffen conception, ended up nevertheless sandwiched by the Allies and surrendered in May 1945. Also Japan ended up sandwiched by Americans and Soviets although its surrender in August 1945 was the result of the atomic bombs dropped in Hiroshima and Nagasaki. The Second World War was over and so was British hegemony.[23]

So Long to the Global Train!

The "Global Train"of the two couples of twins pulled by a locomotive named Britain was finally derailed by 1945 after a series of blows coming from the hegemonic party spoilers. Two rounds of total war with German-led coalitions, the loss of financial leadership and the Global Depression originated on Wall Street, the new political horizon of self-determination set by the nascent U.S. hegemon, and the inspirational model for political organization that the failed Global Communist Revolution provided globally—all these led to the Big Brexit. A brave new world lay ahead in which every society would dedicate itself to launching its own national train. The pursuit of catching up was now seemingly open for all! Or would it be better to move in cars rather than trains? That is, into American cars?

NOTES

1. Peter Hart, *The Great War: A Combat History of the First World War* (Oxford: Oxford University Press, 2015). ProQuest Ebook Central, https://ebookcentral.proquest.com/lib/pitt-ebooks/detail.action?docID=1192584.
2. Gordon Alexander Craig, ed., *World War I, A Turning Point in Modern History: Essays on the Significance of the War* (New York: Knopf, 1967).
3. Richard Pipes, *The Russian Revolution: 1899–1919* (London: Collins Harvill, 1990), 386–391.
4. Vladimir Lenin, *State and Revolution* (London: Penguin Books, 1992).
5. G. F. Krivosheev, in *Soviet Casualties and Combat Losses in the Twentieth Century*, 7–38 (Greenhill Books, 1997).
6. Eric Hobsbawm, *The Age of Extremes* (New York: Pantheon Books, 1994), 64.
7. Silvio Pons, *The Global Revolution: A History of International Communism 1917–1991* (Oxford: Oxford University Press, 2014). ProQuest Ebook Central, https://ebookcentral.proquest.com/lib/pittebooks/detail.action?docID=1767696, 7–42.
8. Ralph Darlington, *Syndicalism and the Transition to Communism: An International Comparative Analysis* (Farnham, UK: Ashgate Publishing, 2008), 185.
9. Alexander J. De Grand, *Fascist Italy and Nazi Germany: The "Fascist" Style of Rule* (New York: Routledge, 2004).
10. Michael Dillon, *China: A Modern History* (London; New York: I.B. Tauris, 2010), 145–187.
11. Michael L. Conniff, ed., *Populism in Latin America* (Tuscaloosa: University of Alabama Press, 1999), 75–96.
12. Diane P. Koenker, William G. Rosenberg, and Ronald Grigor Suny, eds., *Party, State, and Society in the Russian Civil War* (Bloomington: Indiana University Press, 1989), 58–80.
13. Lewis H. Siegelbaum, *Soviet State and Society: Between Revolutions, 1918–1929* (Cambridge University Press, 1992), 90.
14. Spain under Capitan General Miguel Primo de Rivera (1923–1930), Portugal (1926–1974), Poland (1926–1939) under the

First Marshal of Poland Józef Pilsudski and his Sanation ("healing") Movement, Lithuania under the ultra-nationalist anti-Communist Antanas Smetona (1926–1940), Albania (1928–1939) under the President then King Ahmet Zogu, Yugoslavia (1929), Hungary (1932), Austria (1933), Estonia (1934), Latvia (1934), Bulgaria (1935), Greece (1936), and Romania (1938).

15. Cyrus Ghani, *Iran and the Rise of the Reza Shah: From Qajar Collapse to Pahlavi Power* (I.B.Tauris, 2001).

16. Lawrence A. Clayton et al., *A New History of Modern Latin America* (Berkeley, CA: University of California Press, 2017). ProQuest Ebook Central, https://ebookcentral.proquest.com/lib/pitt-ebooks/detail.action?docID=4811719, 258–274.

17. António Costa Pinto, *Latin American Dictatorships in the Era of Fascism: The Corporatist Wave*, Routledge Studies in Fascism and the Far Right (Routledge, 2019). ProQuest Ebook Central, https://ebookcentral.proquest.com/lib/pitt-ebooks/detail.action?docID=5789260, 27–114.

18. Arthur O. Lovejoy, *The Great Chain of Being: A Study of the History of an Idea* (Cambridge, MA: Harvard University Press, 1964).

19. United States. President (1913–1921: Wilson). Address of the President of the United States: Delivered at a Joint Session of the Two Houses of Congress, January 8, 1918. Washington: [Govt. print. off.], 1918. Erez Manela, *The Wilsonian Moment: Self-Determination and the International Origins of Anticolonial Nationalism* (Oxford: Oxford University Press, 2007).

20. John E. Moser, *Global Great Depression and the Coming of World War II* (Taylor & Francis, 2015). ProQuest Ebook Central, https://ebookcentral.proquest.com/lib/pitt-ebooks/detail.action?docID=3384679.

21. Ian Kershaw, *The Nazi Dictatorship: Problems and Perspectives of Interpretation* (London: Arnold, 1985). Eric Hobsbawm, *The Age of Extremes* (New York: Pantheon Books, 1994), 93.

22. David White, *Bitter Ocean: The Battle of the Atlantic, 1939–1945* (New York: Simon & Schuster, 2008), 2.

23. Andrew N. Buchanan, *World War II in Global Perspective, 1931–1953: A Short History* (Wiley, 2019). ProQuest Ebook Central, https://ebookcentral.proquest.com/lib/pitt-ebooks/detail.action?docID=5683100.

CHAPTER 4

When We Became Americans (1946–1973)

THE WORLD SERIES

Soccer is known as a gentleman's game played by hooligans, rugby as a hooligans' game played by gentlemen. Both make the shortlist of the six most popular sports in the world: first place for soccer, sixth for rugby. In between these two, a couple more British globally launched branches figure prominently: cricket and tennis.[1] None of these, though, are shortlisted among the United States' most popular sports. Americans apparently prefer first the "World Series." In this series, the "world" is limited to the champions of the American and National League baseball teams that exist only in the United States and Canada. Second, or first

---

By "America" is meant the United States of America. Although the name America also refers to the entire continent ranging from the North to the South poles, one of the privileges that comes with world hegemony is the appropriation of the name in exclusivity and the recognition of this appropriation by the rest of the world. Such appropriation can be contested by referring specifically to the United States. However, the name United States can also allude to the United States of Mexico or the United States of Brazil. Only the full name United States of America singles out properly the United States of America. But then again, the appropriation of the continent's name to itself remains in place.

© The Author(s), under exclusive license to Springer Nature Switzerland AG 2021
D. Olstein, *A Brief History of Now*,
https://doi.org/10.1007/978-3-030-82420-4_4

depending on the rankings' measures, comes football, that is, American football. The World League of American Football, at one time a subsidiary of the National Football League, was more ambitious in its geographical scope than the "World Series." It included teams from Germany, the Netherlands, Spain, and the United Kingdom, besides those from the United States and Canada. But it lasted, a bit off and on, only from 1991 to 2007. Today's NFL (National Football League) consists of 32 U.S.-based teams.

It is telling that cricket and baseball belong to the same family of bat and ball games. Their similarity is comparable to that of rugby and (American) football, whose name conflicts with what the rest of the world calls football. While we were all becoming Brits, Americans asserted themselves, not only by "tweaking" existing sport branches but also by creating brand new ones, most prominently basketball, an American-created game popular worldwide. Basketball ranks as the second most popular sport in the United States and worldwide. In contrast to the United Kingdom, the United States has managed to preserve a clear-cut leadership in the sport it has disseminated throughout the world. Since the end of the Cold War the U.S. basketball team has been the regular gold medalist at the Olympic Games, except for an astounding defeat to Argentina in 2004.

The U.S. sports scene tells us three things about the nation's place in the world. First, Americans rejected British hegemony from early on and asserted their political, economic, and cultural independence with determination. Second, sports passions capture the historic inclination of the United States toward isolationism. Third, U.S. world hegemony took hold through channels different from those of British world hegemony. And indeed, the U.S. world hegemony that has emerged and unfolded since the end of the Second World War was different not just in its sports of choice but in many regards from the British one that preceded it.

The secret of success that catapulted Great Britain to its position was the unleashing of twin synergic revolutions: the industrial and democratic. The birth of the United States in 1776 is a primary instance of the democratic revolution, and a century later the Industrial Revolution took off quickly in the new nation—so much so, that by 1916 U.S. industrial output had already overtaken that of the entire British Empire.[2] And so, the nascent world hegemon of the twentieth century had fully incorporated and become a leader of the synergic revolutions that were a prerequisite to pursuing and attaining world hegemony. Similarly, after the Second World War, the United States embraced the other twins of world hegemony, the ideologies and policies of free trade and comparative advantage. The adoption of these two was undertaken after a long trajectory of protectionist policies pursued by the United States. Starting with Alexander Hamilton's *Report on the Subject of Manufactures* (1791), protectionism escalated after the Civil War (1861–1865) and in the wake of the Great Depression (1929). But the departure from protectionism to free trade was a prominent signal of having achieved world hegemonic status: let us all freely compete and let us, the world hegemon, alone prevail.

However, the two sets of twins that built British world hegemony during the nineteenth century—the synergic revolutions and the pair of ideologies and policies—while necessary to sustain world hegemony during the twentieth century, were not sufficient. More innovations were to be expected from the world hegemon standing at the cutting edge of the economy, technology, politics, and culture. Moreover, the different historical trajectories of Great Britain and the United States invited different hegemonic approaches as did their disparate global circumstances. The combination of these factors accounts for the emergence of a new world hegemonic style led by the United States.

Hegemony and Empire: Great Britain

Great Britain became the world hegemon of the nineteenth century after having pursued a global empire for three centuries. The establishment of Jamestown, Virginia in 1607 signaled the successful beginning of the British colonization of North America, which resulted in the consolidation of the Thirteen Colonies. Similarly, the founding of Newfoundland in 1610 represented the beginnings of what, by 1841, had become the United Province of Canada. The colonization of the islands of St. Kitts, Barbados, and Nevis spearheaded the British presence in the Caribbean starting in the 1620 s. A couple of decades before the American Revolution (1776), the British managed to assert their presence in India as the East India Company established its capital in Calcutta (1757) and appointed its first governor-general. A century after the outbreak of the American Revolution, Queen Victoria was crowned, in 1876, Empress of India.[3]

By the time that the thirteen colonies were finally lost to the American Patriots in 1783 work was already underway to begin the colonization of Australia, effectively launched in 1788. The Treaty of Waitangi signed in

1840 between the British Crown and Māori chiefs brought New Zealand under British sovereignty. By 1872 an uprising of discontented Māori tribes was fully suppressed.[4] In 1874 the Pangkor Treaty paved the way for British control over Malay rulers exactly 50 years after the Dutch ceded their partial control of the Malay Peninsula to the British.[5] In exchange, the Dutch retained their possessions in the Dutch East Indies (present-day Indonesia). By 1884 the Netherlands, Germany, and Great Britain agreed to carve up the island of New Guinea. That same year the Berlin Conference came to address European competition for colonizing Africa: the Scramble for Africa (see above, pp. 60–64). At the Conference's beginning, about 10% of Africa was under European colonial control. By 1914, less than 10% of Africa fell *outside* of European control. Great Britain commanded the largest share, further enlarged in 1919 with the takeover of the German colonies in the aftermath of the First World War. All in all, Great Britain held onto most of the eastern half of the continent from South Africa to Egypt as well as the most populated areas in the Western half of the continent, in the littoral of the Gulf of Guinea (Nigeria, Cameroons, Gold Coast, and Sierra Leone). Finally, also in the wake of the First World War, Great Britain enlarged its hold on the Middle East. To its existing possessions in the southern Arabian Peninsula, the Gulf of Oman, and the Persian Gulf, it added in 1919 the Fertile Crescent in the form of League of Nations mandates on Palestine, Transjordan, and Mesopotamia; Jamestown in 1607, Jerusalem in 1917: 310 years of global empire-building preceding or intertwined with its rise to world hegemony. Intertwined, but different from.

For Great Britain, ruling over one-fifth of the world's landmass and population was a necessary but insufficient condition to becoming the world hegemon. The rest of the world would be beyond its reach if not for its entanglement with Britain's informal empire, granted by its appealing economic, technological, and cultural leadership or conversely by its military might, which was facilitated by the defeat of its opponents. The first and foremost in this list was the French Empire, knocked down in the Seven Years War (1756–1763) and knocked out by the end of the Napoleonic Wars (1803–1815). The Seven Years War dismantled the French Empire in North America and India, whose possessions were incorporated by the British Empire. The Napoleonic revanche aimed at first to disrupt Britain's reach for its Jewel in the Crown by capturing Egypt (1798) en route to India. After that failed attempt and starting in 1803, Napoleon successfully overran continental Europe until an all-encompassing European coalition led and financed by Great Britain brought about his demise in 1815.[6] At that point, Britain's most long-lasting nemesis, France, fell into line. That same year, the resentful former colony, the United States, ratified the Treaty of Ghent that brought the second round of warfare between Great Britain and the United States, the war of 1812, to an end. This treaty marked the beginning of the most strategic of world alliances, that between the to-be-demoted hegemon and the to-become world hegemon, for at least the next two centuries.

With these two former foes now in line, Great Britain embarked on the establishment of its informal empire, that is, its domination of other states and societies by economic dependence, interference in their poli-cymaking, cultural influence, and, when necessary, resort to violence, albeit without lasting occupation.[7] The newly independent states in South America were the first and primary example, with their ruling elites typi-cally partnering willingly with the world hegemon. Except when they did not, as happened with the Argentine Confederation led by Juan Manuel de Rosas, who, starting in 1845, conducted a protectionist economic policy instead of embracing Britain's free trade. The response was a five-year naval blockade and trespass into Argentine rivers that granted British and French merchant fleets access. Yes, this was a British-French blockade, meaning that this episode also marks the first instance in which the former archenemies began enjoying their cordial understanding or *Entente Cordiale*.[8] This exception to the Latin American free-trade poli-cies was the rule rather than the exception in the Chinese context. In that theater, British merchants were not trading competitive manufactures that the Middle Kingdom (i.e., China) refused to take. Instead, they were drug dealers proffering opium. The Chinese stance against free trade, or drug trafficking, was firm and triggered in its turn British gunboat diplo-macy. After two rounds of Opium Wars (1839–1842; 1856–1860), the Chinese Empire unwillingly gravitated toward the British informal empire (see above, pp. 45–46, 49). And, yes, the Second Opium War was also a British-French partnered expedition.

British world hegemony was the ripe fruit of three centuries of British imperial assertiveness. From its modest origins during the sixteenth century scavenging on Spanish treasures and snatching territories beyond Spain's reach, England in collaboration with the other Atlantic powers— Portugal, France, and the Netherlands—defeated Spain and derailed its global power by the mid-seventeenth century (1648; the end of both the Thirty and Eighty Years Wars is a good heuristic turning point). During the next century and a half Great Britain successfully grew its empire while in tandem subordinating (Portugal) or defeating (the Netherlands and France) the other Atlantic powers with which it had collectively displaced Spain. As the sole and indisputable leader in command of the largest maritime empire—with a growing informal empire on top of it, and propelled by the two sets of twins—Great Britain, starting in 1815, in the wake of the Napoleonic Wars, was firmly on its way to fulfilling its long-lasting imperial and hegemonic vocation. By 1851, the British world hegemony was celebrated in the Great Exhibition in London.

HEGEMONY AND EMPIRE: THE UNITED STATES

This combination of formal and informal empire fostered by the two sets of twins that reflected and deepened British world hegemony was also present in the rise and unfolding of the United States. And yet the twentieth century world hegemon wove this combination in its own singular ways. Crucially, U.S. world hegemony did not start by erecting a global empire but rather by pioneering the partial dismantling of one. This anti-colonial foundational moment became the hallmark of the U.S. experience: domestically, for the ethos, soul, spirit, and mindset of the developing nation; hemispherically, for most other Americans beyond the United States, who embarked on their own path of emancipation soon after (1810–1822) or as late as 1898 following the U.S. example; and globally, for the peoples of the world ruled by some half-dozen European colonial empires and striving for their own emancipation. The shot was indeed heard around the world and continued to echo for two centuries after the trigger was pulled.[9] And with such an appealing anti-colonial message to convey to a world yoked by colonialism, the United States was already showing the way to the future, exercising leadership by example, and with that signaling its own world hegemonic potential.

But the anti-colonial nation turned soon enough to establish its own empire. The same Revolutionary War that launched the very first modern decolonization, simultaneously and in parallel, fostered the conquest of native American territories east of the Appalachian Mountains.[10] In fact, part of the Patriots' motivation for the Revolutionary War was overturning the ban on westward expansion imposed by the Royal Proclamation (1763). And so, the same Treaty of Paris (1783) that brought the Revolutionary War to an end not only acknowledged the independence and sovereignty of the United States but also moved its Western border from the Appalachians to the Mississippi River. The Louisiana Purchase (1803) from Napoleon doubled the size of the United States and pushed the Western frontier all the way into the Rocky Mountains. The annexation of the Republic of Texas (1845) at the expense of Mexico, the incorporation of the Oregon Territory (1846) diplomatically partitioned with Great Britain, and—"Poor Mexico, so far from God and so close to the United States!"[11]—the Mexican Cession of its northwestern-most third (1848) completed the westward expansion. These diplomatic achievements vis-à-vis the great powers and the military triumphs over Mexico were matched all the way through by the dispossession and removal of the native societies, who were subjected to overwhelming military defeats. Seventy years after the shot was heard around the world, a continental empire from the Atlantic to the Pacific was in place.

Such continental success seemed to have materialized "Manifest Destiny," the belief that the special virtues of the American people and their institutions should rule over North America if not over the Western Hemisphere at large. Conversely, this accomplishment combined with a nervous realization that the "American frontier"—the open-ended space westward that promoted freedom, democracy, individualism, and entrepreneurship—would come to a close once the Pacific shores were reached; and so the United States embarked in the late nineteenth century on maritime imperialism. The purchase of Alaska from the Russian Empire in 1867 was the first time the expansion of the United States was not made into a territory contiguous to its boundaries. That acquisition also signaled an additional investment in the Pacific Rim as the newly incorporated Department of Alaska not only expanded the Pacific shoreline but also provided a bridge of some 60 islands, the Aleutian Islands, as crucial logistic stops on the way to Asia. Midway Island in the Pacific, occupied by the United States that same year, further expanded this logistical platform. This new expansionist trend reached its zenith in 1898, the year in which the United States became a global maritime empire by annexing the Hawaiian archipelago and conquering from Spain the Philippines and Guam in the Pacific Ocean as well as Cuba and Puerto Rico in the Caribbean Sea. The Western Samoa Islands became an American protectorate two years later. And so, the United States entered the twentieth century as a continental and maritime empire while nurturing its informal empire as well.

The seeds of the United States' informal empire were planted as early as 1823 when President James Monroe warned that further efforts by European nations to take control of any independent state in North or South America would be viewed as "the manifestation of an unfriendly disposition toward the United States." This declaration had evolved by the 1840s into the Monroe Doctrine. Interestingly, as the Revolutionary War did before, the Monroe Doctrine combines anti-colonialism and imperialism.[12] The anti-colonial dimension of the declaration clearly shows in its text: "The Americas for the inhabitants of the Americas!" Not the European powers. And for that, Latin American patriots expressed their gratitude.[13] The imperialist, or more precisely the non-formal imperialist dimension, resides in its subtext: "The Americas for the United States of America!" Blocking European powers' imperial access to the Western Hemisphere facilitated the development of a U.S. informal empire in the Western hemisphere.

These prospects were quite acceptable to the world hegemon, Great Britain, interested in blocking any attempts by European countries to retake their colonial possessions in the Americas. And indeed, its Royal Navy was the only possible tool to execute this doctrine. And so, aspirations of European power in the Americas were curtailed while the strategic allies emerging from the Treaty of Ghent (1814)—Great Britain and the United States—tacitly carved out their respective zones of influence in the Western hemisphere. Mexico and most of Central America were for the United States; South America was for Great Britain; and the Caribbean basin remained as a bone of contention. Hence, when the British took over the Malvinas Islands, renamed Falklands, from the United Provinces of the River Plate (contemporary Argentina) in 1833 the United States remained silent despite the Monroe Doctrine. And equally silent it remained during the above-mentioned British blockade and naval campaign against protectionist Argentina during 1838 and up to 1850 (see above, pp. 126–127).[14] The United States did not remain silent, though, when France under Napoleon III conquered Mexico in 1862. As soon as the American Civil War was over (1865), President Andrew Johnson demanded the French evacuation, imposed a naval blockade, and supplied arms and ammunition to the Mexican insurgency led by Benito Juarez.

Almost to the end of the nineteenth century, the United States abstained from interfering with Great Britain's activities in South America. That held true until a territorial dispute arose in 1895 between Venezuela and Great Britain, which aimed to expand its colony British Guiana westward at Venezuela's expense. This time the United States did stand in the way of Great Britain by imposing its arbitration. This arbitration, though, ended up granting most of the disputed territory to Great Britain.[15] However, it was a foundational moment for the U.S. assertion of its zone of influence. This assertion was magnified by the Spanish-American War (1898), with which the United States added a maritime empire to its continental one and enhanced its informal empire in the Western hemisphere. Since then the United States has proactively engaged in diplomatic, military, covert, and indirect operations throughout Latin America; the list of about 70 such interventions is too large to unpack.

By the dawn of the twentieth century, the United States was accumulating many of the attributes that made Great Britain the world hegemon: full-fledged synergic revolutions and a combination of a global and informal empire. However, whereas Great Britain had jockeyed for the global top position for three centuries, the United States was ambivalent about such an aspiration from the get-go. To begin with, the United States was embedded in its anti-imperialist/imperialist duality. The anti-imperialism of its Revolutionary War fits uneasily with the imperialism of the American Frontier, Manifest Destiny, and the erection of a continental empire all the way to the Pacific coast. The explicit anti-imperialism of the Monroe Doctrine in caring for the independence of its fellow new republics in Latin America contrasted with the implicit imperialism of the subtextual Monroe Doctrine in carving out the Western Hemisphere as its exclusive sphere of influence. Moreover, beyond this crucial anti-imperialist/imperialist duality, the Monroe Doctrine, even in its imperialistic sense, was too limiting in its scope—the Western Hemisphere only—to be plausible for a would-be world hegemon.

Such a self-imposed limitation relates to two additional conditions that distinguish the U.S. trajectory from that of Britain. First, by the time the United States had fulfilled the necessary conditions for becoming a global empire, the globe was pretty much already carved up by the European global empires and an undisputed world hegemon was sitting at the top of this world order. Were the United States interested in reshuffling the allocation of global empires and directly confronting the world hegemon, it would have to follow a trajectory not too different from that of Germany. Similar to Germany, the United States already had a protectionist economy that resulted in surpassing British industrial output and ambitions of naval expansion as the necessary tool for global empire and commerce.[16] But the United States did not take anything resembling Germany's confrontational road. Rather, as an alternative to the imperial division of the globe, it articulated and fostered its own alternative in its approach to one of the last unconquered prime locations: China. Whereas European imperial powers and Japan were getting ready to partition China, the United States launched and successfully imposed the Open Door Policy (1899–1900). According to this policy, no foreign power would occupy Chinese territory nor displace the Chinese administration. Instead, free trade with China would be equally granted to all interested parties. The anti-imperialist half of the American duality influenced the Open Door Policy: no more imperial conquests. However, the Policy also illustrates an emerging feature of the American incipient world hegemony: informal empire through the imposition of free trade.

This alternative road, embedded in the vision of the Open Door Policy, reflects not only the anti-imperialist component of the American duality but also its growing confidence in its economic might. As with Britain when it became the workshop of the world, free-trade ideology stands for "let us all compete freely in the world market and let only us, the most powerful industrial economy, prevail in it." This American choice at the turn of the nineteenth century was indicative of its hegemonic twentieth century to come.

But the limiting character of the Monroe Doctrine, circumscribed to the Western Hemisphere only, and the articulation of the Open Door Policy in China were not solely the products of a world already carved up by European powers. Rather, the second condition that prompted imperialist restraint and a non-confrontational attitude vis-à-vis Europe came directly from a core vision on foreign affairs since the very inception of the United States. In George Washington's farewell address of 1796, the first U.S. President established the foundation of American foreign policy for a century and a half to come. In this document, he urged the United States to extend commercial relations to all nations while having as little political connection with them as possible. He specifically alerted the United States to steer clear of the protracted conflicts among European nations.[17] With that solid piece of advice, the founding father established non-interventionism as the landmark of American foreign policy, at least with regard to European states. Washington's successors followed this line. Amid the Napoleonic War that pitted the "tyrant of the land" (France) against the "tyrant of the Ocean" (Great Britain), President Thomas Jefferson had declared in his 1801 inaugural address that one of the essential principles of the United States was "peace, commerce, and honest friendship with all nations, entangling alliances with none."[18] This idea and even the very phrasing echoed all the way up to 1941, when protesters carried anti-war signs reading "NO FOREIGN ENTANGLEMENTS."[19]

"No foreign entanglements" is better known as American isolationism, the standard attitude of the United States in foreign policy amid not only the world war between France and Great Britain in the early nineteenth century (the Napoleonic Wars) but also during the unfolding of the earlier phases of the First and Second World Wars in the first half of the twentieth century. Two years into the First World War, President Woodrow Wilson won his second term under the slogan "He kept us out of war." It took the German announcement of its unrestricted submarine warfare policy and an intercepted German secret telegram inciting Mexico to attack the United States to move Woodrow Wilson from praising himself on his neutrality to entering the war in April 1917. Eighteen months later, the gridlock of the war was dislodged by the United States. It had become the new world hegemon: economic, technological, and military leadership as well as cultural appeal—both formal and informal empire. It had it all to become the new world hegemon—everything but vocation and will. In 1919, Woodrow Wilson was awarded the Nobel Peace Prize for establishing and promoting the League of Nations as the first international organization envisioned to maintain world peace. But the U.S. Senate refused to join the League and in so doing it restored disentanglement, non-interventionism, and isolationism.[20]

Napoleon had led the French revanche (1779–1815) in the wake of the French defeat in the Seven Years War (1756–1763). Hitler had led the German revanche following the Reich's defeat in the First War World and its humiliation in the Treaty of Versailles. As the dark clouds of war were looming on the European horizon in the 1930s, the U.S. Congress proactively engaged in projecting American isolationism. Between 1935 and 1939, Congress passed and Franklin Delano Roosevelt (FDR) signed four different "neutrality acts" prohibiting the sale of arms and war matériel to any belligerent party, forbidding loans to states at war, and banning the transportation of any passengers or articles to belligerents onboard U.S. ships. With this last act in particular, Congress got ready to resist an entanglement of the First World War kind in which Germany's unrestricted submarine warfare was so decisive in precipitating the U.S. intervention. FDR, however, managed to include in this act the "cash and carry" amendment allowing the allies to pay in cash and transport their own war matériel. Moreover, in September 1940 he signed an executive agreement with Great Britain known as the "destroyers-for-bases" deal, which did not require Congressional approval, that swapped 50 U.S. navy destroyers for military base leases in British colonies. Finally, in March 1941, Congress approved "An Act to Promote the Defense of the United States," which effectively supplied the allies until the end of the war with food, oil, and war matériel for the equivalent of 745 billion of today's U.S. dollars. Still, this time around, the direct intervention of the United States in a World War resulted not from U-boats but from airplanes. The Japanese navy air force attacked Pearl Harbor and in its wake both Japan and Germany declared war on the United States, imposing a major foreign entanglement.[21]

It was only the Second World War and its aftermath that produced a paradigmatic shift in the legacy of the founding fathers and their interpreters regarding the core premises of foreign policy. Disentanglement, non-interventionism, isolationism, and a self-imposed limitation to the Western Hemisphere proved to be outdated and unviable in the more tightly connected world of the twentieth century where world hegemony was being contested. By the end of the Second World War, there was no room to turn back to isolationism but only to global entanglement and world hegemony. With that, the lineage of Manifest Destiny and American expansionism would come to the fore at an entirely new level[22] (Map 4.1).

Two Centuries at Odds—And Counting

In attaining world hegemony, Great Britain needed first to overcome its challengers, which it accomplished by overwhelmingly defeating France and strategically allying with the United States. But there was more to it, because there was another mighty opponent to British world hegemony: the Russian Empire. Whereas the Atlantic Empires—Portugal, Spain, the Netherlands, England, and France—collided from the get-go amid their maritime expansions across the oceans, the Russian Empire sprinted alone across the Asian continent all the way to the Pacific. It was only then, with Vitus Bering entering into the strait that now bears his name (1728) and Mikhail Gvozdev reaching Alaska (1732) that the Russian monopolistic road of territorially contiguous imperial expansion collided with the contested route of maritime expansion taken by the Atlantic Empires.

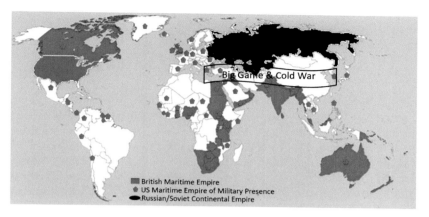

Map 4.1 Two successive world hegemons vs. one lasting counter-hegemon

This means that the Western shores of North America were contested not only by Spain and Great Britain, as was the case in so much of the Western Hemisphere, but also by Russia.

Moreover, as the Russian expansion moved not only westward into the Pacific but also southward into and beyond Central Asia, Russia and Great Britain competed over prospective zones of influence. Great Britain's goal was to contain the Russian Empire by preventing its access to the Indian Ocean and Mediterranean Sea through support for a line of buffer states running from the Ottoman Empire in the west through the Persian Empire, the Khanate of Khiva, the Emirate of Bukhara, and the Emirate of Afghanistan in the east.[23] Multiple wars were fought for that stake including two wars in Afghanistan, two in Punjab and Kashmir, and the Crimean war.

This contest was the Great Game of the nineteenth century (1830–1895). At its core, it was a global geostrategic confrontation, but it also had ideological undertones. As the world hegemon riding the wave of progress, Great Britain was the self-proclaimed champion of liberalism. Its ideological nemesis, then, was despotism perceived as embodied by the Oriental despotism of China (Britain's Opium Wars enemy), and first and foremost by Russia, the mightiest autocracy in Europe. The principles of a parliamentary monarchy fostering freedoms around the world—personal freedom, freedom of property, entrepreneurial freedom, free trade, and free markets—was incompatible with an autocracy devoid of any degree of accountability and based on the institution of serfdom. These sharp differences in ideology, political regime, and economic institutions were particularly stressed and highlighted at moments in which the global geostrategic confrontation reached its peaks.

However, not everything was peaks in this confrontation. For all the irreconcilable character of that confrontation on principle, ideological enmity was prone to convenient accommodation in view of pragmatic considerations. In fact, these geostrategic and ideological enemies shared an interesting sequence of collaborations amid their confrontations. Great Britain had set the ideological rift aside during the Napoleonic Wars to establish its winning coalition with the Russian Empire, together with which (as well as with others such as Prussia and Austria) the Napoleonic war effort was sandwiched to death (1815). But then, by 1854 with post-Napoleonic France under its belt and embarked in their joint British-French *Entente Cordiale*, the central phase of confrontation between Great Britain and Russia opened with the Crimean War (see above, pp. 44–46) and was followed by the Great Game in Asia.

And yet again, with a new force threatening the balance of power in continental Europe, Great Britain and Russia resumed their collaboration after settling their Great Game differences in a series of agreements in 1907. The threat this time came from Germany, which, since its unification in 1871, was by the beginning of the twentieth century the strongest industrial economy in Europe and a competitor for global empire. The Anglo-Russian Entente prepared to sandwich the German threat as had previously been done to the French a century before. And this vision of imposing a double front on Germany was indeed executed during the First World War, this time around with a limited degree of success, and only for as long as the Russian Empire existed. The Bolshevik revolution, however, brought the Anglo-Russian Entente to its end. After Communist Russia withdrew from the First World War, Great Britain together with the allies and even German troops intervened in the Russian Civil War, aiming to topple the Communist regime.

This occasion was also the entry point in the relationship between the United States and Communist Russia. From these troubling beginnings, the relationship continued unfolding and further deteriorating because the United States, like Great Britain before, also had a self-perception of being the world champion of liberalism. And what could be more despotic than a Communist dictatorship that not only concentrates political power but also nationalizes and collectivizes private property?

Interestingly enough, the new foes found in each other several points to emulate. Lenin was a strong enthusiast of Taylorist industrial management techniques albeit in a Communist property rights regime. Later, Franklin D. Roosevelt's administration expressed interest in statist intervention in the economy, but in a capitalist framework. Aside from these points of interest, however, at core the U.S. intervention in the Russian Civil War opened up a grim relationship between these two states that came to represent, as no other pair, the global alternatives of communism and capitalism.

And yet, for all of this irreconcilable ideological conflict, the United States—as with Great Britain before—demonstrated pragmatic flexibility when the time came to join with the Soviet Union to squeeze Nazi Germany to death. The Second World War and its consequences were radically transformative. For one, the war consummated the Big Brexit already launched with the outbreak of the First World War. Great Britain, having lost important tracts of its empire, recovered some of them through American intervention, but it lost credibility across its informal empire where many pro-British ruling elites lost their grip on power or changed their orientation to survive. Finally, the war made evident that Great Britain was no longer leading either set of twins that had made it the world hegemon to begin with. Its leadership was over.

However, on the eastern front, the USSR, although economically devastated and demographically decimated (the Soviet Union lost about 26 million people during the Second World War),[24] emerged from the Second World War as a major military, political, and ideological power. After almost two decades invoking "socialism in one country" as its goal and policy, the Soviet Union led the establishment of Communist regimes throughout Eastern Europe. Also, in Mediterranean Europe— France, Italy, and Greece—Communism, in this case, led by local parties, was making inroads. The same was true in Asia with Communist forces proclaiming the Democratic Republic of Vietnam (1945) and fighting for power in China. Moreover, with anti-colonial and anti-imperialist effervescence intensifying after the Second World War, the Soviet Union was a model to aspire to and an anchor to rely upon. Anti-colonial and anti-imperialist fighters made their own interpretations of Communism, usually entwining it with nationalism. The Soviet Union appeared, then, as a potentially viable new world hegemon. It commanded a huge continental empire, held unto an informal empire—clearly in Eastern Europe and potentially in many states willing to follow its lead—and represented an ideological vision that was globally appealing. However, it did not become a maritime empire, and for all of its economic and technological accomplishments, its leadership was limited and its cultural appeal circumscribed to ideological sympathizers. Its way of life was far less inspiring than the American, and although at first it was seen by some as the wave of the future, its faltering economy since the mid-1950s indicated that its major accomplishments were already behind it. With such a mixed balance sheet, its prospects for world hegemony were unlikely. Yet this balance sheet was strong enough for the Soviet Union to assert its presence as a firm counter-hegemonic force able to contest the world hegemon.

Under these new post-Second World War circumstances, the foes of the Great Game found themselves once again neck and neck from the Mediterranean Sea to the Pacific Ocean, but this time around, the former leading horse, Great Britain, was exhausted. The underdog, instead, as injured as it was, had the will and the power to run at full speed. Had a race between Great Britain and the Soviet Union taken place, the winner of this round of secular confrontation between the mightiest maritime and continental powers would have been, for the first time, the latter. There is only one way for Great Britain to prevent it—to make this race a "relay race" with the reluctant would-be world hegemon finally committed to stepping in for the declining world power. And this is indeed what happened during the second half of the twentieth century: the United States came to replace the fading Great Britain.

Already before the outbreak of the First World War, the United States had become the world's industrial leading power. Yet the unprecedented level of devastation that Europe brought on itself by fighting two world wars catapulted the United States toward an indisputable economic, technological, military, and cultural leadership. The history of the first half of the twentieth century in the North Atlantic can be summarized as the phase in which after four centuries of confrontation over world hegemony, Europe finally self-destroyed, unintentionally crowning the United States as the new emerging world hegemon.

Hence, when a new round of confrontation started unfolding between the mightiest maritime and continental powers in the wake of the Second First World War, it was the turn of the United States to assume the lead role in confronting Communist Russia. After a parenthesis of pragmatic collaboration to defeat two rounds of German challenge, the Big Game reemerged. However, this time the "game" was bigger, global, fateful for the survival of life on planet Earth, and known as the Cold War.

Granted, the two games shared many features. In particular, at the core of each was a strategic geopolitical struggle disguised but enhanced as an ideological, irreconcilable battle, even if at times pragmatism bridged the irreconcilable. However, the Cold War unfolded for the most part in an age of atomic bombs and ballistic missile parity between the contending superpowers. The United States, having enjoyed a monopoly on atomic weapons for almost half a decade, made no preemptive strikes. By 1949 the Soviet Union had conducted its first atomic bomb test. Atomic bomb parity made this war "cold," because a head-on "hot" war of the kind that Great Britain and Russia conducted during the Crimean War was unaffordable. As the Cold War unfolded, the superpowers attained the commanding stage of MAD (mutually assured destruction). And although they were on the brink of madness during the Cuban missile crisis (1962), they backed down into a détente, an easing of hostilities. Stockpiling atomic missiles, conducting proxy wars in Asia and the Middle East—through the same fracture lines as the Big Game—and intervening in domestic politics around the world were the hallmarks of this atomically restrained global war (Table 4.1).

But for this relay competition to happen at all, the United States had to put aside its long-held inclination to isolationism, disentanglement, and hemispheric confinement. The Roosevelt administration was becoming ripe and ready to make the move. Great Britain was urging the United States to make the move. And Soviet intentions and actions, as much as the ways in which they were perceived or misperceived, pushed the United States to make the move. As stated above, the United States had all the ingredients to become the world's leader. The moment that U.S. isolationism ended, a new world hegemon was born. With a mighty counterforce (the USSR) cohabitating in the world order, however, the United

Table 4.1 Maritime world hegemons vs. continental counter-hegemon

World hegemon	Ideological conflict	Geopolitical conflict	Pragmatic collaboration
Great Britain	Liberalism vs. Despotism (Russia)	Big Game	Coalition against Napoleonic France Coalition against Imperial Germany
United States	Capitalism vs. Communism (USSR)	Cold War	Coalition against Nazi Germany

States was left to exercise its hegemony in a bi-polar world in which only some world societies would be willing or induced to follow its lead. In that regard, U.S. world hegemony differed from British hegemony. But then, haven't we all ended up being Americanized nevertheless?

A FOURFOLD BIG STICK

U.S. world hegemony was different from its British predecessor not only because of its stubbornly reluctant beginnings and its forced cohabitation with a firm and long-lasting counter-hegemonic power that imposed a bi-polar world order. The United States was fundamentally different in its foundational arrangements. Unlike Britain, the United States lacked a formal global empire. True, it had a continental empire, but it was one that evolved to be a federal nation-state composed of 50 states, a federal district, and five territories (Puerto Rico, Virgin Islands, Guam, American Samoa, and Northern Mariana Islands). The maritime colonies acquired through the Spanish-American War devolved either into part of the United States (Puerto Rico, 1899) or into its informal empire (Cuba, 1902; Philippines 1946). Indeed, with no empire as such at its disposal it was the informal empire that became the leading modality for the establishment of world hegemony. But the U.S. informal empire came with a twist. Military might was followed neither by colonization nor lasting rule. Rather, the establishment of military bases brought about U.S. global coverage.

Franklin Roosevelt's "destroyers-for-bases" deal with Great Britain represented not only a profoundly symbolic but also a concrete moment in the "relay race," signaling the transition from the former to the new world power. By the end of the Second World War, the United States had 2,000 military outposts around the world. By the end of the Cold War in 1991, there were 1,600 global U.S. military bases remaining. Today the United States still maintains nearly 800 military bases in more than 70 countries.[25]

Another "relay race" moment came in 1944 when Roosevelt authorized the creation of an intelligence service modeled after the British Intelligence Service MI6 (Military Intelligence, Section 6). The Office of Strategic Services (OSS) became active during the last stages of the Second World War but was dismantled soon after and replaced in 1947 with the Central Intelligence Agency.[26] The CIA supported the U.S. empire of bases by providing them with information. Conversely, the CIA received information from the military intelligence. But it was also tasked with providing national security information not just to the military but to the President and other policymakers. To fulfill this goal, the organization counts on offices dedicated to the analysis of open sources (e.g., media, academic publications), technologically gathered intelligence (e.g., reconnaissance satellites imagery), and closed human intelligence (i.e., spies), in regions throughout the world. Finally, beyond its intelligence gathering and processing capabilities, the CIA engages in covert action aimed at inducing or producing favorable political changes. Its history is rich in such interventions.[27]

The Second World War ended not only with 2,000 U.S. military outposts around the world but also with the United States having dropped atomic bombs on Hiroshima and Nagasaki on August 6 and 9, 1945. Detonating the bombs brought about the unconditional surrender of Japan and signaled to the world and the Soviet Union, in particular, that the U.S. monopolistic possession of a doomsday power was new and indisputable. Surprisingly, though, this monopoly came to an end soon enough when in 1949 the Soviet Union conducted its first nuclear weapon test. The new world hegemony became constrained by the bipolar world of the Cold War. And yet, side by side with the loss of its monopoly on atomic weapons (additional atomic powers: Great Britain, 1952; France, 1960; China, 1964; Israel, undeclared; India, 1974; Pakistan, 1998; and North Korea, 2007), the United States produced more than 70,000 nuclear warheads, more than those of all other states combined.[28] Similarly, the United States possessed the widest set of nuclear weapon delivery systems, including long-range bombers, intercontinental ballistic missiles, nuclear submarines, and tactical weapons such as nuclear artillery and human-portable special atomic demolition munitions. All the delivery systems were, of course, supported by its global empire of military bases.[29]

1949 was also the year in which Western European and North American nations signed the North Atlantic Treaty, which established a system of collective defense known as the North Atlantic Treaty Organization (NATO). It was in the wake of the Communist takeover of Czechoslovakia and the Berlin Blockade by the Soviet Union, both during 1948, that Great Britain fostered this alliance "to keep the Russians out, the Americans in, and the Germans down."[30] The terms of the treaty compelled its members to regard an armed attack against anyone as an attack against all. This British initiative was the final gesture of handing over its relay baton. The United States had finally rejected its traditional "splendid isolationism" and agreed to become an informal "empire by invitation."

Based on NATO's transatlantic collaboration, the idea of collective defense to contain the Communist threat was applied globally. In 1951 the United States bound Australia and New Zealand in a collective security agreement, the ANZUS Treaty, for military cooperation in the Pacific Rim.[31] In 1954, the three nations came together to compose the core of the Southeast Asia Treaty Organization (SEATO) until 1977, when it ceased operations. Thailand, the Philippines, Pakistan, East Pakistan (since 1971 Bangladesh), and France and Great Britain were also part of the Southeast Asia Collective Treaty.[32] From 1955 until 1979 Pakistan, Iran, Iraq, Turkey, and Great Britain formed the Central Treaty Organization (CENTO). Although fostered by the United States, the treaty—also known as the Baghdad Pact—did not include the United States as a member. Nevertheless, the United States supported this alliance militarily and economically and participated in its military committee.[33]

By 1955, a decade into the post-World War era, there was a U.S.-led collective defense agreement for every slice of the globe. Westward across the Pacific Ocean, bilateral treaties with countries formerly occupied by the United States—Japan (1951) and South Korea (1953)—were in place. Moving southward into Australia and New Zealand, ANZUS stood firm. From there across South East Asia and the Indian Ocean up to Pakistan, SEATO was in place. Pakistan also served as the easternmost point of CENTO that ran all the way westward to Turkey, which, since 1952, was a member of NATO. Spread across the European continent, the Atlantic Ocean, and to the eastern coast of North America, NATO brought collective defense agreements full circle. Meanwhile, in the Western Hemisphere, and in the best tradition of the Monroe Doctrine, most Latin American countries, in 1947, signed onto the Inter-American Treaty of Reciprocal Assistance or TRIAR (following the Spanish acronym) to provide hemispheric defense.

The U.S. empire rested on a combination of a global military presence, the largest arsenal and widest delivery systems of doomsday weapons, the long reach of its covert intelligence operations, and organizations for collective defense under its leadership. By threatening and beating its fourfold big stick, the United States projected its naked power, but its hegemony was most crucially about a large carrot—the large carrot of its giant economy.

A Huge Carrot Named the U.S. Economy

At the end of the Second World War, the U.S. economy represented about a third of the world's entire economy. It accounted for half of all manufacturing and held two-thirds of the world's gold reserves: a third, half, two-thirds! Such prominence was never attained by Great Britain, which at its peak represented about 10% of the world economy. But more typically and since the fully fledged industrialization of Germany and the United States, Great Britain represented around 8% of the world economy.[34] Several factors accounted for the superlative economic success of the United States. In absolute terms, it had the largest industrial economy in place already by 1916. The First World War catapulted the economy further due to GDP growth and relative to the Europe's war-damaged economies. By 1918, the United States had already become the workshop as well as the bank of the world.

This decisive economic leadership is clearly recognizable by the global economic debacle triggered by Black Tuesday (October 29, 1929) on Wall Street. From that date until mid-1932, the Dow Jones Industrial Average lost 89% of its value and the American financial system collapsed. Soon after, financial systems around the world collapsed. Without available credit, industrial production sharply declined around the world. Without industrial production, the demand for raw materials evaporated in the non-industrialized world. Without jobs there were no salaries for some 20–30% of the workforce, depending on the country. And without salaries consumption spiraled downward. The U.S. Great Depression led to the devastation of the world economy.

The U.S. Senate response to the crisis came quickly in June 1930 in the form of the Smoot-Hawley Tariff, which raised tariffs on over 20,000 imported goods; the United States had reacted to the crisis by turning its back on the world economy.[35] The economies of the world followed suit. The global economy created by the twin forces of the Industrial Revolution and democracy came to a close.

And yet by the end of the Second World War, the U.S. economy had reached full steam once again. In absolute numbers, industrial production had exploded as part of the war effort. In contrast, the economies of Europe, the Soviet Union, and Japan were thoroughly devastated by that same war. Under these conditions, the United States launched an assertive global leadership, whose goal was now to rearticulate the global economy it had previously helped to dismantle. This time around the nascent world hegemon deployed new and multiple tools including new global financial institutions, direct plans for investment, the expansion of its multinational corporations worldwide, and a consumerist way of life.

In July 1944, almost a year before the end of the war, the United Nations Monetary and Financial Conference gathered delegates from 44 nations at Bretton Woods, New Hampshire. What the "destroyers-for-bases" deal represented for the transition of military world hegemony, Bretton Woods represented for the inception of a new economic world hegemony. Great Britain and the United States, as chief partners, led the conference. The handover involved affixing a value of US$35 for an ounce of gold, mimicking the role British sterling had before the beginning of the Big Brexit. With the dollar's value set, each nation's currency was pegged to the U.S. dollar, enthroning it as currency king. The dollar became "as good as gold," granting the United States mighty leverage for years to come. All it took for the United States to meet its economic obligations abroad was to print more dollar bills. By 1958, the accumulated foreign holdings of U.S. dollars had surpassed U.S. gold reserves, yet newly printed bills continued to fulfill American economic commitments.[36]

The monetary exchange system aimed to facilitate international trade. To this end, Bretton Woods also resulted in the establishment of the International Bank for Reconstruction and Development (IBRD) and the International Monetary Fund (IMF) in 1945. The IBRD was created to finance the reconstruction of Europe. In 1960, the creation of the International Development Association (IDA), which offered loans to developing countries around the world, complemented the IBRD. The IBRD and IDA combined to form the World Bank (WB), which financed at preferential interest rates human development, infrastructure, agriculture, industrialization, environmental protection, and governance.[37] While the primary goal of the World Bank was lending to foster development, the IMF's goal was to promote the stability of exchange rates, balance of payments, and financial flows. It gathered statistics, conducted analyses, surveilled member economies, and demanded particular policies.[38] Finally, WB lending and IMF steering combined in 1947 with the General Agreement on Tariffs and Trade (GATT), an agreement geared toward free trade that promoted the reduction or elimination of trade barriers such as tariffs or quotas. Free trade and comparative advantage were launched once again on a new global tour.

Although the governance of the WB and IMF is shared by all state members, the United States has a predominant role in their leadership. The President of the WB has always been a U.S. citizen, and the United States holds 15.85% of the voting power. The President of the IMF has always been a citizen of a European state, but the United States holds 16.73% of the voting power. The headquarters of both institutions are in Washington, DC. When Pierre Charles L'Enfant developed the urban plan for the city of Washington back in 1791, he placed the White House at arm's length from Congress. The two miles separating the buildings represented both a practical constraint and a symbolic gesture to highlight the importance of the division of power between the executive and legislative branches of government. The headquarters of the WB and the IMF are just two blocks away from the White House.

When the Great Depression hit in 1929, the protectionism of Smoot-Hawley was not the only salient counter-measure applied in the United States. Even more prominently, Roosevelt offered a New Deal. In essence, this deal was about state intervention in economic activity, aiming to bring economic recovery by expanding public spending, providing relief to those in need, and regulating the financial system to prevent a future crisis.[39] Whereas the protectionist policy fostered by Smoot-Hawley was reversed after the Second World War by the free-market policies stimulated by the WB, IMF, and GATT, the New Deal's basic tenet of economic recovery and immediate relief through state funding was expanded by the United States into a global New Deal.

Beginning in 1948 and for the next four years, the United States launched the European Recovery Program, better known as the Marshall Plan, providing Western European states with over US$13 billion (equivalent to nearly 139 billion dollars in 2020). This economic support sought relief for war-torn Europe and the recovery of its industries. It also imposed free-trade regulations forging close transatlantic economic ties. Whereas NATO was devised to contain Soviet-led Communist expansion via military means, the Marshall Plan intended to prevent a domestic surge of Communism by enhancing productivity, prosperity, and trade unionism: a strong stick at the borders of Western Europe, a huge carrot within those borders. Moreover, these arrangements also relaunched economic, political, and military cooperation between Western European states, which later proved to be a necessary point of departure for subsequent European integration. Starting in 1951 and for the next decade, the

United States continued providing approximately 7.5 billion dollars annually through the Mutual Security Agency, which in 1961 was replaced by a globally ambitious USAID (United States Agency for International Development) still active today with a US$39 billion current budget.[40]

In this way, the foundational transatlantic collaboration was expanded globally as were military partnerships. In the years immediately following the war, the United States provided generous aid packages to multiple Asian states: Japan obtained 2.44 billion dollars, Nationalist China (after 1949, Taiwan) and South Korea received around one billion dollars each, the Philippines 803 million, India 255 million, Indonesia 215 million, Pakistan 98 million, Israel 282 million, and 196 million to the rest of the Middle East (all these amounts stated in at the time US$. Their equivalents to today's value are almost ten times).[41]

While international institutions provided a framework, guidance, incentives, and surveillance for a new globally articulated economy based once again on free trade and comparative advantage and a global Keynesian approach, the United States provided the seed money to restart the global economy. But it was the private sector of the U.S. economy that made the major breakthroughs in opening up closed national economies and bringing in foreign investment. At the core of this dual accomplishment lay a powerful economic institution: the multinational corporation.

A multinational corporation is an economic enterprise comprising a base company with subsidiary units in more than one country but with all of them operating under the same system of governing bodies. Hence, despite its transnational dimension, a multinational corporation has its headquarters, its cutting-edge technologies, patents, research, and development, as well as the bulk of its capital, shareholders, and the destination of most of its revenues and profits based in one nation only. And that nation in the post-World War order was, for the most part, the United States.

Terminology aside, multinational corporations were first and foremost, American corporations. Yet their transnational nature opened up national markets in which they operated as if they were local corporations (i.e., free trade) and at the same time made available for these mostly U.S. corporations the cheaper labor, raw materials, and favorable regulations that these national economies could offer (i.e., local comparative advantages). In other words, by virtue of their declared multinationalism, U.S. corporations succeeded in penetrating the protectively enclosed national economies of the post-Great Depression world economy, bringing free trade, comparative advantages, and the flow of international investments to a higher level. They accounted for the bulk of international investment and world trade.

And with such an unprecedented scale of international investment promoting mass production and world trade, all that was needed was a matching force of prospective consumers. In this regard, too, the United States had something to offer to the world: a way of life in which consumerism reigned. The U.S. economy confronted the problem of mass production becoming overproduction—that is, production beyond consumer demand—early on. Consumerism became the answer for tackling this problem. In essence, it consisted of stimulating the purchase of goods and services using specific business strategies, media advertisement, and socialization more broadly.

A well-known business strategy to induce consumption was planned obsolescence, the periodic redesigning of a given product that makes the previous design obsolete and hence less desirable. The Ford Motor Company was famous for the mass production of the Model T. The model, launched in 1908 and continued through the 1920s, was a primary example of the success that mass scale assembly lines had in making an affordable product and driving sales. But mass production on its own can bring sales up only to the point in which the market becomes saturated. And here comes what made General Motors famous: the vision of an annual model-year design. Basically, it was a yearly facelift on the body of the same car, which would generate renewed consumer demand. This was the strategy that allowed General Motors to surpass Ford's sales in the 1930s, and it was a strategy that enhanced consumerism in a society that otherwise could have had its needs covered by mass production.[42]

To inculcate obsolescence by forging the link between newly designed products and satisfaction, if not personal fulfillment, industries harnessed the powers of advertisement. The consistent bottom-line idea of advertisement is that the recipient of the message needs some product that will successfully bring about the fulfillment of their aspirations: beauty, health, wealth, status, marriage, happiness, acceptability, popularity, and many more, all of which are achievable only if that advertised product is purchased. A multiplicity of visual and audio mass media was progressively embraced to enhance consumerism, including announcements in all graphic platforms, billboards, radio, and TV commercials. Mass media advertising was so successful in instilling the basic consumerist equation "consumption = happiness" that it became deeply engrained in social relations. Parents to children, relatives to relatives, lovers to lovers, friends to friends could offer satisfaction, happiness, and love via consumption. To this day, it is how many people expected to obtain satisfaction, happiness, and love and hence is what they demand. And once the demand is in place, business will go out of its way to meet it and even offer more. To the large department stores opened in the wake of the Industrial Revolution in the nineteenth century the explosion of consumerism in post-Second World War United States added the shopping mall with its cornucopia of goods and entertainment, many of which were iconically American, from head to toe (baseball caps, t-shirts, jeans, and sneakers) and from breakfast to dinner (doughnuts, cheeseburgers, fried chicken, cola drinks, and milkshakes).[43]

By the end of the Second World War, the United States had fundamentally shifted gears not only in the political arena by ending its long-lasting isolationism that had been aggravated by the First World War, but also by reversing its equally long-lasting protectionist economic policies, exacerbated since the Great Depression. Now was the time once again to bring as much of the world economy as possible into global free markets. The WB, IMF, and GATT were launched with this goal in mind. However, New Deal policies (direct state intervention in economic life) that were originally aimed at bringing the economy out of depression continued to be implemented. Moreover, a sort of a global New Deal was offered to many states that unequivocally sided with the United States in the Cold War-created bi-polar world.

And yet for all the importance of globally disseminated governmental seed monies, it was the U.S. economy through its multinational corporations that brought the largest share of international investments and trade. As national economies grew their own multinational corporations, these economies increasingly reached levels of consumerist prosperity as the crucial components—planned obsolescence, ever-present advertising, consumption = happiness, the shopping mall, and iconic American items—were adopted. That was too much of an attractive huge carrot not to be willingly followed. And so it was that the domestically unconvincing slogan of the Great Depression, "there's no way like the American Way," ended up becoming globally convincing in the second half of the twentieth century. That is hegemony!

An Alluring Dream Named the American Dream

In sharp contrast with the British case, U.S. world hegemony was not based on a global empire but on the powerful combination of a fourfold big stick and an enticingly appealing carrot. And yet as if this winning combination were not sufficient to ensure clear global leadership, the United States also relied on an alluring dream, a true empire of the imagination. Disneyland and Disneyworld with their characters, Hollywood with its stars and blockbusters, superheroes from the comics to the screen, comedians, TV series, miniseries, and sitcoms produced a comforting environment of entertainment, emotional uplift, awakened desires, and manufactured fantasies. For the last five generations, U.S. culture has introduced values and behaviors to the citizens of the world from cradle to grave. At the same time, idiosyncratic assortments of jazz and blues, rock and roll and pop music, metal and punk, and hip hop have constituted a big chunk of the personal soundtracks of young and old alike around the globe, sometimes complementing, sometimes supplanting their native musical backgrounds.

Worldwide, the last five generations have been only more or less aware of the extent to which NATO, SEATO, ANZUS, CENTO, TRIAR, IMF, WB, and GATT shaped their lives. For these same generations, however, individual consciousness has been molded by storylines, visual, and audio memories brought by the Three Stooges, the Addams Family, Batman, Superman, Wonder Woman, Zorro, Indiana Jones, Mickey Mouse, Donald Duck, Dumbo, Bugs Bunny, Nemo, Woody, Buzz, and so many others! Regardless of our location, we have all been Americanized. And this, this is hegemony too!

This huge empire of the imagination is not only fictional and artistic but also made of scientific and technological creativity. The United States was and is home to the best universities in the world, in which most of the leading cutting-edge research has been conducted. As such, they brought to the world many of the major scientific breakthroughs and crucial technological innovations of the second half of the twentieth century—for example, nuclear fission, the polio vaccine, DNA structure, the television, personal computers, the Internet, GPS satellites, and air conditioning. Conversely, the world has been sending many of its best and brightest students and scholars to the U.S. universities. This phenomenon produces an international "brain drain" and an American "brain gain" that continues fostering innovative research and development, made in the United States.

In this way, the tangibles modalities of U.S. world hegemony—military and economic power combined and translated into political influence—are supplemented by the infatuating powers of the imagination, which generate multiple versions of the American Dream. From the sublime ideals of liberty and the pursuit of happiness to the mundane goals of a house, a car, and additional fantasies of consumerism and opulence, the United States is the country in which the most immigrants live: almost 50 million! That is, 20% of all immigrants in the world live in the United States. This is equivalent to the total of the five countries with the next-largest numbers of immigrants (Saudi Arabia, Germany, Russia, Great Britain, and the United Arab Emirates).[44]

Similarly, the United States is the top earning country in international tourism receipts, with about 206 billion dollars spent by 75 million tourists a year. Once again, it takes the next four countries with the largest incomes from tourism (Spain, Thailand, China, and France) to match the United States.[45] And many more people from around the world would have traveled to the United States if only they could, either as immigrants or tourists. Such is the power of U.S. culture that even fast food attracts the international sojourner!

Conversely, the arrival of such a huge number and proportion of immigrants, which makes up more than 14% of the American population (as opposed to a global average of 3%), synergizes powerfully with the American empire of the imagination. An army of scholars, researchers, engineers, programmers, artists, entrepreneurs, and workers—all self-selected by their drive to fulfill the American dream and scrutinized by the U.S. Citizenship and Immigration Services—fosters this empire of the imagination with its new ideas, projects, initiatives, and cultural diversity. And this is not even the major synergy in town.

THE SWIRLING SYNERGY OF THE AMERICAN TRIPLETS

In fact, as much as two sets of twins had made Great Britain the nineteenth century's world hegemon, a set of triplets—the fourfold big stick, the huge carrot, and the alluring dream—worked in tandem to enhance U.S. power. Think, for instance, about a powerful multinational corporation such as International Telephone & Telegraph (ITT).

A modest telephone company formed in 1920 became a huge conglomerate through hundreds of acquisitions in the communication sector and beyond for more than 50 years. This New York-based company first made inroads in Puerto Rico and Cuba, acquiring the Puerto Rico Telephone Company, the Cuban-American Telephone and Telegraph Company and a half-interest in the Cuban Telephone Company. Then it moved into Europe, buying a number of telephone companies there, starting with Spain's Telefónica. A series of electric and electronic companies came next including the Belgian Bell Telephone Manufacturing Company, the French Compagnie Générale d'Electricité, British International Western Electric, and German Standard Elektrizitätsgesellschaft. In the post-Second World War era, the number of acquisitions grew exponentially incorporating not only international telecommunications manufacturing subsidiaries across the globe but also hotels, bakeries, car-rentals, insurance companies, and timberlands.[46]

Such an overwhelming economic success story of the huge carrot enhanced the strength of the fourfold big stick by contributing a large lump sum of tax dollars, communications infrastructure, and cutting-edge technologies to the empire of military bases, the CIA, and partners associated with U.S. collective defense organizations. Similarly, this economic success nurtured the dreams and aspirations of many bright minds hoping to realize the potential of their talents and ideas. That seems to be the case, for example, of Charles Kuen Kao, the "Father of Fiber Optic Communications" and the visionary of trans-oceanic submarine communications via fiber optic cables. Kao was a Chinese-born (1933) electrical engineer and physicist at University College London. He started his groundbreaking work at the research center of Standard Telephones and Cables, a subsidiary of ITT. By 1974 he joined ITT in Virginia; in 1982 he became the first ITT executive scientist and was stationed mainly at the Advanced Technology Center in Connecticut. He served as an adjunct professor and Fellow of Trumbull College at Yale University. In 1986, Kao became the corporate director of research at ITT.[47]

Dream for some, nightmare for others; ITT's presence was also well felt in Chile when Socialist Salvador Allende was elected President in 1970. Back then ITT owned 70% of the Chilean Telephone Company, had investments in telephone equipment, assembling and manufacturing, directory printing and international communications, and operated hotels. No wonder that Harold Geneen, ITT's CEO at the time, communicated his concern to the U.S. State Department in view of the prospects of possible nationalization of private assets.[48] For three years the CIA mounted covert operations to destabilize the democratically elected government of Allende, setting the stage for a military coup in 1973.[49] In its wake, 40,018 dissidents and their families were tortured, including 3,065 killed.[50] But Chile was made safe for ITT and U.S. multinational corporations. The synergy of the triplets swirls also in this direction. Such is the way of the U.S. world hegemony. As powerful as each of the three triplets is in its turn, it is in their swirling synergy that they are at the peak of their might.

Great Britain: 20—United States: 34.
A Different Model for World Hegemony

And so, it is the case indeed that underneath the prominent divergence in sports passions, there are crucial distinctions between the British and American world hegemonies. To begin with, their roads were completely different. England, and then Great Britain, had proactively spent three centuries building a global empire while encroaching, meddling, containing, or totally defeating the other global maritime empires (Spanish, Portuguese, Dutch, French) and the largest continental one (Russia). The resulting nineteenth century British Empire provided the solid and wide springboard from which British world hegemony was launched by the articulation of its informal empire and its economic, political, military, and cultural leadership.

The U.S. trajectory to world hegemony was remarkably different. From its inception and throughout its trajectory, the United States unfolded as an anti-imperialist imperialist state. The political global grip ended up crystallizing not as a formal empire but as the mightiest military entity in world history with global reach and coverage: an empire of military bases. The American industrial-military complex furnished these bases with conventional and atomic weapons and the American allies throughout the world provided ground, forces, budgets, and commitments through regionally based organizations of collective defense.

Its strongest and widest springboard was its huge economy, not its empire. Economically the United States had embraced, internalized, and disseminated the original two sets of twins that promoted Great Britain to world power in the nineteenth century. The U.S. Industrial Revolution was fostered mostly in northeastern states amid protectionist policies;

the democratic revolution gradually unfolded starting with the anti-monarchic Revolutionary War. Free trade was embraced by the United States once it became the world industrial powerhouse in the second decade of the twentieth century, dramatically restrained since the outbreak of the Great Depression, and promoted worldwide in the post-Second World War U.S. world order. This same chronology applies to its handling of the principle of comparative advantage.

Yet aside from surpassing its master on its own turf, the United States also led in expanding the reach of the Industrial Revolution by fostering electrification, the internal combustion engine, the chemical industries, new techniques of mass production (e.g., Taylorism and Fordism), and finally nuclear energy. These breakthroughs in industrial production were matched by catapulting consumerism into a way of life: "I consume, therefore I am." Increasingly, multiple societies around the world wanted to embrace this way of life. The United States was ready not only to point toward the horizon of what might await them but actually to pave the way. The wider the consumerist world, the more powerful the consumers' demands on the world factory and world bank.

This global consumerism entailed not only tangible goods such as refrigerators, television sets, dishwashers, and cars but also cultural products such as music, movies, and TV series. Those captivated the minds and hearts of millions around the world from the tenderest of ages and throughout their lives. It is probably this intangible empire of the imagination that has been Americanizing the world more than anything else. It took some effort to make the argument on Britainnization in Chapter 1 (see above, pp. 1–23). The links between shepherd's pie and pastel de papa or the samosa and empanada were not easily demonstrable. It takes no effort whatsoever to convey that the notion of Americanization has been alive apparently since 1901, fully kicking since 1945, and on the rise ever since through mass media, the universities, technological innovation, the brands of pretty much everything, and fast food chains.[51] In fact, the pervasiveness of Americanization is recognizable by the proliferation of its multiple synonyms or metonyms: "Cocacolonization," "Disneyfication," "Walmarting," and "McWorldization."[52]

Conversely, the milder cultural Britainnization of the nineteenth century unfolded in a decidedly globalized world economy. The British-led Industrial Revolution created a world market of global interdependence relying on train networks; steamship routes foreshortened by the Suez, and later the Panama canals; the telegraph and its International

Telegraph Union; the Universal Postal Union; and agencies of world news. All of these covered a great part of the world by the 1870s. British world hegemony, hence, brought about not only Britannization but also globalization in ways that, aside from the matter of volume, speed, and intensity, are comparable to our contemporary world. The United States, for all of the decisiveness with which it brought about Americanization, did that in a world split in two by the Cold War. The Russian Empire with which Great Britain played the Great Game swung back and forth between confrontation and collaboration. If worse came to worst, Great Britain could defeat the Russian Empire on the battlefield, as indeed it did in the Crimean War. By contrast, the Soviet Union, its satellites, and the political regimes worldwide that it supported or inspired blocked the possibility of a global world market. No back and forth fluctuations between confrontation and collaboration took place; at most a détente was achieved. And worse coming to worst meant mutually assured destruction. Globalization under U.S. world hegemony could fully emerge, then, only with the end of the bi-polar world of the Cold War and the demise of the Soviet Union after 1990.

British hegemony was anchored in its empire, which ruled over more than 20% of the planet and population. U.S. world hegemony relied on its 34% share of the world economy. The two sets of twins—the industrial and democratic revolutions and free trade and comparative advantage—made us all Brits to some degree even with only a thin coat of Britainnization. And they certainly made us part of a globalized world. The three triplets of the U.S. world hegemony—the fourfold big stick, the huge carrot, and the alluring dream—powerfully fostered Americanization until they ran into a wall. Or perhaps we should say a curtain: the Iron Curtain in Eastern Europe and the Bamboo Curtain in East Asia. These barriers prevented the articulation of a full-fledged globalization.

For all of their differences, both these hegemons led the world into the future by the attraction and emulation that they inspired and by the conditioning or forcefulness with which they proceeded. Each remains indispensable to understanding our world and its trajectory for the last 200 years. Moreover, because of their shared culture, a compounding effect ensued as the United States succeeded Britain. The clearest expression of that was the rise and growth of English as a global language.[53]

But then, given the compounding powers of British and U.S. world hegemonies and more specifically the overwhelming powers—military, political, economic, technological, and cultural—of the United States, why would nation-states and societies refuse to follow the lead of, or yield to, the world hegemon's directions? This is the straightforward question that awaits a straightforward answer.

NOTES

1. *25 World's Most Popular Sports (Ranked by 13 factors)*, Total Sportek, http://www.totalsportek.com/most-popular-sports/.
2. Adam Tooze, *The Deluge: The Great War, America and the Remaking of the Global Order, 1916–1931* (Penguin Books, 2014).
3. Barbara Daly Metcalf and Thomas R. A Metcalf, *A Concise History of Modern India* (New York: Cambridge University Press, 2006), 56–91.
4. James Belich, *The New Zealand Wars and the Victorian Interpretation of Racial Conflict* (Auckland: Penguin, 1986), 204–205.
5. Barbara Watson Andaya and Leonard Y. Andaya, *A History of Malaysia* (New York: Palgrave Macmillan, 1984).
6. Alan Palmer, *Alexander I: Tsar of War and Peace* (London: Weidenfeld & Nicolson, 1974), 86.
7. G. Barton and B. Bennett, "Forestry as Foreign Policy: Anglo-Siamese Relations and the Origins of Britain's Informal Empire in the Teak Forests of Northern Siam, 1883–1925," *Itinerario* 34, no. 2 (2010): 65–86. https://doi.org/10.1017/S0165115310000355.
8. Muriel E. Chamberlain, *Pax Britannica? British Foreign Policy 1789–1914* (New York: Routledge, 2014): 88.
9. "Here [Concord, Massachusetts, 1775] once the embattled farmers stood, and fired the shot heard round the world." Hymn: Sung at the Completion of the Concord Monument, April 19, 1836," in *The Complete Works of Ralph Waldo Emerson, Vol. 9*, ed. Edward Waldo Emerson (Boston; New York: Houghton, Mifflin, 1903–1904), 159.
10. Ray Raphael, *A People's History of the American Revolution: How Common People Shaped the Fight for Independence* (New York: The New Press, 2001), 244.
11. Ralph Keyes, *Who Said What, Where, and When* (New York: St. Martin's Griffin, 2006), 387.
12. Jay Sexton, *The Monroe Doctrine: Empire and Nation in Nineteenth-Century America* (New York: Hill and Wang, 2012).

13. John A. Crow, *The Epic of Latin America*, 4th ed. (Berkeley: University of California Press, 1992), 676.
14. George C. Herring, *From Colony to Superpower: U.S. Foreign Relations Since 1776* (New York: Oxford University Press, 2008).
15. Otto Schoenrich, "The Venezuela-British Guiana Boundary Dispute," *American Journal of International Law* 43, no. 3 (July 1949): 523–526.
16. Dirk Bönker, *Militarism in a Global Age: Naval Ambitions in Germany and the United States before World War I* (Ithaca, NY: Cornell University Press, 2012).
17. John Avlon, *Washington's Farewell: The Founding Father's Warning to Future Generations* (New York: Simon & Schuster, 2017).
18. Thomas Jefferson, "First Inaugural Address," (March 4, 1801), in *The Papers of Thomas Jefferson* (Princeton, NJ: Princeton University Press, 2006).
19. Frame from Frank Capra (dir. And producer) "Prelude to War" documentary film, part of the W: Why We Fight series (War Activities Committee of the Motion Pictures Industry, 1942).
20. Christian Tomuschat, ed., *The United Nations at Age Fifty: A Legal Perspective* (Boston: Brill, 1995), 77.
21. James MacGregor Burns, *Roosevelt: The Lion and the Fox* (New York: Harcourt, 1956), 438. William Hardy McNeill, *America, Britain, and Russia: Their Co-operation and Conflict, 1941–1946* (New York: Oxford University Press, 1953), 772–790.
22. For a comparison between the two world hegemons emphasizing differences see Niall Ferguson, *Empire: The Rise and Demise of the British World Order and the Lessons for Global Power* (New York: Basic Books, Reprint edition, 2004) and Niall Ferguson, *Colossus: The Rise and Fall of the American Empire* (New York: Penguin Books; Reprint edition, 2005). For a comparison between the two world hegemons emphasizing similarities see Julian Go, *Patterns of Empire: The British And American Empires, 1688 To the Present* (New York: Cambridge University Press, 2011).
23. Edward Ingram, *In Defense of British India: Great Britain in the Middle East, 1775–1842* (London: Frank Cass & Co, 1984), 7–19.
24. Ingram, *In Defense of British India*; also Michael Ellman and Sergei Maksudov, "Soviet Deaths in the Great Patriotic War: A Note," *Europe Asia Studies* 46, no. 4 (1994), 671–680.

25. David Vine, "Where in the World Is the U.S. Military?," *Politico*, July/August 2015. https://www.politico.com/magazine/story/2015/06/us-military-bases-around-the-world-119321. David Vine, "The United States Probably Has More Foreign Military Bases Than Any Other People, Nation, or Empire in History. And It's Doing Us More Harm than Good," *The Nation*, September 14, 2015. https://www.thenation.com/article/the-united-states-probably-has-more-foreign-military-bases-than-any-other-people-nation-or-empire-in-history/.

26. Tim Weiner, *Legacy of Ashes: The History of the CIA* (New York: Doubleday, 2007), 702.

27. William Blum, *Killing Hope: U.S. Military and C.I.A. Interventions Since World War II – Updated Through 2003* (Monroe, ME: Common Courage Press, 2008).

28. Christopher E. Paine, Thomas B. Cochran, and Robert S. Norris, *The Arsenals of the Nuclear Weapons Powers: An Overview*, Canberra Commission Issue Paper (Washington, DC: Natural Resources Defense Council, January 4, 1996).

29. Amy F. Woolf, *U.S. Strategic Nuclear Forces: Background, Developments, and Issues* (Washington, DC: Congressional Research Service, August 8, 2017). https://fas.org/sgp/crs/nuke/RL33640.pdf.

30. David Reynolds, *The Origins of the Cold War in Europe: International Perspectives* (New Haven, CT: Yale University Press, 1994).

31. Joseph Gabriel Starke, *The ANZUS Treaty Alliance* (Melbourne: Melbourne University Press, 1965).

32. John K. Franklin, *The Hollow Pact: Pacific Security and the Southeast Asia Treaty Organization* (Fort Worth, TX: Texas Christian University, 2006).

33. Elie Podeh, *The Quest for Hegemony in the Arab World: The Struggle over the Baghdad Pact* (Boston: Brill, 1995). Michael J. Cohen, "From 'Cold' to 'Hot' War: Allied Strategic and Military Interests in the Middle East After the Second World War," *Middle Eastern Studies* 43, no. 5 (2007): 725–748.

34. Angus Maddison, *Monitoring the World Economy, 1820–1992* (Paris: Organization for Economic Cooperation and Development, 1995). Angus Maddison, *The World Economy: A Millennial*

Perspective (Paris: Organization of Economic Cooperation and Development, 2001).

35. Douglas A. Irwin, *Peddling Protectionism: Smoot–Hawley and the Great Depression* (Princeton University Press; 2011).

36. Michael H. Hunt, *The World Transformed: 1945 to the Present* (New York: St. Martin's, 2003), 194–195.

37. Donald Markwell, *John Maynard Keynes and International Relations: Economic Paths to War and Peace* (Oxford: Oxford University Press, 2006); Benn Steil, *The Battle of Bretton Woods: John Maynard Keynes, Harry Dexter White, and the Making of a New World Order* (Princeton, NJ: Princeton University Press, 2013).

38. Jonathan Schlefer, "There is No Invisible Hand," *Harvard Business Review*, April 10, 2012. https://hbr.org/2012/04/there-is-no-invisible-hand.

39. Carol Berkin et al., *Making America, Volume 2: A History of the United States: Since 1865* (Boston: Cengage Learning, 2011), 629–632.

40. Martin A. Schain, *The Marshall Plan Fifty Years Later* (New York: Palgrave MacMillan, 2001). Tony Judt, *Postwar: A History of Europe since 1945* (New York: Penguin, 2005). USAID, *USAID Congressional Budget Justification, FY2020* (U.S. Department of State, Foreign Operations, and Related Programs, 2020), https://www.usaid.gov/results-and-data/budget-spending.

41. All data from U.S. Bureau of the Census, *Statistical Abstract of the United States: 1954 (1955).* Table 1075, 899–902 online edition file 1954-08.pdf, https://www2.census.gov/library/publications/1954/compendia/statab/75ed/1954-08.pdf?#. https://www.usinflationcalculator.com/.

42. Bruce W. McCalley, *Model T Ford: The Car That Changed the World* (Iola, WI: Krause Publications, 1994). David Reynolds, *America, Empire of Liberty: A New History of the United States* (New York: Basic Books, 2009).

43. Vicki Howard, *From Main Street to Mall: The Rise and Fall of the American Department Store* (Philadelphia: University of Pennsylvania Press, 2015). Lisa Scharoun, *America at the Mall: The Cultural Role of a Retail Utopia* (Jefferson, NC: McFarland, 2012).

44. United Nations, *International Migration Report* [highlights] (United Nations 2017), https://www.un.org/en/development/

desa/population/migration/publications/migrationreport/docs/
MigrationReport2017_Highlights.pdf.
45. UNWTO, *Tourism Highlights* (UNWTO, 2017), https://www.e-unwto.org/doi/pdf/10.18111/9789284419029.
46. Robert Sobel, *ITT: The Management of Opportunity* (New York: Times Books, 1982). Robert Sobel, *The Rise and Fall of the Conglomerate Kings* (New York: Beard Books, 1999).
47. Jeff Hecht, *City of Light: The Story of Fiber Optics* (New York: Oxford University Press, 1999).
48. "ITT in Chile," NACLA, September 25, 2007, https://nacla.org/article/itt-chile.
49. Christopher Hitchens, *The Trial of Henry Kissinger* (New York: Verso, 2001). Peter Kornbluh, *The Pinochet File: A Declassified Dossier on Atrocity and Accountability* (New York: The New Press, 2003), 171. Tim Weiner, *Legacy of Ashes: The History of the CIA* (New York: Anchor Books, 2007), 361. Peter Winn, "Furies of the Andes," in *Century of Revolution*, eds. Greg Grandin and Gilbert Joseph (Durham, NC: Duke University Press, 2010), 239–275.
50. "Report of the Chilean National Commission on Truth and Reconciliation" vol. I/II, xxi–xxii (Notre Dame, IN: University of Notre Dame Press, 1993) (Digitized and posted by permission of the University of Notre Dame Press, February 22, 2000). https://www.usip.org/sites/default/files/resources/collections/truth_commissions/Chile90-Report/Chile90-Report.pdf. "The Valech Report" (officially The National Commission on Political Imprisonment and Torture Report, Comisión Asesora para la calificación de Detenidos Desaparecidos, Ejecutados Políticos y Víctimas de Prisión Política y Tortura (archive.org). "Chile Recognises 9,800 More Victims of Pinochet's Rule," *BBC News*, August 18, 2011, https://www.bbc.com/news/world-latin-america-14584095.
51. Samuel E. Moffett, "The Americanization of Canada" (PhD dissertation, Columbia University, 1907). W. T. Stead, *The Americanization of the World* (New York: Horace Markley, 1901). Volker R. Berghahn, "The Debate on 'Americanization' Among Economic and Cultural Historians," *Cold War History* 10, no. 1 (February 2010): 107–130. Ralph Willett, *The Americanization of Germany, 1945–1949* (New York: Routledge, 1989).

52. Alan E. Bryman, *The Disneyization of Society* (Thousand Oaks, CA: Sage, 2004). John Dicker, *The United States of Wal-Mart* (New York: TarcherPerigee, 2005). Steven Flusty, *De-Coca-Colonization* (New York: Routledge, 2004). George Ritzer, *The McDonaldization of Society* (Los Angeles: Pine Forge Press, 2009). Reinhold Wagnleitner, *Coca-Colonization and the Cold War* (Chapel Hill: University of North Carolina Press, 1994).
53. David Northrup, *How English Became the Global Language* (New York: Palgrave Macmillan, 2013).

CHAPTER 5

Or Else (1946–1973)

A Very Straightforward Global Story for a Very Straightforward Answer

Many nation-states and societies followed the leadership of the mightiest world hegemon ever, the post-Second World War United States. Many others, though, were unable or unwilling to follow the lead and even stood determined not to yield to the swirling synergy of the U.S. triplets, the fourfold big stick, the huge carrot, and the alluring dream. Such impossibility or unwillingness resulted from the constraints, possibilities, and opportunities opened up by the Second World War and the Cold War.

Let's recapitulate. During the second half of the nineteenth century a "Global Train" pulled by a locomotive named Great Britain brought the societies of the world and the global economy tighter together than ever before. But by the turn of that century and into the second decade of the twentieth century the three spoilers of the British world hegemony—Germany, the United States, and a global communist revolution—had been seriously disrupting the train's progress.

By 1945 these three spoilers had indeed managed to derail the "Global Train" in the wake of a globally convoluted interplay made of two world wars, the Great Depression in between them, and the spinning carousels of revolution and reaction. Great Britain lost its world hegemonic stance and was about to enter the process of losing its empire, too. Also, the

D. Olstein, *A Brief History of Now*, https://doi.org/10.1007/978-3-030-82420-4_5

global economic integration that Great Britain did so much to create was in shambles and the First Wave of Democracy was over. Germany, the leading spoiler and major architect of the derailment, was conquered and in ruins. Hence, by the end of the Second World War only two major forces remained in the hegemonic ring: the United States and what was left of the global communist revolution in the wake of the failure of the Comintern and the adoption of "socialism in one country," the Soviet Union. The alliance between these two lasted not much longer than the four years they joined forces against Nazi Germany and Showa Japan. Unconditional surrender of the Axis powers resulted soon in alienation between the former allies spiraling into a Cold War and a bipolar world order.

A brave new bi-polar world emerged in which there was not only one world hegemon, the United States, showing the path toward the future, but also a counter-hegemonic state, the Soviet Union. The latter not only carved out its own sphere of control (i.e., the Eastern Bloc) and influence (i.e., Communist regimes around the world) but also provided an alternative road for non-Communist regimes across the globe. In this bi-polar framework, world societies and states found the space to maneuver with national and social projects geared toward self-transformation aiming to catch up with developed economies, while trying to assert their presence in the world division of labor, capital, and power. In doing that, nation-states around the world were inspired by the breakthroughs made by Great Britain and its synergic revolutions: industrialization and democratization. They discarded, though, the other twins, the ideologies and policies of free trade and comparative advantage. Instead, nation-states around the world were inspired by the ideologies and policies of the triumphant hegemonic spoilers, the United States and the USSR. The principles of self-determination and socialism fostered by the United States and USSR, respectively, became the new ideology and policy twins touring the world since 1946. That set of twins remade the global socio-political-economic scene.

Self-determination was key for the colonial world as it paved the way for political independence. But self-determination also encouraged formerly independent states to reassert their sovereignty. In both cases—independence and sovereignty—self-determination entailed nationally tailored political projects. By contrast, socialism was originally intended to be an international project. It was for the workers of the world, led by the International, to unite and foster. The bitter experience of the First

World War, however, demonstrated that national allegiance prevailed over class unity as workers fought for their nations rather than their social class across national lines. In the wake of this experience notions of socialism were nationalized in Fascist Italy and National Socialist Germany. The Stalinist transition to "socialism in one country" in 1926 nationalized socialism even at the epicenter of the previously intended communist world revolution. In short, for first wave reactionary and revolutionary anti-hegemonic party states alike, the nation (or the race in the case of Nazi Germany) became the subject of some form of socialism.

This amalgamation of nationalism and socialism produced by first wave, post-First World War anti-hegemonic party states became a core legacy adopted by the anti-hegemonic party states of the second wave, after the Second World War. Alongside the amalgamation, a strategy of duplicating state and party overlapping institutions sought to mobilize society from within to confront the world order outside. During the three decades that followed the end of the Second World War, this amalgamation was fostered by many of the former republics, empires, and colonies upon which Britain had foisted free trade in the nineteenth century. That is, once the "Global Train" that had been pulled by the locomotive Britain was finally derailed in 1945, those second and third-class carriages at the tail aimed to become their own locomotives traveling on their own rails. They did so inspired by the new political horizon of self-determination set by the nascent American world hegemon as well as by the inspirational model for political organization and economic transformation provided by the world counter-hegemon, the Soviet Union.

Hence, instead of a "Global Train" metaphor, this second episode of world hegemony is better represented by multiple national attempts to build their own railways, with the counter-hegemon's train—the USSR—incentivizing these enterprises while at the same time pulling with its own locomotive as many wagons as it managed to hijack. Under these circumstances, and unlike the original "Global Train," lead by Great Britain, the hegemon locomotive—the United States—could pull only some of the world's wagons, those able and willing. But still, being the hegemon locomotive, it did its utmost to have those unwilling wagons hooked in line by using its carrot, stick, and dream.

Indeed, as much as the replacement of the British hegemonic world order by an American-Soviet bi-polar world made room for world societies and states to foster transformative national and social projects, the

Cold War also resulted in constant interventions worldwide by the super-powers seeking to influence, support, steer, or derail these projects. For all of the room that states and societies around the world gained for independent maneuvering—with national and social projects aiming for sovereign assertion and economic catch up—in the long run the hegemonic interventions, particularly those by the United States, prevailed. This "national free room versus superpower intervention" duality resulted in a two-stage sequence in the fate of political regimes in many states. At first, due to the lack of an uncontested world hegemon, a new wave of anti-hegemonic party states bloomed. Next, this second wave of anti-hegemonic party states was followed by a new wave of authoritarian dictatorships backed by U.S.-directed interventions.

Three decades after leaving their own national train stations, these forays aiming to catch up with the most developed nation-states had fallen short of their economic goals and were politically defeated or transformed. By then this brave new world of the national-socialist ideologies and policies had become outdated and was soon displaced by a new iteration of liberalism and comparative advantage. By the mid-1970s a new age of globalization and hegemony was on the brink of being reborn. This second round was to create a neoliberal global world.

From War to War to Cold War

The Second World War is very different from the First not only in its salient military characteristics—very dynamic versus mostly static; total war versus trench warfare—but also in its consequences. The First World War was the original trigger for the emergence of anti-hegemonic party states as well as the disruption of the hegemonic order and the globally integrated economy. Economic globalization was momentarily restored in that war's aftermath. However, the anti-hegemonic party states were there to stay, at first in the Soviet Union and Fascist Italy, later in Communist Mongolia, Kuomintang China, and Cardenist Mexico. And then, with the outbreak of the Great Depression of 1929 the global economic ties were severed more drastically. The emergence of a game-changing anti-hegemonic party state, Nazi Germany, was triggered, and the hegemonic order entered its terminal condition with the outbreak of the Second World War.

The immediate consequence of the Second World War, by contrast, was the overwhelming demise of most anti-hegemonic party states. The opening of the theater of operations in Asia in 1937 brought the end to Kuomingtang China as an effective anti-hegemonic party state following the Japanese invasion. Mongolia, also, lost its character as an anti-hegemonic party state, as the Japanese invasion brought it under Soviet control and it became an authoritarian satellite under the direct control of the Soviet Union. Across the Pacific, the anti-hegemonic party state in Mexico under Cárdenas' Partido de la Revolución Mexicana ruling from 1934 to 1940 was also brought to its end in the context of the Second World War. Cárdenas' succeeding President, Manuel Ávila Camacho, strongly aligned with the United States and resumed diplomatic relations with Great Britain. This shift in foreign policy coincided with a rearrangement of the ruling party domestically. By purging the militant cadres of Cárdenas' party and replacing them with a conservative bureaucracy, Ávila Camacho succeeded in demobilizing the Mexican society. Last but certainly not least, military defeat in the Second World War brought about the collapse of Fascist Italy, Nazi Germany, and Showa Japan. In short, the Second World War wiped out all the anti-hegemonic party states that emerged in the wake of the First World War except for the Soviet Union.

The First World War was sealed by a series of treaties imposed at the Paris Peace Conference in 1919 by the victorious allies. Great Britain preserved its hegemonic stance, France remained self-interestedly aligned with it, and the United States remained reluctant to engage with world hegemony and yielded to its European allies. The Treaty of Saint-Germain partitioned the Austro-Hungarian Empire into its successor states, the Treaty of Sèvres partitioned the Ottoman Empire, and the Treaty of Versailles dealt with the fate of the leading spoiler of British hegemony: Germany was forced to disarm, to make substantial territorial concessions, and to pay large reparations.

In sharp contrast, there was no peace treaty at the end of the Second World War and unlike in the First World War, the allied state from the east—the Soviet Union—remained in the war to its end, emerged victorious, and had its own postwar agenda. Three conferences brought the leaders of the displaced world hegemon (GB), the emerging world hegemon (United States), and the emerging counter-hegemon (USSR) to discuss the postwar order in Teheran (November, 1943), Yalta (February, 1945), and Potsdam (July, 1945). As with the end of the First World War the core issue was how to deal with the leading spoiler of the previous world order: Germany. In contrast with 1918, in 1945 there was no agreement between the Allies with regard to German reparations, the linchpin of the Versailles Agreement. This time around the Soviet Union forcefully demanded compensations while the United States showed no less determination in aiming, instead, for a successful reconstruction of Germany. As much as the seeds of the Second World War can be found in the Guilt Clause of the Versailles Agreement, making Germany fully responsible for the outbreak of the First World War and hence subject to pay reparations, the lack of clarity and agreement between the Allies with regard to Germany, its responsibility, and its reparations by the end of the Second World War sowed the seeds of the Cold War.

In this discrepancy, as in the many others that emerged throughout the last stages of the war and in its immediate aftermath, the Soviet Union made the point that it was the Red Army that engaged around 85% of the Wehrmacht and it was the Soviet people who suffered the largest number of casualties (some 24 million dead out of the approximately 60 million killed in total during the war). Conversely, for the U.S. President Harry Truman, who was well aware of the world hegemonic status of the United States given its unmatchable military and economic power, there was no reason why the United States should not get 85% of what it wanted in all important issues. These colliding accounting balance sheets held by the two largest stakeholders combined with mutual suspicion, ideological confrontation, and bad historical blood to pave the way for the next round in the long-lasting conflict between the mightiest world sea power and the largest continental power. This time around it was called the Cold War and consisted of a world order in which two separate spheres—one to the west of the "Iron Curtain" guided by liberal ideology, capitalist economy, and democratic regimes, the other to the east of that imaginary wall and ruled by Communist regimes—remained divided in a latent but permanent conflict. This conflict and the ensuing competition, which was punctuated by bursts of actual warfare (albeit no direct warfare between the two superpowers), was the cornerstone for almost everything that happened globally under the sun.

Overall, the Cold War unfolded in five main stages. It started in Europe soon after the end of the second World War through diplomatic, politic, economic, and technological means. Then, as the 1940s were coming to a close, the epicenter of the Cold War pivoted to Asia. It emerged there as a "Hot" War with a series of massive proxy wars in China, Korea, Vietnam, and Indonesia for the upcoming two and a half decades. By the early 1960s the Cold War had entered a third phase in which it had escalated in its intensity and became globally disseminated—so much so that in 1962 a crisis boiling point brought the superpowers to the verge of atomic warfare. That fateful episode, the Missile Crisis in Cuba, led to easing the tensions for almost 20 years throughout the 1960s and 1970s. This fourth period was known as détente (relaxation). In a final fifth phase the head-on confrontation was resumed starting in 1979 and lasted until the collapse of the Communist regimes in Eastern Europe (1989) and the extinction of the Soviet Union (1991).

The first divisive issue between the Second World War allies was the fate of Poland. There were two competing Polish governments. One, nationalist and anti-Soviet, was in exile in London; the other was based in Poland, in the city of Lublin. This one was forcefully upheld by the Soviet Union, whose leader, Josef Stalin envisioned Poland as a friendly buffer state blocking the path through which Germany had invaded Russia in both world wars. By the end of the war an entire buffer zone had emerged that included not only Poland, but also Czechoslovakia, Hungary, Romania, and Bulgaria, where Communist regimes were also established in the wake of the Soviet occupation. As for Germany and the reparations question, the country was partitioned into four sections (British, French, American, and Soviet) with the agreement that each of the allies was entitled to take reparations out of its zone of control.

By 1949 two German states, the Federal Republic of Germany to the west and the German Democratic Republic to the east, had emerged, each gravitating toward its respective sphere of influence. At this point they were clearly crystalizing at this point as rivals, with the West under the wings of the Marshall Plan (1948) and NATO (1949) and the East coordinated by the Cominform (Communist Information Bureau, 1947, which succeeded the Comintern's dissolution in 1943), the Comecon (Council for Mutual Economic Assistance, 1949), and the Warsaw Pact (the collective defense treaty of the Eastern bloc signed in 1955 in the wake of the incorporation of the Federal Republic of Germany into NATO). This dichotomy was defined from the U.S. standpoint as the "support [of] free peoples … resisting attempted subjugation by armed minorities or by outside pressures." From the Soviet Union perspective, the same dichotomy was characterized as the clashing of an "imperialist and anti-democratic" block with an "anti-imperialist and democratic" one.[1]

In the meantime, two contradictory messages from the United States to the Soviet Union set in motion the Cold War in Asia. At Potsdam (July 1945) the United States had the Soviet Union committed to enter the Pacific theater of war. At Hiroshima and Nagasaki (August 1945) the United States not only ushered the Soviet Union out of the Pacific theater but also disabused it of any pretension of military parity and equal footing in the new world order. However, by means of its military advance throughout Manchuria, the Soviet Union was able to bring about the partition of the Korean Peninsula. The Democratic People's Republic of Korea ruled by a Communist regime was established in the north; the Republic of Korea emerged in the south. The partition of Korea into two competing states nurtured a latent conflict geared for explosion. Moreover, the Soviet presence in the Pacific theater returned through a back door. An Open Door Policy with China had been successfully promoted by the United States since the late nineteenth century to prevent the millenary country from being hijacked by any single colonial power or carved up between several of them (see above, p. 128). As soon as Japan made its attempt in 1937, the United States backed the Republic of China, continuing their support throughout the Second World War. The United States had also subsequently supported the ruling Kuomintang against the Communist Party in the ensuing Chinese Civil War (1945–1949). And yet, in October 1949 the United States sat down for breakfast, only to learn that a new Communist regime now ruled China, i.e., the Peoples Republic of China. From this moment on both the biggest and the most populated countries that also happened to share one of the longest boundaries in the world were communist!

Such a conjunction would be definitely worrisome for any mind concerned with theories of domino effects—i.e., one Communist regime leading to another and another. Such was the case of Kim Il Sung, the North Korean leader, who in June 1950 crossed the 38th parallel that divided the Korean Peninsula into two states and transformed the Cold War into a hot one. His army's sprint toward the southern tip of the peninsula came to a halt once the UN forces, led and financed by the United States, reversed the direction of the battle and brought it to the north instead. But just as the UN forces had Chinese territory in sight, the Chinese army rolled the UN forces back. A year after the outbreak of the war the foes were bogged down around the starting line (the 38th parallel). By 1953 an armistice was signed. The Koreas were devastated, having sustained a toll of about four million lives.

It was not too much later that the sparks to reignite the Cold War in Asia started flying again as the people of Vietnam strived to achieve self-determination. Yes, this was the self-determination that Woodrow Wilson announced to the world in 1918 and that Ho Chi Minh came to unsuccessfully demand from him at Versailles. Some three decades and a half had since passed and in 1954 it was the Vietnamese military success that brought France, the colonial power, to the negotiating table at an international conference in Geneva and soon afterward out of Vietnam, Laos, and Cambodia. Vietnam was temporarily divided at the parallel 17th with its northern section ruled by the triumphant Communist Party and the southern section due to have elections in two years time to determine its regime. This election never took place and instead an authoritarian regime was imposed and sustained by the United States for a decade. With resistance rising and the authoritarian regime faltering, the United States launched its military intervention in 1964. The Vietnam War ensued for another decade. Vietnam, Laos, and Cambodia were devastated and sustained a toll of as many as three and half million lives.[2] This time there was no return to the starting line (the 17th parallel). The Socialist Republic of Vietnam instead unified the north and south halves under a Communist regime.

Involvement in distant Vietnam concerned President Lyndon Johnson from the start, while public disaffection with that war continued to grow.[3] A different matter, however, was to have a Communist regime emerging next door, literally 90 miles away. Since U.S. independence, tight commercial relations had been maintained with Cuba. Thomas Jefferson thought Cuba was "the most interesting addition which could ever be made to our system of States" and urged the U.S. Secretary of War "at the first possible opportunity, to take Cuba."[4] In 1854 a document known as the Ostend Manifesto provided the rationale for the United States purchase of Cuba from Spain while implying that the United States should declare war if Spain refused to sell.[5] War on Spain was indeed launched in 1898 leading to Cuban independence from that moribund colonial state and dependence on the rising U.S. power (see above, pp. 127, 136). That dependence lasted until 1959 when a revolution led by Fidel Castro and Che Guevara brought the rule of "our son of a bitch" (Fulgencio Batista) to an end.[6] A failed CIA-orchestrated invasion of Cuba in 1961 sent the revolutionaries to look for Soviet protection, which by 1962 arrived in the form of missile installations. Those were discovered by an American aircraft reconnaissance, leading to the establishment of a naval blockade to prevent any further Soviet delivery of atomic missiles to Cuba. With that delivery en route approaching the blockade line, the Cold War was on the brink of becoming an atomic war. An agreement prevented that by having all Soviet offensive weapons in Cuba dismantled while the United States publicly committed to refrain from another invasion of the island and secretly agreed to dismantle its medium-range ballistic missiles deployed in Turkey.

The Cuban Missile Crisis had the paradoxical result of spurring the nuclear arms race between the superpowers while at the same time setting the tone for easing the tensions to reduce the dangers of an atomic Armageddon. On the eve of the crisis the atomic power balance sheet stood at 7,200 to 500 strategic warheads in favor of the United States. A decade later the balance had changed to 8,400 to 2,400. Twenty years after the crisis the superpowers almost reached parity in the number of warheads accumulated: 11,000 to 10,000.[7] On the other hand, new venues of communication between the superpowers were opened, beginning with the establishment of a "red telephone," a direct hot line between Washington, DC and Moscow. This initial step of readiness for direct talks at a moment of urgency to prevent future crisis was later expanded to regular interactions that led to the signing of treaties aiming the limitation of strategic arms: the Strategic Arms Limitation Talks or SALT I (1972) and SALT II (1979 but never ratified). In short, the crisis ended up in this paradoxical mood of "if you want peace [détente], prepare for war" ("Si vis pacem, para bellum" Vegetius, *De re militari*, fourth or fifth century).

At the same time the crisis had shown the determination of the superpowers to intervene in the domestic affairs of states around the world as well as the limits of such interventions. As much as détente efforts were envisioned to avert the strategic threat of a nuclear war, competition between the superpowers to enlarge their respective portions of this bi-polar world continued. As much as Khrushchev promoted Soviet support and influence throughout the newly independent nation-states until immediately before the Cuban Missile Crisis, Andropov wanted the Soviet Union to continue supporting revolutionary causes throughout the world right to the bitter end of the détente Cold War phase. Needless to say, the United States was never shy about stepping into domestic affairs throughout the world carrying its own double-edged sword of support and influence before, during, and after détente. Indeed, the presence of the two superpowers (the world hegemon and the counter-hegemon), the dual world order they established, and the checks and balances that each imposed on the other allowed for states and societies around the world to attempt their own transformative national and social projects. A double delicate balance then emerged. On the one hand there was the balance between the degree of free maneuvering that every single nation-state could allow itself to exercise before running into the counterbalancing acts of a superpower intervention. In the Cuban case that is illustrated by the establishment of a revolutionary regime confronted by a CIA-led counter-insurgency intervention. On the other hand, there was an additional balance between the degree to which one of the superpowers was able to foster its policies before reaching the counterbalancing acts of its superpower foe, as illustrated by the dynamics of the Cuban Missile Crisis in the wake of the CIA-led intervention. This double balancing act describes a great deal of what happened throughout the age of U.S. world hegemony in a bi-polar world order.

ON THE RIGHT SIDE OF THE WORLD HEGEMON

By the end of the Second World War Italy, Germany, and Japan were devastated and disrupted. Since the beginning of the twentieth century these three nation-states had striven to upgrade their place in the British-led hegemonic world order. However, each of them adopted a different strategy. For Germany the strategy was head-on confrontation resulting in defeat (1914–1918) after defeat (1939–1945). For Japan the strategy was associated with the British at first (1914–1918) followed by disappointment with the perceived meager fruits of that successful association and a head-on confrontation against the world hegemonic coalition of the former and emerging world hegemons, Great Britain and the United States, and their partners, France and the Netherlands. If association brought unsatisfying gains to Japan, confrontation brought utter destruction (1941–1945) as epitomized by the dropping of two atomic bombs in Hiroshima and Nagasaki by the U.S. Italy swung back and forth in both world wars, alternately confronting and associating with the hegemonic world order. Until 1915 Italy partook in the Triple Alliance with Germany and Austria-Hungary, although remaining neutral till then when it flipped sides in favor of the British-French-Russian Triple Entente. And yet, as in the Japanese case, the Italians were disappointed by what the prevailing powers delivered as a reward by the end of the First World War. Hence, in a revanchist mode comparable to that of its new partners, Fascist Italy united in the Rome-Berlin-Tokyo Axis with Nazi Germany and Showa Japan and confronted the hegemonic world order head-on during the Second World War until July 1943. Then, Italy flipped sides once again:

Mussolini was briefly arrested (and released by a German commando), the Italian King Victor Emanuel III surrendered to the Allies, and the Germans stepped in to bog down the Allied forces in Italy till the very end of the war.

Italy, Germany, and Japan shared not only their point of arrival by 1945—destruction and collapse—but also some crucial features of their previous trajectories. Domestically they all reached political unification and centralization late in the game, during the 1860s, and all three were latecomers in the quest for a global empire. For around a millennium (962–1808) both Italy and Germany were the sites for two political institutions with claims of universal sovereignty: the Papacy and the Holy Roman Empire, respectively. The conflict between these institutions, each claiming universal power, combined with a multiplicity of wealthy and powerful city-states and principalities and the subsequent interventions and conquests by other empires (Spanish, French, Austrian), prevented the emergence of a unified and centralized monarchy—the way it evolved in Portugal, Spain, England, France, and Russia—or a republican confederacy as done by the Dutch Provinces. All these unified polities threw themselves into global empire-building in tandem with their processes of domestic political centralization. The Atlantic maritime powers did that through the oceans; Russia did that continentally across Eurasia. By the time that Italy and Germany became unified and centralized states in 1871 most of the globe was already carved up by the imperial powers, leaving little room for global empire-building. Such a grievance nurtured the anti-hegemonic stance sustained by Italy and Germany in both World Wars, particularly in the case of the full-fledged industrial power of Germany (Map 5.1).

Albeit in a completely different context, Japan also suffered from the "blocked path to empire grievance" as a result of its protracted domestic centralization and self-imposed isolation. For almost a millennium (1185–1868) Japan was ruled by military dictators or *shoguns* nominally appointed by the Emperors. These shoguns ruled the country through their *bakufu*, or tent government, namely, a pyramid of loyalties between feudal lords (*daimyōs*) and *samurais* from lower to upper rank all the way up to the *shogun* at its top.[8] Starting in 1600 and for the next 260 years, Japan was ruled by the Tokugawa Shogunate or *bakufu* as all *shoguns* were members of the Tokugawa clan. Power was split between this clan based in Edo (contemporary Tokyo) and the *daimyōs* and *samurais* in the provinces who conducted an independent administration while

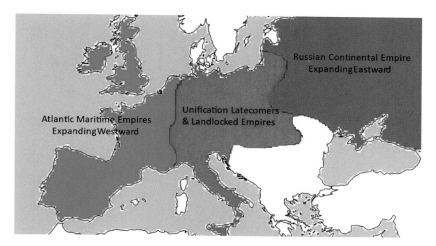

Map 5.1 Maritime and continental empires by centralized polities versus limited empires by landlocked centrifugal polities

remaining loyal to the *shogun*. This regime introduced in 1635 the Seclusion laws, or *Sakoku*, that severely restricted trade and contacts with the outside world. Isolation was violently brought to an end at cannon point as Commodore Mathew Perry showed up with a four-ship squadron at Edo Bay in 1853 (see above, pp. 50–51). Forcefully opened up to foreign trade, Japan coped by quickly and thoroughly transforming into an industrializing economy, an urbanizing society, an outwardly looking state aiming to establish its own empire, all of it under a modern and centralized political regime. This radical transformation that started in 1868, known as the Meiji Restoration, brought about the modernization of Japan and its empowerment. As a freshly industrialized economy Japan approached imperial assertion through collaboration, which did not yield the expected imperial gains by the end of the First World War. Hence, as a self-confident full-fledged industrial power in the second round Japan did so by head-on confrontation. The Japanese empire, then known as the "Co-Prosperity Sphere," engulfed for as long as it could Korea, large stretches of east China, South East Asia in its entirety, Taiwan, the Philippines, and the Indonesian archipelago up to the Solomon Islands. By August 1945 all of that was over, with significant portions of the country in ruins as was the case with its Axis partners (Map 5.2).

Pro-Hegemonic (till 1930)   Anti-Hegemonic (1930-1945)   Pro-Hegemonic (since 1945)

Map 5.2 Japan's geopolitical oscillations: Pro-hegemonic (till 1930); anti-hegemonic (1930–1945); pro-hegemonic (since 1945)

Finally, Italy, Germany, and Japan shared not only some crucial features of their previous trajectories—namely, the inhibition of a successful expansionist policy due to a late centralization of their polity that resulted in anti-hegemonic latecomers' blasts—as well as their point of arrival by 1945—destruction and regime collapse. By 1945, all three states started their post-Second World War era under U.S. occupation. Germany was divided into four occupation zones each under U.S., British, French, or Soviet control. The U.S., British, and French administrations merged in May 1949 to form the Federal Republic of Germany that remained occupied till May 1955. Although the original occupation policy envisioned the deindustrialization of Germany, that policy was soon replaced as the Cold War started unfolding and a need for a strong German ally emerged.[9] The economic support provided by the Marshall Plan combined with political support to the conservative Christian Democratic Union administration under Konrad Adenauer up to 1963 paved the way to the *Wirtschaftswunder* or German economic miracle. By introducing a new currency (the Deutsche Mark), removing price controls, drastically cutting marginal tax rates, and bringing inflation under control the productivity of the German economy grew at an average annual pace of 8% during the 1950s and 4.4% during the 1960s.[10] Germany became the European economic powerhouse once again.

The occupation of Japan was also long-lasting, from 1945 to 1952, and it is similarly divided into two periods with the emerging Cold War representing the watershed. As with Germany, at first a punitive approach prevailed. This approach included trials for war crimes, dismantling the army, confronting the political elites with the emperor at the top by imposing a new constitution, and attacking the economic elite by redistributing the land owned by the rich landowners and by breaking up the *zaibatsu* or large business conglomerates. And yet the triumph of communism in China (1949) caused the United States to shift toward a new goal of strengthening the Japanese economy. Another Cold War instance, the Korean War (1950–1953), provided the opportunity to fulfill that goal by transforming Japan into the principal supply depot for the UN forces. In this context and under the administration of the conservative Liberal Party led by Shigeru Yoshida, the large corporations conformed large conglomerates (*keiretsu*) once again. Japanese industry was reactivated. A Japanese economic miracle was underway and Japan became, yet again, the industrial powerhouse in Asia.[11]

Last but not least, Italy faced a similar sequence of occupation and recovery, except that the first was not so prolonged nor the second so dramatic. An Allied Military Government was established in the wake of the invasion and subsequent armistice in 1943 and lasted till the signing of the Italian Peace treaty in 1947. As the Fascist regime that participated in the anti-hegemonic confrontation had collapsed by the time of the allied invasion there was not a punitive phase to this occupation. Rather, the U.S. effort was concentrated on marginalizing the Communist Party and the labor unions within the political system. The CIA's meddling in the 1948 elections accomplished that by enthroning in power the conservative Christian Democratic Party led by Alcide de Gasperi till 1953. As in Germany the Christian Democratic Party was the leading post-Second World War political force, but in Italy it managed to stay in power till 1994.[12] As in Germany and Japan there was a substantial economic growth in Italy that was known as *il miracolo economico*: an average growth of GDP of 5.8% between 1951 and 1963 followed by a yearly average of 5% between 1964 and 1973.[13]

In short, all these three states led by dictatorial regimes that brought about the mightiest anti-hegemonic confrontation only a decade before had become, in the post-Second World War bi-polar world order, democratic regimes firmly integrated as key pillars of the U.S. world hegemony. As such they joined in the broader U.S.-led world hegemonic coalition that included their recent foes, the British and French democracies. These two U.S. allies were not destroyed to the extent that the Axis powers were. Also, they were the major recipients of American support through the Marshall Plan, with 26 and 18% shares of total contributions, respectively.[14] After some five years of austerity, their economies experienced a booming growth and a substantial rise in living standards. These eras were known in Britain as the *golden age* and in France as *Les Trente Glorieuses* or *la révolution invisible* (The Thirty Glorious Years or the Invisible Revolution, 1946–1975).[15]

The Iberian states traveled a similar path. They were neutral during the war but were ruled by the authoritarian regimes of Salazar and Franco with their fascist paraphernalia. For Portugal as a faithful British ally the incorporation into the hegemonic sphere was smooth. It was a recipient of Marshall Plan benefits and a NATO founding member in 1949. In contrast, Francoist Spain had been fully backed by the Axis Powers and displayed during the war years many characteristics of a reactionary anti-hegemonic party state. As a result, the United States applied at first an isolation policy. But as observed in the "reverse course" taken by the United States both in Germany and Japan, as the Cold War loomed in the horizon, authoritarian Spain was also embraced by the world hegemon in 1953. Down the road, even if a few years later (1959–1974), Spain's *el milagro español* was underway. All the other European states, either allied with the United States during the war (Belgium, Netherlands, Luxemburg, Iceland, Norway, Denmark, Greece, and Turkey) or neutral (Ireland, Sweden, Switzerland), and ruled either by democratic regimes (Ireland, Belgium, Netherlands, Luxemburg, Iceland, Norway, Denmark, Sweden, and Switzerland) or authoritarian regimes (Greece and Turkey), also fell on the right side of the world hegemon and enjoyed similar conditions.

This co-emerging global economic bonanza, often called the *Golden Age of Capitalism*, was the biggest carrot provided by the world hegemon through its multi-layered globalKeynesianism: (1) structuring a stable world economic order based on the institutions established in Bretton Woods; (2) setting a model of state intervention in the economy combined with state-sponsored welfare policies that provided the example to be followed and locally adapted by the following countries; (3) providing the seed money to jump-start the economic reconstruction; (4) leading in technological breakthroughs that enhanced economic productivity and diversification; and (5) generating a large demand for its huge domestic market as well as its military and geopolitical needs, namely, the handling of the Cold War including its hot blasts such as the Korean War.[16]

The second commonality for both the former Axis Powers and Western Allies of the United States in the wake of the Second World War was the loss of their respective empires. The Axis Powers lost them throughout the process of their military defeats during the war. The Western Allies started losing them to the process of decolonization soon after the end of the war and throughout the next two decades. Also in this regard, the U.S. world hegemon had shown its partners the way. The Wilsonian vision of self-determination, which was applied only selectively to the European continent at the end of the First World War (see above pp. 106–108), now was executed globally. And yet the fulfillment of self-determination for colonial societies was not necessarily detrimental for the former imperial powers. Following the lead of the world hegemon, they embraced informal empire as their principal tool of domination, displacing their historical taste for empire.

In 1949, Great Britain established the modern British Commonwealth to include not only its settler colonies (Canada, Australia, New Zealand, South Africa, Irish Free State, and Newfoundland), as constituted in 1931, but all previous colonial domains which grew in the wake of decolonization to become 54 sovereign states.[17] France developed its own stick and carrot policies in regard to its former colonies in Africa. Known as the *Françafrique,* this post-colonial set of policies aimed to preserve access to strategic raw materials and local markets as during colonial times. Friendly African regimes got the carrots, uncooperative ones the sticks. Since 1960, France has intervened militarily more than 30 times in Africa, where its army has a presence in at least ten countries. And then, it was not only that the world hegemon's allies managed to keep a hold on their previous empires through these neo-colonialist configurations. It is also the case that the previous foes of the emerging world hegemon, Japan and Germany, got to foster their regional domination by replacing military means with economic power. With the exception of the East Asian communist states (The People's Republic of China, North Korea, and Vietnam), Japan's economy came to dominate what once was the Co-Prosperity Sphere. Similarly, Germany's failed attempt to subdue Europe by conquest was succeeded by its preponderant role in the European Union.

The failing phase of the British hegemony after the First World War left a devastated economy spiraling down into Global Depression and an open contestation for empire. The rising phase of the American hegemony in the wake of the Second World War launched an era of a booming economy, the burial of empires, and the blooming of informal empires. All these three in the world hegemon's own image and likeness gave birth to the hegemonic sphere.

On the Wrong Side of the Counter-Hegemon

The Soviet Union was the very first anti-hegemonic party state and the sole survivor of the first wave of anti-hegemonic party states (see above, pp. 80, 92–97). By the end of the Second World War a mixed bag of fortunes was rolled through its door. On one hand, the country was demographically, physically, and economically devastated by the war; on the other hand, its military, political, and ideological powers were at an unprecedented high. This combination provided the opportunity to revisit the "Socialism in One Country" policy adopted by Stalin back in 1926 that abandoned the attempt to export the Communist Revolution beyond the boundaries of the Soviet Union. The result of such reconsideration was a hodgepodge too. On the one hand, Communist insurgencies fighting civil wars to achieve power were suppressed or divested, as in Spain on the eve of the Second World War and in Greece in its immediate aftermath, respectively. Moreover, communist takeovers of power were discouraged in countries with influential Communist parties such as Italy and France. On the other hand, most of those countries occupied by the Red Army where the Russian Empire once stood—Estonia, Latvia, and Lithuania—were incorporated into the Soviet Union while in those countries occupied by the Red Army but beyond the reach of the former Russian Empire—Rumania, Bulgaria, Czechoslovakia, and the eastern portion of Germany—local Communist parties responding to the orders of Moscow were enthroned in power. That was also the fate of Poland, largely part of the Russian Empire before 1914. This dual approach of establishing Communist regimes subservient to the Soviet Union while blocking communist takeovers where inconvenient to the Soviet Union's foreign policy represents, in fact, the reaffirmation of the "Socialism in One Country" policy. For the second time, the foundational vision of a world communist revolution that would bring about a communist world order was buried (see above, pp. 97–99). The communist anti-hegemonic stance against the capitalist world order was replaced by the entrenchment of the Soviet Union and its own informal empire as a counter-hegemonic sphere. That is to say, it was a self-enclosed domain determined to reject the world's hegemon big carrot, fighting back its mighty fourfold stick, and desperately blocking its alluring dream while at the same time fostering its own counter-hegemonic triplets.

Throughout the three decades that followed the end of the Second World War (1945–1975) the Soviet Union underwent manifold vicissitudes that can be succinctly summarized by pointing to a handful of major transitions. If we were to economize and pick one major transition only throughout this period, then we would highlight the transition from totalitarianism to post-totalitarianism. Under Stalin, the Soviet Union was a totalitarian state led by one leader revered by a single mass party that thoroughly mobilized society and economy to bring about its transformation. To do this it used ideological indoctrination through the state-controlled mass media, formal (e.g., schooling) and informal (e.g., youth movement) education, and mass surveillance and widespread use of terror. In the wake of the Second World War, these features were further enhanced as Stalin and the Communist Party were credited for the victory over Nazi Germany and the postwar reconstruction efforts demanded much mobilization primarily channeled to the development of heavy industry and energy. Stalin's firm grip on power ended only with his death in 1953. That event marks the beginning of the post-totalitarian phase in the Soviet regime. In this phase, despite the intent to control society as closely as possible, the head of the state was not as revered (in fact, the personality cult would be suppressed); the single party lost ground among the masses; and its cadres and bureaucrats immersed themselves in partisan quarrels. The results? A diminished drive and ability to mobilize society and economy while at the same time relaxing the intensity of the use of surveillance and terror and dialing back the indoctrination of an ideology that was losing its appeal.[18]

Moving into a less conceptual and more descriptive account of these three decades, we can differentiate two transitions—the transitions between the rule of Stalin (till 1953) and Khrushchev (1953–1964), and then from Khrushchev to Brezhnev (1964–1982). These three terms are characterized as the phases of late Stalinism, attempted reforms, and reaction to reforms, respectively. In 1956 Khrushchev started to denigrate Stalin, his personal rule, and personality cult as well as to denounce the crimes and atrocities committed by this dictator. A wide range of reforms included the end of terror by the political police, a measure of decentralization of the command economy by devolving power to regional authorities while simultaneously encouraging a participatory approach to local government politics, and a degree of liberalization in artistic and intellectual censorship. These reforms, compounded by failures in agricultural production and foreign policy resulted in Khrushchev's replacement in 1964 by a backlash personified in Brezhnev. Most reforms were undone, conservatism replaced reformism, and stagnation paved the way to the Soviet Union's demise. The Soviet Union had its own train metaphor that bitter Soviet citizens would secretly tell: The moment the Soviet train came to a halt Stalin had the driver shot for sabotage; Khrushchev brought the co-driver back from the prison camp, but the train still did not move; finally, Brezhnev ordered that all the blinds be drawn across the windows and declared: "Now the train is moving!".[19]

But for all of the travels with the Soviet train, the empowerment of the Soviet Union in the wake of the Second World War was clearly attested by the emergence of the Eastern bloc—its own informal empire in a brave new global world of informal empires. By 1948, the establishment of this bloc was complete, accomplished through the formation of Communist one-party states modeled and controlled by the Soviet Union. As such, these Communist one-party states were by no means anti-hegemonic party states aiming for their reassertion in the world order. Rather, they had emerged out of the Soviet conquest, occupation, and tutelage. These regimes did not rely on a broad social coalition but on the Soviet army. Their goal was not to relocate their nation-states in the world division of labor and power but to follow the directives from Moscow as an integral part of the counter-hegemonic sphere. Their resemblance to anti-hegemonic party states is only a formal one, due to the use of the Soviet Communist one-party state regime model. At their core, however, these Communist one-party states were diametrically opposed to the mobilizational and revisionist anti-hegemonic party states. The Communist one-party states of the Eastern bloc were plain authoritarian political regimes. Their belated authoritarian character became apparent, time and again, when grassroots social mobilization forced the real power behind the regimes decisively to step out into the open.

In the wake of Stalin's death (1953), a widespread uprising against the Communist regime took place in the German Democratic Republic. The tanks of the Group of Soviet Forces in Germany violently suppressed the uprising.[20] Three years later a revolt broke out in Hungary. This time a new government deposed the communist one, taking Hungary out of the Warsaw Pact. The Hungarian revolt became a fully-fledged revolution.

Twelve divisions of the Red Army invaded the country to join the five divisions already stationed there. In a matter of two weeks the Hungarian revolution, the resistance to the Soviet informal empire, the attempt to escape the counter-hegemonic sphere, was over.[21]

Such a forceful suppression made anti-Soviet revolts unlikely until 1968. In January of that year, a reformist politician, Alexander Dubček, was elected Secretary of the Communist Party of Czechoslovakia. His reforms, which aimed to loosen the grip of the command economy and one-party rule, the so-called Prague Spring, were to the dislike of the Soviet Union. By August 2,000 tanks and 200,000 troops of the Warsaw Pact brought the reforms to an end.[22] It took more than a decade for another attempt of opposition to get underway. In 1981 Solidarity, a grassroots movement formed by trade unions, dared to do so in Poland. This time around the commander-in-chief of the Polish People's Army, Wojciech Jaruzelski, stepped in to establish the Military Council of National Salvation. It was as if the Polish Army had learned the lessons of the previous uprisings and in a preemptive coup d'état of sorts had signaled to Moscow: "No need for you to come over here, we'll handle that alone."

Most communist one-party states in the Eastern bloc were covered-up military dictatorships whose masks were removed at times of social and political mobilization amidst demands for change. Only communist Yugoslavia and Albania (and Rumania to some extent) managed to detach themselves from the Soviet tutelage and pursue their own independent assertion in the world order. In this way, they represented a communist type of anti-hegemonic party states (Map 5.3).

Aside from the Soviet Union's informal empire in central and eastern Europe, the Soviet counter-hegemonic sphere was further enhanced by additional Communist regimes that emerged in Korea (1945), China (1949), and Vietnam (1954). However, these three states were independent communist anti-hegemonic party states whose degree of alliance with the Soviet Union fluctuated over time.

The Soviet Union and China

Since the global tour of the synergic twins, the effects of the Catch-22 dilemma on the gunpowder empires—modernize or perish, modernize and perish—had been becoming acute (see above, pp. 43–44). The Chinese empire collapsed in 1911, the Russian in 1917. These two

Map 5.3   The Soviet counter-hegemonic order 1945–1989

of the former gunpowder empires were replaced by newly established anti-hegemonic party states. The Soviet Union, the very first anti-hegemonic party state, for all the devastation that it sustained during the Second World War, had emerged as a powerful counter-hegemonic force in a bi-polar world order. The fate of the anti-hegemonic party state in China lead by Chiang Kai-Shek and his Kuomintang Party was completely different. A comparison of these two trajectories highlights some circumstantial similarities and crucial differences.

Initially, in both countries the revolution and establishment of an anti-hegemonic party state spiraled down into a civil war. Unlike Russia, though, in China the nationalist forces of the Kuomintang Party and the Chinese Communist Party fought side by side against the landowning aristocrats or warlords in a campaign known as the Northern Expedition (1926–1928). It was only after this triumph in a first civil war that the Kuomintang doubled down on persecuting the Chinese Communist Party, bringing about its near-extinction during the 1930s. Secondly, as in the Soviet Union, the post-revolutionary civil war in China was followed by an additional herculean challenge, the outbreak of the Second World

War. China was invaded in 1937 by Japan and, as in the Soviet Union in 1941 following the German invasion, the invading forces proved to be unstoppable. However, in contrast with the theater of war in the Soviet Union, in China there were no military reversal of fortunes at any point during the war and the Japanese army held the upper hand all the way through. Unable to mount an effective resistance to the Japanese invasion, the Kuomintang was removed from its political power bases in the lower Yangzi region. In contrast, the communists resisted behind the Japanese lines, gaining popular support. By the end of the Second World War a second and now full-blown civil war took place in China between the decaying first anti-hegemonic party state ruled by the Kuomintang and the emerging second Chinese anti-hegemonic party state led by the Chinese Communist Party. With that outcome, the trajectories of the Soviet Union and China grew more similar: the largest and the most populated gunpowder empires of the nineteenth century became the mightiest anti-hegemonic party states under communist rule of the twentieth century. And there were more similarities to follow (Table 5.1).

On October 1, 1949 Mao Zedong declared the founding of the People's Republic of China. This second anti-hegemonic party state in China was more thorough in power concentration and relentless in the repression of opponents, wider in geographic terms, and deeper in its dominance over society and economic planning. As was the case after the Communist Revolution in Russia, the most burning problem in an overwhelmingly rural society was the fate of the landless peasants. By the end of the civil war, the Communist regime transferred land ownership to the poor peasants, gaining their support and making them the social backbone of the emerging regime. From 1947 to 1952 the agricultural sector went through a land reform that redistributed 40% of China's arable land to 300 million peasants. The number of landlords executed has been estimated from 800,000 up to around 2 million. This radical reshuffle of land allocation gave 90% of the rural population ownership of 90.8% of the arable land.[23]

And yet, as in the case of the early stages of the Soviet Union, the quest was not just about bringing equality to a rural society. The quest actually was to liberate that society from the Catch-22 dilemma that it had faced since the days of the global tour of the synergic set of twins by transforming it into an industrial society. The land reform addressed the domestic risk of disruption by social discontent. However, the risk of

Table 5.1   Russia's and China's trajectories compared—Phase one (in **Bold**: Commonalities; in *Italics*: Singularities)

Russia	*China*
Both conservative Gunpowder Empires defeated by Great Britain and France	
Crimean War (1853–1856)	*Opium Wars (1839–1860)*
Both military defeats prompted reforms insufficient to fully catch up with foes	
Subsequent military defeats ended in anti-monarchic revolutions	
The First World War triggered Liberal Revolution (February 1917). The Provisional Government toppled by a Communist Revolution (October 1917)	*Consecutive defeats at the hands of Japan and Western Powers fostered a Republican Revolution that established the Republic of China (January, 1912)*
Civil War	
After the Communist Revolution a civil war confronted Communists vs. anti-Communist (1917–1923)	*After the Republican Revolution a civil war confronted Republicans and Communists vs. regional Warlords (1926–1927). Subsequently the Republicans suppressed the Communists. A civil war between the two was averted due to their collaboration during the Japanese invasion (1937–1945). After the end of the Second World War a civil war between Republicans vs. Communists ensued (1945–1949)*
Communist Regime	
A Communist regime was established in the former Russian Empire in 1917 that consolidated by the end of the Civil War in 1923	*A Communist regime was established in the former Republic of China in 1949 by the end of the Civil War*

foreign invasion would remain until China became a full-fledged industrial economy. As a matter of fact, it was the fast industrialization of the Soviet Union that allowed it to prevail in the Second World War and escape the Catch-22 dilemma that had brought about the demise of the Russian Empire amidst the First World War. By contrast, it was the failed attempt of the Kuomintang anti-hegemonic party state to industrialize that allowed for the Japanese military success in China during the Second World War and brought about the state's demise.

Now, the communist anti-hegemonic party state in China was determined to industrialize. Building on the partial accomplishments of its predecessors—the Kuomintang and the Japanese occupation—all existing industries were nationalized. Nationalization was followed by a developmentalist economic policy relying on the Treaty of Friendship, Alliance and Mutual Assistance signed with the Soviet Union in 1950. (This treaty replaced a previous one signed between Stalin and Chiang Kai-shek.) According to the terms of this treaty an extraordinary planned transfer of technology was implemented by 10,000 Soviet specialists visiting China and 50,000 Chinese engineers, trainees, and students visiting the Soviet Union. These exchanges resulted in the construction of 250 industrial projects and the transfer of thousands of industrial designs. However, the linchpin of Mao's industrial policy was his vision of a Great Leap Forward, his second five-year plan that ran between 1958 and 1962. The sequence of the plan is reminiscent of the logic of the first five-year plan in the Soviet Union: in order to enable industrial workers to run factories they must be properly supplied. To guarantee such supply, rural productivity must increase, and its delivery cannot be compromised. To fulfill this intermediate goal, private farms were collectivized (see above, pp. 98–99). As in the Soviet Union the results were catastrophic for the rural population, except on an even larger scale. If the cost of lives in the Soviet Union amounted to six to seven million victims during the 1933 starvation, the death toll of the Great Chinese Famine of 1959–1961 ranged between 15 and 55 million people.[24]

As in the Soviet Union the goal was to catch up with and even surpass the world hegemon, present and past, respectively. In 1957 Khrushchev aimed to surpass the U.S. economy in 15 years, while Mao aimed to surpass that of Great Britain.[25] Both dreams failed to deliver. Moreover, and different from the first five-year plan in the Soviet Union (1928–1932), the ultimate project of fostering industrialization in China was a total failure too. In fact, during this period the Chinese economy shank. Instead of the big scale industrial projects marshaled by the Soviet Union, Mao envisioned a small-scale industrialization led by people's communes without the "interference" (i.e., technical expertise) of suspicious professionals prone to fostering class stratification. In this way industrialization would unfold side by side with the construction of a Communist society. The state made huge investments. The people in the communes burnt their furniture, doors, and trees to melt down their pots, pans, and whatever other metal objects they could find in "backyard furnaces." The resulting pig iron was worth next to nothing.[26]

In the Soviet Union, the upheavals caused by the first five-year plan, including forced collectivization, its resulting famine of 1932–1933, and the growing criticism within the Communist Party (real and perceived) were some of the triggers for the Great Purge (1936–1938). In it,

Stalin through his subservient secret police (NKVD) executed 950,000 to 1,200,000 people: former small farmers (*kulak*s), members and leaders of the Communist Party, the commanders and commissars of the Red Army, and non-Russian nationalities within the Soviet Union.[27] In China, the Great Leap Forward was not only a tremendous human tragedy but also an economic colossal failure. Under these circumstances, Mao resigned his presidency and stepped aside from policymaking. But after a short absence he made his triumphal comeback in 1966 by launching his Great Proletarian Cultural Revolution. This new undertaking was in effect a massive purge of the rank and file of the Chinese Communist Party who, Mao feared and in some cases with good reason, were disrespecting and marginalizing him. As in the Great Leap Forward, Mao's appeal was for the actions to emanate from below instead of originating from professionals as in the Soviet Union. So, Mao appealed to the young generation of party members who became the Red Guard to purge from the Communist Party its senior members as well as workers, military, professionals—all suspected of revisionism—and ethnic minorities. Some 36 million people were persecuted, of whom 1.5 to 3 million were killed. This second great initiative of Mao's also spiraled down into destruction, disruption, economic contraction, and chaos.[28]

By 1971 the Cultural Revolution was over. In 1976 Mao died. Soon after, Deng Xiaoping started to emerge as the new undisputed leader. Unlike Stalin's successor Khruschev, Deng Xiaoping never denigrated Mao or denounced the crimes and atrocities he had committed. At most he dared to assert that "Mao was 70 per cent right and 30 per cent wrong."[29] Khrushchev's radical criticism of Stalin (1956) ended up backfiring eight years down the road resulting in a conservatist backlash that stagnated the Soviet Union and incubated its collapse. In contrast, Deng Xiaoping's measured criticism of Mao paid off in the sustainability of his program of reforms that would transform China beyond recognition in the upcoming decades. This would make for a drastic divergence in the trajectories of these giant states that otherwise shared so much in their historical unfolding—first as huge gunpowder empires and next as communist anti-hegemonic party states implementing their own versions of "Socialism in One Country," that is, socialism and nationalism combined (Table 5.2).

Table 5.2 Russia's and China's trajectories compared—Phase two (in **Bold**: Commonalities; in *Italics*: Singularities)

Russia	*China*
Both Communist Regimes aiming to catch up with industrialized powers	
Their shared sequence has a three decades gap based on the date of the regime emergence, 1917 vs. 1949	
(see above, Table 4.1: Russia's and China's Trajectories Compared—Phase One)	
Collectivization of land & centralized Industrialization: First Five Year Program (1928–1932)	*Collectivization of land & people's communes Industrialization: Great Leap Forward (1958–1962)*
Disastrous Results	
1933 Starvation: 6–7 million victims	*1959–1961 Great Famine: 15–55 million victims*
Leadership's fear of criticism (real or perceived)	
1936–38: Great Purge	*1966–1971 Great Proletarian Cultural Revolution*
Leadership Transition following Leader's Death	
Khrushchev's confrontational approach led to failure of reforms (1956–1964)	*Deng Xiao Ping's pragmatical approach led to success of reforms (1980–1989)*

THE COUNTER-HEGEMONIC TRIPLETS: POWERFUL, BUT NOT AS MUCH

When confronted with the three triplets of the U.S. world hegemony—the fourfold big stick, the huge carrot, and the alluring dream—the lesser powers of the competing counter-hegemonic triplets of the Soviet Union were very apparent. Yes, the Soviet Union had its own big stick, but it was not fourfold. The Soviet Union did not have a global empire of military bases; its military was limited to its own huge territory and that of its Eastern European satellites. The Soviet Union had its own intelligence agency, the MGB from 1946 to 1953 and the KGB from 1953 to 1990. However, these agencies were deeply vested in domestic intelligence for the sake of confronting enemies within the gates, real or imaginary. True, international espionage was also conducted and occasionally very successfully as in, most prominently, the stealing of the atomic bomb secret. Yet, even this success reflects the need to catch up with the world hegemon instead of taking the lead. At times, however, and in specific fields the Soviet Union did take the lead, most emblematically with the launching of the Sputnik (1957), the first artificial Earth satellite, which took the CIA by surprise. However, what truly set the two intelligence bodies apart was the global range of the CIA covert operations to topple or prop up political regimes favorable to the United States around the world. That was something that the MGB and KGB could not accomplish beyond their direct sphere of influence.[30] Neither did the Soviet Union have a system of collective defense for every slice of the globe, except for its own immediate zone of influence, the Warsaw Pact. Ultimately, what made the Soviet Union stick big, even if not fourfold, was its nuclear arsenal that held the world hegemon captive to the madness of MAD (mutually assured destruction).

There was no huge carrot that the Soviet Union could offer, either. The Soviet Union ended the Second World War as a mighty military force that had significantly expanded geographically. However, the Soviet Union was devastated after the war. An estimated 24 million Soviet soldiers and civilians perished in the war, the heaviest loss of life of any of the combatant countries. The war also inflicted severe material losses throughout the vast territory that had been included in the war zone. Roughly a quarter of the country's capital resources had been destroyed, and industrial and agricultural output in 1945 fell far short of prewar levels. Under these circumstances the Soviet Union compelled Soviet-occupied Eastern Europe to supply machinery and raw materials. This arrangement amounted to a "reverse Marshall Plan" of sorts in which the net outflow of resources from Eastern Europe to the Soviet Union was approximately $15 billion to $20 billion in the first decade after the Second World War. The Soviet Union rebuilt quickly after the war. However, its postwar five-year plans focused on the arms industry and heavy industry at the expense of consumer goods and agriculture. And so, whereas a decade after the war steel production was twice its 1940 level, the production of many consumer goods and foodstuffs was lower than it had been in the late 1920s.[31] There were not many carrots to lure followers and neither was there an alluring dream to live for.

Instead of the alluring dream offered by the United States, the Soviet Union offered an alluring mirage. The distinction here is between an aspiration that can be made true—at least to some extent, at least for some—and an optical illusion viewed at a distance and unable to materialize. The communist ideology had offered people around the world for generations the desirable dream of a classless society without exploitation—a society in which every member contributes according to her possibilities and receives according to her needs. This enticing vision, first articulated in writing, was presumably to be materialized by its leader, the Sun of the Nations, Joseph Stalin. Tender children in the Soviet Union cheerfully thanked Comrade Stalin for a happy childhood only to realize the grim reality in adulthood. Stalin's supporters in Europe became disenchanted as the Soviet tanks rolled over Budapest (1956) and Prague (1968). More Stalinists around the world became disenchanted after the collapse of the Soviet Union (1991). A mirage can only be perceived at a distance. As the distant horizon becomes closer the mirage vanishes, with only die-hard Stalinists still allured by the mirage.[32]

However, in the aftermath of the Second World War and for a couple of decades to come the mirage loomed sufficiently distant in the horizon to be alluring enough for many. People around the world had been impressed by the fast economic growth of the Soviet Union before the war, specifically during the Great Depression, as well as by its fast recovery after the war. Even among economists in the United States the expectation was for the Soviet Union and its command economy to overcome the American economy in terms of its gross national product. According to the Nobel laureate Paul Samuelson, that was projected to happen sometime between 1984 and 1997.[33] It is unsurprising then that the centralized command economy, or at least some of its features such as the nationalization of strategic sectors of the economy and the packaging of its economic goals and programs into five-year periods became inspiring templates worldwide. Moreover, the Soviet Union encouraged followers not only through leading by example, but also, in some cases, by providing generous support. And so it was that amidst the process of decolonization in the wake of the Second World War, liberation movements around the world embraced some sort of interpretation of socialism combined with nationalism as they strove to emancipate themselves from the old empires. Similar attempts were conducted by older nation-states aiming to escape the claws of informal empires.

Under the Tracks of Entwined Nationalism and Socialism: Perón, Evita, and the Socialist Fatherland

On the eve of October 17, 1945, thousands of workers made their way rather spontaneously to the Plaza de Mayo in Buenos Aires, Argentina. They came to demand the liberation of Colonel Juan Domingo Perón. For the last two years, in his capacity as the secretary of labor in a military government, Perón had sanctioned a series of decrees on compensations, retirement, and working conditions that were favorable to the working class. Anxious due to the mutual empowerment of Perón and the labor organizations, the members of the military junta pressed Perón into resignation, which was then followed by his imprisonment. But this series of events did not work out for the junta. In a week, the broad mobilization of the workers in the capital city and nearby locations resulted in the liberation of Perón and his overwhelming return to the political scene.

A highly contested election campaign followed. All major political parties, including the Conservative and Communist Parties at both right and left ends of the political spectrum, gravitated toward the Democratic Union, a political coalition actively sponsored by the United States. According to this coalition, the electorate's choice was between democracy or "Nazi-Peronism." For Perón and his supporters, the choice was "Braden o Perón," a reference to Spruille Braden, the U.S. ambassador to Argentina and Truman's Assistant Secretary of State for Western Hemisphere Affairs. On election day, February 24, 1946, Juan Domingo Perón obtained 56% of the popular vote and won the national elections in 22 of the 23 provinces. His presidential mandate, prolonged by winning the subsequent election in 1952 and thereafter interrupted by a military coup in September 1955, profoundly transformed the history of Argentina.

Domestically, Perón's regime fostered the development of Argentina by industrializing its economy. Since the nineteenth century, the ruling elite had been operating a highly profitable economy based on the exporting of its agricultural produce. Half of Argentina's production, especially beef and cereals, was purchased by Great Britain, which also transported most Argentinean exports and imports. In this context, transportation, storage, distribution, prices, wages, and working conditions were out of the control of the Argentinean government. The Global Depression since 1929 with its resulting sharp decline for Argentinean produce called this agro-exporting model into question. Moreover, the outbreak of the Second World War ten years later divested the international merchant flotillas from the South Atlantic. The services of British, American, Spanish, and Swedish companies sharply declined. Those of German, Italian, and Japanese companies were banished altogether.

These new circumstances demanded both the development of local industries in order to replace the lost imports and the construction of an Argentinean merchant fleet to give exports an outlet. In this way, the global constraints planted by necessity are the seeds for import substitution industrialization, that is, the development of local industries to provide for the goods that were previously imported from the industrial economies. These seeds blossomed, under Perón's leadership, into a full-fledged economic policy that was the linchpin of the regime's support. Once again, as observed in the cases of the Soviet Union and Communist China, industrialization would demand the transfer of resources from the agricultural sector. In the Argentinean case, however, Perón's regime was not disruptive to agricultural production. Rather, the regime heavily invested in agricultural technology, resulting in an increased output. A heavy-handed taxation policy on the exports of this produce became in turn the major source of funds for the industrializing policy.

In 1947 Argentina's first five-year program was launched, aiming to bring the transportation and communication infrastructures under state control as well as fostering industrialization. Telephone and railroad companies were purchased from their foreign owners, mostly British and French, and nationalized. The build-up of a merchant fleet began by purchasing Italian, German, Swedish, and French ships beached in Argentinean ports during the Second World War. Also a national aviation company was established. Controls on transportation came hand in hand with the development of the steel, shipping, aeronautic, and light industries. Conversely, the fostering of these industries relied upon an energy policy that brought about the nationalization and fostering of the oil industry, the construction of hydroelectric plants, and the development of a nuclear power plant. Aside from their contribution to the economy, these developments also entailed a significant strengthening of the Argentinean military forces on land, air, and sea.[34]

With regard to foreign policy, and amidst the unfolding Cold War between the world hegemon and the counter-hegemon, Perón articulated his "Third Position," that is, "neither capitalist nor communist" as a way to disentangle himself from both superpowers and relate to the states outside their direct sphere of influence. This approach was eventually adopted by other countries with the establishment of the non-aligned movement in 1956 by Josip Broz Tito of Socialist Yugoslavia, Jawaharlal Nehru of India, Sukarno of Indonesia, Gamal Abdel Nasser of Egypt, and Kwame Nkrumah of Ghana. But for Perón's regime this organization arrived too late. In 1955 Perón's regime was toppled by a military coup that began a cycle of alternating military dictatorships and low-effectiveness democracy regimes until 1983. A thorough repression of the military dictatorships brought the Perónist national and socialist aspirations to an end. However, at the same time across the globe similar attempts were made by many states that ended up clustering around the non-aligned movement. This movement brought about the coalescence of a "Third World," that is, a third global block amidst the bi-polar world order created by the world hegemon and the counter-hegemon.

Entwined Nationalism and Socialism Throughout the Latin American Oligarchic Republics

Perón's regime in Argentina shares important similarities with a simultaneous regime to its north, in Brazil, run by Getulio Vargas. To begin with, both Perón and Vargas amassed political power in the framework of an authoritarian regime. In the case of Vargas, power accumulation occurred during the days of his authoritarian regime proclaimed as the *Estado Novo* (New State, 1937–1945). However, by 1950 Vargas was able to reach power through democratic elections propelled by the *Partido Trabalhista Brasileiro* that he established in 1945 to mobilize the urban workers. Hence, both leaders managed to establish a broad social basis of support and gained legitimacy through democratic elections despite military attempts to hold them back. Second, once in power, both regimes attempted industrialization through the nationalization of resources and infrastructure as well as import substitution, aiming to transform the agro-exporting economies of their countries. This transformation occurred while protecting the interests of the working class by shifting the balance of power between capital and labor, favoring the latter.

Finally, in 1954 under the threat of an imminent military coup, Vargas committed suicide. Perón was overthrown by the military a year later. In both cases, military dictatorships ensued for decades afterward. As a result, these economic and social transformations were curtailed and a political cycle of alternation between military dictatorship and low-effectiveness democratic regimes was set in motion. The *Partido Trabalhista Brasileiro* reemerged into power from 1961 until 1964 when a tougher military dictatorship lasting for over two decades (1964–1985) brought its government to an end. In Argentina the Perónist Party was banned for a decade and a half. A partial removal of that ban in 1970 brought back the Perónist Party to power and subsequently Perón from exile. On March 24, 1976 a military coup brought to an end the rule of

Perón's widow Eva (Evita). A murderous dictatorship unfolded for eight years (1976–1983).

Such comparable experiences of popular regimes supported by mass parties aiming to transform their economies and societies while espousing some forms of nationalism and socialism actually were far more extensive throughout the Latin American oligarchic republics. In Guatemala Jacobo Árbenz assumed the presidency in 1951 following his electoral victory as the candidate of the *Partido de Integridad Nacional*. A year later an agrarian reform bill was passed by the National Assembly. This reform redistributed land uncultivated by large landowners to landless peasants (some 500,000 individuals constituting about a sixth of the population) while compensating the former according to the value that the landowners had declared for taxation that same year. Despite the social justice and economic improvements brought by this major reform, or because of them, the American United Fruit Company, a major landowner with annual profits twice the size of the Guatemalan government, prodded the U.S. State Department into action. In 1954 the CIA staged a coup that overthrow Árbenz, repealed the agrarian reform, and set Guatemala into a path of political violence, civil war, and massive repression for four decades to come (1960–1996).[35]

In Bolivia the *Movimiento Nacionalista Revolucionario* rose to power via a revolution in 1952. The movement's leader, Víctor Paz Estenssoro, carried out a sweeping land reform, rural education, and nationalization of the country's largest tin mines. Paz Estenssoro was overthrown by a military junta in 1964.[36] A far more consequential revolution brought Fidel Castro and his *Organizaciones Revolucionarias Integradas* to power in Cuba in 1959. Although the Cuban revolutionary regime began as another instance of a nationalist-socialist blend with a characteristic land reform and state intervention in the economy, a failed CIA-organized coup à la Árbenz in 1961 fully entangled it within the framework of the Cold War. By the end of that year Fidel Castro had announced his allegiance to Marxist-Leninist communism. In 1962 the alarm of "another Cuba" was heard by the ruling elite of the Dominican Republic and the Johnson administration in Washington as the *Partido Revolucionario Dominicano* led by Juan Bosh prevailed in the first elections after three decades of Trujillo's murderous authoritarian dictatorship (1931–1961). Land redistribution and nationalization of foreign holdings were on the agenda of its short-lived mandate that ended by virtue of a CIA-backed military coup in 1963. A very different military coup made by the *Revolutionary Government of the Armed Forces* in Peru? in 1968 brought to power a general, Juan Francisco Velasco Alvarado, who ran on a platform of agrarian reform, the nationalization of multiple companies and infrastructures, and a policy of import substitution. At the same time, Peru's foreign policy shifted to a partnership with Cuba and the Soviet Union. In 1975 general Velasco was deposed by a military coup.[37] Very similar domestic and foreign policies were simultaneously applied in neighboring Chile by Salvador Allende, who by contrast had reached power by legitimate elections in 1970 but similarly was ousted by a military coup in 1973 (see above, pp. 147–148).[38]

As it turns out, the emergence of Perón's regime was just the first occurrence of an overall phase in Latin American history, running since the end of the Second World War and throughout the 1970s. In this phase, certain forms of nationalism and socialism were espoused to support policies of nationalization, import substitution industrialization, centralized planned economies, and wealth redistribution. Such policies aimed to dislodge the grip of the landed oligarchies on the Latin American republics, catch up with the industrialized world, assert their self-determination, and improve their position in the global arena. This phase got started at a time in which the attention of the world hegemon was elsewhere, in Europe and Asia, but not in its "backyard." As the nationalist and socialist regimes in Latin America represented a threat to American interests and became entangled with the Cold War in the eyes of the American administrations, they were thoroughly suppressed by military dictatorships supported by the United States. An unholy alliance between the leader of the free world and a large cluster of authoritarian regimes in Latin America was forged (Map 5.4).

This phase is often depicted in the literature as the age of classical Latin American Populism. In this age, governments were in the hands of charismatic leaders supported by wide social coalitions attempting social reforms by political intervention, economic regulation, increased spending, and public ownership. The historical roots of this governance modality are attributed to the shared legacies of colonial and independence experiences. The colonial legacy is represented by the mining or agro-exporting model consisting of the export of raw materials and the import of manufactured goods, perpetuated by the rule of a landed aristocracy. The independence legacy is represented by the figure of the *caudillos*, the powerful charismatic leaders who in the wake of the political vacuum opened by the collapse of the colonial empires led the nascent

Map 5.4   Nationalism and socialism throughout Latin America: Justicialismo, Argentina 1946–1955; Partido Trabalhista Brasileiro, Brazil 1951–1954; Árbenz, Guatemala 1951–1954; Movimiento Nacionalista Revolucionario, Bolivia 1952–1964; Organizaciones Revolucionarias Integradas, Cuba 1959–; Partido Revolucionario Dominicano, Republica Dominicana 1963; Frente Popular, Chile 1970–1973

nations. Similarly, the social legacy of patronage, the quid pro quo mechanism of distributing economic favors for political support, deeply rooted since colonial times, could be identified as the source of reminiscent practices by Populist regimes. And yet, for all of these plausible regional lineages of post-Second World War entwined nationalism and socialism in Latin America, a long list of additional cases from around the world makes clear that despite the regional idiosyncrasies, this phenomenon was genuinely global.

ENTWINED NATIONALISM AND SOCIALISM
IN RECENTLY EMANCIPATED COLONIES
THROUGHOUT THE MIDDLE EAST

Throughout the Middle East, six major cases of entwined nationalism and socialism emerged after the end of the Second World War and throughout the 1970s: Iran (1951–1953), Egypt (1956–1970), Syria (1958–1970), Iraq (1958–1979), Libya (1969–2011), and Algeria (1963–1978). This new tour, launched by Perón's Argentina and Vargas' Brazil, expanded not only throughout Latin American but also beyond that region. For instance, an informative comparison can be made between Perón's regime and that of Colonel Gamal Abdel Nasser in Egypt (see above pp. 185–189). Like Perón, Nasser first came to power through a military coup (1952). Yet, in 1956 his rule gained legitimacy by a public referendum that reflected his broad popular support. Even though social mobilization was not carried out by a highly dynamic political party—as the *Partido Justicialista* had for Perón—national rallies fulfilled this function: first the Liberation Rally, then the National Unity, and finally the Arab Socialist Union. Moreover, social support was also achieved by a tightly controlled trade union, the Confederation of Egyptian Workers, and other professional associations under state control—similar to the role played by the labor federation, the *Confederación General de los Trabajadores*, in Argentina. Yet the concentration of power was mainly achieved by an impressive enlargement of the state apparatuses, i.e., bureaucracy and security forces, which was reflected in the government's expenditures on the army and paramilitary police, increasing from 18.3% of the budget in 1954–1955 to 55.7% in 1970.

This combination of an enlarged state machinery backed by the mobilized social sectors was in charge of implementing measures aimed at achieving economic development: a land reform (already started by 1952) that by 1961 expropriated a seventh of all cultivated land from large landowners and distributed it among small proprietors and landless peasants; the decision to build the Aswan High Dam in order to make the large area between Cairo and Alexandria suitable for cultivation; and the formation of the Helwan Iron and Steel Complex (1954). At the same time, the evacuation of British troops from the Suez Canal (1954) ended in the nationalization of the canal, while the Anglo-French-Israeli invasion (1956) resulted in the nationalization of foreign property. These initial steps developed by 1960 into a full-fledged five-year plan (1960–1965), which included the nationalization of private banks, foreign investments, and factories.

A series of similarities and differences are easily recognizable in making the contrast between Perón's and Nasser's regimes. Both leaders gained power as colonels participating in a military coup. Both managed to become the most acclaimed figures of the regimes installed by these coups. Both gained legitimacy by popular suffrage. Once in power, they both launched similar economic and social policies—for example, nationalization, property reforms, and five-year programs—aiming to transform their countries by catching up with the industrialized world. On the other hand, Nasser relied first and foremost on the army that backed his regime all the way through and up to the Arab Spring in 2011. Perón, instead, based his support on a political party and was ousted from power by the army. The armies that challenged Nasser's regime were foreign—British, French, and Israeli—reflecting the difference between a country like Argentina, which experienced decolonization at the beginning of the nineteenth century, and a country like Egypt, where decolonization was still a work in progress by the 1950s. And yet amid these differences, it is very telling that Perón's Third Position ("neither capitalist nor communist") foreign policy became a full-fledged political stance vis-à-vis the Cold War powers as Nasser and others established the Non-Aligned Movement by 1961.

The anti-hegemonic party state software was exported from Egypt to Syria during 1958–1961 through the creation of the United Arab Republic, and to Iraq after the revolution of 1958 and during its Arab union policy from 1963 to 1964. In both countries a parallel set of policies regarding centralization of power, economic development, and determined foreign policy can be observed. As in Egypt, also in Syria and Iraq the state enormously increased its personnel; in the Syrian case it raised from 34,000 to 251,000 state employees between 1960 and 1975. A land reform, which expropriated the landed elite, redistributed about a fifth and almost a half of cultivable land in Syria and Iraq, respectively, while keeping the rest to be administrated directly by the state and the party through a village council, a branch of the party, the Peasant's Union, and even by officials from the ministry of agriculture who provided instructions regarding the types of crops, and the methods to be employed in their growth and marketing. Similarly, the state oversaw programs of large-scale industrialization and nationalization of industries in order to substitute the importation of simple consumer durables and to pursue the catching up by producing iron, steel, and later on machinery. The major difference compared to Egypt, however, is that a well-structured party, the *Ba'ath Party* (the *Renaissance or Resurrection Party*), played a crucial role. The singularity of this party, in contrast to the multi-class features observed so far, resides in its reliance on the support of a particular religious and ethnic group concentrated in particular regions of the country. This was the case of the Alawite minority in coastal Syria since 1966 and that of the Sunni minority in the region between Baghdad and Tikrit in Iraq.

All these occurrences of entwined Nationalism and Socialism in the Middle East unfolded under the broader ideological umbrella of Pan-Arabism, that is, the assertion of the unity of the Arabs from Iraq to Morocco as a single nation. Still in the Middle East but beyond the scope of Pan-Arabism, as the revolution in Egypt was taking its very first steps, a significant transformation in similar directions was already underway in Iran. There, in 1951, Mohammad Mosaddegh became prime minister of the constitutional monarchy presided over by the Shah Mohammad Reza Pahlavi. His administration introduced similar socioeconomic reforms to those ubiquitous elsewhere: a land reform that established collective farming and government land ownership, higher taxes on the wealthy and wealth redistribution through social security, and nationalization. Most prominently, the nationalization of the oil industry developed since 1913 by the Anglo-Persian Oil Company (see more above, pp. 47–48). In 1953, the CIA and MI6 implemented a coup that led to the replacement of Mossadegh by an Iranian General, Fazlollah Zahedi, who unsurprisingly restituted the oil industry to its former owners.[39]

By contrast the Pan-Arabist regimes were not toppled by foreign interventions but underwent drastic transformations from within. The anti-hegemonic party state in Egypt became an authoritarian regime simultaneously with Sadat's alignment with the United States in 1976. The *Ba'ath Party* regime in Syria was transformed into an authoritarian regime by Hafez al-Assad in the wake of his military coup in 1970. Also in Iraq the *Ba'ath Party* regime was transformed into an authoritarian regime following Saddam Hussein's takeover in 1979 leading to the purge of the party's leadership and cadres, the terrorizing of society, and the alignment with the United States and its hegemonic coalition (Map 5.5).

The Latin American republics experimented with the entwining of nationalism and socialism after some 150 years of decolonization. The Middle Eastern republics did so only after 15 years. Many of the former

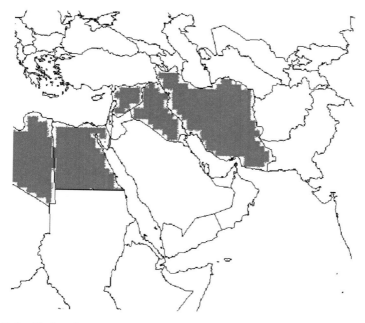

Map 5.5 Nationalism and socialism throughout the Middle East: Mosaddegh's Iran 1951–1953; "free officers," Egypt 1952–1970, "free officers"; Iraq 1958–1963–1979, Ba'ath Party; Syria 1958–1970, "free officers"; Libya 1969–2011

colonies in South Asia, South East Asia, and Africa moved straight forward from decolonization into entwined nationalism and socialism.

Straightforward: From Decolonization into Entwined Nationalism and Socialism in South Asia, South East Asia, and Africa

The independence of India in 1947 is the turning point from which the process of emergence of new nation-states in Asia and Africa evolved. The most notable political development in India since its independence was the stability of its parliamentary democracy. However, since Britain transferred the power to the Indian National Congress, for all but three of India's 42 years of independence until 1989, the successors of the Indian National Congress—the Congress Party and its continuation Congress

Party (I)—were the ruling party in New Delhi. Therefore, the case of India amounts to a one-party state, even if under a democratic regime, whose political organization, economic and foreign policies amounts to a particular case of an anti-hegemonic party state. Its peculiarity derives, to a great extent, from the singular social coalition that sustained the regime. Thus far, the anti-hegemonic party states relied either on a coalition composed of workers and peasants or a coalition composed of industrialists, landlords, lower middle class, and small state owners. The case of India adds to these self-excluding types of coalition a third one characterized by the crucial role of the middle class as the cornerstone of the social coalition, whose power and success progressively attracted landlords and industrialists on the one hand and weak and despised groups (e.g., untouchables, Muslims) on the other hand. The preeminence of the Congress Party and the social coalition behind it enabled the sustainability of parliamentary democracy—instead of a "people's democracy" or the open rejection of democracy—without resorting to typical measures used by anti-hegemonic party states. Opposition parties from left and right, regional and national, secular and religious operated freely. It was rather the lack of effective alternatives, particularly at parliamentary elections in the Union, which was the primary reason for the failure of the opposition. There were fair elections, free press, independent judiciary, and an un-politicized civil service. However, as soon as the preeminence of the Congress Party was at stake, as in 1975 when a court declared Indira Gandhi guilty of campaign abuses, a state of "national emergency" was established. Political parties were banned, civil rights were suspended, and the press controlled with the government holding the monopoly on the news and interpretation. As democracy was re-established in 1977 the Congress Party was defeated in the sixth general elections for the first time. Since then, the Congress Party (I), although still the most prominent political party, lost its exclusivity as a government party being defeated again in the ninth general elections (1989), in 1996, in 1998, and in 1999. Similarly, since 1989 there have been non-Congress Party governments in most states of the Union. The erosion of the Congress Party position as the head of the Indian anti-hegemonic party state is concomitantly related to the transformation of its defining economic and foreign policies.

The Indian anti-hegemonic party state, in consonance with this political strategy, held the "commanding heights" in its hands. The government has been the dominant or monopolistic producer and/or supplier of military ordnance, iron and steel, ships, heavy engineering and foundry goods, energy from all sources, telecommunications and broadcasting, and railroad and air transport. Public sector corporations produced automobiles, cement, electronic goods, and warehousing, among others. This economic structure was developed since 1951 through sequential five-year plans issued by the Indian government's Planning Commission. Its aim was the industrialization of India through a policy of import substitution while preventing the concentration of wealth and with the means of production providing for all citizens social and economic justice. And yet, the protectionist policy suited also the great industrial houses, which prospered below the state level in the framework of a mixed economy. The liberalization policies applied by the Congress Party since the second half of the 1980s opened the displacement process of the state from the "commanding heights," which sealed the fate of the Indian anti-hegemonic party state.

The primary concern of India's foreign policy has been Pakistan. The conflict between the two centered on Kashmir conflated with the Cold War, Sino-Indian hostilities, and Sino-Soviet tension. The strongest feature of India's foreign policy amidst these situations has been "non-alignment." In the Cold War context, Pakistan became an ally of the United States in the 1950s. Unsurprisingly, even though formally non-aligned, India strengthened its relationship with the Soviet Union. Although "non-alignment" paid off as both the United States and the Soviet Union came to India's side during the Sino-Indian war (1962), the general trend was further strengthening the relationship with Moscow as reflected by the Indo-Soviet treaty of friendship and cooperation (1971). Backed by this treaty, the Indian navy asserted its position at the Bay of Bengal vis-à-vis the U.S.navy during the third Indo-Pakistani war (1971). This stance reflected the Indian anti-hegemonic stance facing the predominant position of the United States in the Indian Ocean. In short, backed by the Soviet Union the Indian anti-hegemonic party state developed a formidable military capacity not only for self-defense purposes but for gaining a predominant role in South Asia at the expense of the hegemonic power.

This same pattern of direct transition from colonial rule to nation-state rule by an anti-hegemonic party state regime, opened by India's decolonization, was observed across much of Africa. 1947, the year of India's independence, was also the year of the foundation of the United Gold Coast Convention under the leadership of Nkrumah aiming at the immediate achievement of self-government. Its successor, the Convention People's Party, founded in 1949, became preeminent after a landslide victory in the legislative assembly elections, under British administration, in 1951. By the time that Ghana's independence was achieved, in March 1957, Nkrumah's party held an undisputed leadership validated by the Presidential elections of 1960 (in which Nkrumah obtained 90% of the votes) and sealed in 1964 by constitutionally establishing Ghana as a one-party state. Opposition was silenced from 1958 through the exercise of the Preventive Detention Law that enabled the regime to detain and imprison several hundred opposition members. On the other hand, the Convention People's Party mobilized society through the party institutions (whose membership encompassed 15% of the population) ranging from the central organs through the regional and local units, supplemented by organizations such as the National Council of Ghana Woman, the Young Pioneers youth organization, the trade union movement, and the United Ghana Farmer's Council. In 1963 it was announced that all officer cadets had to apply for party membership. In 1964 plans for the introduction of political commissars were announced. But these attempts to strengthen the party position also failed. It is from this state apparatus that the blow that brought Ghana's anti-hegemonic party state to its end came in 1966 through a military coup that established a military dictatorship.[40]

Since his first administration in 1951, even under British rule, Nkrumah worked out ten different Development Plans of which four were fully implemented. The British colonial administration initiated in 1951 the ten-year Plan for the Economic and Social Development of the Gold Coast to mitigate anti-colonial agitation, on the one hand, and to increase the production of agro-mineral raw materials needed by metropolitan industry, on the other hand. However, Nkrumah's empowerment following the elections of this same year led to a reformulation of the developmental program. The increase of agricultural productivity, mainly of cocoa and oil seeds (the traditional products of colonial economies) was only the immediate and preliminary aim, whose strategic target was industrialization. The industrialization program was envisaged to rely in its earlier stages on foreign capital except in strategic sectors such as electricity supply, railway transport, and steel. The future nationalization of private enterprises would be compensated according to a pledge in the national constitution binding every government. Following this general framework, the second five-year development plan, the first for independent Ghana scheduled for 1959–1964, aimed at raising the yields of the cocoa industry, establishing large acreages of rubber and banana plantations, and increasing the yields of cereals using irrigation and fertilizers. The subsequent seven-year development plan, scheduled for 1964–1970 but interrupted in 1966 by the military coup, aimed to produce domestic substitutes for manufactured staples so far imported, while at the same time attempting to foster the manufacture and processing of agricultural and mining commodities before export. Regarding the results, the attempts to modernize agriculture through the establishment of cooperatives under the guidance of the United Ghana Farmers' Co-operative Council engulfed some 870 cooperatives and 123 State Farms with a total membership by 1965 of 15,300 and 20,000 farmers, respectively. Considering that by then over 70% of Ghanaian production consisted of subsistence-based smallholder production, the low likelihood of the achievement becomes evident. In the industrial sector the program appeared to be too ambitious and therefore it was abandoned in 1961. Following this experience, the emphasis of the seven-year development plan was on manufacturing local raw materials, while the investment in infrastructure, light, and heavy industries failed, resulting in heavy foreign debt.

The financing of industrialization attempts highlights the foreign dimension of Ghana's anti-hegemonic party state. In his industrialization efforts, Nkrumah persistently sought assistance from the socialist camp. The Soviet Union and its subsumed Eastern Bloc provided Ghana with favorable credits refundable in twelve-year periods with interest rates of 2–3%. China offered free interest loans that included a grace period. Simultaneously, Nkrumah approached Western countries as well in order to finance his development plans. It is this twofold orientation toward the Communist bloc and the Western powers for bargaining assistance, aid, and support that is one of the main characteristics of anti-hegemonic party states in peripheral states. In the case of Ghana, this twofold orientation became a Damocles' sword. Ghana's heavy indebtedness coincided with the fall of cocoa's price. While the Communist bloc granted Ghana a three-year payment moratorium, extension on credits, and enlargement of cocoa importation, hegemonic creditors conditioned further help on an agreement with the IMF. This agreement included cutbacks in government expenditure, removal of subsidies to state-owned enterprises, reduction of the price of cocoa, discarding the monopoly of Ghana's Shipping Line (Black Star Line), reduction of trade with the socialist block, and the creation of a more liberal climate for Western investment. Two days after Ghana's Finance Minister made public the rejection of these reforms, Ghana's anti-hegemonic party state was overthrown by the army[41] (Map 5.6).

Map 5.6 Nationalism and socialism throughout Africa: Algeria 1954–1988, "National Liberation Front"; Ghana 1957–1966, Convention People's Party; Guinea 1958–1984, Parti Démocratique de Guinée; Mali 1960–1968, Union Soudanaise du Rassemblement Démocratique Africain; Tanzania 1964–1985, Tanganyika African National Union; Uganda 1966–1971, Uganda People's Congress; Madagascar, 1975–1982, Avant-garde de la Révolution Malgache, Supreme Revolutionary Council

ENTWINED NATIONALISM AND SOCIALISM AROUND THE WORLD: THE GLOBAL RISE OF ANTI-HEGEMONIC PARTY STATES

Every region visited by this global tour under the tracks of entwined Nationalism and Socialism beyond the hegemonic and counter-hegemonic spheres clearly has its own characteristics. Moreover, each state had its own idiosyncrasies and even each of the regimes in power underwent distinctive phases. And yet several underlying commonalities can be highlighted as well. All of these regimes displayed a twofold reliance on state institutions and party apparatuses. This was combined with the mobilization of society and economy inspired by a collectivist ideology that, espousing nationalism and socialism, aimed to transform these societies and economies in order to catch up with the industrialized world as improve their position within the world order.

The ways in which each of these regimes unfolded are similar on several counts. Their trajectories got started by a political force opposing a prevailing political regime. At some point in their development, these political forces become a well-organized party, a mass movement, and eventually the ruling regime (although not necessarily in this order). Once holding state power, these parties transitioned from being at the outskirts of the previous political regime to the center of power. Also, once in power, the resulting regimes accumulated and concentrated power by the apparatuses of the state and the party organizations, imposing internal unity. One approach was developing conciliatory policies between social classes in order to form a broad social coalition. A different approach was a thorough repression of dissidents in order to eliminate opposition. These measures were derived from and/or justified by the leading collectivist ideology, a concoction of some nationalistic and socialist ideas. Also, the economic and social policies were derived from these collectivist ideologies. These policies consisted of a persistent cluster of measures that typically included land reform, nationalization, economic protectionism, import substitution industrialization, central planning, five-year plans, and wealth redistribution programs. These policies were put in place with the ultimate goals of catching up with the industrialized world, reshaping the social structure, and improving the stance of the nation within the world order. These are the underlying commonalities present in the above examples as well as in multiple additional cases[42] (Map 5.7).

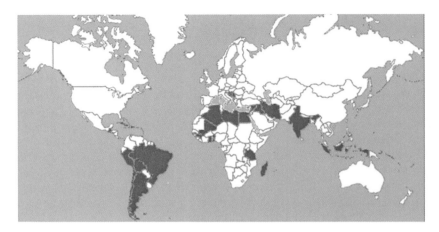

Map 5.7 The anti-hegemonic sphere—Anti-hegemonic party states around the Third World

By visualizing this global trend in the aftermath of the Second World War and for the subsequent three decades on top of the already bi-polar world of the hegemonic and counter-hegemonic spheres, there should be no wonder that the economic globalization disrupted in the wake of the 1929 Global Depression was very slow to recover. With nationalizations, import substitution industrialization, and economic protectionism directing the policies of so many states outside of the bi-polar world of the Cold War there was only room for a slow re-globalization of the world economy.

Pyramids into Diamonds

During the period between the Great Depression (1929) and the mid-1970s, states around the world had adopted a strong interventionist approach on their economies. That was the case with the expansion of global Keynesianism within the hegemonic sphere, the consolidation of the communist counter-hegemonic sphere, and the explosion of anti-hegemonic party states throughout the rest of the globe. This development constrained the relative de-globalization of the world economy and coincided with the shrinking of socioeconomic inequality both within nation-states and between them.

Within nation-states a significant shift occurred as social structures metaphorically similar to a pyramid—with the vast bulk of the population in the lower ranks of society and a small privileged elite atop—were replaced by diamond-shaped societies, in which a significantly enlarged middle classes made up the bulk of the population with smaller groups of elites atop and lower ranks below. For instance, before 1929 the richest 1% in the United States claimed 45% of the nation's wealth and the upper class made of the highest 10% echelon of wealth owned 80% of it. The numbers for Europe are even more extreme, where the highest 1 and 10% echelons amassed 65 and 90% of their societies' wealth, respectively. These pyramid social structures were drastically transformed into diamonds by 1970, in which the richest 1% owned a mere 8% of the nation's wealth while the vast bulk of it was distributed across a broad middle class.[43] Throughout the world the share of wealth owned by the richest echelons drastically diminished and was redistributed to a rapidly growing middle class.[44] Far more drastic was the collapse of wealth owned by the richest echelons in societies that underwent the establishment of Communist regimes such as the Soviet Union and the Eastern Bloc, China, North Korea, Vietnam, and Cuba, where private property was expropriated, nationalized, and collectivized. The long-standing pyramid social structures in these mostly agrarian pre-revolutionary societies were transformed in the wake of the revolutions into diamond structures in which the bulk of the population shared highly egalitarian conditions; a minority of forcefully exploited and suppressed dissidents were at the bottom; and a ruling elite was at the top point. Finally, also throughout the Third World the emergence of anti-hegemonic party states was conducive to the narrowing of socioeconomic inequality, even if the interventionist measures were not as drastic as in the Communist regimes or the sources of taxable wealth available for distribution was not comparable to those that narrowed the inequality gap in the hegemonic sphere. And yet, for all the different gradations in the reduction of domestic socioeconomic inequality, it represented an overall global trend, referred as the "Great Compression"[45] (Diagram 5.1).

The reason for this transition from pyramids to diamonds was state interventionism and relative de-globalization. Either in the form of global Keynesianism within the sphere of the hegemonic order, communism in the counter-hegemonic sphere, or following the recurring redistributive policies adopted by anti-hegemonic party states throughout the Third World, state intervention in all cases brought about wealth and income

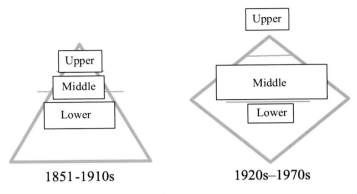

Diagram 5.1   The Great Compression

redistribution. Global Keynesianism accomplished that by fiscal policy, labor policy, and the establishment of the welfare state. Progressive tax codes made the rich pay much more, as much as 90% for the top marginal tax in the United States under Franklin Delano Roosevelt's New Deal (1929). Even during Nixon's years (1969–1974) it never went below 70%. At the same time salaries grew significantly not only in absolute terms but also relative to capital gains. As for the welfare state, education and health services, public housing, and social security systems were provided to the citizens by the states, which at the same time generated much employment by running the extraction of natural resources such as mines, infrastructures such as utilities and transportation, and industries in manifold areas.

These generous provisions and the decrease of economic inequality more widely were outgrowths of the Great Depression, the World Wars, and the Cold War. One way of making sense of the Great Depression, aside from the standard bubble-to-burst account (see above, pp. 108–110), is to look at the staggering rate of socioeconomic inequality on its eve. With 80–90% of the wealth concentrated in the hands of the richest 10% alone, demand for goods and services was doomed. In other words, the Great Depression was a crisis of demand because the bulk of the population had diminishing ability to consume. Hence the solution to the crisis was redistributing wealth to stimulate demand and in so doing make the economy grow again.[46] That redistribution of wealth was made by global Keynesianism and its corollary, the development of the welfare state. As for the World Wars, the critical way in which they brought about the narrowing of socioeconomic inequality is the sheer devastation that they brought about. Such devastation to economies and properties meant wiping out the riches of the highest socioeconomic echelons, making the socioeconomic playing field more level. That is why these wars are included in the list of the "great levelers" of socioeconomic inequality.[47] The Second World War and the Cold War further motivated the development of welfare states. Aside from the demand crisis exploding in 1929, welfare states were also a way to compensate populations that underwent the tremendous sufferings caused by the Second World War while still being mobilized by their states and carrying out their orders and demands for further sacrifices. Moreover, as the Cold War took shape, welfare states provided an alternative to the communist lure of an egalitarian society in the context of devastated post-Second World War Europe where communist parties were powerful and on the rise. Indeed, an alternative in the form of the welfare state needed to be extended to the less privileged members of society if they were to be distanced from the communist dream—an experiment in social engineering that only in hindsight turned out to be a nightmare. As for the anti-hegemonic party states throughout the Third World, tackling inequality within their societies was also very high on their agendas. In many cases, these agendas were what brought them to power in the first place; they delivered by implementing policies such as land reforms, fiscal reforms, wage raises, public housing, education and health services, social security systems, and a wide range of social plans.

Interestingly, the metaphor of a transition from pyramid to diamond social structures within nation-states also applies to the ongoing changes in the levels of inequalities between nation-states. During the times of British global hegemony, the socioeconomic structure of the global society was arranged as a pyramid with colonies, mandates, and protectorates throughout Africa and Asia at the bottom, global European empires at the top, and crumbling Eurasian gunpowder empires and Latin American oligarchic republics somewhere in between. By the time the Big Brexit was consummated in the wake of two World Wars and the unfolding of decolonization, this global pyramid was reshaped into a diamond in which the bulk of societies throughout the world strived to achieve or reassert political sovereignty combined with economic strategies envisioned to catch up with the industrial nations at the top of the pyramid. In so doing, they reshaped the global society into a diamond structure. Moreover, the leading industrial nations, for their part, suffered major devastation during the World Wars and lost their empires, contributing in these ways to the shrinking of the wealth gap between nation-states.

As much as the transition from pyramids to diamonds within societies was propelled by state interventionism and relative de-globalization, the same is true for the narrowing inequality gap between societies. This was particularly prominent throughout the Third World, namely, former colonies, mandates, and protectorates, some of the former gunpowder empires, and the Latin American oligarchic republics. The combination of nationalizations of natural resources and infrastructures with protectionist policies matched by import substitution industrialization as applied by anti-hegemonic party states resulted both in blocking global economic integration and in narrowing the socioeconomic gap with the fully developed economies of the hegemonic sphere. These effects are clearly visualized by the trends observed since the dismantling of these anti-hegemonic states. Domestically, GDP per capita had reversed course from sustained growth throughout the 1960s and 1970s into stagnation in Latin America starting in the 1980s and collapse in Africa back to pre-1960s levels. Regarding inequalities between these regions and the leading world economy, since the demise of the anti-hegemonic party states the gap in per capita GDP between the United States and the Middle East, South Asia, Latin America, and Africa grew by 154, 196, 206, and 207%, respectively, between 1960 and 2014.[48]

Within the hegemonic sphere, the narrowing of inequalities between countries, as well as those within countries, was accomplished through global Keynesianism. Starting from the U.S. support for reconstruction in Europe and Japan and the establishment of international financial and trade institutions (IMF, WB, GATT) that tightened financial and commercial relations, this economic paradigm articulated a mutually beneficial economic integration throughout the hegemonic sphere. The industrialized nations relaunched and enhanced their industrial economies. Although nation-states the hegemonic sphere also held a firm grip on the economic steering wheel by way of interventionist policies, given that their goal was economic integration they headed for export-oriented industrialization as opposed to the import substitution industrialization of the anti-hegemonic party states. This export-oriented strategy allowed for industrial specialization and convenient integration into an international division of labor. By contrast, import substitution policies applied throughout the Third World were instrumental in launching industrialization projects, nurturing domestic markets, and diminishing the socioeconomic gap with the economies of the hegemonic sphere. However, in the longer run import substitution policies that aimed to diversify their production in order to widely replace imports did not manage to establish industries able to sustainably compete without the strong stance of the anti-hegemonic party states interventionism. Finally, in the counter-hegemonic sphere it was the centralized command economy that brought about formidable industrialization and post-Second World War reconstruction in the Soviet Union and the Eastern Bloc and, by contrast, complete disruption of the Chinese economy, in all cases at a tremendous human cost.[49]

The above triangulation of economic policies, economic globalization, and socioeconomic inequalities in the wake of the First World War, the collapse of the British global hegemony and the emergence of the U.S. global hegemony indicates a global rise in state interventionism, a relative de-globalization of the world economy, and the diminishing of socioeconomic inequalities within and between nation-states. This is the triad trend that characterized most prominently the 1945–1976 period in which the U.S. global hegemony was limited by the communist counter-hegemonic sphere and the anti-hegemonic party states in the Third World. The states in each of these three blocks applied different strategies domestically and abroad—global Keynesianism, centralized command economy, or economic nationalism. And yet, each of these strategies had redistributive effects within their societies and contributed to narrow the socioeconomic gaps between societies. However, as the second half of the 1970s was underway the tide was about to turn. A new set of economic and political shocks would bring this transition from pyramids to diamonds to an abrupt halt and eventually revert it from diamonds back to pyramids.

NOTES

1. David McCullough, *Truman* (New York: Simon & Schuster, 1992), 547. Michael Hunt, *Crisis in U.S. Foreign Policy: An International History Reader* (Yale University Press, 1996) 159.
2. R. J. Rummel, "Statistics of Vietnamese Democide," Charlottesville, Virginia: Center for National Security Law, School of

    Law, University of Virginia, 1997, http://www.hawaii.edu/pow erkills/SOD.TAB6.1B.GIF.

3. Michael A. Hunt, *A Vietnam War Reader: A Documentary History from American and Vietnamese Perspectives* (The University of North Carolina Press, 2010), docs. 76, 79, 83.

4. Arthur Schlesinger, Jr., "The American Empire? Not so Fast," *World Policy Journal* 22, no. 1 (2005), http://www.worldpolicy. org/journal/articles/wpj05-sp/schlesinger.html.

5. Lars Schoultz, *Beneath the United States: A History of U.S. Policy Toward Latin America* (Cambridge, MA: Harvard University Press, 1998), 39–58.

6. Allegedly President Franklin D. Roosevelt coined the expression "our son of a bitch" in reference to either ruthless Nicaraguan dictator Anastasio Somoza (the father) or the brutal Dominican dictator Rafael Trujillo. That was an expression of American realistic approach to foreign policy. Hugh Thomas, *Cuba: The Pursuit of Freedom* (Picador, 2001), 650.

7. Gerald Segal, *The Simon & Schuster Guide to the World Today* (Simon & Schuster, 1987), 82.

8. Jeffrey Mass and William Hauser, eds., *The Bakufu in Japanese History* (Stanford University Press, 1985), 189.

9. Frederick H. Gareau, "Morgenthau's Plan for Industrial Disarmament in Germany," *The Western Political Quarterly* 14, no. 2 (June 1961): 517–534.

10. T. van de Klunder, and A. van Shaik, "On the Historical Continuity of the Process of Economic Growth," CEPR Discussion Paper Series No. 850 (1993).

11. Hans Brinckmann and Ysbrand Rogge, *Showa Japan: The Post-War Golden Age and Its Troubled Legacy* (Tuttle Publishing, 2008).

12. Paul Ginsborg, *A History of Contemporary Italy: Society and Politics, 1943–1988* (Penguin, 1990).

13. Nicholas Crafts and Gianni Toniolo, eds., *Economic Growth in Europe since 1945* (Cambridge University Press, 1996), 428.

14. Martin Schain, *The Marshall Plan: Fifty Years After* (Palgrave MacMillan, 2001).

15. David Kynaston, *Austerity Britain, 1945–1951* (London: Bloomsbury Publishing, 2010).

16. Nicholas Crafts and Gianni Toniolo, eds., *Economic Growth in Europe since 1945* (Cambridge University Press, 1996). Frances

Cairncross and Alec Cairncross, *The Legacy of the Golden Age: 1960s and Their Economic Consequences* (Routledge, 1994). Stephen A. Marglin and Juliet B. Schor, *The Golden Age of Capitalism: Reinterpreting the Postwar Experience* (Oxford University Press, 1992). Michael John Webber and David L. Rigby, *The Golden Age Illusion: Rethinking Postwar Capitalism* (Guilford, 1997).

17. W. David McIntyre, "Britain and the Creation of the Commonwealth Secretariat," *Journal of Imperial and Commonwealth History* 28, no. 1 (January 2000): 135–158.

18. Juan Linz and Alfred Stepan, *Problems of Democratic Transition and Consolidation: Southern Europe, South America, and Post-Communist Europe* (Baltimore, MD: Johns Hopkins University Press, 1996), 93–94.

19. Christie Davies, "Jokes as the Truth About Soviet Socialism," *Electronic Journal of Folklore* 46 (2010), 18, http://www.folklore.ee/folklore/vol46/davies.pdf.

20. Richard Millington, *State, Society and Memories of the Uprising of 17 June 1953 in the GDR* (Palgrave Macmillan, 2014). Jonathan Sperber, "17 June 1953: Revisiting a German Revolution," *German History* 22, no. 4 (2004), 619–643.

21. Jenõ Györkei, Alexandr Kirov, and Miklos Horvath, *Soviet Military Intervention in Hungary, 1956* (New York: Central European University Press, 1999), 350.

22. Matthew Ouimet, *The Rise and Fall of the Brezhnev Doctrine in Soviet Foreign Policy* (Chapel Hill; London: University of North Carolina Press, 2003). Tony Judt, *Postwar: A History of Europe Since 1945* (Penguin Press, 2005).

23. Walter Scheidel, *The Great Leveler: Violence and the History of Inequality from the Stone Age to the Twenty-First Century* (Princeton, NJ: Princeton University Press, 2017).

24. Sheila Fitzpatrick, *The Russian Revolution*, 3rd ed. (Oxford: Oxford University Press, 2008), 140. Leslie Holmes, *Communism: A Very Short Introduction* (Oxford: Oxford University Press, 2009), 32. Jisheng Yang, "The Fatal Politics of the PRC's Great Leap Famine: The Preface to Tombstone," *Journal of Contemporary China* 19, no. 66 (2010), 755–776. Yang Jisheng, *Tombstone: The Great Chinese Famine, 1958–1962* (Farrar, Straus and Giroux, 2013). Peng Xizhe, "Demographic Consequences of the Great Leap Forward in China's Provinces," *Population and Development*

Review 13, no. 4 (1987), 639–70. Frank Dikötter, *Mao's Great Famine: The History of China's Most Devastating Catastrophe, 1958–62* (Walker & Co., 2010).

25. Nikita Khrushchev, *Khrushchev's Memoirs* (Little Brown & Company, 1970), 250–257.

26. Dwight Perkins, "China's Economic Policy and Performance," in *The Cambridge History of China, Volume 15*, eds. Roderick MacFarquhar, John K. Fairbank and Denis Twitchett (Cambridge: Cambridge University Press, 1991), 483–493.

27. David R. Shearer, "Social Disorder, Mass Repression, and the NKVD During the 1930s," *Cahiers du Monde russe* 42/2–4 (2001), 505–534. http://journals.openedition.org/monderusse/8465; https://doi.org/10.4000/monderusse.8465. Michael Ellman, "Soviet Repression Statistics: Some Comments," *Europe-Asia Studies* 54, no. 7 (2002): 1151–1172.

28. Roderick MacFarquhar and Michael Schoenhals, *Mao's Last Revolution* (Cambridge, MA: Harvard University Press, 2006), 262. Jung Chang and Jon Halliday, *Mao: The Unknown Story* (London: Jonathan Cape, 2005), 569.

29. Helwig Schmidt-Glintzer, "The Politics of Memory. 70 per cent good, 30 per cent bad. China Has Found a Simple Formula to Assess Mao Zedong's Legacy," *International Politics and Society* 10.08.2017. https://www.ips-journal.eu/in-focus/the-politics-of-memory/article/show/70-per-cent-good-30-per-cent-bad-2216/.

30. Oleg Gordievsky, *KGB: The Inside Story of Its Foreign Operations from Lenin to Gorbachev* (Harpercollins, 1992).

31. Mark Kramer, "The Soviet Bloc and the Cold War in Europe," in Klaus Larres, ed., *A Companion to Europe Since 1945* (Wiley, 2014), 79.

32. Graeme Gill, "The Soviet Leader Cult: Reflections on the Structure of Leadership in the Soviet Union," *British Journal of Political Science* 10 (1980): 167. Catriona Kelly, "Riding the Magic Carpet: Children and the Leader Cult in the Stalin Era," *The Slavic and East European Journal* 49 (2005): 206–207.

33. David M. Levy and Sandra J. Peart, Sandra J., "Soviet Growth and American Textbooks: An Endogenous Past," *Journal of Economic Behavior & Organization* 78, nos. 1–2 (2011): 110–125. Paul

A. Samuelson, *Economics: An Introductory Analysis*, 5th ed. (New York: McGraw-Hill, 1961), 830.

34. Mario Rapoport, *Historia económica, política y social de la Argentina* (Buenos Aires: Emecé-Colihue, 2007).

35. Piero Gleijeses, *Shattered Hope: The Guatemalan Revolution and the United States, 1944–1954* (Princeton, NJ: Princeton University Press, 1992). Richard H. Immerman, *The CIA in Guatemala: The Foreign Policy of Intervention* (Austin, TX: University of Texas Press, 1982). Stephen M. Streeter, *Managing the Counterrevolution: The United States and Guatemala, 1954–1961.* (Athens, OH: Ohio University Press, 2000).

36. Forrest Hylton and Sinclair Thomson, *Revolutionary Horizons: Past and Present in Bolivian Politics* (London; New York: Verso, 2007), 78–79.

37. Daniel M. Masterson, *Militarism and Politics in Latin America: Peru from Sánchez Cerro to Sendero Luminoso* (Westport, Ct: Greenwood Publishing Group, 1991), 228–248. Enrique Mayer, *Ugly Stories of the Peruvian Agrarian Reform* (Durham, NC: Duke University Press, 2009). Cristobal Kay, "Achievements and Contradictions of the Peruvian Agrarian Reform," *Journal of Development Studies* 18, no. 2 (1982): 141–142.

38. Peter Winn, "The Furies of the Andes: Violence and Terror in the Chilean Revolution and Counterrevolution," *A Century of Revolution: Insurgent and Counterinsurgent Violence During Latin America's Long Cold War*, eds. Gilbert Joseph and Greg Grandin (Durham, NC: Duke University Press, 2010), 239–275.

39. William Cleveland, *A History of the Modern Middle East* (Boulder, CO: Westview Press, 2016). Mark J. Gasiorowski and Malcolm Byrne, *Mohammad Mosaddeq and the 1953 Coup in Iran* (Syracuse, NY: Syracuse University Press, 2004).

40. Trevor Jones, *Ghana's First Republic 1960–1966: The Pursuit of Political Kingdom* (London: Methuen, 1976).

41. Ansa Asamoa, *Socioeconomic Development Strategies of Independent African Countries: The Ghanaian Experience* (Accra: Ghana Universities Press, 1996), 48–87.

42. List of additional cases: In Latin America: Justicialismo (Argentina, 1946–1955); Partido Trabalhista Brasileiro (Brazil, 1951–1954); Movimiento Nacionalista Revolucionario (Bolivia, 1952–1964); Arbenz (Guatemala, 1951–1954); Organizaciones Revolucionarias

Integradas (Cuba, 1959–); Partido Revolucionario Dominicano (Dominican Republic, 1963); Frente Popular (Chile, 1970–1973). In Asia: Communist Party (Vietnam, 1945–1986); Sukarno's Indonesia (1945–1967); Indian National Congress (India, 1947–1985); Communist Party (China, 1949–1976). In the Middle East: Mosaddeq's Iran (1951–1953); "free officers" (Egypt, 1952–1970); "free officers" and Baath Party (Iraq, 1958–1979); Baath Party (Syria, 1963–); "free officers" (Libya, 1969–2011). In Africa: National Liberation Front, Algeria 1954–1988; Convention People's Party, Ghana 1957–1966; Parti Démocratique de Guinée (Guinea, 1958–1984); Union Soudanaise du Rassemblement Democratique Africain (Mali, 1960–1968); Tanganyika African National Union (Tanzania, 1964–1985); Uganda People's Congress (Uganda, 1966–1971); Avant-garde de la Révolution Malgache (Madagascar, 1975–1982).

43. Jason Hickel, *The Divide: A Brief Guide to Global Inequality and its Solutions* (New York: W. W. Norton & Company, 2018), 99–100, 119.

44. Thomas Piketty, *Capital in the Twenty-First Century* (Harvard University Press, 2017).

45. Scheidel, *The Great Leveler.*

46. Samuel Bowles, David M. Gordon, and Thomas Weisskopf, *Beyond the Wasteland: A Democratic Alternative to Economic Decline* (Verso Books, 1985).

47. Scheidel, *The Great Leveler.*

48. Hickel, *The Divide,* 53–54, 150.

49. David Turnock, *The East European Economy in Context: Communism and Transition* (Routledge, 1997).

CHAPTER 6

All Together Now: Becoming Global Citizens (1968–2003)

THE REVOLUTIONARY PROCESSES (1968–1991): E PLURIBUS UNUM (ONE OUT OF MANY)

British and U.S. world hegemonies differ in many regards. One way to encapsulate them is by pointing to the "hegemonic-globalization paradox:" much globalization with limited hegemony versus much hegemony with limited globalization. During the nineteenth century, Great Britain led a full-fledged economic globalization with a diminishing share in the global economy and a limited degree of cultural Britannization. After the hegemonic impasse of 1914–1945, the U.S. economy and U.S. lifestyles made their presence felt all over the world, yet post-Second World War globalization had a limited reach. That limited reach was the direct result of the consolidation and expansion of the Soviet counter-hegemonic sphere and the emergence and growth to global proportions of the anti-hegemonic sphere throughout the Third World. For as long as these two spheres were to remain firmly in place, it seemed that the U.S. world hegemony could effectively blossom within its limited hegemonic sphere only. And yet, by 1968 all three spheres were shaken to their cores and were set to undergo major transformations that would unleash in a matter of three decades the reach of economic globalization under U.S. hegemony to a genuine planetary stage.

By 1968, the anti-hegemonic party states on the rise since the immediate aftermath of the Second World War were being toppled

© The Author(s), under exclusive license to Springer Nature Switzerland AG 2021
D. Olstein, *A Brief History of Now*,
https://doi.org/10.1007/978-3-030-82420-4_6

one after the next for more than a decade. A wave of authoritarian regimes had replaced them, wreaking havoc on the anti-hegemonic party states' leaderships, supporters, constituencies, and legacies of entwined nationalism and socialism. In their turn, many of these authoritarian regimes, as well as pre-existing ones, paved the way for the establishment of democratic regimes that started emerging during the 1970s and onward into the 1990s. As for the communist counter-hegemonic sphere, with Khrushchev's ascent to power in 1954, the fracture between the Soviet Union and China fully developed by 1968 and had redirected China toward collaboration with the United States by 1972. Subsequent domestic reforms in each of these Communist states—starting in China by 1979 and less than a decade later in the USSR—transformed them and most of the latter's satellites beyond recognition by the 1990s (Map 6.1).

Meanwhile, sweeping changes were also underway in the hegemonic sphere. The "golden age" of capitalism, that period of multiple "economic miracles" (1946–1973) was approaching its disruptive end. With global Keynesianism, deeply rooted and naturalized for almost three decades as the way of running economy and society, being called into question, an old–new alternative known as neoliberalism gained ground quickly. By the 1990s, a series of technological breakthroughs in computation, communication systems, and automation had transformed economy and society beyond recognition.

These 30 years of profound global transformations were propelled by multiple local shocks: revolts and wars, reforms and revolutions, and technological innovations. 1968 signaled a year of worldwide protests by youth disaffected with the brave postwar bi-polar new world. 1973 brought a regional war—the Yom Kippur or Ramadan War—that played out as yet another proxy war in the context of this bi-polar world order, except that this war triggered a major global economic crisis of transformative proportions that ended up dethroning global Keynesianism. In 1978 Mao Tse-Tung was succeeded in power by formerly purged leader Deng Xiaoping, who was soon to launch a transformation that cascaded beyond China's borders. During April to June 1982 a war unfolded in the South Atlantic, in which Argentina temporarily recovered its Malvinas Islands and then Great Britain secured back its Falkland Islands, the names with which Argentines and British, respectively, call the same islands located 700 kilometers off the Argentine shore, 12,800 kilometers from Britain (see above, p. 126). This limited and presumably self-contained military conflict had, however, tremendous global implications by saving

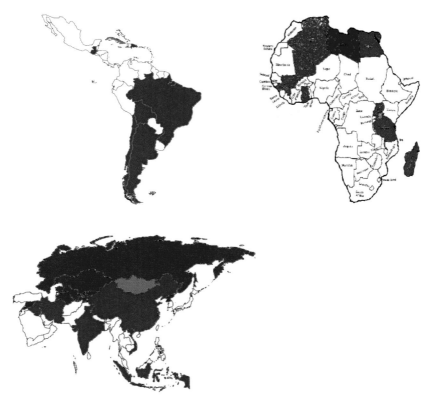

Map 6.1 The Anti-hegemonic and counter hegemonic spheres liquidated by military coups and/or neoliberal Reforms.[1] Compare with Maps 5.4–5.7, above, pp. 191–202 and Maps 6.2 and 7.1, below, p. 265 and p. 311

the prospects of neoliberalism success on the one hand and turning the page on authoritarian regimes on the other.

In 1985, a generational shift in the leadership of the Soviet Union, personified by the rise of Mikhail Gorbachev, took place. Soon after, transformative political (*Glasnost*) and economic (*Perestroika*) reforms were underway. These reforms cascaded in 1989 and 1991 into the demise of the Eastern Bloc and the Soviet Union, respectively. The brave bipolar new world had come to an end. Another brave new world came to the fore, a global and neoliberal one. With the decline of anti-hegemonic party states throughout the Third World and the collapse of the communist counter-hegemonic, the hegemonic sphere expanded its global reach. Starting in 1991, as illustrated by the First Gulf War, U.S. world hegemony was no longer limited. A consistent overlap between the reign of a world hegemon and a globally integrated world economy materialized, as in the days of the British-led first globalization. The "hegemonic-globalization paradox" was over.

Moreover, with these momentous political and socioeconomic changes, major technological breakthroughs in information and communication were simultaneously underway. The conflating effects of these new technologies—satellite communication, computational systems, and the Internet—and the adoption of the new ideologies and policies of neoliberalism by most nation-states had created by 1991 a global economy working in real time that also fostered the development of a global society, global culture, and a myriad of responses to them. It was then that it became official: globalization as we now know it had begun!

1968, A Global Revolt

For more than two decades, the brave new world that had emerged in the wake of the Second World War had been experiencing demographic and economic growth combined with growing social equality within and between societies. The demographic growth, known as the "Baby Boom," accounts for the growth of the world population from around 2.2 to 3.5 billion people between 1945 and 1968.[2] The economic growth, known as the "Long Boom," ranged between 5–6% yearly (as opposed to 2–3% a year since).[3] The growing social equality during these decades is known as the Great Compression and transformed social structures from pyramids into diamonds. These major trends combined were consolidated on the eve of 1968 when the best-nurtured and educated cohort of young people in world history thus far was coming of age. This generation had enjoyed higher standards of welfare than any previous generations in terms of housing, nutrition, health care, and education. Moreover, on top of these fundamental needs the first generation coming of age in the brave new world had also developed a youth culture of fashion and design, pop culture and consumerism, ideological underpinnings, and lifestyles.

Yet, not all was rosy in this booming brave new world. Probably the first to realize that and take stock of it was precisely this coming-of-age privileged generation. Affluence, fashion, pop culture, and consumerism aside, the brave new world also was the world of the Cold War that carried the maddening latent prospect of mutually assured destruction (MAD). Nuclear warfare was a plausible scenario that this generation had internalized through emergency drilling at school, definitely an unsettling experience that cast doubts on the viability of the otherwise rosy brave new world. Tense episodes throughout the Cold War such as the Cuban Missile Crisis showed how quickly tensions could escalate to brinkmanship. But even without reaching such Armageddon proportions, the world order offered by the Cold War was disturbing enough through its proxy wars and military interventions.

By 1964, U.S. President Lyndon Johnson escalated the late John F. Kennedy's limited intervention in Vietnam into a full-fledge war. And yet, for all of the devastating power of the fourfold big stick of the world hegemon, on the eve of the 1968 Vietnamese New Year, the T′êt Holiday, the North Vietnamese People's Army, and the Việt Cộng (or National Liberation Front based in South Vietnam) had launched a major military offensive against the South Vietnamese Army of the Republic of Vietnam and the U.S. Armed Forces. Although this attempt by the Communist camp ended up in military defeat, the offensive sent shockwaves throughout the world, portraying the determination of the Vietnamese revolution to confront the world hegemon. Shortly before, on October 9, 1967, Comandante Ernesto Che Guevara—leader of the Cuban Revolution and failed revolutionary attempts in Congo and Bolivia—was executed by the CIA-backed Bolivian army. In subsequent months Che Guevara became a powerful inspirational global icon who captured the youth imagination. The perceived injustices in distant latitudes throughout the Third World soon combined with the injustices experienced on the very hegemonic sphere societies: youth disenfranchisement, gender inequality, gay and lesbian repression, and, in the United States, the segregation of Black Americans. Injustices conflated by authoritarian regimes triggered protests throughout the Third World. Finally, the communist counter-hegemonic sphere was not an exception to the trend; protest against the Communist authoritarian regimes backed by the Soviet army was ready to break out too.

And so it was that a generation coming of age amidst material well-being, relative peace, and political stability; alien to the hardships of the previous generations that suffered two world wars and a global economic depression in between; equipped with the intellectual tools provided by systems of mass education running all the way from pre-school to universities; and informed by burgeoning mass media that made the world a global village took to the streets throughout the world to demand change. In the United States, peace activists, students, women's movements, and hippies persistently protested the Vietnam War in Washington D.C., throughout city centers, on university campuses, and in rallies and demonstrations, pickets and occupations, walks-out and sits-in, several of which were forcefully and even fatally suppressed by the security forces. Simultaneously, the Vietnam War was being protested throughout the hegemonic sphere in Europe, Japan, and Latin America. These worldwide protests coincided with locally driven demands, some of which had been building up for decades and were reaching a fever pitch in 1968.

In the United States, most prominently, it was the civil rights movements that lead nonviolent strikes and marches against a segregation regime known by the euphemism "separate but equal" to which Black Americans were subjected. The movements that had been emerging since 1954 reached a boiling point in 1968 amidst riots in more than 150 American cities in the wake of Martin Luther King Jr.'s assassination. By then, President Johnson's administration finally acknowledged that the United States was "moving toward two societies, one black, one white, separate and unequal" (the report of the Kerner Commission, appointed by Johnson to examine the causes of race riots). A second Civil Rights Act was signed amidst the riots. That same year, Cesar Chávez, leader of the National Farm Workers established in 1962 to defend the rights of agricultural workers, many of Latino and Filipino origins, launched the first of his "spiritual fasts" in preparation for a civil disobedience campaign by farm workers.[4] Also in 1968 Women's Liberation groups on the rise for some time became prominent by targeting the Miss America Beauty Contest as an emblem of sexist social norms and roles.

Similarly, throughout Western Europe the protest against the Vietnam War became the battle cry against the U.S.-led hegemonic post-Second World War world order and the rejection of the domestic socioeconomic and political order. Laurel and Hardy, the Three Stooges, The Addams Family, and Jerry Lewis were not funny any longer while U.S. carpet-bombing devastated Vietnam. The tenderness of Lassie, the collie dog that the European post-Second World War generation grew up loving, was replaced by the horrors of Lazy Dog, a cluster bomb that was part of the 7.5 million tons of bombs that the United States dropped in Indochina (compared to 2.25 million tons it dropped in all the Second

World War). In a matter of one generation, the Star-Spangled Banner passed from being proudly flown on the balconies of grateful Western Europe, since the days of the liberation from Nazi Occupation and throughout the unfolding of the Marshall Plan, to be set on flames during 1968 by a new generation of Europeans in one city after the next.

In March that year, the Italian students had occupied all their universities but one demanding change within and beyond the campus. In Germany, students demanded curricular reform in the universities as well as a more democratic society and a public debate on the country's recent past domestically, and the betterment of life conditions in the Third World. In May 1968 the movement of students and workers' unions reached its peak, mobilizing 80,000 demonstrators in the capital Bonn against the German Emergency Acts. This law, aimed at limiting the basic constitutional rights in a state of emergency, was nevertheless passed by the Bundestag signaling the beginning of the end of the students' movement. But it was in France where May 1968 reached fever pitch with student demands triggering a major revolt in Western Europe. At first students demanded a say in the administration of their institutions and teaching curriculum. The police intervention at the Sorbonne University resulted in mass confrontations in which some 50,000 people took part in street fights against the riot police. Soon some ten million workers joined the students occupying factories, going on strike, and multiplying the number of protesters throughout the streets of Paris tenfold to some 400,000–500,000 strong. It took President Charles de Gaulle three weeks of large movements of troops, control over the media, and cooptation of several workers' unions to divide and rule.

By June the *Revolutionary Socialist Student Federation* was established in Great Britain. The iconic creative slogans of Paris' walls, such as *Pouvoir à l'Imagination* (*Power to the Imagination*) and *Soyez réalistes, demandez l'impossible* (*Be realistic, demand the impossible*), were supplanted by the systematization of a strategic agenda: "opposition to the control of education by the ruling class, support of all anti-imperialist struggles and solidarity with national liberation movements, opposition to racialism and immigration control, and workers' power as the only alternative to capitalism."[5] A series of school occupations ensued through July. In August, the Northern Ireland civil rights movement held its first civil rights march of very many to come. One of them, in Derry, in October was violently suppressed resulting in more than 100 injured. Another march in 1972, again in Derry, cost the lives of 14 protesters. This "Bloody Sunday" unleashed the violence of "the Troubles," the irregular low-level intensity war that lasted till 1998.[6]

Beyond the North Atlantic, major protest movements exploded throughout the world. In Japan, the 1968 revolt embodied a similar pattern and sequence as those described above. In June students barricaded the University of Tokyo and Nihon University (representing some 10% of Japan's total university student population) against police intrusion and established "All-Campus Joint Struggle Councils" (*Zenkyōtō*) demanding greater academic and personal freedom. The roots of the process are reminiscent of those of North Atlantic societies. First, economic growth brought a rise in college enrollments—from 8% of high school graduates in 1960 to 20% in 1968. This resulted in intense entrance examination competition and tensions over rising tuition. In short, it was a Japanese version of the ubiquitous protest against "Mass Production Education."[7] And yet again, as in other societies, what started up as demands for reforming academic institutions grew to encompass broader political goals such as protesting the United States–Japan Security Treaty, opposing the Vietnam War, and fomenting a social revolution. This radicalization sent students out beyond the campus. In Japan, *Zenkyōtō* collaborated with The Citizens League for Peace in Vietnam (*Beheiren*), with the campaign against the United States–Japan Security Treaty, and with workers' unions. But at the same time, this radicalization alienated many of the students involved in the movements, inhibited wider social support, and induced the government to forcefully suppress the protests. By 1969, students' activism began to wane and it was almost entirely suppressed by 1970.[8]

An opposite and extraordinary outcome in the entire global wave of 1968 protests was reached by students and workers in Pakistan, where they were able to topple Ayub Khan's dictatorial regime. Established in 1958 the regime was set to celebrate its "Decade of Development." That was a decade of more than 5% of average yearly GDP growth. However, this growth went hand in hand with wealth and income inequalities. Accordingly, the National Students Federation decided to celebrate Khan's "Decade of Decadence" instead. In October, protests broke out in Karachi, Rawalpindi, and Peshawar. A spiral of lethal repression by the security forces and growing mass mobilization by the students ensued. Citizens joined the protests, organizing boycotts refusing to pay for bus and railway fares. Soon after, a wave of strikes and marches had the economy paralyzed. Industrial workers organized *gheraos*, that is the encirclement of factories and mills. Confrontations spread to the rural areas, where peasants attacked and killed landowners, money lenders, cattle rustlers, and police officers. This violence led to further repression from the government. After imposing martial law on the country, Khan came under harsh criticism from intellectuals and journalists. Social mobilization kept growing from November 1968 to March 1969 with constant marches, sit-ins, strikes, publications, films, and protest songs. In contrast with all scenarios of mass protests above mentioned, these grassroot movements in Pakistan were harnessed by a strong oppositional political party, the Pakistani Peoples Party. This was a democratic socialist party established and led by Zulfikar Ali Bhutto, who became Pakistan's first elected prime minister in 1970 once mass revolt, atypically, resulted in regime change.[9]

Also in Mexico there was a crucially important party known by its oxymoronic name Institutional Revolutionary Party (*PRI*). However, far from being a party galvanizing and capitalizing on social protest it was instead the target of those. Having established itself in power since 1929, the *PRI* asserted itself further as a single party state. As in Pakistan, this authoritarian regime ruling on top of a socioeconomically polarized society was also geared for celebration. Aiming to put a nice international face on these unsettling realities of authoritarianism and flagrant inequality, Mexico's *PRI* was getting ready in October 1968 to host the Olympic Games. As in Pakistan at the same time, a large student movement came to the fore to protest and was violently suppressed by the state. On the eve of these games the security forces massacred hundreds of protesters (the estimated death toll ranges from 300 to 400) in the *Plaza de las Tres Culturas*, in Mexico City. A thorough repression of the opposition by the state, known as the Mexican Dirty War, ensued in which as many as 3,000 people were disappeared and extrajudicially executed.[10]

Another Latin American Dirty War—that in Argentina—resulted in some 30,000 people disappeared and extrajudicially executed. Its departure point was the popular protests starting on May 1969. The unfolding of the process seemed to entwine some of the aspects observed in the Pakistani and Mexican trajectories. As in Pakistan the protests gained momentum as time went by and gravitated toward a popular oppositional party and charismatic leader. Between 1969 and 1972 some 18 major outbreaks of popular protest across the country eventually lead to the collapse of the military dictatorship, an electoral process, and the return to power of a popular party and leader, in this case that of Perón, in exile since 1955 (see above pp. 185–188). However, this result was short-lived. In 1976 a new more extremist and determined military dictatorship took power again and, as in Mexico except tenfold larger, fostered a Dirty War that decimated civil society by carrying out a politicide (a systematic annihilation of political adversaries).[11] A military coup in 1977 in Pakistan brought back a military dictatorship to power there too, bringing these comparable trajectories full circle.

At the same time, the counter-hegemonic sphere also became a theater in which more freedoms were demanded and mass demonstrations, protests, and strikes were launched. On January 1968, the reformist leader Alexander Dubček was elected First Secretary of the Communist Party of Czechoslovakia. A series of reforms aiming to expand civil rights such as freedom of speech, press, and movement as well as a degree of democratization and partial decentralization of the economy ensued. That was just the beginning of the implementation of a political program named "socialism with a human face." The new freedoms opened the public sphere for the flow of opinions on how the economy should be run, what the domestic and foreign risks for liberalization are, and how the recent past of the country should be revisited with critical eyes. The Communist Party of Czechoslovakia, for its part, aimed to consolidate the direction of the reforms by gathering a Party Congress that would incorporate the reforms program into the party statutes and would elect a new Central Committee.[12]

The optimism, enthusiasm, and socio-cultural effervescence resulting from these reforms and its prospects soon expanded outside Czechoslovakia's borders. Throughout March 1968 a series of protests and strikes by students, intellectuals, and factory workers unfolded in all major Polish academic centers, cities, and towns. All of them were thoroughly repressed by the state by the end of April. In the wake of this suppression, anti-student and anti-intellectual campaigns were launched by the Polish United Workers' Party authoritarian regime. An antisemitic campaign was fostered too resulting in the expulsion of some 15,000 Polish Jews.[13] Albeit detached from Soviet tutelage, also in Communist Yugoslavia a wave of student protests broke out in June 1968 reaching multiple capital cities of the Yugoslav republics. As elsewhere, students demanded more freedom and a feasible economic path for their future in view of rising unemployment. A mixed bag of forceful suppression and cooptation brought also these protests to an end.[14] Yet, the most drastic and dramatic suppression in Eastern Europe occurred in Czechoslovakia. In

August some 200,000 troops and 2,000 tanks of the Warsaw Pact invaded the country bringing the "Prague Spring" and its reforms to its end by sheer intimidation.[15]

This global survey of mass protest, revolts, demands for reform or revolution during 1968, while touching upon several prominent epicenters in the hegemonic, counter-hegemonic, and Third World spheres, is by no means exhaustive; there were multiple additional sites of protest worldwide. However, it suffices to unequivocally conclude that 1968 was a year of global revolts. Most of these outbreaks were just as much the results of home-brewed conditions as they were catalyzed, triggered, and/or enhanced by developments elsewhere globally broadcast by the mass media. This atmosphere of a global revolt was present in all societies involved. For a new generation of "baby boomers" raised during the economic Long Boom and the "Great Compression" of inequality, expectations were on the rise. Expectations to have access to the comforts achieved by fully developed industrial economies or economies apparently in the process of becoming so. Expectations, aside from these material conditions, to further individual and collective freedoms and rights. Expectations that such a basket of material well-being, liberties, and rights would be granted regardless of race, ethnicity, gender, sexual preference, or location on the planet.

In the short run, domestically, the global revolt of '68 ended up being, for the most part, a political non-starter. In fact, a reactionary backlash sent right-wing rulers to power—by election in democracies, by appointment in dictatorships, or by sheer violence where new dictatorships appeared to be the response. More constructive was the impact of the global revolt in the international arena. The domestic threat that these revolts posed for governments across the Cold War divide had contributed to the superpowers' willingness to ease the tensions, or détente, between them. And so, starting in 1969 diplomatic efforts were made to de-escalate tensions, promote dialogue, and open negotiations over arms control. This yielded bilateral agreements between the United States and the Soviet Union in 1972 (SALT I) and 1979 (SALT II) and a multilateral declaration in 1975 (the Helsinki Accords) aiming to improve relations between the hegemonic and counter-hegemonic spheres. And yet, it is in the longer run where the global revolt of '68 made its strongest imprint. It turns out that the liberties and rights component of the '68 expectations would constitute a resilient political agenda for decades to come, particularly aiming to make these liberties and rights equitable to people worldwide regardless of race, ethnicity, gender, sexual preference, and country of origin. And that is what makes the 1968 global revolts relevant up to this very moment.[16]

1973, The Yom Kippur or Ramadan War

One of the exceptions to the 1968 global revolts was the Israeli society. There, the memories of the Second World War and the Holocaust were stronger than ever in the wake of Nazi criminal Adolf Eichmann's trial in Jerusalem in 1961. Moreover, the buildup of an Egyptian siege by a naval blockade of the Straits of Tiran, the mobilization of Egyptian forces along the border with Israel, the expulsion of the United Nations observers from Gaza and Sinai, and Nasser's charismatic invitation for a crushing war against Israel across the Arab world during 1967 generated an atmosphere of such deep fear that those memories and the perceived prospects of imminent annihilation became entwined. It was out of this dark mode that the Israeli society retorted in jubilation when in June 1967 the Israeli army defeated the armies of Egypt, Syria, and Jordan in a matter of six days. After such a collective consternation and mobilization, the only youthful marches in Israel in 1968 were the celebratory army parades. But the military's overwhelming victory of 1967 was followed by an Arab retribution in 1973.

On October 6, 1973 on Yom Kippur (Atonement Day), the holiest day in the Jewish calendar, the joint forces of Egypt and Syria attacked Israel by surprise. For three days the attackers had an upper hand moving into the Sinai Peninsula from west to east and through the Golan Heights from east to west. By the third day of the war with the Israeli army now fully mobilized the Arab double offensive was halted and pushed back. In a matter of a week Israeli artillery was shelling the outskirts of Damascus. A week later Israeli forces had crossed the Suez Canal moving south and west toward the city of Suez. On October 25, a ceasefire was jointly imposed by the United States and the Soviet Union, as suitable to a bi-polar world order. In the subsequent peace process (1977–1978) that normalized the relations between Egypt and Israel this war had its most momentous regional consequence. However, this regional war had far more consequential repercussions on the global scene.

With the outbreak of the war the U.S. States established an airbridge to supply the Israeli army to confront the Soviet-furnished armies of

Egypt and Syria. In response, the Arab members of OPEC (Organization of the Petroleum Exporting Countries) had the price of oil raised fourfold and declared an oil embargo against the United States and later extended to additional states (Canada, Japan, the Netherlands, Great Britain, Portugal, Rhodesia, and South Africa) triggering a global energy crisis, a global recession, a global debt crisis, and ultimately a makeover of the world economy and world societies.[17] The immediate effect of this first "oil shock" sent oil prices from US$3 to US$12 a barrel and destabilized the regular oil supply.[18] In the mid-run the repercussions of this energy crisis led to the end of the Long Boom, the Great Compression, global Keynesianism, and worldwide entwined nationalism and socialism. In short, the post-World War era, already challenged and shaken on social grounds by the 1968 global revolt, was pushed toward its end in 1973 on economic grounds.

The "Global Train" of the British hegemony ran on coal. The cars of the U.S. hegemony ran on oil. Immediately after the First World War American oil production accounted for almost two-thirds of the global production. By the end of the Second World War, the U.S. share had exceeded two-thirds and the United States met all domestic needs independently until 1955. Yet, from this peak American oil production went downhill in the subsequent two decades by which time its output had declined by 16.5% despite the constant increase in demand. The unsurprising result was an increasing dependence on foreign oil imports. Between 1970 and 1973 American imports of crude oil nearly doubled, reaching 6.2 million barrels per day in 1973. At the same time, the strongest economies of the hegemonic sphere in Europe and Japan were fully dependent on the Middle Eastern oil supply.[19]

It is against this backdrop that the Arab members of OPEC (Organization of the Petroleum Exporting Countries) turned to "oil weapon" by raising the oil price fourfold and declaring an oil embargo on countries supporting Israel. Expectedly, these economies sustained a double toll as a result of this "oil weapon" dual move. With a fourfold increase in oil price, prices for all goods and services relying in some way on oil—which means virtually everything—skyrocketed. If the rising prices brought high inflation, the shortages in oil, and its insecure supply reduced productivity. With that the entire economy and the prospects for economic growth slowed down.[20] It was then that the bright Long Boom reached a new gloomy destination: stagflation, that is, slow economic growth (stagnation) and high rate of price increase (inflation).

But economic crises bring winners as much as losers. The oil weapon did not prove to be effective, at least in the short run, because Israel prevailed in the October 1973 war and did not withdraw to the 1949 Armistice Line as demanded.[21] However, the oil weapon definitely proved to be highly profitable. For OPEC countries the export of oil started in October 1973 to generate many more dollars than before. The term coined for this additional revenue was "petrodollars." Regionally, this increased revenue allowed Saudi Arabia to fund groups and institutions aligned with its fundamentalist interpretation of Sunni Islam, known as Wahhabism. This funding allowed for the proliferation of clerics and religious schools that nurtured cohorts of believers ready to fight nonbelievers and heretics. The repercussions of this process were to become apparent in the ensuing decades on a global scale.[22]

First, however, these petrodollars were quick to take the world, particularly the Third World, by storm in their chase for profitable investment outlets. From 1974 to 1981 OPEC members accumulated US$450 billion petrodollars. A portion of them were invested in U.S. Treasury securities and other financial markets of the strong economies of the hegemonic sphere. However, due to the recession in these economies, many of the petrodollars flowed through the U.S. and European commercial banks as loans to Third World countries.[23] Third World countries were in desperate need of petrodollar-generated loans to finance their imports of ... oil! Moreover, they were encouraged to take low interest rate loans to foster monumental infrastructural projects. Low interest rate ... but not *fixed* interest rate. When the U.S. Federal Reserve reversed its policy of low interest rates in 1979, Third World economies became overwhelmed by foreign debt. It is this sequence of moves that marks the beginning of the indebtedness crisis to which Third World countries would be subject for decades to come. Any debt relief program extended by the international financial institutions, the World Bank and the IMF, would come with strings attached. Namely, any traces of entwined nationalism and socialism must be eliminated. In this way, this economic crisis brought additional unexpected losers as much as winners.

Another unexpected winner of the energy crisis was the Soviet Union and its counter-hegemonic sphere as the high oil prices brought to its stagnated economy a new lease on life. As the Soviet economy faltered throughout the 1960s and early 1970s with lack of flexibility to harness the new technological breakthroughs, it became more and more dependent on the extraction and export of oil and gas. As the price of those soared during the energy crisis the Soviet economy, along with those of the other oil exporting countries, seemed to be booming. Oil exports jumped from 111 million tons on the eve of the crisis to 183 million by the end of the decade. The revenues from oil and gas hiked from under 10 billion (in 2011 U.S. dollars) to 300 and 400 billion, correspondingly, in less than a decade.[24] With that, salaries and hence consumption were boosted. Western imports arrived to meet the rising demands for car manufacturing technologies, synthetic fiber, and additional consumer goods. The Soviet Union became more actively engaged in foreign trade with countries from the hegemonic sphere, particularly West Germany as a consumer of natural gas and Japan as a consumer of oil. At the same time, the Soviet grip on its counter-hegemonic sphere was tightened, this time in contrast to 1968, not by its rolling tanks but by tankers with subsidized fuel.

Subsidized fuel allowed the economies of the Eastern Bloc to keep running. Subsidizing fuel enabled the Soviet Union to sustain its control on them. Exporting oil pulled the Soviet Union out of its long recession, boosting its foreign trade and domestic consumption. As for trade, one of the import items in demand by the Soviet Union was animal feedstock. As for consumption, this specific import is directly associated with the happy days of state-run shops with plentiful sausage products at subsidized prices. Those were the days of the energy crisis as experienced in the Soviet Union, in the short run. In the longer run, oil exporting dependency made for the demise of the Soviet Union. The end of the energy export bonanza in the 1980s resulted not only in depleting state-run shops but also in grinding down the economies of the Eastern Bloc and ultimately bringing about the collapse of the Soviet Union.[25]

And so, throughout the three worlds that inhabited the Cold War era, the oil shock of 1973 was highly impactful. It generated stagflation in the hegemonic sphere, promoted indebtedness throughout the Third World, and granted a pyrrhic victory to the counter-hegemon. Its effects were further compounded by a second oil shock in 1979. This time the price of crude oil more than doubled in the course of one year as a result of a decrease in the oil output. The reason: the Islamic Revolution in Iran (1978–1979). Since 1905, alongside the other gunpowder empires, the Persian society had been striving to bring its autocratic rule to an end. The first attempt ended in 1908 by the actions of the autocratic ruler, Mohammad Ali Shah, backed by the Russian and British empires. Autocracy was further rooted in the wake of Reza Khan's military coup in 1921 that enthroned the Pahlavi dynasty for the next almost six decades. Halfway through this period a popular prime minister, Mohammad Mosaddegh, was deposed in 1953 by the Shah, Mohammad Reza Shah Pahlavi, backed by the United States and Great Britain (see above, p. 194). All in all, except for these frights, Iran remained a stable country under the thumb of an autocrat backed by the world hegemons that extracted its oil. But then, in February 1979, after more than a year of marches, demonstrations, strikes, and protests, millions gathered in the streets of Tehran to greet Ayatollah Khomeini, an expert (*Mujtahid*) in Muslim Law (*Sharia*) exiled for more than 14 years. In no time, and after armed street fights, a theocratic republican constitution was approved, and Iran became an Islamic Republic.

In a matter of weeks, the hegemonic sphere had lost an ally and its economy a vital oil supplier.[26] This represented a momentous political change, in which the pro-hegemonic authoritarian regime of the Iranian Shah was replaced by an anti-hegemonic party state. The U.S. support of the Iraqi dictator Saddam Hussein in his war against the Islamic Republic (1980–1988) proved futile after almost eight years of stalemate, attrition, and hundreds of thousands of deaths.[27]

In tandem with the Islamic Revolution in Iran another fundamental political transformation was unfolding in Communist China during the very same days of 1978–1979. In this case, however, the transformation worked the other way around. A long-standing anti-hegemonic party state in China, although remaining in power, was about to change its nature into a pro-hegemonic authoritarian regime.

1978, DENG XIAOPING MEANS "SOCIALISM WITH CHINESE CHARACTERISTICS"

Another exception to the 1968 global revolts was the Chinese society but for very different reasons than in Israel. In this case it was because the students' mass movement known as the "Red Guards" had already peaked in 1966 and throughout 1967 was thoroughly suppressed by the Chinese army, reaching the point of marginalization by the summer of 1968. Put differently, the students' mass movement in China preceded, announced, and for many also inspired what was about to come during the global revolt of 1968. In that, the relationship between the Chinese Cultural Revolution of 1966—and the key role of students in it—and the global revolt of 1968 was an astonishing case of becoming lost in translation. At core the "Red Guards" was a students' mass movement instrumented from above by Mao Zedong in order to purge the Chinese Communist Party of its senior members as well as workers, military, professionals—all suspected of "revisionism," i.e., not following the party line according to Mao—and ethnic minorities (see above, p. 182). For the uncritical eyes of students across the world, the televised images of the "Red Guards" marches, destructive actions, and violent attacks represented a revolt against the institutionalized authority of government officials, university professors, and more broadly of an older conservative generation that harbored the "Four Olds" (old customs, old culture, old habits, and old ideas). As they saw it, these older generations urgently needed to be replaced by a new generation ready to revolutionize society and culture. By the time Mao reaped the benefits of the purges and the terrorizing of society at large, yet a moment before China descended into absolute chaos, the "Red Guards" were forcefully suppressed. By then, however, a romanticized image of them became ingrained in the minds of many students worldwide who aspired to bring "imagination to power."[28]

One of these purged "revisionists" was Deng Xiaoping, a revolutionary veteran who participated in the Long March (1934–1935), served as Secretary-General of the Communist Party throughout the 1950s, and played a key role in trying to deal with the catastrophic consequences of Mao's Great Leap Forward (1957–1960, see above p. 182). That last deed was what made him a deserving target for the "Red Guards." He was sent to the Xinjian County Tractor Factory in rural Jiangxi province to work as a regular worker. In 1974, Deng was rehabilitated by Premier Zhou Enlai, who appointed him as First Vice-Premier. With Enlai's death in January 1976, however, Deng was removed from his position again. His second comeback took place in the wake of Mao's death (September 1976) in July 1977, this time to become the leader of the People's Republic of China. In December 1978, during the Third Plenum of the 11th Central Committee Congress of the Communist Party of China, Deng took the reins of power. Soon, the reasons for his previous constant suppression by the party's old guard became apparent as Deng Xiaoping was headed toward a total makeover of Communist China.

If the 1968 global revolt was made famous by its phrases and slogans (see above p. 219), Deng Xiaoping's reforms were no less so: "*Kai fang!*" ("open up!"), "A basic contradiction between socialism and the market economy does not exist,"[29] "It doesn't matter if the cat is black or white as long as it catches mice,"[30] "Let some people get rich first,"[31] "To get rich is glorious!"[32] All of them were very indicative of what became to be known as "Deng Xiaoping Theory"—self-described as a continuation, not a rejection, of "Mao Zedong Thought"—and of Deng Xiaoping's reforms in practice, a "Reform [that] is China's second revolution."

"*Kai fang*!" ("open up!") sounds self-explanatory. An enclosed autarkic economy was now to be opened up to the world economy for investment, trade, and technological transfers. That move was made possible because "a basic contradiction between socialism and the market economy does not exist." In practice, this meant that the contradiction was averted at first because the Chinese market economy opening up to the world was circumscribed to specific locations, the so-called "special zones." In 1979, the first four special zones were established in four cities in the Guangdong and Fujian provinces. Fourteen additional coastal cities were opened up as special economic zones in 1984. In 1988 Hainan Island became the biggest special economic zone while the existing ones were enlarged. This gradual process of expanding into additional regions never stopped unfolding. It has only accelerated, transforming China into a country in which there is nothing special about free trade. As for the potential contradiction, who would argue against the tremendous economic success of almost 10% GDP growth between 1979 and 2010? "It doesn't matter if the cat is black or white as long as it catches mice." That is, who cares if it's communism or capitalism as long as it works?[33]

"Some people [were allowed to] get rich first" was true not only in the special economic zones but also in the countryside. The rural system of communes was gradually dismantled and the farmers obtained freedom to manage the land and sell their products on the market. Agricultural output increased and farmers became rich enough to stimulate industrial development through their demand for manufactured products. Subsequently, in the late 1980s state-owned industry started undergoing a process of privatization. First, the companies were restructured into joint stock corporations. Then, large portions of the shares were granted to the companies' managers. Finally, the workers were compelled to sell their few shares. "To get rich is glorious!"[34]

Such momentous transformations completely reshaped China. Moreover, the opening and growth of the Chinese economy coincided with stagflation in the hegemonic sphere, indebtedness throughout the Third World, and the last lease on life of the counter-hegemonic sphere. All of these elements were about to fall into place, causing a momentous trans-formation that completely reshaped the world. But for that to happen, some additional crucial developments were required.

1982, MALVINAS/FALKLAND ISLANDS WAR

The Argentinean society was no exception to the 1968 global revolt, even if social protests didn't break out until 1969. A long-lasting stalemate between revolutionary and reformist forces on one hand and conservative and reactionary forces on the other ended up in the establishment of a murderous military dictatorship in 1976. By 1982, and amidst economic crisis, the military junta was totally discredited. In a move to gain legiti-macy the generals attempted to mimic an anti-hegemonic party state by confronting a hegemonic power, thus aiming to mobilize society from within. On April 2, 1982 an Argentinean amphibious landing took posses-sion of the Malvinas/Falkland Islands. The intended effect was achieved. By exploiting the long-lasting grievance caused by Britain's usurpation of Argentinean sovereignty over the islands (see above, p. 126), the dicta-torship managed to mobilize the public opinion in its favor. But the effect was short-lived. By April 5 a British naval task force was charged by Prime Minister Margaret Thatcher with retaking the islands. On May 2 the "Iron Lady" gave the green light to torpedoing the cruiser ARA General Belgrano, sinking the ship and, in the process, also the nego-tiations to avert a war. On May 1 the British assault on the islands began from the air and sea. By June 14 the Malvinas/Falkland War was over, with the islands back in the possession of Britain.[35] Soon after, mass protests broke out in Buenos Aires. In a matter of days, the mili-tary regime in Argentina collapsed. In so doing it signaled the arrival of Third Wave Democracy—initiated in the Mediterranean basin (Portugal, 1974; Greece, 1974; and Spain, 1977; see above and below, pp. 11–12, 264–266)—in Latin America.

No less consequential were the political repercussions in Great Britain. The Iron Lady owed her nickname not to her determination in the South Atlantic conflict but to her domestic policies. Aiming to tackle an inflation peaking at 27% before her appointment in 1979, Thatcher implemented a monetarist policy, slowing the money supply by increasing interest rates and by reducing expenses on social services such as housing and educa-tion. These monetarist policies, which hampered the less privileged the most, could be and have been justified as a painful but necessary cure for the inflationary disease. However, such an argument barely could hold when it came to her generous fiscal policy favoring the wealthy at the expense of the rest of society. The Iron Lady launched a series of regressive tax reforms that fell off significantly on the tax share of the upper income earners and burdened the population at large with higher and new taxes, such as the increase in the sales tax and the per-head "poll tax," respectively.

If the ultimate goals of the monetary policies were somewhat hidden in the dark, the fiscal policies shed a clear light on them. Thatcher's administration aimed to remove the social protections provided by global Keynesianism throughout the welfare state and state intervention in the economy. It is in this regard that her legacy is the strongest: the state-owned, that is the publicly funded, assets were divested in one of two ways. Whatever was a clearly worthy asset, such as the National Freight Corporation, British Aerospace, British Rail, Associated British Ports, Rolls Royce Aircraft Engines, British Airports Authority, British Petroleum, British Steel, and several water, power, communications, cable, and wireless utilities, was sold to private investors and corporations at substantially reduced prices. Whatever was deemed to be a liability more than an asset—coal pits, mines, and manufacturing plants—was closed down.

The application of some of these policies had managed, by 1981, to decrease inflation to around 10%, raise unemployment to over 3 million people for the first time since the Global Depression of the 1930s, and drop Thatcher's own rate of popular approval to 23%, the lowest recorded rate for any previous prime minister in Great Britain. And in response to that, the Iron Lady declared: "To those waiting with bated breath for that favorite media catchphrase, the U-turn [namely, reversing the above-listed policies], I have only one thing to say: You turn if you want to. The lady's not for turning." And, indeed, as May 68 and Deng Xiaoping before her, Margaret Thatcher was notorious for her sayings. They were different from the vagaries of the French May proverbs but similar to Deng Xiaoping's assertions in being closely entwined with concrete policies. For example, her tax cuts for the wealthy were encapsulated by the phrase "…The larger the slice taken by government, the smaller the cake available for everyone." With regard to the divestment of social expenses and dismantling of the welfare state she coined the phrase "The problem with socialism is that you eventually run out of other people's money."

And for the hollowing out of the assets accumulated by the intergenerational work of a whole society through its privatization as well as the frontal charge against the social support provided by state-based institutions such as schools, universities, hospitals, utilities, and pensions, she simply said: "There is no such thing as society: there are individual men and women, and there are families." By 1982 this very determined transformative agenda led to a very low rate of popular approval for Thatcher. She declared, "You may have to fight a battle more than once to win it." In her case, the path to prevailing in her domestic battle passed through her military victory in the Malvinas/Falkland Islands.

At the sound of "God Save the Queen" and "Rule Britannia, Britannia rule the waves!" the return of the triumphant naval task force to the British ports filled the hearts of the Britons with the jingoism of past glories after having barely defeated an army dedicated to the suppression of its own citizenry. Under the wings of this triumphalist atmosphere the Conservative Party under Thatcher's leadership won the 1983 elections in the most decisive electoral victory since 1945 and with the Labor Party having its worst electoral performance since 1918. Thus bolstered, the Iron Lady was ready to battle over her economic agenda once more and win. "We had to fight the enemy without in the Falklands. We always have to be aware of the enemy within, which is much more difficult to fight and more dangerous to liberty," she declared in a 1984 speech.[36] By 1985, she had 25 unprofitable coal mines closed, paving the way for the closure of 150 mines throughout the subsequent decade.[37] The privatized industries started showing improvements in performance.[38] Inflation receded from its 27% peak in 1979 to a mere 4% by 1987, the early 1980s recession was replaced by an economic growth above an annual 4% on average, and, consequently, unemployment was more than cut in half by 1989, reaching 1.6%.[39] As the 1980s were coming to a close this new economic phase in the history of the British economy was dubbed the "British economic miracle."

The "Falkland spirit," as she liked to refer to it, allowed Thatcher to be reelected not only once but twice (in 1987 she was elected for the third time). In this longer time span her originally widely repudiated policies ended up either leading to or coinciding with (that is a matter of controversy[40]) an economic boom. In this fashion her policies, or Thatcherism, consisting of regressive tax cuts, divestment of social services, deregulation, privatization, and flexibilization of labor markets became inspirational on a global scale, representing the alternative economic model to both global Keynesianism and soon after even to Soviet Communism.

1985, Gorbachev Means Glasnost and Perestroika

Neither was the Soviet society exempt from the 1968 global revolt. Its effects permeated through the suppression of Prague's Spring and the resulting Brezhnev's Doctrine. This doctrine articulated a determined policy geared toward the forceful intervention in any Communist regime within the counter-hegemonic sphere whenever any attempts of reforming, opening up, or liberalizing occurs, to ensure that a country once socialist always remains socialist. This was the last move toward ossification by a conservative leadership willing to undo the short-lived penchant for reform under Nikita Khrushchev (see above, pp. 182, 241). An era of stagnation ensued, the "Brezhnevian Stagnation," characterized by a failing economy unable to address the mounting needs for consuming goods (e.g., food, clothing, housing), an asphyxiating censorship that clamped down on creativity, and a nostalgia for the atrocious Stalinist era.

This lamentable condition was subsequently compounded by the descent of the Soviet regime into a gerontocracy, the rule of the elderly, i.e., an oligarchic rule by leaders older than most of the adult population. Leonid Brezhnev was 58 years old when he became General Secretary of the Communist Party of the Soviet Union in 1964 and ruled until his death aged 75, even though his deteriorated health precluded him from effectively managing his duties since 1973. After his death in 1982, his successor Yuri Andropov, former KGB chairman, was appointed at the age of 68 and lasted a bit more than one year in power before dying. His successor, Konstantin Chernenko, was 73 years old when he reached power and ruled during the last 13 months of his life. At this point it became evident that stagnation and gerontocracy were spiraling the Soviet Union down extremely fast. A much-needed alternative finally arrived in 1985, represented by the appointment of a young figure of the Communist Party to the highest office and the resulting disruption of the conservative approach responsible for the stagnation.

The 53 years young appointee was Mikhail Gorbachev, a full member of the Soviet Communist Party since 1952. Back then, as a student at the law school of Moscow State University, Gorbachev was close friends with

Zdeněk Mlynář. The two were committed Marxist-Leninists who grew increasingly concerned about the Stalinist regime. They had the opportunity to enthusiastically support a series of political and economic reforms during the so-called Khrushchev Thaw (see above, pp. 182, 241). But they also got to witness how these reforms cost Khrushchev his removal from power by the party hardliners. In 1968, Zdeněk Mlynář would become the secretary of the Czechoslovak Communist Party during the Prague Spring and authored *Toward a Democratic Political Organization of Society*, a political manifesto that championed the need for combined political and economic reforms.[41] In 1985, Gorbachev, by then a full member of the Central Committee of the Soviet Communist Party, set course to replace gerontocracy and stagnation with *glasnost* and *perestroika*.[42]

Glasnost—literally meaning openness and transparency—referred to the need for an honest open conversation about the bleak situation of the Soviet Union by bringing to the table the relevant issues and problems as well as the plausible prospective solutions. Such a proposition entailed the possibility of a degree of criticism of the state leadership, policies, and institutions. Life experience, and Khrushchev's failure, had taught Gorbachev that reforms would encounter the resistance of the party officials. Hence, with *glasnost* he aimed to break through the party encirclement by winning over the Soviet civil society. However, it was quite unclear how much freedom of opinion, speech, and mass communication would be actually granted in a society that has never had a real taste of that. The result of this tension between possibilities and constraints made for a very ambiguous situation that was difficult to navigate.[43]

Perestroika—literally meaning restructuring—referred to the need to reshape and adjust the economic system to better meet the needs of the population. The idea was to allow some wiggle room for a market to develop amidst the Soviet command economy. Such an entwinement of two economic principles would not be new to the Soviet system given the former experience with Lenin's New Economic Policy (see above, pp. 97–98). Indeed, just as did the epoch-making leaders above-mentioned, Gorbachev had his maxims too. A memorable one says: "The market came with the dawn of civilization and it is not an invention of capitalism. [...] If it leads to improving the well-being of the people there is no contradiction with socialism."[44]

Starting in 1987, a new law—the Law on State Enterprise—allowed state companies, provided that they had fulfilled the state orders first, to determine output levels based on demand from consumers and other enterprises. Conversely, this allowance came with the condition of self-sustainability: each state company became accountable for its own balance of revenues and expenses without state intervention filling in the negative balances of unprofitable companies. An additional couple of tools were provided to the state companies to make their balances positive: they gained freedom to trade with foreign partners and could establish joint ventures with foreign investors. Finally, the companies were no longer to be directed by state officials but instead by company workers elected by their peers. A further step was taken a year later when a new law on cooperatives allowed the establishment of private businesses in the manufacturing, foreign trade, and services sectors. Sixty years since the abolition of the New Economic Policy by Stalin and 30 years since the more moderate reforms by Khrushchev, private property made its way back to the Soviet Union. At the same time, these freedoms of enterprise also weakened the party's absolute control of the economy.

For decades, Stalinist Soviet Union and Maoist China had undergone parallel trajectories, except 20–30 years apart. Both moved from agricultural collectivization (1928 in USSR/1947 in China) to commanded industrialization (1928 in USSR/1958 in China); from catastrophic famines as a result (1933 in USSR/1959–1961 in China) to mass repression as a preventive measure to challenges to the leadership (1936–1938 in USSR/1966–1968 in China); and from the passing of the tyrants (1953 in USSR/1976 in China) to the introduction of reforms by the successors (1956 in USSR/1979 in China). But then, reforms in the Soviet Union encountered an unsurmountable resistance that sent the country into 25 years of deep freeze (see above, p. 234). Hence, when Gorbachev defrosted stagnation the parallel trajectories of the Soviet Union and China resumed, this time synchronously.

Deng Xiaoping's economic reforms in China were wholehearted, fully opening the economy to foreign investment and trade from without and to the emergence of a capitalist class from within. Gorbachev's *perestroika* was partial, gradual, wary, and hesitant: foreign investment and trade were far more regulated and there was no privatization process leading to the emergence of a domestic capitalist class. The *perestroika* ended up being more instrumental in disrupting the state command economy than in providing a functioning alternative. In China, economic growth skyrocketed to a sustained average of 9.5% GDP yearly growth, whereas in the Soviet Union the GDP yearly growth during the *perestroika* days amounted to −1.3%.[45] Similarly hesitant was the ambivalent *glasnost*. In China, by contrast, policies in this regard were clear-cut. Liberalizing political reforms simply did not exist. And that is what made Gorbachev so popular among Chinese students.

1989, A GLOBAL REVOLUTION

Twenty years had passed by then since the 1968 global revolt and the Prague Spring. In January 1989 Czech activists gathered to commemorate the 20th anniversary of the death of Jan Palach, a student who had immolated himself as his ultimate protest against the suppression of the Prague Spring. The memorial escalated very quickly into a series of demonstrations against the Communist regime. The "Palach Week" was forcefully suppressed by the armed forces. In hindsight, however, this 20th anniversary commemoration of an incident of the 1968 global revolt signaled the outbreak of a global revolution in 1989.

One signal is that, 20 years after the Prague Spring, the new leader of the Soviet Union clearly implied, at the United Nations General Assembly, that the Brezhnev Doctrine was over by announcing a substantial reduction in Soviet troops throughout Eastern Europe. Another is that instead of military support, what Gorbachev offered his allies was *glasnost* and *perestroika*. Although neither of these propositions looked very appealing to the Communist dictators, both resonated very well at the grassroots level.

That was clearly the case for the Polish workers organized around their union Solidarity despite being suppressed since 1981 (see above, p. 177). In the fall of 1988, they launched a prolonged strike that came to an end only in early April 1989 after two months of negotiations. These negotiations resulted not only in some compromises on the economic demands but most crucially in the legalization of Solidarity and the announcement of future semi-open elections. This breakthrough for a peacefully negotiated transition from Communist authoritarianism to democracy would become the round table model later applied in Hungary and Bulgaria. But first, on June 4, 1989 Solidarity overwhelmingly won those elections signaling a pivotal shift in Polish history. Soon after the country transitioned into a short-lived power-sharing arrangement between Solidarity and the Communist Party, paving the way to Solidarity's full command of the Polish government by August.

This exact same time window of mid-April to June 4, 1989 encompassed the dramatic failed attempt of Chinese students to bring about change in their country. As in 1968, students were at the forefront of the protests driven by a comparable blend of ideology and constraints. On the ideological side, it seemed that Deng Xiaoping had shown the way to students and intellectuals: "*Kai fang*!" ("open up!"). If that was true for the economy that should be also true for politics and society. If the command economy was to blame for China's disastrous Great Leap Forward and subsequent poverty and underdevelopment, its twin, a command political regime, should be the culprit for China's disastrous Cultural Revolution and its legacy of intellectual suppression and scientific stagnation. Throughout university campuses around the country the ideas of freedoms, human rights, and democracy became widespread, led by itinerant professors and discussed by locally grown study groups. "Open up!" suddenly was turned into "Open up in all directions!".

Already in 1986, this undercurrent had grown sufficiently to openly start calling for political reforms in Hefei, Beijing, Shanghai, Nanjing, and another 11 cities across 150 university campuses (out of 1,016). But these early expressions of discontent were also rooted in concrete constraints, concerns, and grievances, in addition to the abstract values and ideals. The students were anxious about their professional and occupational futures. In a privatized economy companies no longer needed to employ students assigned by the state after graduation. The job market offered only limited options for students, particularly for those specializing in the humanities and social sciences. And for whatever opportunities that existed, the impression was that a political system tainted with nepotism, favoritism, corruption, and cronyism siphoned those off for the insiders and blocked access for all others.[46]

Hu Yaobang, the General Secretary of the Communist Party in 1986, let the demonstrations wind down on their own, which happened in less than a month (12/1986–1/1987). Yet, the discontent among the Party leadership about Hu Yaobang's soft approach toward the students' protests costed him his position. The students, however, did not forget Hu Yaobang's patience and moderation and were appalled by his dismissal, which they came to believe two years later was the cause of his sudden death on April 15, 1989. With the spread of this news students started to gather in large numbers to honor his memory and asked to revive his legacy. In a matter of days, the calls shifted toward the demand of fundamental political reforms: freedoms, rights, democracy. The Communist regime's response was hesitant at first, shifting from antagonizing to conciliatory; perhaps Hu Yaobang's "wind down on their own" approach was right after all? Indeed, protests were dying out as April 1989 reached its end.[47]

By mid-May, however, the protests gained a new lease on life as a very high-stakes state visit was on the agenda. The Soviet premier was about to visit after 30 years of the Sino-Soviet split. The world attention was concentrated on this summit, which did not escape the attention of the students' movements. After all, the official guest was no less that the hero of glasnost and perestroika! So, the students stayed put at the very center of the welcoming ceremony location, Tiananmen Square, waiting for him and the world press with a hunger strike. By then, the protests had also expanded throughout the country to some 400 cities. Now in view of the mounting challenge the regime came to react drastically by declaring martial law and mobilizing some 300,000 soldiers toward Beijing. After a couple of weeks in which the protesters blocked the army vehicles from accessing the city, Deng Xiaoping and the party leadership decided to terminate the protests.[48] During the night of June 4, the People's Liberation Army rolled its tanks toward Tiananmen Square and opened fire on the protesters. The Tiananmen Square Protests soon became the Tiananmen Square Crackdown and ended up as the Tiananmen Square Massacre, with an estimated toll ranging from 1,000 to 10,000 deaths and 40,000 injured.[49] The Goddess of Democracy and Freedom, a ten meter tall statute reminiscent of the American Statute of Liberty, was destroyed, aptly symbolizing the end of the hopes for democracy and freedom in Communist China.[50]

This resounding suppression in China did not bring the 1989 global revolution to a stop, even if a Tiananmen Square-style massacre was considered by dictators and feared by the citizenry.[51] Already by June, the negotiated transition to democracy in Hungary allowed for a massively attended and solemn funeral in Budapest's largest square for Imre Nagy, the 1956 Hungarian prime minister hanged for treason. On October 23, 1989, on the 33rd anniversary of the 1956 Hungarian Revolution, the Communist regime was formally abolished.

In the meantime, the dismantling of the border fence between Hungary and Austria allowed some 30,000 East Germans to escape to the West via Hungary. By early September, demonstrations started rolling in the city of Leipzig in ever-growing numbers. reaching some

120,000 people by mid-October and 300,000 after the deposition of the General Secretary of the Socialist Unity Party that had ruled the German Democratic Republic. When demonstrations reached Berlin on November 4, half a million people gathered in Alexanderplatz. Five days later East Berliners were crossing toward the Western half of the city via existing border points as well as through improvised new ones opened with hammers and chisels. The Berlin Wall had collapsed. In less than a year Germany was reunified. Bringing 1989 full circle, demonstrations against the Communist regime were once again forcefully suppressed by the armed forces in Prague in mid-November.

Except that the world had now changed. The snowball of demonstrations kept rolling this time during the second half of the month bringing 200,000, then 500,000, then 800,000 protesters to Letná Square. Bringing the 1968 Prague Spring full circle, Alexander Dubček, the deposed First Secretary of the Communist Party, was elected speaker of the federal parliament.

The 1989 global revolution was powerfully and rapidly underway to consummation. Its next stations were Bulgaria and Romania during December 1989, Mongolia in 1990, Yugoslavia started breaking apart in 1991, and the end of the Communist regime in Albania in 1992.

And yet, its definitive instance was the collapse of the Soviet Union. At first the union started to unravel at its fringes. The Baltic republics—Lithuania, Estonia, and Latvia—and Armenia declared independence in 1991. Next the union imploded at its very center. In view of growing separatism, Gorbachev envisioned a new union treaty that would redefine the Soviet Union as a federation of independent states with a common president, foreign policy, and military. As the signing of such a treaty became imminent, the conservative leadership attempted a coup d'état in August 1991 that failed after three days due to popular opposition. Gorbachev's position, though, became unsustainable. The separatist unraveling and the implosion at the center continued spiraling for four additional months. More and more republics asserted their independence. Less and less power remained in the hands of Soviet institutions. With whatever little power was left, on December 26, 1991, the Union's Supreme Soviet voted itself and the Soviet Union out of existence. With that, the 1989 global revolution was consummated[52] (Table 6.1).

"'68–'89," 1968 and 1989 were the two crucial years in the dismantling of the post-Second World War global order that marked the opening and close of that process. One stark contrast between the two is that

Table 6.1 Russia's and China's trajectories compared—Phase three (in **Bold**: Commonalities; in *Italics*: Singularities)

Russia	China
Both Communist Regimes aiming for reforms	
Their shared sequence starts with a twenty-five years gap based on the date of initiation of reforms, 1956 vs. 1980. Twenty years of backlash and stagnation in the USSR led to the almost full synchronization of the sequences	
(see above, Table 5.1:Russia's and China's trajectories compared—Phase one)	
Khruschev's attempts at reforms (1956–64) backlashed into "Brezhnevian Stagnation," until the rise of Gorbachev (1985) and his Glasnost and Perestroika. Partial and hesitant economic reforms	*In 1980, Deng Xiaoping launches his economic reforms unfolding since in a full fledge way, making China a state capitalist economy. No reforms liberalization comparable to Glasnost occurred*
Social response to reforms	
Top-down attempt to remove Gorbachev from power to back pedal his liberalizing reforms	*Grass roots movements demand political liberalization*
Communist Regimes' dealing with responses	
The backlash against Gorbachev's reforms failed	*Brutal repression in Tiananmen Square (1989)*
Reforms' results	
End of Communist Regime, USSR, and Eastern	*Communist Party perpetuated in power Block*

the first was a global revolt, while the second was a global revolution. One prominent similarity is their global scope and impact, even though that global reach unfolded differently. Most of the 1968 revolts broke out in response to local conditions throughout the hegemonic, counter-hegemonic, and Third World spheres. Some of these conditions were shared—the blend of grievances and expectations of the best-nurtured generation—while the global mass media contributed to making local outbreaks contagious elsewhere. However, the revolutions of 1989 occurred in the counter-hegemonic sphere alone, the local conditions were shared only in its perimeter and the media's contagious effect also remained circumscribed.

And yet, the impact of these 1989 revolutions seemingly confined to the counter-hegemonic sphere actually was global. For one, there was a spillover effect into Communist regimes elsewhere in Africa, Asia, and Latin America. Moreover, the collapse of the Soviet Union not only signaled the demise of communism specifically as a type of political regime but also of the anti-hegemonic party state more broadly. The Soviet

Union was the first state in which this political strategy of mobilization from within and confrontation from without, guided by a political party and its collectivist ideology, was implemented in 1917. Since then, the strategy had become a global trend reaching its peak during the post-Second World War world order (see above pp. 201–202). Hence, the demise of the Soviet Union also represented the swan song for the anti-hegemonic party states worldwide.

Even more fundamentally, the global reach of the 1989 revolutions brought to a close the post-Second World War world order, which rested on the Cold War tension. A new world order was ready to emerge.

1991, Hegemony and Globalization Reconciled

The final demise of the Soviet Union and its counter-hegemonic sphere signaled the end of the Cold War. However, it was the intensification of the Cold War that hastened the Soviet Union toward its demise. 1989 was also the year in which the Soviet invasion of Afghanistan came to an end after almost a decade of war. That was not a focused and short military intervention, as Brezhnev naively expected by deploying his standard "once socialist, always socialist" doctrine (Afghanistan had been under the rule of the Communist Party since 1978). Instead, the intervention brought the détente to an end and gradually turned out to be a protracted and weakening by proxy war in which the United States—along with some of its allies, crucially Saudi Arabia and Pakistan—found the opportunity to retribute in kind with an economic drain, politically demoralizing reverse, and military resounding defeat for the effective Soviet support of North Vietnam a decade earlier.[53] The war in Afghanistan was the linchpin of the Cold War by proxy wars during the 1980s, a decade prominent for its multiple and global reaching ongoing proxy wars throughout the Third World: in Ethiopia–Eritrea, Angola, and Mozambique; in Thailand-Laos, East Timor, and Yemen; and in Nicaragua, El Salvador, and Guatemala, to name several. And yet, as resource-draining as the 1980s proxy wars were, they were just one front in the new military offensive launched by the world hegemon that brought economic attrition to the counter-hegemon to an entirely new level.

Under his Rollback Doctrine, U.S. President Ronald Reagan adopted the strategy of prompting the Soviet Union military production up to its breakpoint.[54] It was to that end that not only the above-mentioned proxy wars were escalated, but also U.S. missiles Pershing II pointed at the

Soviet Union were deployed in Western Europe, conventional and nuclear arms were stockpiled, and massive military exercises were performed in multiple scenarios. This included the simulation of a nuclear attack, "Able Archer 83," arguably the closest the world came to nuclear war since the Cuban missile crisis in 1962.[55] Also in 1983, Reagan initiated a new program called the Strategic Defense Initiative (SDI). Its goal was to end the MAD (mutually assured destruction) situation that governed the strategic relations between the two superpowers. In order to break this stalemate, the program aimed to develop the capability of intercepting and disrupting any intercontinental ballistic missiles that the Soviet Union could launch while they were still flying high above the planet. Attaining such capability would entail the deployment on the ground and in outer space of weaponry-firing nuclear X-ray lasers, subatomic particle beams, and projectiles, all under the central control of a supercomputer system. Aptly, the program was dubbed "Star Wars."

As soon as the plan was announced, the Soviet leadership accused the United States of aiming to disrupt the MAD situation by denying the Soviet Union the possibility of retaliating against an American first strike (or striking first). Gorbachev's level of concern with this program and the tremendous burden that the military budget imposed on the Soviet economy came to the fore during the Reykjavík Summit in 1986. In that summit Gorbachev went so far as to propose banning all nuclear weapons within a decade on the condition that SDI would be confined to laboratory research only during that time. Reagan did not concede, and the negotiations stalled. Eventually, an Intermediate-Range Nuclear Forces Treaty eliminating all short-, medium-, and intermediate-range (500–5,500 km) missiles was signed, ratified, and executed in 1987, 1988, and 1991, respectively. For Gorbachev, however, that came as too little too late. By then, the toll of this "Second Cold War" and the poor results of his reforms had spiraled the Soviet Union to its collapse.[56]

As successful as this Second Cold War was for the world hegemon, Reagan's Rollback Doctrine against the "Evil Empire" was in stark contradiction with his economic policies, known as "Reaganomics." For all of his talk of shrinking the state, Reagan heavily relied on the state to finance the intensive arms competition of his making. Yet, at the same time his number one economic priority was to cut taxes. Corporate taxes were significantly reduced and the top personal tax rate was cut from 70 to 28%. The result: the largest budget deficit in U.S. history.[57] A second priority for Reaganomics was to reduce double-digit inflation by continuing to raise interest rates, which ultimately reached 19%. That triggered the appreciation of the dollar and automatically sent import prices down and export prices up. In those years, between 1979 and 1984, the U.S. economy inadvertently took the path of deindustrialization, which would continue for decades to follow—and up to the present—in tandem with the increase of automation and the transfer of manufacturing either abroad or into the non-unionized U.S. Southeast.

Strikingly, it was industrialization that had set Great Britain on the path of world hegemony more than two centuries earlier. But now, on the verge of becoming the uncontested world hegemon, the United States embarked on the dismantling of its own industry. This process is most prominently viewed in the strip of land running from the northeastern shore, between Massachusetts and Maryland, all the way throughout the Great Lakes states and up to Iowa and Missouri. These vast stretches of land previously known as the Industrial Heartland with huge industrial complexes that had been rusting for decades now were renamed the Rust Belt. Within it, many cities such as Chicago, Buffalo, Detroit, Milwaukee, Cincinnati, Toledo, Cleveland, St. Louis, and Pittsburgh suffered from unemployment and population loss as mines, mills, and factories closed, followed by declining tax revenues and cuts in education and welfare services, while drug use and crime went up.[58]

But then, if everything went so badly for the U.S. economy how did remain the rising undisputed world hegemon? Clearly there was a flip side to military spending and high interest rates. One component of military spending consisted of investments in research and development. As the Cold War unfolded, the state had been funding technological innovations all along. In the wake of the Soviet launching of Sputnik—the first artificial Earth satellite—in 1957, President Eisenhower had created the Advanced Research Project Agency (ARPA). This U.S. Department of Defense agency collaborated with universities, corporations, and other government agencies aiming to expand the frontiers of science and foster technological innovation. Probably the brightest child of ARPA (renamed DARPA in 1993, with the D standing for defense) was ARPANET… the foundation of the Internet.[59] But there were many more bright children, including: Project MAC (responsible for groundbreaking research in computation, operating systems, and artificial intelligence); Multics (a computer operating system that had influenced all subsequent operating systems); Transit (the first satellite navigation system and predecessor to the Global Positioning System [GPS]); Aspen Movie Map (a hyper-media system that provided a virtual tour through the city of Aspen, Colorado, paving the way for virtual reality); and Shakey the Robot (the first general-purpose mobile robot able to reason about its own actions).[60]

All of these information and communication innovations contributed to a major technological revolution, the Information Revolution that thoroughly transformed economy and society by growing the availability, storing, dissemination, and roles of information in all aspects of social life. In so doing, the Information Revolution was creating a post-industrial society that superseded the declining industrial one. During the Reagan years the fruits of this state-funded technological revolution were handed over to the private sector which channeled them into marketable goods, making personal computers and the internet increasingly available to most.[61]

As with defense spending, punishingly high interest rates had their bright side. The same high interest rates that derailed U.S. industry by dropping import prices, raising export prices, and disinvesting the industrial sector, also happened to attract national and foreign investors into the U.S. financial system. High interest rates are, hence, responsible for the beginnings of contemporary financialization. Financialization refers to the increase in the size and importance of the financial sector relative to the economy as a whole. On the eve of Reaganomics, the financial sector comprised around 3% of the U.S. gross domestic product (GDP). In its wake it doubled its GDP share.[62] The deregulation of the sector launched by Reagan allowed deposit banks to function as investment banks (following the repeal of the Glass–Steagall Act) and the creation of new financial instruments, such as mortgage-backed securities and derivatives. In this way, the U.S. industrial economy was superseded not just by the new information economy but also by financialization. And then, as in so many previous instances, the two rising phenomena became entangled in a spiraling synergy that sent the U.S. stock market into a stratospheric rise throughout the last decade of the 20th and first decade of the twenty-first century. Part of the investments went directly into the new high-tech information economy in the form of high-tech companies' stocks and venture capital supporting the launch of startup companies. At the same time, the new information and communication technologies enabled the growing of financial activities with a global reach.

In this way the world hegemon reached the finishing line of the Cold War not only as the victorious military superpower but also as the reinvigorated economic powerhouse. The hegemon subsequently transformed the entire world into a global economy working in real time, facilitated by opening up economic policies, and articulated by communication and information superhighways. In the process it also led to creating a global society and culture, as well as a myriad of local responses to them. 1991 is the point when it became official: globalization as we know it had begun!

That same year, in the wake of Saddam Hussein's miscalculated invasion of Kuwait that transformed him from U.S. ally to foe, the hegemon was able to form a global coalition under its leadership that comprised 39 nations.[63] The 1991 swift military victory over Iraq in the First Gulf War brought the emerging new world order to its first test.[64] Its result was a resounding reaffirmation of the U.S. world hegemony more assertive and powerfully than ever before. By 1991 hegemony and globalization had become fully reconciled!

Everything Falling into Place

In the aftermath of the Second World War a brave new world order had emerged. It was a tripartite world made up of the contestation between the hegemonic and counter-hegemonic spheres as well as a Third World in search of its own path and maneuvering in the wiggle room opened by that contestation. For all the differences and singularities between and within each of these three blocks, one underlying feature served as a common ground for societies in all three: some form of entwinement between nationalism and socialism.

The socialist component revolved around some form of wealth and/or income redistribution for the members of the collective defined as the nation, which represents a nationalistic worldview. The tool to implement this entwinement was the state—that is, the key institutions on top of the societies in all three blocks: the Keynesian state in the hegemonic sphere, the communist state in the counter-hegemonic sphere, and the anti-hegemonic party states throughout the Third World. These modalities, individually and as a combination, brought about the Long Boom of sustained economic growth as well as the Great Compression of social inequality within and between societies. With that it seemed that this paradigm of *statism*, namely the deployment of a significant degree of state control over economic and social policy, had become second nature and would continue reigning supreme for years to come. And then, seemingly out of the blue sky, the clouds started to gather.

The 1968 global revolts confronted the world hegemony, most prominently with regard to its brutal intervention in Vietnam, as well as the counter-hegemon for its imposed authoritarianism throughout its sphere of influence. But the 1968 global revolts also contested the domestic authoritarianism of the state mechanisms run by an older generation, most prominently reflected in the education systems. Demands for larger freedoms, against massification, and against homogenization ran against the grain of statism and the collectivism that it entailed. At the same time, the 1968 global revolts had also awakened the dormant forces of privilege and reaction that for years had acquiesced to an interventionist state willing and able to redistribute some of their wealth widely across society. Now, with large and growing sectors of society in fear as a result of perceived potential threats nurtured by the 1968 global revolts, a window of opportunity was opened for these privileged and reactionary forces to roll back the interventionism of the state in economic and social matters. The timing became even more propitious once the economic model ran into serious travails as a result of the 1973 oil embargo and the second oil shock in 1979. The Long Boom credentials of the statist models were gone and had been replaced by stagflation. The need to address the gloomy economic situation and the motivation to displace the state as an agent of wealth redistribution merged in a set of policies first trialed by military dictatorships in the Third World and then attempted in democracies in the hegemonic sphere.

This set of policies came to dismantle the socialist-nationalist entwinement as both components were confronted head-on. The socialist side of the equation was tackled by cutting taxes, particularly those on the wealthy. With a diminished fiscal base, the concomitant results were cuts on public expenses such as education, health, social programs, and infrastructures. The shrinking of the state was pursued further by putting the assets that it had accumulated over decades—infrastructures, utilities, companies—into the hands of wealthy individuals and corporations, a process known as privatization. The position of wealthy individuals and corporations was further enhanced by another key process known as deregulation, namely, the elimination or reduction of rules constraining business activities, such as lending rules, labor conditions, and environmental considerations. With that, the state lost its role as a watchdog of economic activity.

The extension of deregulation to the sphere of interaction with the world economy was a frontal attack on the nationalist side of the equation. National markets were opened to imports of goods and services, foreign financial investments, while the exchange rates of national currencies were left to float freely. With that, states lost their grip on their national economies, which became part of a global economy and its fluctuations.

When these unpopular policies were applied by military dictatorships in the Third World and generated discontent and resistance, martial law and state terror paved the way for their implementation. However, when these unpopular policies were applied in democracies in the hegemonic sphere those measures could not be part of their toolbox. So which measures did they use?

The two democracies that led in the application of this set of policies were no other than the historic world hegemon, Great Britain, and the contemporary one, the United States. As hegemons, past and present, they were meant to lead, and so they did. In Great Britain, Margaret Thatcher was on the verge of losing her reelection due to the unpopularity of her economic policies. The serendipity of a military operation that turned into a full-blown war in the South Atlantic in 1982, allowed for jingoism to reverse her electoral fate. Ronald Reagan was similarly experiencing his lowest rate of approval bottoming out at 35% as his third year in office got started in 1983. Then, jingoism arrived to boost his popularity.[65] In October 1983 the United States launched its largest military campaign since Vietnam and invaded Grenada, a 135 square mile island in the Caribbean Sea, populated back then by 96,000 people, and ruled since 1979 by an anti-hegemonic party state. The island was subdued in four days. "Operation Urgent Fury" seems to have been urgent indeed and was a tremendous success. Ronald Regan ended 1983 with a 55% approval rate.

The support thus gained despite the unpopular economic policies and their extension in time ended up coinciding with an improvement of the British and American economic performances: inflation started to decline and economic growth took off. With that the model was claimed to be the much-needed replacement to the statist paradigm. Moreover, as unhappy as workers might have been with their minimum salaries frozen at $3.35 an hour, the flexibilization of the labor market with the job insecurity that generated, and the defeat and marginalization of unions, they could rather be thankful that their job had not been automated, outsourced, or offshored.[66]

Indeed, two other key components in the new policies package were outsourcing—transferring an activity performed by one company to another—and offshoring—the relocation of business activity to another country. And what better timing to start sending jobs abroad than when the most populous country in the world opened its locked gates to the world economy? The Deng Xiaoping reforms in China coincided with the reshaping of the U.S., British, and Western European economies more widely. Manufacturing jobs were sent to the recently opened special economic zones on the Chinese shores. Conversely, a growing wave of inexpensive products made in China based on the local inexpensive labor was imported by Western countries, driving the prices of consumer goods down. In the meantime, the once-hostile political relations between the hegemonic sphere and communist China started to shift into a symbiotic economic relationship.

For its part, the Soviet Union led by Mikhail Gorbachev sought to reform not only its economy (as with China) but also its political regime. Deng Xiaoping, in full command of the Chinese Communist Party, was able to harness the entire party in fostering his envisioned economic reforms. Gorbachev, aware of the reluctance of the Soviet Communist Party to support his envisioned economic reforms and mindful of the fate of the previous reforms attempted by Nikita Khrushchev, tried to articulate civil society as a counterweight to the party. Neither *perestroika* nor *glasnost* performed well. The satellite regimes of the counter-hegemonic sphere were left by the failing Soviet Union to their own devices. In 1989, they collapsed one after the other. In 1991 came the turn of the Soviet Union to collapse.

With that the brave bi-polar world of the Cold War came to an end. Moreover, the counter-hegemonic model, even if only a chimera, was gone by implosion. The model of state interventionism and wealth redistribution was allegedly proven wrong and as such could not serve any longer as an aspirational horizon. The aspirational horizon shifted toward a model that gets as far as possible from the reported illnesses that brought about the Communist demise: state ownership, state interventionism, and wealth redistribution. By 1991 the new aspirational horizon was in full swing and it was all about the new synergy comprised by the shrinking of the state, the Information Revolution, and financialization.

For more than 20 years since the global revolt of 1968, the brave new world of the post-Second World War order had been experiencing multiple turbulences aligned as bus lines in subsequent stops: 1968, 1973,

1978, 1982, 1985, 1989, 1991. Each of these turbulences had their epicenters in different regions of the world but they sent rippling effects of varying magnitudes across the globe. Around 1991 everything was falling into place for a new world order to fully emerge. The diverging trajectories of statism-led entwinement of socialism and nationalism across the Three Worlds were now converging into varieties of the new paradigm taking root in the entire globalizing world. One paradigm, one world out of the many, *E Pluribus Unum*.

THE REVOLUTIONARY RESULTS: NEOLIBERAL REFORMS, STRONGER THAN REVOLUTIONS

The new paradigm coming to displace the statist-led entwinement of socialism and nationalism, consisting of taking the state out of the way of a corporate world with global outreach, came to be known as *neoliberalism*. It was a new wave of liberalism, the same ideology that in the nineteenth century guided Great Britain as the world hegemon. The same hegemonic ideology until the Big Brexit challenged it, sending the state to center stage, in multiple forms of statism. The same ideology that had bloomed in the absence of anti-hegemonic threats during the nineteenth century and that withdrew in the face of the counter-hegemonic and anti-hegemonic threats of the twentieth century. The same ideology whose core principles are free trade and comparative advantage. The same ideology, except that now it needed to confront and downsize a state machine that had been enlarging itself for almost a century.

Neoliberalism added a couple more ideologies and policies, supply side economics and monetarism, and in so doing became new. The supply side idea maintains that economic growth is most effectively created by lowering taxes and diminishing the regulation of economic activity. Under such conditions the suppliers of goods and services can deliver better products at lower prices, increasing employment and benefiting consumers. Monetarism states that the only desirable state intervention in the market should be that of the central bank control on the supply of money into the economy. Such supply should be moderate in order to prevent inflation, because the more money is out there chasing goods or services, the higher prices will rise.

This logic is the opposite to that of the demand side practiced by global Keynesianism. That view, that reigned since the Great Depression and up to the advent of neoliberalism, maintained that it is the role of the state to ensure sufficient demand of goods and services for the economy to grow. Such a demand will occur if the state stimulates demand by being a major consumer itself and by allowing the population to consume by redistributing wealth through taxation and social welfare and even by continuing to print money when necessary.[67]

In short, the old nineteenth-century set of twins met a newer, late twentieth-century couple of ideologies and policies, which together resulted in a full-fledged package of economic policies. This package included tax cuts, privatization of state-owned assets, deregulation and liberalization of economic activity for the sake of a freer corporate world and freer consumers, and cuts to social and public expenses for society at large.

Beginning in the early 1970s, the neoliberal set of policies started touring the world as the nineteenth-century set of twins had previously done (see above, pp. 41–64). At first, preliminary experiments with the ideologies and policies developed by neoliberal economists in ivory towers were carried out in societies under military rule: Chile under the dictatorship of Pinochet and Argentina under a military junta lead by Videla. Then, by the late 1970s, the official launch of neoliberalism on center stage took place in Great Britain, the United States, and China—that is, in the previous world hegemon, the contemporary world hegemon, and the maybe-future one. In fact, neoliberalism became such a dominant unmovable force in these countries that its tenets remained in place regardless of changes in national governments. When the Labor Party prevailed in Great Britain after almost two decades of Conservative rule in 1997, Tony Blair continued fostering neoliberal policies. When Bill Clinton brought the Democratic Party back to the White House in 1993 after two terms by Ronald Reagan followed by another Republican term by George Bush, neoliberal policies continue steering the American economy. Back in his inaugural address in 1981, President Reagan memorably stated "… government is not the solution to our problems, government is the problem." Fifteen years later, when President Clinton addressed Congress with the State of the Union, he indelibly announced: "… the era of big government is over." Subsequent shifts in these two bipartisan systems did not change the neoliberal course.

Similarly, the one-party state system in China had been continuing and deepening the neoliberal policies inaugurated by Deng Xiaoping. And neoliberalism became such a dominant unmovable force in these countries that its tenets grew to encompass the entire world with only a few exceptions (e.g., Syria, North Korea). The synergy produced by the past-present-future world hegemons triad and the leadership provided by the uncontested world hegemon since 1991 amidst the collapse of the counter-hegemonic sphere, the defeat of the anti-hegemonic party states throughout the Third World, and the willingness of most nation-states to follow the lead gave this new paradigm a global reach at record speed. In a matter of one decade, the last one of the twentieth century, the new paradigm of neoliberalism had taken the world by storm.

These transitions from every form of national-social entwinement with its statist interventionism—whether global Keynesianism in the hegemonic sphere, communism in the counter-hegemonic sphere, or an eclectic blend throughout the anti-hegemonic party states of the Third World—toward the new neoliberal paradigm amounted to a series of radical shifts throughout all domains of social life. Despite all of the regional and national variations some overall trends became very prominent. To begin with the economic domain, a fundamental change was the shift of the basic referential unit of activity. Unsurprisingly, the leading referential unit for economic activity in the national-social entwinement was … the nation-state. This fundamental domestic orientation had crucial consequences for the ways in which goods and services were produced and consumed. National economies were designed to produce most of the nation-state's needs while their domestic markets were targeted as the main outlet for their production. In this way, whatever manufactures had been imported during the first reign of free trade and comparative advantage during the British hegemonic nineteenth century, were envisioned—in the wake of the Big Brexit and throughout the twentieth century—to be substituted by the output of growing national industries. In turn, these industries would sustain a well-paid national workforce able to consume whatever was domestically produced. Such was the basic structure of a nationally closed-circuit economy.

However, by the 1990s the enthronement of neoliberalism meant throwing away the national leg of the national-social entwinement by displacing the nation-state as the main referential unit of economic activity and adopting the world economy as its alternative unit. This alternative economic unit, the world economy, is based on the international division of labor, that is, a world in which each nation-state specializes in the production of whatever it comparatively excels in. In this old/new economic framework, the old ideologies and policies of comparative advantage and free trade (see above, pp. 38–39) became front and center once again. In short, the idea of producing all or most manufacturers nationally for domestic consumption was displaced by the old/new idea that each national economy should export what it excels at and import all the rest. In this fashion, a globally open-circuit world economy swiftly displaced the nationally closed-circuit economies of the world.

Such momentous transformations had tremendous consequences. On the production side, industries deemed uncompetitive were closed or offshored to rentable locations abroad. On the consumption side, laid-off workers from such industries were removed or marginalized as consumers from the domestic market, unless they manage to reconvert and join enterprises on the right side of their economy's comparative advantage. Because, indeed, many industries and services that suited the principle of comparative advantage bloomed. The demand for their output was not restricted to the domestic market any longer, and the demand from the global market kept growing stronger. Concomitantly, workers in such activities enhanced their consumption possibilities due to their rising purchase power as well as because imported goods enabled by free trade that fulfilled the principle of comparative advantage were more competitive and, therefore, carried lower prices.

In this way, for example, millennial kids grew up with far more toys than did baby boomers. The former accumulated plentiful, even if short-lived, toys cheaply imported from China, while the latter had only a small selection, albeit long-lasting ones, made by their national industries. Generation Z adolescents had stacks upon stacks of T-shirt, hoodies, and sneakers for every occasion produced in Bangladesh, Vietnam, or Indonesia, while Generation X adolescents had far fewer of these items, made by their national industries. The rising affordability of goods and services that came with free trade and comparative advantage also had a profound effect on lifestyles, radically shifting the balance from more frugal toward more consumerist values, attitudes, and practices. Whereas mass consumption was the trademark of the middle classes in the hegemonic sphere since the Long Boom, most people throughout the counter-hegemonic sphere and Third World societies were notable for their frugality. The swiping changes brought by the globally open-circuit world economy also opened access in all societies to join the mass-consumption lifestyle—at least for some of their members.

NEOLIBERALISM MEANS GROWING
INEQUALITIES: THE "GREAT BIFURCATION"

For some, but not for all. There was a sharp divergence in the life paths of those employed by comparatively advantageous enterprises and those that were not and as a result experienced unemployment, underemployment, or demotion. And this is just one of the multiple sources of the growing socioeconomic inequality brought by the neoliberal paradigm leading to the Great Bifurcation, namely, the sharp growth of socioeconomic inequality resulting in social polarization. A second source of growing inequality, even for those on the right side of comparative advantage, had to do with the bifurcating effect of global competition. On one hand, corporations had been competing for the most effective CEOs and pathbreaking innovative talents, sharply raising their incomes. On the other hand, this same global economy had united workers from all around the world ... in their competition for a job! The result is that their salaries were kept at low levels due to the actual or prospective outsourcing, offshoring, or automating of their jobs. Besides, their consumption force was not absolutely required any longer given the global reach of prospective consumers.

Finally, these two effects of global competition fully synergized. Who is the most effective and better paid CEO if not the one who keeps workers' salaries low? Between 1978 and 2000 the gap between the incomes of CEOs and workers in the United States, for example, grew by a factor of 13.75. That is, whereas in 1978 the average pay for CEOs in the S&P 500 was $1.5 million, by 2000 it had jumped to $20.6 million, while workers had moved from earning $48,000 in 1978 to $48,300 in 2000 (in constant dollar values). In other words, while CEOs earned on average 31 times as much as workers did on the eve of neoliberalism, by the time neoliberalism was in full swing CEOs earned on average 426.5 times as much as workers did.[68] These two sources of inequality are based on salary income. On top of these two, there is the additional gap between the have and have-nots in terms of access to extra-salary income from returns on investments. Unsurprisingly, there is a clear overlap between the higher levels of salary income and the existence of investment income that further contributes to making social polarization a Great Bifurcation.

These growing inequalities resulting from the old/new ideology and policy twins—free trade and comparative advantage—that brought about the replacement of the nationally closed-circuit economies with a globally open-circuit world economy were further compounded by the effects of the newer ideology and policy twins—supply side contraction and monetarism—that resulted in the decline of the redistributive role of the state. At the same time that only enterprises on the right side of comparative advantage were surviving, the salaries of CEOs and highly qualified workers skyrocketed, financial investors' incomes rose, and taxation went down—drastically down for the upper income brackets. This is because the enthronement of neoliberalism meant not only throwing away the national leg of the national-social entwinement but discarding the social leg as well.

Amidst tax reductions and monetarist policies, states drastically diminished their capabilities to redistribute income and wealth and moved away from that role and vocation. Hence, to the winners-and-losers divide generated by the transition from nationally closed-circuit economies to a globally open-circuit world economy, an additional and often overlapping divide was added demarking the winners and losers resulting from tax cuts. For the upper deciles of most economies tax cuts were succulently enriching. However, for most members in each society the withdrawal of the welfare state was keenly felt as they moved down the social ladder, with the poor being damaged the most. As a result of this double condition—the transition from nationally closed-circuit economies to a globally open-circuit world economy and the decline in the redistributive role of the state—wealth and income disparities within societies soared. A huge gap of income and wealth between the upper decile—and particularly the upper 1%—and the rest of the population in each society kept growing ever larger.

These inequalities resulting from the neoliberal core principles of liberalization and deregulation of trade and investments as well as its commitment to diminish the state role by undercutting its fiscal basis, privatizing its assets, and curtailing its obligations to its citizens were further enhanced by an emerging technological divide. Gradually emerging since the late 1947—yes, another "gradualution" except significantly faster—by the 1990s the powers of a new technological revolution were fully unleashed. This new technological breakthrough was the Information Revolution, consisting of the growing availability, storage, dissemination, and roles of information in all aspects of social life enabled by the transition from mechanical and analog electronic technology to digital electronics. Among the pillars embodying this revolution there are the digital computers, satellite communication, cellular phone, and the internet. These technological innovations amounted to a revolution that totally transformed the economic landscape. As such, these technological innovations—alongside and often overlapping with both the effects of free trade and comparative advantage and the supply side and monetary policies—created their own social divide, the digital divide. Simply put, those having access to the information and communication technologies and the tools to process and leverage the information obtained are better-off than those who have limited or no access and skills for optimizing the use of the information. All these three sources of income and wealth inequality—the revival of free trade and comparative advantage (the old ideologies and policies), the application of supply side economics and monetarism (the new ideologies and policies), and the new technological revolution—seemed to reinforce each other, resulting in a prominent socioeconomic polarization within each society, a neoliberal "Great Decompression" mirroring the Great Compression brought about by entwined nationalism and socialism.[69] Such is the domestic dimension of the Great Bifurcation.

But the growth of inequality was not just a domestic proposition in the transition from entwined nationalism and socialism to neoliberalism. The inequality abyss also kept growing larger between societies, for some of the same reasons. That is clearly the case with the digital divide between developed and developing countries. As in the first globalization of the nineteenth century, the emergence of contemporary globalization correlates not only with the undisputed leadership of a world hegemon but also with a major technological breakthrough led by that hegemon. The steam engine and the Industrial Revolution did that for British world hegemony and nineteenth-century globalization. The Information Revolution was the technological breakthrough unfolding in tandem with the global reach of the U.S. world hegemony and contemporary globalization.

As back then, a major divide unfolded and continues to unfold between those economies that had already fully embarked on this revolution and those that lagged behind.[70] Since the outbreak of this new technological revolution there are huge and growing gaps in terms of the necessary infrastructures, equipment, services, and skills to materialize the potentials of the information and communication revolutions. These gaps may be as wide as presence versus complete absence of these technologies or less extreme gaps such as the quality, reliability, and speed of the technologies. For example, 50% of all the bandwidth through which information travels is concentrated in just three countries—China, the United States, and Japan—and 75% of it is concentrated in just 10 countries.[71] 2018 is the benchmark year in which access to the internet reached half of the world population. Yet, that half included around 80% of the population in Europe but only 20% of the population in Africa.[72] This global digital gap amplifies multiple additional gaps between societies in, for example, education, health, productivity, and wages.

These effects of the global digital gap have been compounded by the two sets of ideology and policy twins, the older free trade and comparative advantage and the newer supply side and monetarism. The effects of the newer couple, responsible for the decline of the redistributive role of the state domestically, were propagated globally through impositions made by the International Monetary Fund (IMF) and the World Bank (WB). In their attempt to pay back loans that often dated back to the 1970s and 1980s petrodollar indebtedness (see above, p. 226), Third World countries had appealed to these two international financial institutions created in 1944 at Bretton Woods to foster global Keynesianism (see above pp. 140–142). By the 1980s, however, the IMF and WB had become leading tools of global neoliberalism. Hence, their rescue packages were extended with strings attached, the so-called structural adjustment programs. These programs included the demand for balancing national budgets by raising taxes while cutting government spending. The immediate implications of these "austerity plans" are deep cuts in education, health care, social programs, and the removal of subsidies on basic consumption items such as bread and oil.

Aside from these internal changes, structural adjustment programs also demanded external changes, crucially reduction of trade barriers and deregulation of external trade, opening the door for the older set of twins. Such a long way had these old twins of free trade and comparative advantage traveled since the days in which Britannia ruled the waves! Back then these two had opened up the world for trade and assigned regional specializations introduced by colonialism, informal empire, and opium wars. The emergence of the U.S. world hegemony since 1945 corresponded to the waning of colonialism as the new world hegemon pressed self-determination forward and a plethora of newly independent countries were established. The access of the old twins to these new states as well as older ones—most of which were in the midst of fostering their own policies of entwined nationalism and socialism—was achieved by the enthronement of authoritarian regimes willing to collaborate with the world hegemon in opening up for free trade and yielding to comparative advantage. But then, in the wake of Third Wave Democracy, authoritarianism gradually expired. The world became one of the independent states ruled by democratic regimes. With both colonialism and authoritarianism—the previous gate openers of the old liberal twins—gone, this role was effectively played by the IMF and the WB through indebtedness and structural adjustment programs. Among the demands of these programs there were the reduction of trade barriers (welcome back, free-trade twin!) and making the economies export-oriented (welcome back, comparative advantage twin!).

This new global tour of the old twins enlarged socioeconomic inequalities between societies in tandem with the growing socioeconomic inequalities within societies. A globally open-circuit economy based on the old twins sent every society to specialize in what it could export best (comparative advantage) while importing the rest (free trade). By following these principles, there very quickly emerged a hierarchical world division of labor based on the amount of capital and power accumulated by each society with its corresponding technological strengths and political leverages. Societies whose economies are based on quasi-monopoly products, that is products that this economy alone or only a few others can deliver given the amount of available capital and cutting-edge technologies necessary for their production (e.g., latest-generation information, communication, transportation, pharma, and bio-technologies), are located at the top of this global hierarchy. Conversely, societies located at the bottom of this global hierarchy are characterized by economies based either on raw materials and/or on products facing strong competition, that is, products that many other economies can deliver (e.g., textiles, food, furniture, toys). The margin of profits on these competitive goods, whose prices go down due to competition, are lower than those of quasi-monopoly goods, which do not confront as much competition. These conditions tend to perpetuate low capital accumulation and lagging technology in economies producing competitive commodities and goods, contrasted with high capital accumulation and cutting-edge technologies in economies producing quasi-monopoly goods.

The spinning of these vicious and virtuous cycles contributes decisively to the growth in socioeconomic inequality between societies. By the mid-1990s the balance of trade between the hegemonic sphere of the Cold War era and the Third World, now usually referred as the Global North and the Global South, was US$2.66 trillion a year in favor of the former. The overall payment balance between the Global South and Global North resulting from the re-emergence of the old twins since 1980, including not just trade but all payment flows in both directions, such as South to North debt servicing and North to South aid, amounts to $26.5 trillion transferred from the former to the latter by 2016.[73]

As in the levels of domestic inequalities, for precedents of such levels of socioeconomic disparities between societies it is necessary to go all the way back to before the days of the Great Compression, to the first globalization of the nineteenth century when Great Britain and these same ideology and policy twins reigned supreme. Neoliberalism was able to undo the Great Compression brought about by entwined nationalism and socialism.[74] Its alternative Great Decompression represents the Great Bifurcation between economies taking off and economies taken down. Two decades into neoliberalism, the new global paradigm that replaced the post-second world war paradigm of entwined nationalism and socialism, the average income of the citizens living in the world hegemon were around nine times higher than that of those living in Latin America, 21 times higher than those in the Middle East and North Africa, 52 times higher than those in sub-Saharan Africa, and 73 times higher than those living in South Asia. Similarly, the socioeconomic inequality gap between the Global North and the Global South, as measured by average per capita incomes has roughly tripled since 1960. And the ratio between the per capita income between the poorest and richest country has shifted between 1960 and 2000 from 1:32 to 1:134.[75]

There is one crucial and huge exception to this overall trend of growing inequality between the Global North and the Global South: China. Since the opening up of the Chinese economy in 1978, the GDP of China grew at an average pace of 9.7% during the first decade, 10.1% during the second decade, and 10.5% during the third decade. All of this growth compounded means that the size of the Chinese economy surged from below $150 billion in 1978 to some US$8.2 trillion in 2012.[76] This means that the size of the Chinese economy model 2012 was almost equivalent to 55 Chinese economies of model 1978! The same calculation applied to the U.S. economy shows that its 2012 model equals the size of about 5.5 U.S. economies model 1980. At a tenfold faster pace of growth, China has indeed been experiencing its "Greatest Inequality Compression" with respect to the Global North at the very same time that the Great Decompression has been setting the Global North and the Global South ever more apart. This was done by neoliberalism too.

And yet, this is neoliberalism with Chinese characters! In essence, the transition from a nationally close-circuited to a globally opened economy was achieved in China while statism remained firmly in place with both state and party intervening in economic development. This did not, however, mobilize the Chinese society in the ways that the Chinese Communist anti-hegemonic party state did under Mao throughout the Chinese Civil War, the Great Leap Forward, and the Cultural Revolution. Communist China since the leadership of Deng Xiaoping had embraced capitalism and integration into the global economy, removing in tandem the mobilizational component from within and the anti-hegemonic stance in foreign affairs. With these two features gone, the Chinese Communist party state became an authoritarian regime in which domestic socioeconomic inequality rose at the fastest rate in the world, moving in the Gini scale for inequality (perfect equality $= 0$; maximal inequality $= 1$) from 0.30 in 1980 to beyond 0.50 by the early 2010s. Clearly, this statist regime is no longer dedicated to wealth and income redistribution. It is entirely dedicated, though, to the protection of its economic interest. As such, the Chinese state did not allow the IMF and WB— or any other international organizations—to interfere with the Chinese economy. Hence, there was no access for any structural adjustment plans in China. In this sense, the crucial and huge exception represented by China actually serves as the exception that reconfirms the rule: no access to the older twins, no falling behind the growing socioeconomic inequality gap between countries. Quite to the contrary, China had contributed much to shrink that gap. It seems that the memory of the Opium Wars had not faded away.

From Melting Pot to Salad Bowl

This Great Bifurcation within and between societies is, aside from the digital divide, to a significant extent the result of the withdrawal of the state from the economic and redistributive dimensions of social life. In tandem with that withdrawal, the downsized neoliberal state also drew back from the cultural sphere. More than two centuries earlier, the Democratic Revolution had transformed subjects of autocracies into citizens of states (see above pp. 31–32). Conversely, states had strived since then to mold their citizens in their image and likeness by shaping their identities in a uniformed, standardized, and homogeneous fashion. All citizens were induced to use the same language, internalize the same values, ideals, symbols, and a myriad of behaviors that amounted to a whole way of life shared by the collective, the nation.[77] This process of top-down collective identity formation intrinsic to the Democratic Revolution was enhanced and upgraded in tandem with the growth and empowerment of the state into statism. The entwinement of nationalism and socialism addressed and fostered its collective constituency as nationally unified and socially cohesive.

This process of molding a uniform, standardized, and homogeneous national and social collective around a shared identity that encompasses a myriad of meanings and behaviors is best captured by the metaphor of a "melting pot." Imagine a container in which many different substances are melted down, blended into an homogenic solution, poured into many identical molds, and ... voilà! The many different substances have turned into a uniformed, standardized, and homogeneous collection of items belonging in the same category. Such visualization simplifies what state interventionism meant for the cultural sphere: socializing people from diverse national, racial, ethnic, religious, linguistic, cultural, gender, sexual orientations, and/or socioeconomic backgrounds into a firmly internalized homogenous collective identity.

So thorough was the striving for homogeneity that very little room, if at all, was left for diversity of any sort. A left-handed boy would have his hand tied behind his back in order to conform in a right-handed writing class, and the mere notion of left-handedness would become stigmatized as denoting clumsiness, awkwardness, and ruggedness. The homogenizing days of the statist melting pot were very comforting for those able and willing to conform. It provided a sense of belonging in a collective that functioned within a more or less closed-circuit economy and amidst different degrees of fomented cohesiveness throughout income and wealth redistribution. It was, at the same time, a very tough proposition for those unwilling or unable to conform.

Among the many state assets that neoliberalism discarded—infrastructures, utility plants, factories—it also discarded the melting pot. In downsizing the state, neoliberalism de-prioritized investment in creating a collective identity of national unity and social cohesiveness. That was the cultural logical outcome of downsizing the state, opening up the economic circuit to a global extent, and reducing the state obligations toward its citizens by way of reducing income and wealth redistribution.

Under the neoliberal paradigm, there was no place for uniform, standardized, and homogeneous individuals; neither in practice nor in spirit.

Rather, these individuals became costumers that deserve efficiency, effectiveness, and accountability from a state that collects their taxes to deliver services. These individuals were also the consumers of the corporations that the neoliberal state enabled to grow and expand. And, as is well known, the costumers are always right. Hence, whatever individualized preferences costumers may have based on their diverse backgrounds should be … accommodated. In an increasingly global, mass-consuming, market-driven economy, these individualized preferences represent desirable market segments to be targeted, nurtured, and catered to. And so, in the absence of the homogenizing juggernaut known as the statist melting pot, in tandem with the rise of global markets that are, by definition, heterogeneous, and amidst the identification of a rainbow of varied, idiosyncratic, and heterogeneous domestic market segments, diversity became beautiful! And who would want to discard the colorful beauty of diversity?

Indeed, the growing sense was that diversity should be promoted and enhanced by fully displacing the melting pot idea with a salad bowl metaphor. In this case, imagine a container in which many different ingredients are brought together, mixed into a salad, and … voilà! Here is the salad bowl made of many different ingredients, each of which keeps its specific properties while contributing its unique color, fragrance, flavor, and hint to the whole. Such visualization illustrates the effects of leaving people alone to socialize as they see fit in accordance with their diverse backgrounds. At the same time, the market segment strategy fostered by the corporations enhances this diversity, resulting in the unlearning of previously internalized homogenous collective identities.

So thorough was the striving for diversity that there was very little room for collectivity on a national scale. Rather, collective identities were scaled down from the national setting to building communities based on national or regional origin, racial, ethnic, religious, linguistic, cultural, socioeconomic backgrounds, gender, sexual preferences, and/or any common interests of any sort. A left-handed girl would be left alone writing in her mostly right-handed writing class. The stigmatizing connotations of left-handedness would be severely criticized, bringing awareness to this discriminatory bias, and a new word would replace left-handedness altogether by calling it instead, say, special-handedness. A special-handedness community would emerge. The comforting days for those able and willing to conform to the homogenizing melting pot were gone along with the sense of belonging to a national collective. At the same time, though, it was a tremendous liberating process for all those unwilling or unable to conform to the melting pot demands but willing and able to bloom in a salad bowl.

The process of displacing the melting pot policies and their homogenizing consequences in favor of the salad bowl model and its individualism combined with community building is another example of how processes started in 1968 fell into place after 1989. The anti-authoritarian and anti-massification components of the 1968 global revolt also represented, to a significant extent, an attack against the melting pot, a key tool of massification based on an authoritarian conception. The liberties and rights component of the 1968 agenda and its goal to make people equitable worldwide regardless of race, ethnicity, gender, sexual preference, gender, and country of origin gained much terrain when statism was displaced by neoliberalism.

Amazingly enough, the socio-liberal progressive, pluralistic, and inclusivist legacy of the global revolt of 1968 and the economic-neoliberal regressive, elitist, and exclusionist agenda ended up finding a common ground and synergizing to produce the new cultural paradigm of multiculturalism. This paradigm is based on a positive and assertive attitude toward diversity of cultures emanating from different national origin, racial, ethnic, religious, or linguistic, backgrounds, gender identities, and sexual orientations. It is exemplified by the changing ways in which immigrants relate to their linguistic and cultural legacies. In the melting pot days of statism immigrants would give their newborns local names and speak with their children in the local language, thick accent and all. In the multicultural environment of the salad bowl, immigrants would give their newborns heritage names and speak with their children in their own mother tongue. Not doing that, in a society sufficiently multiculturalist, would deprive their children from a heritage-informed cultural identity and prevent them from effortlessly acquiring an additional language. Personal and communal heritage are important, and an additional language is a valuable asset in a global world. The melting pot approach was propitious in a nationally closed-circuit economy, but that was no longer the situation. A globally open-circuit economy exposes itself to the cultural diversity worldwide and, hence, is conducive to embracing diversity at home. President Clinton, a baby boomer who came of age amidst the global revolt of 1968 and reached power soon after 1989, clearly articulated this dynamic in one of his speeches: "... Our diversity [within the United States] can be a source of strength in a world that is ever smaller."[78]

Ultimately, the period of 1968–1989 created a synergy between compensating losses (e.g., an increase in socioeconomic inequality) and gains (e.g., the rise of identity politics and empowerment of diverse communities). At best, this empowerment of diverse identity groups supported the emergence of multiculturalism—that is, the openness and appreciation for each and every culture and the willingness to partake in them all. However, this same empowerment of diverse identity groups could, at worst, pull societies apart into tribalized sections. As these opposite possibilities played out amidst the Great Bifurcation, there was a propensity for the emerging well-accommodated global middle class to enrich itself with the cultural wealth offered by multiculturalism. By contrast, those people left behind by the Great Bifurcation were further entrenched within their own identity community along with alienation from—if not outright hostility toward—others.

THIRD WAVE OF DEMOCRACY

Authoritarianism was also pushed back in the more fundamental wave of regime change throughout the world. This massive political shift is the Third Wave of Democracy. This was the most decisive global turn toward the establishment of democratic regimes. The wave got started in Southern Europe (Portugal, Spain, Greece) in the mid-1970s, continued during the 1980s throughout Latin America (only Costa Rica and Venezuela were peacefully democratic by 1978 and only Cuba and Haiti remained authoritarian by 1995), the Asian Pacific (Philippines, South Korea, and Taiwan), and in 1989 it merged with the global revolution in Eastern Europe and reached the Soviet Union by 1991. Between the years 1974 and 1991 more than 60 countries throughout the world transitioned toward democratic regimes. Since 1989 the wave also arrived in sub-Saharan Africa (Map 6.2).

The collapse of the Soviet Union brought new momentum to the Third Wave of Democracy. The end of the bi-polar world of the Cold War was a decisive hegemonic moment. With the counter-hegemonic sphere gone, the prospects for new anti-hegemonic attempts seemed doomed. The assertion of the U.S. world hegemony encompassed this double synchronization: not only were hegemony and globalization reconciled, but also economic (neo)liberalism was aligned with political democracy.

Map 6.2   Political Regimes during the 1990s—Democracies (black) and none-democracies (white). Compare with Map 3.2, above p. 105

The unholy democratic-authoritarian strategic alliance from the Cold War days was finally exorcised and the world hegemon started to shape states around the world according to its own image and likeness—societies that not only exercised the U.S.-led principle of self-determination but that were also ruled by democratic regimes. This was an idealistic feat that the British world hegemony ruling over colonies, mandates, protectorates, and informal colonies never dreamt of accomplishing.

Throughout this process of changing its ways in order to finally put its political acumen where its principles, concerns, and/or rhetoric on human rights were, the United States transformed many of its former author-itarian allies, such as Galtieri, Pinochet, Noriega, Saddam Hussein, and Sukarno, into newer foes who were indirectly or directly confronted and ultimately collapsed. This pattern of transmuting friend into foe would come back in the future to hunt the world hegemon (i.e., Al-Qaeda).

Throughout the1990s the traces of the brave new world of the post-Second World War became so indistinct that they seemed to be completely gone. A new global neoliberal world had fully displaced it. This is yet another brave new world in which, after the end of the Cold War, the

assertion of world hegemony and the global reach of economic globalization had come to fully correspond. It was a world in which the
world hegemon succeeded in disseminating the core principles of liberalism extensively across the world in the form of the old and new sets of
twins (free trade and comparative advantage; supply side economics and
monetarism), a prolonged Third Wave of Democracy, and the unleashing
of individualism and communitarian identity assertion. This was also a
world in the midst of a powerfully transformative technological revolution
that generated a post-industrial society and continues to grow. And this
was a world in which socioeconomic inequality has dramatically grown
both within and between societies. Each of these results, in turn, became
the points of departure for new processes that right now are calling the
global neoliberal world into question.

NOTES

1. In Latin America anti-hegemonic party states were removed by
   military dictatorships supported by the United States or even
   by its direct intervention. The AHPS in Guatemala (1954) was
   overthrown by the U.S. intervention. In Brazil (1954, 1964),
   Argentina (1955), Dominican Republic (1963), Bolivia (1964),
   Chile (1973) AHPS were overthrown by military dictatorships.
   In Asia, instead only one military coup brought the Indonesian
   AHPS under Sukarno to its end in 1967. The other major AHPS
   in Asia transformed themselves by liberalizing their economies
   and entering the global economy and hegemonic order amidst
   institutional continuity. China adopted this road following Mao's
   death in 1976, India since 1985, and Vietnam since 1986. Also in
   the Middle East internal transformation produced by the regimes
   themselves resulted in the end of AHPS party states. Although in
   contrast with Asia the main driving force was not economic liberalization. The AHPS in Egypt became an authoritarian regime simultaneously with Sadat's alignment with United States in 1976. The
   Ba'ath AHPS in Iraq was transformed into a authoritarian regime
   by S. Hussein in 1979 by purging the Bath Party, terrorizing
   society, and aligning with the United States and its hegemonic
   Coalition. Also in Syria the Ba'ath anti hegemonic party state was
   transformed into an authoritarian regime. Therefore, only the first
   anti-hegemonic attempt essayed by Mosaddeq was defeated by an

external force orchestrated by the C.I.A. in 1953. The demise of AHPS in Africa provides examples of the several fates observed in the rest of the areas of the world. AHPS in Ghana (1966) and Uganda (1971) were brought to their end by military coups. AHPS in Guinea (1984), Tanzania (1985), and Madagascar (1982) adopted a rapprochement policy with IMF in face of their desperate economic situation in which their policies resulted. The AHPS in Algeria succumbed in 1988 to mass protest.

2. "World Population by Year," *worldometer*, http://www.worldomet ers.info/world-population/world-population-by-year/.

3. "GDP growth (annual %)," The World Bank, https://data.worldb ank.org/indicator/NY.GDP.MKTP.KD.ZG.

4. Gastón Espinosa and Mario Garcia, *Mexican American Religions: Spirituality, Activism, and Culture* (Durham, NC: Duke University Press, 2008), 108. Mario Garcia, *The Gospel of Cesar Chavez: My Faith in Action* (Sheed & Ward Publishing, 2007), 103.

5. "From the Archive, 15 June 1968: British Students Talk About a Revolution," *The Guardian*, Saturday, June 15, 2013, https://www.theguardian.com/theguardian/2013/jun/15/student-pol itics-lse-revolution-1968. Anthony Barnett, "A Revolutionary Student Movement," *New Left Review* 53 (January–February 1969).

6. Rex Cathcart, *The Most Contrary Region* (The Blackstaff Press, 1984), 208. Kenneth Lesley-Dixon, *Northern Ireland: The Troubles: From The Provos to The Det, 1968–1998* (Barnsley, UK: Pen and Sword Books, 2018), 13.

7. Eiji Oguma, "What Was "The 1968 Movement"? Japan's Experience in a Global Perspective," *The Asia–Pacific Journal: Japan Focus*, June 1, 2018, https://apjjf.org/-Oguma-Eiji/5155/art icle.pdf.

8. Eiji Oguma, "Japan's 1968: A Collective Reaction to Rapid Economic Growth in an Age of Turmoil," *The Asia–Pacific Journal: Japan Focus*, March 23, 2015, https://apjjf.org/-Oguma-Eiji/4300/article.pdf.

9. Talukder Maniruzzaman, "'Crises in Political Development' and the Collapse of the Ayub Regime in Pakistan," *The Journal of Developing Areas* 5, no. 2 (January 1971), 221–238. Riaz Ahmed Shaikh, "1968—Was It Really a Year of Social Change in Pakistan?"

Sixties Radicalism and Social Movement Activism (New York: Anthem Press, 2012).

10. Fernando Herrera Calderon and Adela Cedillo, *Challenging Authoritarianism in Mexico: Revolutionary Struggles and the Dirty War, 1964–1982* (New York: Routledge, 2012).

11. Juan Carlos Cena, ed., *El cordobazo: una rebelión popular* (Buenos Aires: La Rosa Blindada, 2000). Beba C. Balvé and Beatriz S. Balvé, *El '69: huelga política de masas–rosariazo, cordobazo, rosariazo* (Buenos Aires: Razón y Revolución and CISCO, 2005). James Brennan, "Working Class Protest, Popular Revolt, and Urban Insurrection in Argentina: The 1969 'Cordobazo'," *Journal of Social History* 27 (1993): 477–498.

12. Kieran Williams, *The Prague Spring and Its Aftermath: Czechoslovak Politics, 1968–1970* (Cambridge: Cambridge University Press, 1997).

13. George Katsiaficas, *The Imagination of the New Left: A Global Analysis of 1968*, (South End Press, 1999), 66–70.

14. Madigan Fichter, "Yugoslav Protest: Student Rebellion in Belgrade, Zagreb, and Sarajevo in 1968," *Slavic Review* 75, no. 1 (2016): 99–121.

15. Kieran Williams, *The Prague Spring and Its Aftermath: Czechoslovak Politics, 1968–1970* (Cambridge: Cambridge University Press, 1997), 153–58.

16. Jeremi Suri, *Power and Protest: Global Revolution and the Rise of détente* (Cambridge, MA: Harvard University Press, 2003).

17. Roy Licklider, "The Power of Oil: The Arab Oil Weapon and the Netherlands, the United Kingdom, Canada, Japan, and the United States," *International Studies Quarterly* 32, no. 2 (1988): 205–226.

18. A short video on the long gas lines during 1973–1974 visually puts the point across: https://www.youtube.com/watch?v=hmG5KcinVSI. One dimension of the crisis is the rise of prices. The video seemingly shows the price of a gallon at US$ 0.44, which is a very desirable price nowadays. However, before the embargo the price of the gallon stood at US$ 0.38. By June 1974 it reached US$ 0.55. The other dimension is productivity. On that, one of the comments to the video reads: "[I] remember those days! I remember missing a day of work because I couldn't find any gas!".

19. David S. Painter, "Oil and Geopolitics: The Oil Crises of the 1970s and the Cold War," *Historical Social Research/Historische Sozialforschung* (2014): 186–208. Daniel Yergin, *The Prize: The Epic Quest for Oil, Money, and Power* (New York: Simon and Schuster, 2008), 570–594.

20. Robert B. Barsky and Lutz Kilian, "Oil and the Macroeconomy Since the 1970s," *The Journal of Economic Perspectives* 18, no. 4 (2004): 115–134.

21. Roy Licklider, *Political Power and the Arab Oil Weapon: The Experiences of Five Industrial Nations,* Studies in International Political Economy (Berkeley, CA: University of California Press, 1988).

22. David Commins, *The Wahhabi Mission and Saudi Arabia* (London and New York: I.B. Tauris, 2006), vi–viii.

23. Ibrahim M. Oweiss, "Economics of Petrodollars," in Haleh Esfandiari and A. L. Udovitch, *The Economic Dimensions of Middle Eastern History* (Westerham, UK: Darwin Press, 1990), 179–199. David Spiro, *The Hidden Hand of American Hegemony: Petrodollar Recycling and International Markets* (Ithaca, NY: Cornell University Press, 1999), 74–75.

24. Clifford Gaddy and Barry Ickes, "Russia's Dependence on Resources," in *The Oxford Handbook of the Russian Economy*, Michael Alexeev and Shlomo Weber, eds. (Oxford University Press, 2013), 543–550.

25. Michael Ross, *Oil Curse: How Rich Oil and Gas Raw Material Deposits Shape Development of States* (Moscow: Gaidar Institute, 2015), 155–157.

26. Nikki Keddie, *Modern Iran: Roots and Results of Revolution* (New Haven, CT: Yale University Press, 2003).

27. James G. Blight et al., *Becoming Enemies: U.S.–Iran Relations and the Iran–Iraq War, 1979–1988* (Rowman & Littlefield Publishers, 2012). Bryan R. Gibson, *Covert Relationship: American Foreign Policy, Intelligence, and the Iran–Iraq War, 1980–88* (Westport, CT: Praeger Publishers, 2010). Bruce Jentleson, *With Friends Like These: Reagan, Bush, and Saddam, 1982–1990* (New York: W. W. Norton, 1994). Mark Phythian, *Arming Iraq: How the U.S. and Britain Secretly Built Saddam's War Machine* (Boston: Northeastern University Press, 1997).

28. M. Meisner, *Mao's China and After: A History of the People's Republic Since 1949* (Free Press, 1986), 334–366.

29. Daily Report: People's Republic of China, Editions 240–249 (1993), p. 30.
30. Hung Li, *China's Political Situation and the Power Struggle in Peking* (Hong Kong: Lung Men Press, 1977), 107.
31. Quoted in *The Economist*, May 31, 2001.
32. Misattributed or apocryphal. Deng is commonly quoted with this phrase in Western media but there is no proof that he actually said it.
33. Jin Wang, "The Economic Impact of Special Economic Zones: Evidence from Chinese Municipalities," *Journal of Development Economics* 101 (March 2013), 133–147. Ezra Vogel, *Deng Xiaoping and the Transformation of China* (Cambridge, MA: The Belknap Press of Harvard University Press, 2011), 398.
34. David Harvey, *A Brief History of Neoliberalism* (Oxford: Oxford University Press, 2007), 145–146.
35. Max Hastings and Simon Jenkins, Simon, *The Battle for the Falklands.* (Macmillan, 2012).
36. David V. Khabaz, *Manufactured Schema: Thatcher, the Miners and the Culture* Industry (Troubador, 2007), 226.
37. Andrew Marr. *A History of Modern Britain* (Pan Books, 2009), 411.
38. David Parker and Stephen Martin, "The Impact of UK Privatisation on Labour and Total Factor Productivity," *Scottish Journal of Political Economy* 42, no. 2 (1995): 216–217.
39. Kenneth O. Morgan, *Oxford Illustrated History of Britain* (Oxford: Oxford University Press, 2009), 581.
40. Mark Bevir and Rod A. W. Rhodes, "Narratives of 'Thatcherism'," *West European Politics* 21, no. 1 (1998): 97–119.
41. Gail Stokes, ed., *From Stalinism to Pluralism: A Documentary History of Eastern Europe since 1945* (Oxford: Oxford University Press, 1996), 125.
42. William Taubman, *Gorbachev: His Life and Times* (New York: Simon and Schuster, 2017), 91–98.
43. Michael Hunt, The World Transformed: 1945 to the Present (Oxford University Press, 2015), 315–316.
44. Mikhail Gorbachev Statement (June 8, 1990), as quoted in Quentin Grafton et al., *The Economics of the Environment and Natural Resources* (Wiley-Blackwell, 2004), 277.

45. Angus Maddison, *The World Economy. Volume 2: Historical Statistics* (Paris: Development Centre Studies—OECD, 2006), 478–9.
46. Dingxin Zhao, *The Power of Tiananmen: State-Society Relations and the 1989 Beijing Student Movement* (Chicago: University of Chicago Press, 2001), 64, 215.
47. Philip Pan, *Out of Mao's Shadow: The Struggle for the Soul of a New China* (Simon and Schuster, 2008), 273–275. Zhao, *The Power of Tiananmen*, 143–159.
48. Lian Zhang, compiled, Andrew Nathan and Perry Link, eds., *The Tiananmen Papers: The Chinese Leadership's Decision to Use Force, in Their Own Words, Public Affairs*, 2001), 355–362. Alexander V. Pantsov and Steven I. Levine, *Deng Xiaoping: A Revolutionary Life* (Oxford: Oxford University Press, 2015), 400–402. Ezra F. Vogel, *Deng Xiaoping and the Transformation of China* (Cambridge, MA: Belknap Press of Harvard University Press, 2011), 606–608. Julia Kwong, "The 1986 Student Demonstrations in China: A Democratic Movement?" *Asian Survey* 28 (1988), 970.
49. Louisa Lim, *The People's Republic of Amnesia: Tiananmen Revisited* (Oxford University Press, 2014). "China: 15 Years After Tiananmen, Calls for Justice Continue and the Arrests Go On," Amnesty International UK, June 3, 2004. Retrieved May 30, 2009. Kris Cheng, "Declassified: Chinese Official Said At Least 10,000 Civilians Died in 1989 Tiananmen Massacre, Documents Show," *Hong Kong Free Press*, December 21, 2017. Retrieved December 22, 2017. Adam Lusher, "At Least 10,000 People Died in Tiananmen Square Massacre, Secret British Cable from the Time Alleged," *The Independent*, December 24, 2017. Retrieved December 24, 2017.
50. Tsao Tsing-yuan, "The Birth of the Goddess of Democracy," in Jeffrey N. Wasserstrom and Elizabeth J. Perry, eds., *Popular Protest and Political Culture in Modern China* (Boulder, CO: Westview Press, 1994), 140–147.
51. Mary Fulbrook, *History of Germany, 1918–2000: The Divided Nation* (Wiley-Blackwell, 2002), 256.
52. Hunt, *The World Transformed*, 323–324.
53. Gregory Feifer, *The Great Gamble: The Soviet War in Afghanistan* (New York: Harper, 2009).
54. Nicholas Lemann, "Reagan: The Triumph of Tone," *The New York Review of Books*, March 10, 2016.

55. Vojtech Mastny, "How Able Was "Able Archer"? Nuclear Trigger and Intelligence in Perspective," *Journal of Cold War Studies* 11, no. 1 (2009): 108–123.

56. Pavel Podvig, "Did Star Wars Help End the Cold War? Soviet Response to the SDI Program," *Science & Global Security* 25, no. 1: 3–27. https://doi.org/10.1080/08929882.2017.127 3665. Ken Adelman, *Reagan at Reykjavik: Forty-Eight Hours that Ended the Cold War* (Broadside Books, 2014).

57. Harvey, *A Brief History*, 26.

58. Robert W. Crandall, *The Continuing Decline of Manufacturing in the Rust Belt* (Washington, D.C.: Brookings Institution, 1993). Ted McClelland, *Nothin' But Blue Skies: The Heyday, Hard Times, and Hopes of America's Industrial Heartland* (New York: Bloomsbury Press, 2013). Steven C. High, *Industrial Sunset: The Making of North America's Rust Belt, 1969–1984* (Toronto: University of Toronto Press, 2003).

59. Matthew Lyon and Katie Hafner, *Where Wizards Stay Up Late: The Origins of The Internet* (Simon & Schuster, 1999), 27–39.

60. Simson Garfinkel and Hall Abelson, eds., *Architects of the Information Society: Thirty-Five Years of the Laboratory for Computer Science at MIT* (Cambridge, MA: MIT Press, 1999).

61. Mariana Mazzucato, *The Entrepreneurial State: Debunking Public vs. Private Sector Myths* (Anthem Press, 2013).

62. Simon Johnson and James Kwak, *13 Bankers: The Wall Street Takeover and the Next Financial Meltdown* (New York: Pantheon Books, 2010), 63.

63. Afghanistan, Argentina, Australia, Bahrain, Bangladesh, Belgium, Canada, Czechoslovakia, Denmark, Egypt, France, Germany, Greece, Honduras, Hungary, Italy, Kuwait, Morocco, the Netherlands, New Zealand, Niger, Norway, Oman, Pakistan, Poland, Portugal, Qatar, Saudi Arabia, Senegal, Sierra Leone, Singapore, South Korea, Spain, Sweden, Syria, Turkey, the United Arab Emirates, the United Kingdom, and the United States.

64. President Bush's speech to Congress, March 6, 1991 (extracts), https://web.archive.org/web/20110531214717/http://www. al-bab.com/arab/docs/pal/pal10.htm.

65. "File:Gallup Poll-Approval Rating-Ronald Reagan.png," *Wikimedia Commons,* https://commons.wikimedia.org/wiki/File:Gallup_Poll-Approval_Rating-Ronald_Reagan.png.

66. John Peters, "Labour Market Deregulation and the Decline of Labour Power in North America and Western Europe," *Policy and Society* 27, no. 1 (2008): 83–98. https://doi.org/10.1016/j.polsoc.2008.07.007. Jong H. Park, "The East Asian Model of Economic Development and Developing Countries," *Journal of Developing Societies* 18, no. 4 (2002): 330–53.

67. Dwivedi, *Macroeconomics, 3E.* (Tata McGraw-Hill Education, 2010), 372.

68. Ruth Umoh, "CEOs Make $15.6 Million on Average," *CNBC* make it, January 22, 2018, https://www.cnbc.com/2018/01/22/heres-how-much-ceo-pay-has-increased-compared-to-yours-over-the-years.html. "CEO Pay Soars to 361 Times that of the Average Worker," AFL-CIO, May 22, 2018, https://aflcio.org/press/releases/ceo-pay-soars-361-times-average-worker.

69. Martin Hilbert, "When is Cheap, Cheap Enough to Bridge the Digital Divide? Modeling Income Related Structural Challenges of Technology Diffusion in Latin America," *World Development* 38, no. 5 (2010): 756–770.

70. Martin Hilbert and P. Lopez (2011). "The World's Technological Capacity to Store, Communicate, and Compute Information," *Science* 332, no. 6025: 60–65.

71. Martin Hilbert, "The Bad News is that the Digital Access Divide is Here to Stay: Domestically Installed Bandwidths Among 172 Countries for 1986–2014," *Telecommunications Policy* 40, no. 6 (2016).

72. "ICT Facts and Figs. 2005, 2010, 2017," Telecommunication Development Bureau, International Telecommunication Union (ITU). Retrieved May 7, 2019. *Measuring the Information Society Report (itu.int).*

73. Hickel, *The Divide*, 25, 28.

74. Hilbert, "When is Cheap, Cheap Enough".

75. Hickel, *The Divide*, 2, 16.

76. Mark Purdy, "China's Economy, in Six Charts," *Harvard Business Review*, November 29, 2013, https://hbr.org/2013/11/chinas-economy-in-six-charts.

77. Benedict Anderson, *Imagined Communities: Reflections on the Origin and Spread of Nationalism* (Verso, 2016). Eugen Weber, *Peasants into Frenchmen: The Modernization of Rural France, 1870–1914* (Palo Alto, CA: Stanford University Press, 1976).

78. "The Nineties "Can We All Get Along?"," *CNN*, broadcast, minute 18, July 23, 2017, minute 18.

CHAPTER 7

Falling Apart. Back to Nationalism (2003–2020)

HEGEMONY AND GLOBALIZATION RECONCILED BUT SPIRALING DOWN

On September 11, 2001 the Islamic terrorist group al-Qaeda launched four coordinated attacks against the United States, killing around 3,000, injuring some 6,000 others, and causing material damages of $10 billion. In confronting the tragedy, governments, media, and civil societies across the globe responded with expressions of support for and solidarity with the United States. The sole world hegemon, which had galvanized a global coalition in 1991 while confronting Saddam Hussein, had, in 2001, harvested the world's public opinion sympathy in this dark moment of vulnerability masterminded by Usama Bin Laden. In a matter of 17 months, American forces were back in Iraq in full strength confronting Saddam Hussein once again, except this time for no convincing reason and without global support. Suddenly, the long-lasting ascent of the United States as the sole and uncontested world hegemon started spiraling down. Starting with the invasion of Iraq, United States world hegemony seemed to have lost its way, a crisis of its own making. A turbulent period of two decades would follow with radically shifting agendas, from George W. Bush's neoconservatism through Barak Obama's neoidealism and up to Donald Trump's neonativism ("America First").

275

The downward spiral of U.S. world hegemony on geopolitical and diplomatic grounds was compounded by the Great Recession (2007–2009), the most severe economic crisis since the Great Depression (1929–1933). The effects of the crisis reverberated globally till 2016 and particularly affected Europe, where Ireland, Greece, Portugal, and Cyprus defaulted on their national debts. The global Great Recession fundamentally confronted the sole reigning paradigm of global neoliberalism, disseminated starting in the late 1970s and consolidated in the 1990s: "… government is not the solution to our problems, government is the problem," affirmed President Reagan in 1981. "The era of big government is over," President Clinton proudly announced in 1996. Yet the "Washington Consensus" on neoliberal policies had been called into question at its very epicenter. A decade later, when the economic crisis threatened to spiral out of control the solution to the problem was … well …the government and state intervention, for Republicans and Democrats alike.

To begin with, the problem seemed to be "deregulation," that is, the imposition of rules that favored the corporate world. With the eruption of the global Great Recession, and despite the preliminary sidelining of the state as a regulatory institution and its intervention in economy and society, the state was brought back to make taxpayers pay the bill for irresponsible deregulated corporate behavior.

This triggered one of those momentous occasions in which a paradigm shift appears on the horizon. Because in response to the tremendous economic losses sustained by middle and lower classes throughout Euro-America and beyond, neoliberalism had only the same old quid pro quo medicine to offer: new rescue loans …to underwrite new austerity programs! With that, whatever remained from the diamond shapes of world societies seemed doomed to erode once again, making the pyramidal social structures even sharper. These conditions brought about another momentous occasion, that in which the Great Bifurcation of socioeconomic inequalities unfolding since the rise of neoliberalism—locally by the 1970s, globally by the 1990s—became politically charged and turned into a head-on conflict with neoliberal globalization.

For at least two decades, the happy citizens of third-wave democracies—as well as those in well-established democratic regimes—had been exercising their right to vote, alternating governments but not fundamentally altering who exercised power. Neoliberal governance was slightly modified by ruling parties leaning more or less toward the left or the right, but the course of the pro-corporate policies that delivered the Great Bifurcation remained unmodified. With the opening of the twenty-first century, the levels of frustration due to the lack of any major policy changes exploded.

The 2001 Argentinean expression ¡Que se vayan todos! ("All of them must go!") came to express a growing sentiment around the globe. To begin with, the first region in the world forcefully subjected to neoliberal policies—Latin America—embarked in the early 2000s on its "Pink Tide," a radical, post-neoliberal turn to state interventionist and redistributive policies. By the beginning of the second decade of the new century, the worldwide socioeconomic polarization of the Great Bifurcation had reached political maturity, embodied in the rise of an old/new type of political force generically referred to as populism. Under this label, social movements and political parties confronted head-on, and from both right and left flanks, the core tenets of neoliberal globalization.

Since the 1990s, prominently, thoroughly, and globally, neoliberal globalization had been displacing the closed-circuit national economies with an open-circuit world economy. In tandem, neoliberalism, throughout the world and to different extents, brought about the dismantling or reduction of wealth and income-leveling mechanisms. Finally, the comforting melting pot of local mainstream worldviews was displaced by the alternative salad bowl. In short, statism, nationalism, and socialism were drastically marginalized if not all together discarded. Unsurprisingly, then, the backlash against the neoliberal paradigm was made of multiple agendas, each of which sought to bring back its own combination of some of these old and lost elements while adjusting for newly crystallized circumstances.

The confrontational movements and parties, including well-established political parties now fostering populist agendas, were tremendously empowered by some of the bright new offspring of the Information Revolution: smartphones and social media. These same tools, however, also empowered governments and corporations at a much faster pace. This made for a strenuous competition between the three major building blocks of the social fabric: governments, corporations, and civil society. Moreover, the Information Revolution itself was undergoing a crucial fast-paced transformation known as the "Industrial Revolution 4.0," signaling that an entirely new set of technologies was about to take the world by storm in multiple fields: robotics, artificial intelligence, nanotechnology, quantum computing, biotechnology, the internet of things (IoT), 3D printing, fifth-generation wireless technologies (5G), and fully autonomous vehicles.

Clearly history has been accelerating. When the Industrial Revolution coalesced around 1851, when Britannia ruled the waves and led to creating a global economy, the human population of the planet had reached its first billion, and the world economy almost its first trillion (of real 2010 U.S. dollars). By the end of the Second World War, when the United States had become the world hegemon, the world population had doubled, and the output of the world economy had grown fivefold to around $5 trillion. Since then and up to the present, this acceleration has gained speed bringing humankind to some 7.7 billion people, while the output of the world economy is now approaching $70 trillion. That is how the last 75 years came to be known as the "Great Acceleration." And with such ever-growing acceleration, uncertainty—a fundamental existential condition—has intensified, generating anxieties for the present and future.

SHAKEN AMERICAN WORLD HEGEMONY

Great Britain and the United States had reached their pinnacle as world hegemons fostering a world order and economic globalization during 1851–1873 and 1991–2001, respectively. Among the sources of their globally unmatched powers was the prowess of their cutting-edge technologies that brought about the Industrial and Information Revolutions, respectively. And yet, another fundamental feature that had facilitated their rise to world hegemony in the longer run was their geographic insular position. During modern times England at first and then Great Britain (since the Acts of Union, 1707), protected by the English Channel, averted multiple invasions attempted or envisioned by their continental European foes. King Phillip the Second of Spain, the ruler of the world hegemon of the day, had unsuccessfully attempted that in 1588, 1596, and 1597. Future aspirants to world hegemony would only plan but not dare to execute a full-fledged invasion of Britannia. Between Louis XIV (the Sun King) and Napoleon, the French considered the move in vain as many as five times (1708, 1744, 1759, 1779, 1803–9). "Operation Sea Lion," Hitler's plan for the invasion of Great Britain, never came to be implemented, either.

On a continental, rather than an island, scale the U.S grew confidently secluded by the cushioning of huge bodies of water. The immensity of the Atlantic and Pacific Oceans kept the United States protected since the most strategic of all alliances, the alliance between the two world hegemons, was forged in the wake of the British-American War of 1812–15. That war, in which the Congress in Washington D.C. was burnt to the ground and the defense of Fort McHenry gave birth to the verses that became the U.S. anthem, was the last occasion until the twenty-first century in which external attacks caused significant damages in the United States. After 1815, the variety of threats had actually shown the implausibility of inflicting damage on the continental United States. A century later, Pancho Villa, the Mexican revolutionary, set fire to Columbus, New Mexico in 1916, killing eight soldiers and ten residents. Yet, when the Zimmerman Telegram (see above, p. 85) arrived a year later in Mexico from the German Foreign Office inciting Mexico to recover its lost territories of Texas, Arizona, and New Mexico, the possibility was deemed negligible.[1]

Other than that, all that Germany could muster during U.S. neutrality in the First World War was a couple of sabotage actions in New York and New Jersey to prevent the delivery of war matériel to the Allied Powers. That same goal prevailed during the Second World War after 1941, when German submarines sank 609 ships.[2] And 1941 was indeed the major date in the history of attacks on U.S. soil. On December 7 of that year, the Imperial Japanese Navy Service launched a surprise attack against the naval base at Pearl Harbor in Honolulu, the Territory of Hawaii. The attack inflicted heavy losses in human lives, with some 2,500 killed and 1,200 wounded, and substantial amounts of war matériel destroyed or damaged. The following day the U.S. Congress declared war on Japan. And yet, the rule of continental untouchability of the United States since 1815 remained unbroken. The most damage the Japanese forces could achieve in targeting continental United States was to bomb Dutch Harbor in the city of Unalaska in Alaska, as part of their campaign on the Aleutian Islands, and to send some 9,000 hydrogen balloons loaded with incendiary bombs. This was the first-ever transcontinental weapon and it was highly ineffective, with some 1,000 balloons estimated to have reached North America, 284 actually documented as sighted or found, and only one turning lethal when five children played with it, three months and a day before "Little Boy," an atomic bomb, was dropped on Hiroshima.[3]

Such a remarkable track record of secular untouchability since 1815 by a state that had been participating in multiple military conflagrations, including the two world wars and the proxy wars of the Cold War, was dramatically broken on the morning of 9/11, 2001. Al-Qaeda's terrorist attacks on the World Trade Center, the Pentagon, and a missed target in Washington D.C. resulted in the killing of around 3,000 people, injuring some 6,000 others, and causing material damages of some $10 billion.[4] Al-Qaeda's terrorist attacks, in the way that terrorism works, seeded and nurtured fear in the minds and hearts of the American population and beyond. Al-Qaeda's terrorist attacks also ended an age of innocence based on the heretofore well-grounded assumption of untouchability. Al-Qaeda's terrorist attacks also pierced in some quarters in the American public opinion another age of innocence with the realization that "somebody out there in the world really hates us." And yet, for all of the painful grieving, material losses, and unsettling realizations, none of these results of al-Qaeda's terrorist attacks could have come close to shaking U.S. indisputable world hegemony. The realization that "some people out there really hate us" was soon overwhelmed by global expressions of sympathy and solidarity coming from governments and the general public, with but a few exceptions. And even if the assumption of untouchability could not be fully restored, the strong hand and long arm of the U.S. military might be swiftly deployed in chasing the culprits.

In less than a month after the terrorist attacks, by October 7, 2001 military might had converged with global sympathy and solidarity in Afghanistan. It was there that Osama bin Laden, Al-Qaeda's leader, was hiding and the Taliban regime rejected the U.S. extradition demand. Operation Enduring Freedom, carried out by American and British forces, ensued, bringing the Taliban regime to its end in a matter of two months (12/17/2001). Immediately the United Nations Security Council unanimously authorized, that is including Russian and Chinese support, the establishment of the International Security Assistance Force, a NATO-led coalition force of 51 countries. As in the First Gulf War, the United States had asserted its world hegemony by mobilizing a global coalition against an isolated enemy, without the protest, reluctance, or dispute of a single state.

But it was precisely the revisiting of the First Gulf War enemy that started unraveling the as-yet undisputed authority of the U.S. world hegemon. On March 19, 2003, joint U.S. and British forces invaded Iraq. By May 1, President G. W. Bush had declared the end of major combat operations after the country was taken over. This time, however, the invasion and occupation of a targeted country were strongly opposed by some of the U.S. closest allies, such as Germany, France, and Canada and less surprisingly by major world powers such as Russia and China that had so far ambivalently acquiesced in front of the American undisputed world hegemony. The alleged possible links between the 9/11 terrorist attacks and the invasion of Iraq—Saddam Hussein's support of terrorism and the urgency to disarm his weapons of mass destruction—were broadly unaccepted around the world by governments and societies alike. Large-scale protests against the U.S. invasion of Iraq and subsequent war were held around the world. The suggestion that the world was remade as one in which there were once again two superpowers, this time the U.S. and the worldwide public opinion, may be farfetched.[5] However, certainly the erosion of the undisputed U.S. world hegemony had been underway since 2003.[6]

Hegemony is the result of the balance and synergy between coercion and consent, the stick and the carrot. These two factors fluctuate in a zero-sum game interplay, in which the more there is of the one the less the other is necessary or available. Leaning too much on coercion carries the risk of breaking this balance, losing hegemony, and replacing it with naked power, which is conducive to power struggle. And this balance indeed started to break apart for U.S. world hegemony when multilateral consent and collaboration were displaced by President G. W. Bush's unilateralism, that is, one-sidedness in U.S. foreign policy decision making. One-sidedness in U.S. foreign policy decision making was not a new feature in and of itself; U.S. unilateralism has a long pedigree. What was new was the international context in which unilateralism was reinvoked in the aftermath of 9/11. U.S. foreign policy had been unilateral for as long as isolationism was the goal, the practice, and the achievement for most of its history until 1941. Later on, U.S. foreign policy developed its unilateral underpinnings during the Cold War era, in which countries received the message that if they were not with the United States, they were against it. By 2001, however, in the absence of either isolationism or Cold War, unilateralism represented a novel proposition and an unwelcome one, because who likes one-sided impositions? The former and potentially future adversaries, Russia and China, certainly did not. Neither did even some of the closest allies, Germany and France, who galvanized the European Union.

Unilateralism in this new context was a particular and detrimental interpretation by the United States of undisputed world hegemony, according to which the hegemon had the capacity and mandate to police and reshape the world precisely because of its unique position as the sole superpower. As such a hierarchical, top-down, and *fait accompli* relational approach, unilateralism was already ill-received on all these counts by the international community. But on top of all these drawbacks, unilateralism was not embraced by the George W. Bush administration by chance or mistake but deliberately in order to foster an international agenda that held little appeal for prospective partners and collaborators.

Since 2003, unilateralism as an approach came hand in hand with the conceptions of preemptive war and regime change as the final goal. The preemptive-war line of argumentation, nakedly stated, would read: "It's better to wage war now so that we can be sure it's conducted on our foes' ground, rather than leaving open the possibility that we might absorb another attack on our home territory. Such certain war now will have for us a lower cost than the potential cost of a possible attack in the future. The immediate and concrete victims of a certain war abroad concern us less than the potential victims of a possible future attack on our home ground."

Regarding the ultimate goal of regime change, again as with unilateralism there was nothing new in this goal, sought and achieved so many times in the past by U.S. foreign policy. The novelty came in the preference shift for the establishment of democratic regimes as opposed to the standard practice of imposing authoritarian regimes during the Cold War era. The reason behind this shift in the vision for regime change from authoritarian to democratic lies in the presumption that democratic regimes do not fight with one another. Hence, the moment a hostile regime is toppled and replaced by a democratic one, that country will not fight the United States any longer.

The reasonings of unilateralism, preemptive war, and regime change, however, did not resonate for most of the international community, not even for some of the closest U.S. allies. On the eve of the invasion of Iraq, the French intelligence service disputed the U.S. intelligence reports according to which Iraq was developing weapons of mass destruction. The United Nations Security Council had never explicitly approved the 2003 invasion of Iraq. The invasion's legality under international had been challenged from multiple directions, such as the International Commission of Jurists, an independent commission of inquiry set up by the government of the Netherlands, and by the United Nations Secretary-General Kofi Annan, who asserted that the war was illegal.[7]

Since then, the ground wars in Afghanistan and Iraq have continued unraveling up to the present. They devastated these two countries and their populations with human costs as high as an estimated 106,000–170,000 civilians killed,[8] 360,000 dead by war-related causes[9] and about 135,000 fighters killed[10] in Afghanistan, while in Iraq the human toll between 2003 and 2006 alone was as high as 151,000 to 601,027 fatalities.[11] Around 2.6 million Afghans are registered refugees abroad with the UN Refugee Agency (UNHCR) while about one million people are internally displaced.[12] In Iraq, as early as 2007 the estimated number of displaced people amounted to 4.1 million people (1.9 displaced within the country; 2.2 became refugees abroad).[13] According to some moderate estimates, the economic cost of the wars for the United States has been about $738 to $932 billion in Afghanistan, while in Iraq the cost went beyond two trillion dollars, perhaps approaching three trillion. The cost of these two wars combined with their respective spillovers into Pakistan and Syria were reported to total at least $5.6 trillion by late 2017.[14]

Side by side with these high human and economic costs, the first apparent geopolitical result of this dual invasion of Afghanistan and Iraq had seemed to be the scaffolding of a military siege on the Islamic Republic of Iran, the U.S. archrival in the region since the Islamic Revolution of 1979. The reality was the opposite. The destruction of Saddam Hussein's regime amounted to releasing Iran from the influence of the regional gatekeeper that had held it in check—the reason that Saddam Hussein's regime had enjoyed the United States and its allies' support throughout the decades prior to his invasion of Kuwait in 1990. Moreover, the vacuum generated by the destruction of Hussein's regime resulted in the establishment of a government led by the Iraqi majority Shi'a population bonded by coreligionist identity with Iran. From Iraq to Syria, and Lebanon to Yemen, Iran was able to articulate a wide arc of coreligionist solidarities and proxies against its archenemies, Israel and Saudi Arabia, the strategic allies of the United States in the region.

With these grim results, in May 2010, President Obama unilaterally declared that the "War on Terror" was over, specifically the war against al-Qaeda and its terrorist affiliates.[15] Accordingly, by September 2010 the U.S. combat operations in Iraq were officially over and the last U.S. troops left the country by December 2011.[16] By then, the Arab Spring—a wave of mass anti-authoritarian government protest—was underway throughout the Middle East. The Obama administration embraced the situation as conducive for regime change, from authoritarianism to democracy. Accordingly, Obama's administration supported the anti-authoritarian protests by action or omission. By omission, the

U.S. close ally in Egypt, Hosni Mubarak, was left unsupported and ripe to be toppled by the mass protests and the acquiescence of the Egyptian army. In Syria, the United States took actions aiming to topple the Assad regime and bring about regime change; the nonviolent struggle in Syria degenerated after five months into a full-fledged civil war by August 2011. The United States extended its support to the Syrian National Council, a coalition of opposition forces aiming to establish a democratic regime in Syria, and has been providing military support to various anti-government forces since.[17]

However, the one anti-government force that seriously endangered the future of the Assad regime was the Islamic State, a force that emerged in the wake of the U.S. invasion of Iraq and grew in the power vacuum generated by the Obama-led unilateral withdrawal. The collapse of Saddam Hussein's regime and its replacement steered by the United States of a Shi'a-led government triggered a radical reaction among the previously ruling Sunni minority. A civil war ensued in which a Sunni fundamentalist state known as the Islamic State was established in the northwest third of Iraq by an even further radicalized splinter of al-Qaeda in 2014. By late 2015 the Islamic State had also taken over the eastern half of Syria.

The "War on Terror" had proven to have a life of its own beyond anybody's power to unilaterally declare it over. And so, starting in August 2014 the U.S. forces, under the command of President Obama this time, were re-engaging in Iraq, now confronting the Islamic State. By 2018 the Islamic State was defeated in Iraq.[18] Through substantial American and Russian intervention, by March 2019 the Islamic State had lost its territories in Syria too. However, the Islamic State outlived the collapse of its geographical state by inspiring a global network spanning throughout the northern half of Africa, the Middle East, Central and Southeast Asia.[19] And so almost two decades later, Operation Enduring Freedom, the military campaign originally envisioned against Taliban ruled Afghanistan, grew in tandem with the Islamic State network to became a global Operation Enduring Freedom with local branches in Trans-Saharan Africa, the Horn of Africa, and the Philippines. The "War on Terror" and Islamic global terrorism have been spinning for the last two decades.

Throughout the two first decades of the twenty-first century, U.S. world hegemony had been shaken. The recourse to unilateralism had alienated allies throughout Europe and stimulated hitherto acquiesced rivals such as Russia and China into assertiveness. The global public opinion had drastically shifted from massive solidarity with the United States in the aftermath of 9/11 to firm criticism against its policies. The devastation of a big portion of the Middle East, from Syria to Yemen and from Iraq to Pakistan, brought by preemptive wars and regime changes kept nurturing this criticism for two decades. At the same time the inconclusive military results had eroded the prestige and credibility of the unmatched military power of the world hegemon. Moreover, the credibility was further undermined by drastic changes within the U.S. administrations with regard to this "War on Terror."

Russia was the big winner of the war in Syria the way Iran was in the Second Gulf War. Russia had regained power for the Assad regime in most of Syria. Instead of regime change, Russia produced regime continuity in Syria. Nevertheless, the Trump administration asserted its commitment to the opposition in 2018 by announcing an open-ended military presence in Syria. Ultimately, however, in the last spin of the American unilateral zigzagging policies in and out of the various and interrelated Middle Eastern conflicts for almost two decades, a year later Trump ordered the withdrawal of all American troops from Syria. This was a seeming acknowledgment that the U.S. regional rival, Iran, and/or its historical rival, Russia, had the upper hand in this conflict.[20]

It took a large effort for Russia to reassert its presence in the Middle East and to make its policy prevail over that of the United States in Syria and its vicinity. In fact, Russia's intervention in Syria was its furthest-reaching theater of action after having strived for two decades to reassert its presence in its immediate perimeter. As the Cold War was approaching its end in 1990, the Soviet Union was apparently given assurances by the United States that NATO would not reach beyond Germany.[21] With or without reassurances, what once was the Eastern Bloc in the Soviet counter-hegemonic sphere eventually became an integral part of NATO (Poland, Czech Republic, and Hungary in 1999; Slovakia, Bulgaria, and Romania in 2004). Moreover, in 2004 three former Soviet Republics—Lithuania Latvia, and Estonia—finalized their process of incorporation into NATO and two additional former Soviet Republics—Georgia and Ukraine—pursued the opening of their own processes of incorporation into NATO with the support of the United States.

With the rise of in 2004 a pro-Western government in Georgia led by Mikheil Saakashvili—the so-called Rose Revolution that ousted Edward Shevardnadze—this country sought closer ties with NATO. By 2008 President George W. Bush indicated his willingness to incorporate it into the alliance. However, almost 20 years into the post-Cold War era, Putin's Russia was back on its feet. The submissive client state of the world hegemon that Russia was in the aftermath of the Soviet Union's collapse under Boris Yeltsin had been transformed; gone was its acquiescence amidst NATO's expansion. Hence, with the prospects of a NATO member emerging on its southern border in the Caucasus range by 2008, Putin's Russia reignited early 1990s conflicts between Georgia and two of its constituent regions, South Ossetia and Abkhazia, which back in the days of the Soviet Union had been autonomous.[22] On August 1, 2008, South Ossetian separatists and the Georgian army began to exchange artillery fire.[23] This initial shelling announced the outbreak of the first twenty-first-century European war. In a matter of days, the Russian army invaded Georgia by air, land, sea, and cyberspace while opening a second front in Abkhazia. By August 12, a ceasefire agreement was brokered by Nicolas Sarkozy presiding over the European Union. By occupying South Ossetia and Abkhazia since, however, Russia has not only been violating this agreement,[24] but most crucially has been drawing a line in the sand: "NATO watch out! Stay clear of the Russian sphere of influence." And NATO did stand away from Ukraine despite having had its eyes on this country for a Membership Action Plan.[25]

NATO's self-restraint, however, did not preclude the European Union from extending an Association Agreement to Ukraine. In March 2012, such an agreement was initialed between the European Union and the Ukraine fostering cooperation between the parties in the economic, political, social, cultural, and security domains. Simultaneously to the process that should have led to the ratification of this agreement, however, Ukraine was in negotiations with Russia for its collaboration with the Russian-led Eurasian Customs Union. The European Union made clear that it must be one integration or the other, certainly not both. The Ukrainian state and society found themselves between a rock and a hard place, with the major political parties and their constituencies gravitating toward one or the other direction for regional integration and overall national outlook. When the pro-Russian integration President Viktor Yanukovych was toppled by a pro-European Union integration movement, Russia stepped in to draw yet again another line in the sand. In March 2014 Russia had annexed Crimea, whereas in the eastern regions of Ukraine it had been supporting the pro-Russian separatist forces in Donetsk and Luhansk, in the easternmost portion of the country known as Donbas/Donbass (in Ukraine/Russia, respectively). These Russian-backed separatist forces had established the People's Republics of Donetsk and Luhansk. Ukraine, for its part, ended up with what it regarded as three temporarily occupied and uncontrolled territories.[26]

With that the message was finally conveyed: The Russian empire has had its sphere of influence for centuries. The collapse of the Soviet Union was the vulnerable exception that allowed the U.S. world hegemony to snatch vast swaths of that sphere in Eastern Europe and the Baltic Basin. No more. Putin's Russia is back on its feet holding its sphere of influence, a counter-hegemonic sphere, as Russia had been capable of doing since the nineteenth century amidst the rise of Great Britain as world hegemon as well as in the second half of the twentieth century confronting the U.S. world hegemony (see above, pp. 131–132). So much so, that it became capable not only of expanding its sphere of influence into the Middle East as a leading force in the Syrian civil war, but also of conducting a new iteration of confrontation, sometimes referred to as a new Cold War of sorts, against the world hegemon.[27]

Through such lenses, the wars in Georgia, Ukraine, and Syria can be understood as the first by proxy wars of this new round, which also may include an arms race component as in the past, as well as a media, information, and cyber fight—as a substitute for what once was an ideological struggle—and economic warfare. The withdrawing from the Intermediate-Range Nuclear Forces Treaty by President Donald Trump in February 2019 and by Putin in July represents the formal inauguration of a new potential nuclear arm race. The most daring Russian blow, so far, in the media, information, and cyber fight is its interference in the 2016 Presidential election aiming at harming the candidacy of Hillary Clinton, boosting that of Donald Trump, and exacerbating political tensions within the American society. Although the impact of this interference is hard to assess, certainly the interference's goal and the electoral results coincided. Giving the small margin of Trump's electoral victory any little bit of an impact might have helped.[28] Amidst the Russian launching of the twenty-first-century proxy wars and electoral meddling, the United States has been relying on sanctions against Russian individuals, companies, and government agencies with unclear results and prospects.[29] Call it "new Cold War" or not, the emergence of a new Russian counter-hegemonic sphere represents a benchmark in the unraveling of the U.S. world hegemony. While the United States has been self-inflicting wounds in its "War on Terror," other major international players did not stand still but instead have been running their own geostrategic agendas. Although Russia is the most prominent case, and with a long historical lineage, of carving out its own zone of influence as a counter-hegemonic sphere, it is by no means the one and only case nor necessarily the most challenging.

China makes for a second case of hegemonic challenge that even without relying on hard power is potentially more consequential. Differently from Russia, China did not possess during the Cold War a counter-hegemonic sphere of influence at its command beyond its borders. Rather, except for North Korea, China was contained within its national borders. China's economic, political, and demographic powerhouse spreads along the Pacific coastal line, which happens to be encircled by the absolute U.S. command of this ocean. That includes the surveillance and control of the East and South China Seas from the American naval and air bases throughout the arc of islands and peninsulas running from Hokkaido (Japan) in the north throughout South Korea and the Philippines, all the way to Singapore in the south. China's poorer and less populated interior is landlocked. Since the 1990s, however, China has been substantially investing in reverting these two sets of constraints. On the East and South China Seas, China has been disputing maritime boundaries and islands, building new artificial islands and a powerful navy, and exploring oil and natural gas deposits.[30] On the continental landlocked front, China has been developing the New Eurasian Continental Bridge: a railway line that runs throughout China, east to northwest, and crosses to Kazakhstan, from southwest toward northeast, in order to connect with the original Continental Bridge, the Russian trans-Siberian railroad that links Asia with Europe. In time this project grew to connect by land more than 12 Chinese cities and nine European cities: Lianyungang in Jiangsu Province to Rotterdam and Yiwu in Zhejiang Province to Madrid, for example. Given the cost of rail transportation and its duration (around two weeks roundtrip), compared to that of shipping and air cargo, this railway network is not necessarily a cost-effective economic proposition, but it is definitely a geopolitical assertion of outreach.[31]

In 2013, the Chinese leader Xi Jinping has announced this assertion in its full-fledged magnitude by introducing the world to the "Belt and Road Initiative." This global strategy shows that differently from Russia, China is not aiming to reassert a portion of a lost counter-hegemonic sphere of influence, but rather it aspires to world hegemony. The initiative consists of building transportation infrastructures to connect the world, as well as conduct additional investments in the energy sector and beyond.[32] The "Silk Belt" refers to the overland networks for which the New Eurasian Continental Bridge represents its departing point and backbone. The aim, however, is to establish an additional line to the Persian Gulf and West Asia all the way to the Mediterranean Sea and another line headed for Southeast and South Asia. This last branch directly relates to the "Silk Road" component of the initiative. The "Silk Road" consists of maritime lines of navigation aimed at granting China oceanic autonomy. China's tightening collaboration with Pakistan allows China to circumvent the American encirclement of its Pacific coastal line by gaining direct access to the Indian Ocean through the China-Pakistan Economic Corridor all the way to the Pakistani ports on the Arabian Sea, starting with the already functional port of Gwadar. In order to finance this colossal vision, which would position China as the pivot of an Afro-Eurasian and global network, China led in the establishment of the Asian Infrastructure Investment Bank in 2016, a potential alternative to the International Monetary Fund and the World Bank established in 1944 under the U.S. leadership amidst its transition to become the world hegemon (see above, pp. 140–142).

mination in the wake of the 1941 attack on Pearl Harbor when the United States took up a leadership position on a global alliance against the forces of Nazism, Fascism, and Japanese imperialism. Sixty years later, in the aftermath of the 2001 attacks, the United States has embarked since 2003 in a unilateral attack against a misrepresented danger, an ill characterized enemy, and ultimately against an enemy that had emerged and crystallized, to a significant extent, as a result of the U.S. invasion of Iraq. By the time the Second World War was over in 1945, the United States had become the world hegemon. As the "War on Terror" (2001–onward) continues the U.S. position as the world hegemon continues to erode. In between these two points in time, the United States as the world hegemon had already experienced another 20-year bad war, the Vietnam War (1955–1975), in which serious doubts on U.S. policies, values, and military credentials were cast around the world. That experience had informed and nurtured the 1968 global revolt that in the short run had challenged the U.S. role as the world hegemon in a bi-polar world. Paradoxically, in the longer run, it had set in motion the transformation of the post-Second World War order and the emergence of the neoliberal globalized world in which the United States emerged as the undisputed sole world hegemon (see above, pp. 242–246).

In short, the differences between the aftermaths of 1941 and 2001 for U.S. world hegemony could barely be starker. In between these two dates, the cascading repercussions of the Vietnam War for America's place as world hegemon—shaken at first, reasserted next—signals that the long-run consequences of the "War on Terror" on the U.S. world hegemony remain inconclusive even if the immediate impact was severely damaging. With a defense budget four times as big as the next major military spender, China, 15 times bigger than the Russian defense budget, and in fact as large as the combined budgets of the next 13 armed forces, the United States remains the military world hegemon.[33] The fourfold big stick with which the U.S. world hegemony projects its naked power (see above, pp. 136–138) is still there with its global empire of military bases and the largest arsenal with the widest delivery systems of a doomsday weapon. The long reach of its intelligence covert operations, however, appears less prominent than in the Cold War era and, more fundamentally, its leadership in collective defense suffered severe reverses during the multiple iterations of "The War on Terror." As a result, the global geopolitical grip of the world hegemon is currently loosening. Its rivals are getting closer to each other, while its allies are being pushed further apart. In this context, it is worth remembering that one breaking point in the ascent of the United States as the uncontested world hegemon, despite the setback of the Vietnam War, was the snatching of China away from the Soviet sphere and toward a partnership with the United States starting in 1972 (see above, p. 214). These days, we are witnessing the reversal of the process with Russia and China closing lines to counterbalance the American pressures they had been sustaining in their immediate spheres—Eastern Europe and the Caucasus for Russia, the Pacific Ocean for China—gravitating into what may become a new Russian-Chinese strategic collaboration. Conversely, the U.S. partners in Europe and Asia are being called to fend for themselves.

World hegemony is a balancing act that the United States has been performing so effectively in the past, since the end of the Second World War, with its fourfold stick, its huge carrot, and its alluring dream (see above, pp. 136–146). By now, however, U.S. world hegemony has been shaken. And not only because of its detrimental and zigzagging policies of unilateralism, neoidealism, and neonativism as well as the high tolls imposed by the "War on Terror." As high as the economic costs of the wars associated with this term have been, the U.S. economy has been confronting much more serious troubles shaking its second pillar of world hegemony, the huge carrot.

2007 Shaken Neoliberal Globalization

While in the high geopolitical sphere the United States was transitioning from the peak of its world hegemonic role in the 1990s toward a growing contestation since the 2000s, at home the U.S. households were becoming increasingly indebted. In 1990, the ratio of household debt to disposable personal income was already very high at 77%. By the end of 2007, however, it moved off the chart to 127%! The driving force in this growing indebtedness was the purchase of houses by homeowners (about two-thirds of the buyers), or investors (the remaining third). The reasons behind this housing purchase spree were the rise in mortgage lending, even to borrowers with unconvincing credentials for repayment—the so-called subprime mortgages—and an increasing housing bubble that sent prices up as the spree continued. Although these subprime mortgages were made more secure or "securitized" by bundling them into investment packages together with solid mortgages, the share of subprime mortgages grew substantially and from 2004 to 2006 they rose to represent around a fifth of all yearly issued mortgages. By 2007, as the rate of subprime mortgage delinquency rose, some of these "securitized" packages started defaulting. Banks heavily invested in these "securitized" packages were at high risk. Moreover, once the mortgage market was shaken by such defaults the housing bubble burst and properties' value collapsed, further enhancing the mortgage market crisis. The fast-declining value of mortgaged properties was no match for the amounts of debt incurred to purchase them; these became "underwater mortgages." By October 2007, when both home sales and the Dow Jones Industrial Average were reaching their peaks, the wheels of a major financial crisis in the United States were already set in motion. A year later, these same wheels were spinning out of control.[34]

The federal government and the Federal Reserve, on guard for months striving to keep the situation under control, had been extending loans and guarantees to struggling banks, such as the Bear Stearns Companies Inc., which was saved in the nick of time. By the beginning of September 2008, attentive to the combined losses of the Federal National Mortgage Association (Fannie Mae) and the Federal Home Loan Mortgage Corporation

(Freddie Mac)—two government-sponsored corporations specialized in "securitizing" mortgage loans—the federal government took them over under conservatorship to prevent the disruption of the financial market. In a matter of a week, however, when the Lehman Brothers Holdings Inc.—a private firm, the fourth largest investment bank in the United States—waved for help, the federal government refused. The Lehman bank filed for bankruptcy, the largest bankruptcy in American history. In that single day, the Dow Jones Industrial Average lost 4.5% of its value. The effects started to cascade.[35]

Many heavyweight financial institutions, such as Merrill Lynch Bank and American International Group, Inc. (AIG) that had insured trillions of dollars of mortgages were tottering. Morgan Stanley and Goldman Sachs Group Inc. took the precaution to become commercial, rather than investment, banks in order to gain access to credit via the Federal Reserve. Others such as Washington Mutual, Inc.—the largest saving and loan association in the United States—and the Independent National Mortgage Corporation (IndyMac) were too late and collapsed all together. By March 2009, once the dust of the financial earthquake had settled, in Wall Street the Dow Jones had lost more than half of its value (53.4%). The surge of the financial crisis made it difficult to borrow money and with investments derailed the productive sector took the hit. Unemployment roughly doubled to 10% as a result of around eight million jobs lost. Consumption declined in tandem while home evictions and foreclosures, six million of them, were on the rise. With all these trends spiraling down in sync, the U.S. economy entered in the late 2008 and throughout 2009 its first major recession since the 1929 Great Depression.[36]

And so did the world. The financial crisis was instantly transmitted to the Eurozone as the "securitized" investment packages had been widely disseminated around the global financial system. Leading banks such as HBOS, Royal Bank of Scotland, Bradford & Bingley, Fortis, Hypo Real Estate, and Alliance & Leicester suddenly found themselves all on the line. Housing bubbles burst, stock indexes throughout the region started their descent, investment shrank, unemployment rose to peak at 11.6% on average by 2012 with Greece and Spain leading at 27%, and consumption fell.[37] Finally, a global economy, in which its developed core sustains the compounding effects of investment and consumption crunches, reverberated the effects of the recession, to different extents, around the world. With a sharp drop in international trade, China and India experienced a slowdown in their continuous growth. South Korea and Australia barely averted recession but Japan and New Zealand did not. Several economies throughout Asia, Latin America, and Africa were also affected, however, to a lesser extent.[38]

As much as the financial crisis and subsequent recession were global, deeply affecting the Global North, so were the mitigating policies applied by governments around the world. Here again, the United States showed the way by expeditiously coming to the rescue of private banks and manufacturing corporations via bailout. The miscalculated impact of the Lehman's bankruptcy signaled to the federal government and the Federal Reserve that bailing out financial institutions and extending rescue packages to corporations should be the course of action to control the financial crisis. A mere day after Lehman Brothers folded, the Federal Reserve took over AIG. From finance to manufacture, the big three carmakers, General Motors, Ford, and Chrysler received government support too and were bailed out. All in all, various government agencies committed trillions of dollars, perhaps as many as 11 to 16.8 trillion dollars, in loans, purchases, and direct spending. Similarly, the Federal Reserve expanded money supply and cut interest rates to confront the recession.[39] Governments and central banks around the world follow suit: banks were rescued to contain the financial crisis—Benelux partially took over Fortis, the German government bailed out Hypo Real Estate Holding, and the British government pioneered a bank rescue package for 850 billion dollars on October 2008—with subsequent stimulus plans being extended and interest rates lowered to confront the recession.[40]

The massive state assistance coming to the rescue of corporations hit by the financial crisis of their own making and to mitigate the resulting recession managed to contain both the crisis and the recession and bring the world economy to safety. However, the estranged situation had immediately become apparent: How had it reached the point where these private financial institutions ran their casino capitalism for gains but turned back to the state when they encountered losses instead? Wasn't that state acting as a "nanny state," that is a state coming to the assistance of those in need? But isn't "nanny state" the derogative term of choice used by the corporate world to vilify the welfare state? Does this mean that supporting hardworking people living in poverty, providing health care and education, running social programs for populations with special needs, all of that was wrong, but coming to the rescue of wealthy financiers who gambled on speculative financial instruments was right?! How then is it that, all the sudden, a society is being called upon to pay the price of the financial crisis and resulting recession? Wasn't the case that "there is no such thing as society"? (see above p. 233). And so it was, that a society of taxpayers, paid with their tax money the bailout of corporations while they themselves, the members of society, were offered in exchange a newer round of austerity programs that ensured further cutbacks on the "nanny state."

Hence, the immediate response of the neoliberal global leadership, in the heat of the moment, was to instantly turn their skin into global Keynesians. However, the public opinion did not have much stomach for that opportunistic swamp. Throughout the United States, there was an outburst of protests in more than 100 cities. More broadly, aside from that grassroots activism and ahead of the House of Representatives discussion on the Emergency Economic Stabilization Act, which aimed to grant $700 billion of public money to private corporations, the public opinion opposed the initiative.[41] And so did the House of Representatives, except that a huge drop in the Dow Jones (over 777 points, worth 1.2 trillion dollars in market value) and the pressure it generated led to a second vote four days later that reversed the results.[42] Comparable bailout packages were offered throughout Europe and they came hand in hand with new austerity measures. A marriage of convenience between global Keynesianism and neoliberalism made the citizens of many developed economies undergo the worst of both models: more taxes to pay for fewer public services to obtain.

The global financial crisis and recession—running just during 2008–2009 or up to 2016, depending on location and metrics—made unmistakably visible a fundamental condition in the contemporary world economy and unleashed the potential for a radical ideological and political paradigmatic shift. The financial crisis and subsequent recession made the world aware, more than ever, of the financialization of the economy (see above, p. 245). Since the 1970s the financial sector kept growing relative to other sectors of the economy by generating "investment instruments" that would make money from money rather than money from production or (nonfinancial) services. These "investments] instruments" rely on the most fundamental financial activity, namely, lending. Lending by the financial sector may carry the potential of economic growth for the borrower but to begin with it carries the certainty of indebtedness. Depending on the lending conditions, the destination of the credit, and a multiplicity of uncertain factors, the result for the borrower may be, then, economic growth or continuing indebtedness. If the borrower's gains allow her to pay for the debt interests and principal and keep part of the gains, then credit leads to growth. If, by contrast, indebtedness drains the economic gains of the borrower for the servicing of her debt with the financial sector, then credit leads to a debt trap. In this case, the financial sector used these debt service proceedings to grant new loans to the struggling indebted borrower who would continue spiraling down. This is indebtedness coming full circle.

The Third World had been experiencing this full cycle since the Oil Crisis starting in 1973. Back then, the financial sector had obtained an injection of money resulting from the hike in the oil prices. Suddenly, an existing asset—oil—was worth four times more. The petrodollars had catapulted the financial sector in the Global North and had submerged the Global South in a debt trap (see above, p. 226). Starting in the 1980s, the citizens of the Global North started experiencing a debt trap too by servicing their growing credit cards debts, bank, mortgage, student, and auto loans. The decline in purchase power as a result of stagnating salaries and the fast-rising prices of crucial goods and services (e.g., houses, cars, education, and health) led to indebtedness. As with the hike in the oil prices, the basic tool for the growing of the financial sector and indebtedness in tandem was the inflation of prices of already existing assets.

A most prominent case in point is the housing market. According to Zillow Home Value Index, the median home value in the United States in 2019 is $229,000. Adjusted for inflation the median home value in the United States has been $45,490 in 1940, $97,740 in 1970, and on the eve of the financial crises, the median home value adjusted for inflation was $222,600. Home values more than doubled in 30 and 36 years, at 115% and 128% hike, respectively.[43] An even more vertiginous hike in the prices of existing assets is the case of the stock market. In 1979, the total value of stocks in the United States represented 35% of the country's GDP. On the eve of the financial crisis, the value of the stocks represented 137% of the country's GDP. The intangible wealth of stocks had overcome by then the real economy by 37% in the United States. By 2018 it stood at 148.5%. In the long-standing financial center of Switzerland, the value of the stock market was 236.24% of the country's GDP for 2018. A financial hub such as Hong Kong illustrates the point with even starker figures: the capital invested in its stock market represents 1,052.15% of its 2018 GDP.[44]

But beyond inflating prices of existing assets, financialization took on creating value through instruments, which value derives from other assets, and as such, they are called derivatives. These instruments are contracts that specify the conditions under which payments are to be made between two parties for those underlying assets such as commodities, stocks, bonds, market indices, interest rates, or currencies. For instance, a cacao beans producer and a chocolate factory may sign a contract on the price of a given amount of cacao beans throughout a given length of time. Say, on September 16, 2019, the parties signed that during the next two years the producer will sell the manufacturer three metric tons of cacao beans a month for $2,250 the metric ton. In this way, the producer knows that even if the cacao beans' price precipitously collapses to $1,390, as it happened in August 2004, he is covered. The manufacturer, for his part, knows that even if cacao beans' price suddenly skyrockets to $3,530, as it happened in January 2010, she is covered too.[45] Producer and manufacture had hedged each other by reducing their (opposite) risks of price fluctuation.

And yet, this type of derivative instrument can be used, instead, precisely for risk-taking. Consider a contract buying from the cacao beans' producer 10 metric tons of his produce at $3,250 the metric ton on September 16, 2029. That may be an enticing proposition for the producer, given that the highest price for the last 30 years for the commodity he offers was $3,530 and this price did not last for long. Whereas the buyer speculates that given population growth and climate change a decade from today, demand will go up, supply down, and hence prices will break the past celling and reach new heights. Such prospects may interest other risk taker investors, whose expectations may be that chances are that by September 16, 2029, the metric ton of cocoa beans would perhaps cost $4,530, $5,530, $6,530, or $7,530, and therefore it would make perfect sense to try and buy this contract for $4,250, $5,250, $6,250, or $7,250, respectively.

The volume of trade in these financial instruments amounts to as little as $542.4 trillion, according to the Bank of International Settlements, or as much as $1.2 quadrillion, according to some analysts. Add to any amount within that range some $186.26 trillion in deposits, stocks, and bonds (in 2017) and you can start grappling with the sheer size of the financial sector of the economy. To bring that into proportion, contrast it with the global GDP made of all the goods and services produced and delivered during 2018. It has been estimated by the World Bank at around $86 trillion.[46] Now you can appreciate what a remarkable wedge sets apart the tangible productive economy and the intangible speculative one. This is financialization, an economic colossus with a say in world hegemony, socioeconomic inequality, political regimes, and technology.

The good news that financialization brings to the U.S. world hegemony is that the bulk of the financial assets belong in the U.S. economy and most of the financial activity happens in its framework. The bad news for the U.S. world hegemony is that the growing U.S. financial economy comes in tandem with its shrinking share in the global productive economy. Moreover, this inverted relation of a growing share in the world financial economy with a shrinking share in the world productive economy has been already observed during the decline of the British world hegemony. The reverse side of this trend is the Made in China 2025 strategic plan launched in 2015. The goal of this plan is to move China beyond its 1980s–2010s transformation into the world factory to become a technological trailblazer in leading industries including information technology, artificial intelligence, robotics, green energy, aerospace equipment, and medical devices, among others. Those are the sectors particularly targeted by the tariffs imposed by the United States on China in 2018 that resulted in the current trade war between the world hegemon and the aspirant to the position. The American attempt to block the Chinese telecom Huawei from providing 5G technologies around the world is currently the most visible instance of this potentially protracted confrontation.[47]

With regard to socioeconomic inequality, the growth of financialization inflates the giant wedge that further enhances the Great Bifurcation between those who partake in the financial economy and those who only participate in the real economy. The wide social outrage triggered by the financial crisis expanded the collective awareness of the financialization juggernaut and on September 17, 2011, Main Street started showing its determination to confront Wall Street. By then, a social movement had emerged and entrenched itself in Zuccotti Park, in Manhattan's financial district, to denounce the global financial system and the large corporations. The slogan was "We are the 99%," alluding to the huge gap in wealth and income between the highest 1% of the curve and all the rest. The agenda included: tighten banking-industry regulations, ban high-frequency trading, arrest all "financial fraudsters" responsible for the 2008 crash, form a Presidential commission to investigate and prosecute corruption in politics, reduce the influence of corporations in politics, and institute a "Robin Hood Tax," that is, some form of taxation on the wealthy to benefit the poorer.[48] The modus operandi consisted of occupying public spaces for assemblies, deliberations, rallies, and marches while emphasizing the importance of non-violence. In less than a month, the Occupy movement's protests had taken place in more than 600 communities across the United States.[49]

As had the financial crisis and the recession as well as the mitigating policies before, this social movement had instantly reached global proportions by been disseminated worldwide through social media and by joining up with previously existing local movements and protests. By October 9, 2011, Occupy protests were held in almost 1,000 cities across 82 countries. This global movement blended locally with movements already active since the heydays of the financial crisis and throughout the recession. These locally grown movements had been protesting the austerity measures that since 2009 had been cutting back on education, public health, pensions, and additional public services. By 2012, there was a growing awareness of the global Occupy movement as well as growing support in global public opinion. A poll conducted by the global research company Ipsos in 23 countries had shown that 8% of the interviewed were "very familiar" with the movement while 30% were "somewhat familiar." An additional quarter (24%) were "not very familiar," and a significant minority of 38% either had heard of it but "know nothing about it" or had never heard of it. Moreover, 20% of the interviewed "very much sympathize" with the movement while an additional third were "somewhat" sympathetic with the movement, bringing the different levels of sympathizers to more than half (53%); the number of detractors and undecided amounted each to about a quarter of the respondents. In some countries, though, the levels of sympathy were much higher, such as in South Korea (67%), Indonesia (65%), India (64%), Spain (62%), and many others.[50]

In 2012, however, the global Occupy movement started waning. Seemingly, the movement did not bring about any major transformation: "financial fraudsters" were not prosecuted, "Robin Hood Taxes" were not instituted, and the tightening of banking regulations was not necessarily attributable to the protests. And yet, the movement did succeed in making social inequality concerns front and center in the public discourse. Three decades and a half into the reign of the neoliberal paradigm, Occupy's slogan "We are the 99%" had identified, targeted, and denounced the Great Bifurcation.[51] The social, economic, and political foundations of the neoliberal world order had been called into question by a global movement of protest.

Such a development may ring some bells—the bells of similarity with '68–'89 (see above pp. 240–242). Twenty-three years after the establishment of the post-Second World War order the grievances and aspirations of a new generation had exploded in a global wave of protests during 1968. Although the foundations of espoused nationalism and socialism remained in place, the alternative neoliberal world was seeded back then. Twenty-one years later, in 1989, another generation brought about a new outbreak of mass protests. Albeit limited to the counter-hegemonic sphere, the outbreak this time was truly revolutionary in that the Communist bloc collapsed and with that, the espoused nationalism and socialism world order came to its end globally. Neoliberalism became global and had reconciled hegemony and globalization.

And yet again, 22 years later, in 2011, a third generation took to the streets to make its demands: revolutionary demands in a few cases (see above, the Arab Spring, pp. 12, 283), reformist demands in most. Some of these movements succeeded in toppling political regimes (e.g., Tunisia, Libya, and Yemen). Others resulted in the coalescence of new political forces (e.g., Podemos in Spain) or the revitalization of existing parties (e.g., Syriza in Greece). Most, however, did not bring about significant political change. Some of the social movements were locally driven (e.g., Indignados in Spain), others regionally connected (e.g., the Arab Spring), and one major movement, global Occupy, was globally coordinated. The most immediate precedent for such a level of coordination was the global demonstration against the war in Iraq in 2003. Global Occupy had superseded that precedent in creating a movement sustained across time, rather than a one-time occasion. In so doing, it may have established a new way in which a global civil society gets together to confront global challenges and make politics globally. The current climate-action strike movement in 2019 seems to suggest that possibility. By now, however, the most visible impact of the global protests of the early 2010s, as well the economic crises that had triggered it, is the assault on the foundations of the neoliberal global order. The magic formula of neoliberalism for the last almost four decades, shrinking the role of the state for the sake of corporations' and individuals' freedoms has been under fire ever since.

NEOLIBERALISM CHALLENGED AROUND THE WORLD

Even before the 2007 financial crisis and subsequent global recession, some of the economies of South America had been facing major problems since 2002. The Brazilian economy, the largest in the region, was crumbling under its huge public debt that scared investors away making things even worse. Trying to retain foreign investors, the Brazilian government found itself forced to offer higher interest rates on their investments. In order to pay for these lofty returns to the anxious investors, the Brazilian government turned to the International Monetary Fund for loans. The IMF granted Brazil first 15 billion dollars first, then 30 billion dollars. High interest rates were not the only strings attached to these large IMF loans. The standard constraints were also attached: austerity measures. With the presidential elections looming on the horizon merely two months ahead, the disgruntled Brazilian society was ready to cast its vote in October 2002.[52]

Amidst this crisis, the value of the Brazilian currency continued dropping, adding to its sharp decline since 1999 in which it lost more than a third of its value. The devaluation of the Brazilian Real immediately triggered a major problem for the economies of the region: with a much-devaluated Brazilian Real, exports to Brazil, their major trade partner, also dropped. That was just another straw that broke the Argentinean economy's back. From 1998 to 2002 the Argentinean economy shrank by 28%.[53] As a result, the national deficit and external debt continue to increase to the point that the IMF as the country's creditor required the Argentinean government to implement additional austerity measures.[54] A series of cuts in public spending, civil servants' salaries, and pension benefits ensued, but to no avail. Unsatisfied with the looming budget deficits, the IMF refused Argentina the release of a $1.3 billion tranche of its loan and demanded a further 10% cut of the national budget.[55] As concerned Argentineans began withdrawing their bank deposits aiming to convert their Argentinean pesos—artificially pegged to U.S. dollars one to one—into U.S. dollars, the government froze all bank accounts to contain the bank run. Riots and sustained mass protests ensued. In a matter of 17 months, four Presidents were forced to resign. In April 2003, the disgruntled Argentinean society was ready to cast its vote too.

The left-wing anti-austerity measures candidates Luiz Inácio Lula da Silva and Néstor Kirchner were elected in Brazil and Argentina, respectively. The rise of these leaders in the largest economies in South America sparked a region-wide rise of left-wing anti-austerity forces, bringing them to power. The Pink Tide was set into motion. In the subsequent decade, nine more countries in the region joined the tide.[56] Gravitating to different degrees toward the camp of the previously isolated Bolivarian Republic of Venezuela in command of Hugo Chávez since 1999, The Pink Tide had taken South America in the 2000s by storm. The laboratory of neoliberalism in the early 1970s had become its mausoleum with the dawn of the twenty-first century.

The Latin American road toward neoliberalism was paved by authoritarianism and indebtedness. Since the end of the Second World War and throughout the 1970s, most countries in the region had experimented with some form of espoused nationalism and socialism. By the 1970s the regimes that ran such experiments were all gone, toppled by military dictatorships backed by the United States (see above, pp. 213–216). As part of their ties with the world hegemon, these regimes were granted access to hefty loans, whose origins are to be found in the accumulating petrodollars of the 1973 and 1979 oil crises (see above, pp. 226). With indebtedness came the conditions imposed by the IMF. States were urged to increase their exports in order to properly serve their debts. The competitive exports at hand were the traditional agro-mineral commodities that had characterized the Latin American oligarchic republics since inception. Nationalized and centralized import substitution industrialization was displaced by the perennial free trade "export agro-minerals and import all the rest" model. With indebted economies increasing their commodities exports not only throughout Latin America but all around the world, the price of commodities in the world market went steadily down during the 1980s and did not fully recover during the 1990s. That was the age of the "great commodities depression." By 2003, however, more than a decade into a fully globalized economy, conditions had substantially changed. For multiple reasons such as world population growth, the rise of the biofuel technologies, the rise of China and a huge growth in its commodities demand, and climate change damages, the demand for agro-mineral commodities took off and their prices started skyrocketing. This was the "commodities boom" of the 2000s that brought the "great commodities depression" of the 1980s and 1990s to an end.[57]

The timing of this turnaround in the prices of agro-mineral commodities proved to be key in the consolidation of the Pink Tide. Relying on taxing the exports of agro-mineral commodities or the goods produced with them, many of the new left-wing anti-austerity governments of the 2000s were able to introduce a wide range of social policies and programs to improve the living conditions of their impoverished and disadvantaged populations. With that, post-neoliberalism started taking root in Latin America.

However, it is quite difficult to articulate what post-neoliberalism is made of. Starting in the 1970s and in full swing by the 1990s, neoliberalism had dismantled the interventionist state that had been directing entwined nationalism and socialism since the Great Depression. The role of the interventionist state was transferred to the private sector, a myriad of corporations. Nationalism was displaced by globalism and socialism by wild capitalism. As post-neoliberalism started emerging amid the rise of the Pink Tide, all six ingredients from both the post-Second World War order (1945–1973) and the neoliberal world order (1973–onward) were on the table (Diagram 7.1).

In the emerging post-neoliberal order, different Pink Tide governments picked, chose, combined, and balanced idiosyncratically between a more or less interventionist state, between nationalism and globalism, and between social and wild capitalism. As in the post-Second World War order, wealth redistribution policies were put in place along with some policies of nationalization. There was not much import substitution industrialization, and definitely not centralized planned economies. But, as in the neoliberal world order, integration into the global economy was imperative, as were assurances to the corporations. Conversely, no one of the Pink Tide governments envisioned nationalism and globalism as a zero-sum game. The revenues on which their administrations

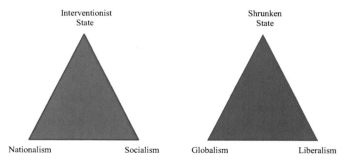

Diagram 7.1   The pillars of post-Second World War and neoliberal world orders

depended came from the global economy—an economy willing to take the commodities and products that the world division of labor had assigned to Latin American economies to deliver. This model of idiosyncratic post-neoliberalism that creatively blended elements of the two previous modes of governance reached the global stage in the wake of the global financial crisis and recession.

As in South America, where the financial crisis and recession was followed by a new devastating round of austerity measures in the early 2000s, also in the wider world, the global financial crisis and recession resulted in an additional tranche of austerity measures in the 2010s. Then, across the world and throughout the 2010s decade, global post-neoliberalism emerged in the same way that it first emerged in South America in the 2000s. However, in the wider world, the post-neoliberal tide is not necessarily "pink," in the sense of a mild tone of red denoting a left-wing leaning. Quite to the contrary, many of the proponents of post-neoliberalism around the globe had right-wing leanings.

In Latin America, globalization was a requisite for the Pink Tide to flourish and it was the global market that had blessed their agro-mining commodities with high prices and outlets. At the same time, Latin America had been conducting long-lasting and recurring experiments with forms of statism that entwined nationalism and socialism (see above, pp. 188–191). The ideological and political legacies of these experiences still inform, condition, and influence the present.

In other latitudes, however, globalization was perceived as a curse rather than a blessing, on either economic or cultural counts, or both. Economically, globalization could have led, in reality or in perception, to the disarray of national economies, at least for some segments of society. Culturally, globalization provided the context in which larger migratory fluxes arrived from abroad while neoliberalism had replaced the homogenizing melting pot by the salad bowl model from within (see above, pp. 260–263). The resulting diversity and heterogeneity were far from being welcomed by all. Rather, they awakened intolerant reactions by wide sectors in many societies.

Hence, a clear visualization of the segments of society disgruntled with the neoliberal paradigm to the point of becoming the backbone of post-neoliberalism around the world emerges by focusing on the varying economic and cultural effects that neoliberalism had on the lives of individuals and groups. For those people economically better-off in the global neoliberal economy and tolerant with, or even enthusiastic about, diversity, neoliberalism offered the best possible path on both counts. A second group were made economically worse-off by the global neoliberal economy but were tolerant of diversity. For this second group, neoliberalism offered a trade-off in which socioeconomic losses might be compensated by identity empowerment and the appreciation of diversity. In this case, contestation to neoliberalism mainly was based on economic grounds, as shown by the Pink Tide in Latin America. A third group includes those economically better-off but intolerant of diversity to different extents of bigotry. For this third group, neoliberalism offers a tense balance with unclear prospects. The burning question in this case is to what extent economic gains would make for unwelcome diversity—or would it be the other way around. Finally, the fourth group comprises those for whom neoliberalism created a worse-off economic situation while at the same time they are intolerant of diversity to different extents of bigotry. It is the social segment belonging to this fourth category that constitutes the backbone of bigoted post-neoliberalism (Table 7.1).

Bigoted post-neoliberalism has been confronting globalization with a surge of nationalism. In the economic arena, nationalism fosters protectionism. In the cultural sphere, nationalism had acquired an ethno-centric, religious, and xenophobic character that confronted any kind of diversity with generalized bigotry. Conversely, the leading component of economic liberalism in neoliberalism, free trade was slashed while some of the prominent features of political liberalism in neoliberalism, such pluralism, freedom of opinion, and freedom of press were curtailed. Interestingly, however, the thorough success of Third Wave Democracy has been such that the global reach of democratic regimes, even if only formally, has mostly remained in place.

Table 7.1 The social origins of post-neoliberalism

Economic dimension	Cultural dimension	
	Pro-Salad Bowl diversity	Pro-melting pot homogeneity
Better-Off	Win–Win: Firm supporter of neoliberalism	Win-Loss: Balance between socioeconomic success and bigotry
Worse-off	Loss-Win: Balance between socioeconomic stress and identity empowerment	Loss-Loss: Firm detractor of neoliberalism

However, democratic regimes were substantially diluted during three decades of neoliberalism. For one, electoral results were deeply impacted by the corporate world funding of the elections. Next, elected governments were highly constrained by the austerity measures imposed by the IMF and WB. Finally, the end result was that the Washington Consensus reigned supreme regardless of the original ideological orientation and agendas of most elected governments. Post-neoliberalism dilutes democratic regimes further by challenging the embedded assumption that democracy is the political regime that embodies liberal values. What the post-neoliberal situation has created is a divorce between these two: democracy and liberalism. Democratic regimes may continue to run according to constitutions and institutions, although more or less modified. But the values informing many of these democratic regimes are not liberal but ethno-religious-nationalist. Those are, then, illiberal democracies that express and foster the bigotry of the ruling party's leadership and constituencies. And bigoted agendas can be deployed only by authoritarian means. The post-neoliberal situation has brought to the fore democratic regimes that espouse some form of ethno-religious-nationalism and authoritarianism. Such nationalistic "demotarianisms," that is, formally democratic regimes with authoritarian attitudes and behaviors fostering nationalist agendas, have been proliferating during the last decade up to the point that the world hegemons, past and present, helped to foster it.

The financial crisis and recession in the early 2000s in South America launched a pro-social variety of post-neoliberalism reflecting the demands and aspirations of constituencies experiencing the "Loss-Win" situation. This was the same type of social base that in the wake of the global financial crisis and recession sent the Coalition of the Radical Left, Syriza, to power in Greece in 2015 to confront the new round of austerity measures. This was the same type of social base that transformed the Indignados social movement in Spain into a political party, Podemos. In the 2015 general election, Podemos became the third-largest party with more than a fifth of the vote (20.65%), almost on par with the well-established parties that have been alternating in the application of neoliberalism since 1982, the Spanish Socialist Workers' Party and the People's Party with 22 and 28.7%, respectively. This was the same type of social base that on a pan-European scale was behind the emergence of Now the People!, a marginal force in the European Parliament. Last but not least, this was the same type of social base that produced or attempted the takeover of neoliberal parties by supporting left-wing candidates as their new leaders. That is what happened in the world hegemons, past and present, with the election of Jeremy Corbyn as the leader of the U.K. Labor Party in 2015 and with Bernie Sanders as the contesting nominee for the U.S. Democratic Party in 2015 and 2019.

However, the world hegemons, past and present, turned out to be embarked in the opposite direction of post-neoliberalism. They were taking the bigoted path, relying on the constituencies experiencing the "Loss-Loss" situation along with additional support coming from the "Win-Loss" and even the "Loss-Win" situations. The global financial crisis and Great Recession brought not only Occupy and wide support for Bernie Sanders in the United States but also the rise of the Tea Party and Donald Trump's shocking victory in the 2016 presidential election. Not only was there Occupy London, Edinburgh, Glasgow, and Cardiff, and Jeremy Corbyn as the leader of the Labor Party in Great Britain, but also the rise of the Independent Party and the shocking victory in the 2016 British referendum to leave the EU. And throughout the EU as well, bigoted post-neoliberalism has been making substantial inroads.

Amidst the migrant crisis that brought more than 1.5 million immigrants from Africa and the Middle East to Europe during 2015–2018,[58] bigoted post-neoliberalism reached power in Italy in 2018 with the short-lived coalition between Beppe Grillo's Five Star Movement and Matteo Salvini's League Nord. In this same context, albeit not as far-reaching, established right-wing parties—such as the French National Front and the Austrian Freedom Party—and newly formed parties—most prominently Alternative for Germany that became the third-largest party in the Bundestag, along with the Dutch Forum for Democracy, the Danish People's Party, and the Sweden Democrats, represented a generalized phenomenon throughout Europe. They were all riding the bigoted post-neoliberal wave that had been steadily growing as evidenced by stunning electoral performances in Western Europe. In Eastern Europe what made the electoral performances stunning was recurring victories and the rise to and perpetuation in power. Such are the cases of Jarosław Kaczyński's Law and Justice party in Poland since 2015 and Victor Orbán's Fidesz party in Hungary since 2010, while other parties with similar ethno-religious nationalist, anti-migration, and Euro-skeptic agendas participated in ruling coalitions, such as the United Patriots of Bulgaria, the Slovak National party, and the National Alliance in Latvia.

Democratic regimes are rare throughout Asia. In the isolated couple of cases in the Middle East, as of 2019, Recep Tayyip Erdoğan and Binyamin Netanyahu had been able to successfully deliver at once globalization and neoliberalism to the better-off and ethno-religious-nationalism to the worse-off in the Turkish and Israeli societies for the last 16 and 10 years, respectively. The social protests in Istanbul in 2014 and Tel Aviv in 2011 led by constituencies coming mainly from the "Loss-Win" condition and entangled with global waves of protests were to no avail.

It takes a large eastward leap and bounce to reach the next democracy in the continent, which happens to be the largest in the world. In India, the Congress Party had transitioned successfully from the implementation of entangled nationalism and socialism embraced since independence in 1947 to neoliberalism starting around 1977. However, the Congress Party was not able to contain the surge of ethno-religious nationalism coming from constituencies experiencing the "Loss-Loss" situation combined with additional support coming from the "Win-Loss" and even the "Win–Win" situations. In 2014 Narendra Modi and his ethno-religious nationalist Bharatiya Janata Party (BJP) reached power which has continued to grow stronger.

It takes another huge leap eastward across the continent, in fact, all the way to the Pacific Ocean into the island nations and a semi-peninsular one to reach a few additional democratic regimes in South Korea, Japan, Taiwan, the Philippines, Indonesia, Australia, and New Zealand. Also from these countries, signals of the advent of ethno-religious-nationalism and demotarianism have been rising up. For example, the Liberal Democratic Party headed by Shinzo Abe aimed to reform the Japanese "Peace Constitution" in order to reinstate the Emperor as chief of state (rather than a symbolic figurehead), grant the Japan Defense Forces the right to launch war, and ensure homage to the national flag and anthem. A demotarianism component is most bluntly exemplified by Rodrigo Duterte's sustained electoral success in the Philippines despite the allegations of thousands of extrajudicial killings and the repression of the press.[59]

Most of the rest of Asia and Africa are ruled by authoritarian regimes that foster ethno-religious-national agendas of their own. For example, in Burma, the Rohingya Muslims are persecuted by a regime whose figurehead was until recently Aung San Suu Kyi, a Nobel Peace laureate. In Thailand, a military dictatorship, the second since 2006 with a six-year democratic interlude in 2008–2014, has insistently tried to suppress the constantly reemerging Thai Rak Thai Party, a party led by the Shinawatra brothers that is reminiscent in its constituencies and agenda to the Pink Tide parties. The list of authoritarian regimes is long. However, the heavyweight cases at the forefront of that list are no other than the mightiest anti-hegemonic states, Russia and China.

The reversal of Russia's geopolitical and international situation, from encroachment and declining power to expanding assertion (see above, pp. 285–287), is directly related to a sharp, swift, and early transition from the neoliberal mode of governance to the post-neoliberalism one. Boris Yeltsin had opened up the Russian economy to foreign investors and the international financial institutions that steered the application of the Washington Consensus in its "shock therapy" version—that is, with the immediate and complete release of all state controls of the economy, such as currency, prices, trade, and banking controls as well as the privatization of public-owned assets and the withdrawal of state subsidies and programs. The results for the Russian economy and society were devastating. Between 1991 and 1994 life expectancy was reduced by five years and by 1998 the GDP had contracted by around 40%.[60] The ascent of Putin to power, as with that of the Pink Tide in Latin America, corresponded with the commodities boom. Under these circumstances, the Russian economy benefited from the export of oil and gas at very high prices that had allowed for the growth of state revenue, with the concomitant re-empowering of the state and reassertion of statism to confront economic impositions from outside and address the social crisis from within. In the process, Putin enthroned himself into an undisputed leadership of, thus far, two decades.

And whatever dispute might be, a thorough suppression of any opposition and freedom of press will make it acquiesce, while maintaining the formalities of democratic appearances. The Russian case was one of the earliest cases of ethno-religious-nationalistic demotarianism and probably the most influential in terms of inspiration, imitation, support, and, perhaps, by meddling. Interestingly, once again the role of showing the world the way to an alternative mode of governance fell on Russia's shoulder. Such was Russia's role in the wake of the Democratic Revolution in France, pulling the Concert of Europe back into its autocratic track amidst the liberal imperialism of world hegemonic Great Britain (see above, pp. 131–132). Such was the role of the Soviet Union by showing an alternative horizon amidst the rising American world hegemony. This horizon was made visible not only to other Communist regimes but also to a plethora of anti-hegemonic party states around the globe. And such is the role of Russia yet again, as we have been globally transitioning from neoliberal globalization to ethno-religious-nationalistic demotarianism since the opening of the twenty-first century. In this crucial case, Putin's Russia delivers a carrot grown on gas and oil, holds a stick informed by a long-lasting authoritarian tradition, and projects a dream of reinvigorated pride streamed online by trolls and offline through the gun barrel.

When it comes to dreams, however, China has a publicly announced one: The Chinese Dream. If the unarticulated Russian dream is about reinvigorating the pride lost with the collapse of the USSR, the Chinese dream has both a long-standing grievance to address and a far more ambitious goal into the future. The Chinese dream confronts the nightmare of two centuries of humiliation by multiple world powers (see above, pp. 45–46, 49) as a result of lagging behind them economically, technologically, and militarily. At the same time, the dream leverages the astounding economic, technologic, and military catching up of the last four decades to envision a full reversal of fortunes. China will become the new emerging world hegemon in the wake of the decline of the United States from such a position. In so doing, China will be restored to its proper position as the Middle Kingdom or the Kingdom at the Center, 中国.

The dream was implicitly announced by Xi Jinping on occasion of his appointment as President in 2013. Although the Chinese dream is portrayed as an extension of the "Socialism with Chinese characters" project envisioned by Deng Xiaoping, the ascension of Xi Jinping to power actually marks the transition from Deng Xiaoping's neoliberalism with Chinese characters to the current ethno-religious-nationalism with Chinese characters. In this case, the regime does not constitute an illiberal democracy or demotarianism, but a long-lasting and full-fledged authoritarian regime.[61]

What is left, then, of the original—once the one and only—world hegemonic American Dream?! In tandem with an eroded fourfold stick that leaves allies in limbo from Europe to East Asia via the Middle East and a financialized huge carrot that leaves behind the financially unprivileged, the alluring American dream is being contested by an appalling American nightmare.

In this nightmare, the well-being conveyed by the hegemonic vision "there is no way like the American way" is replaced by a poisonous atmosphere made of bigotry, racism, xenophobia, antisemitism, and misogyny compounded by a free ride for lethal assault rifles for all that has resulted in multiple tragedies at the borders and inside the country. A nightmare that entails the combination of the largest per capita expenses in health care (almost double compared to other OECD countries) with a growing lack of access to it for 8.5% of its population (as of 2017), amidst a lethal opioid crisis that has been taking an ever-growing number of lives every year (70,237 overdose deaths in 2017), and a slightly declining life expectancy that positions the world hegemon as number 43 world ranking. A nightmare in which the proposition of "one person, one vote" is being skewed by gerrymandering—the strategic redrawing of electoral districts for partisan electoral gains—to the point that, conflated with the Electoral College system, popular majority loses elections. A nightmare in which the proposition of "one person, one vote" is being skewed yet again by granting political personhood to corporations while rejecting campaign financing restrictions, as the Supreme Court did in 2010, to the point that elections have become big-money elections.[62]

Can this land of nightmares be the Land of the Free? How alluring a dream can emanate from these daily realities for people around the world regularly exposed to them by globally broadcasting mass media? In short, the world hegemon is not just loosening the geopolitical grip it once held with its fourfold stick. It is not even the combination of that with a proportionally shrinking carrot challenged by innovative competitors. It is also the loss of the aura of a desirable place—perhaps even the most desirable place in the world, as it used to be for the many people wanting to move there, and also for people rooted in their countries yet trying to replicate whatever attainable elements of the American way of life were possible back home. That phase seems to be dwindling.[63]

Since 2003, the U.S. world hegemony has been unraveling, and its spiraling down is accelerating. Also since 2003, a post-neoliberal world order started to coalesce, with the rise of the Pink Tide and the consolidation of Putin's Russia being two of its earliest and firmest expressions. Almost two decades later, the bigoted version of post-neoliberalism not only has taken deep roots in Russia but around the globe. By contrast, the Pink Tide that announced the beginning of post-neoliberalism in its pro-social variant was not only waning throughout South America but was actually taken over by ethno-religious-nationalist demotarianism. In Brazil, the mightiest state in the region, where the Pink Tide was originally launched in 2003, the citizenry voted bigot post-neoliberalism into power with the election of Jair Bolsonaro as President in 2018. That same year, the election of Andrés Manuel López Obrador in Mexico and his pro-social post-neoliberalism represents the only recent counterpoint to that tendency not only throughout Latin America, but around the world. During the last decade, ethno-religious-nationalist demotarianism has been consolidating as the new mode of global governance for all but a few struggling isolated cases, most prominently the challenged core of the European Union (Map 7.1).

In the long run, this decline of the U.S. world hegemony takes its place in a secular rise and decline cycle of world hegemonic powers. Similarly, the current wave of authoritarianism and illiberal democracy (2003 onward) appears as an additional pendular oscillation, this time away from Third Wave Democracy (1974–2003), which was an oscillation away from the second wave of authoritarian and anti-hegemonic party states (1945–1974) that surpassed "Second Wave Democracy" (1945–1974), just as the first wave of authoritarian and anti-hegemonic party states (1917–1945) had surpassed the First Wave Democracy (1828–1926) (see above, pp. 11–12, 101–103, 201–202, 213–216, 264–266). By contrast,

Map 7.1   Political regimes during the 2020s—Democracies (black), None-democracies (white), and Illiberal democracies (grey). Compare with Map 6.2, above, p. 265

when we come to assess our current technological and environmental conditions, we seem to be on the verge of unprecedented transformations.

A Couple of Trump Cards: Technological and Ecological Disruptions

The tracking of this *Brief History of Now* began around two centuries ago at the time that a momentous technological transformation, the Industrial Revolution, had matured to remake economics, society, politics, and culture. This was a pivotal moment in which for the first time inorganic entities, that is machines, became able to digest energy and channel it into movement. In so doing, machines started competing and displacing the only entities able to do that before, humans and animals whose muscle power had been producing most of the economic output that history had witnessed but for a few exemptions in which water currents and winds were also harnessed for processes of production (see above, pp. 27–28).

Since this clear break, the Industrial Revolution produced permanent innovations that periodically brought about qualitative breakthroughs. This is how the Second Industrial Revolution (1870s–1914) came to the fore, bringing about a series of innovations including electrification, the chemical industries, and scientific methods of work planning and management such and Taylorism and Fordism, all of which resulted in the advent of mass production (see above, pp. 69–70). With mass production in place and growing ever faster, cheaper, and more effective, the next major jump occurred in the fields of information and communication by increasing the availability, storage, dissemination, and roles of these two in all aspects of social life. In so doing, this third round of the Industrial Revolution, also known as the Information Revolution, is not merely a qualitatively upgraded version of the previous one, the way that the second revolution represented an upgraded version of the original one. Instead, it represents a significant departure from the original and second Industrial Revolutions in as much as it not only upgrades manufacturing processes through information processing, automation, and the launching of new electronic manufactures, but also fosters a new economy of services based on information and communication that supersedes the industrial economy and promotes a post-industrial one. This qualitative jump is acknowledged by referring to the Third Industrial Revolution not as such but rather as the Information Revolution (see above, pp. 244–245). The Fourth Revolution now underway is an outgrowth of this original Information Revolution inasmuch as it is driven by the original breakthroughs of information and communication technologies. And yet, as the Second Industrial Revolution represented a qualitative departure from the original Industrial Revolution, this upcoming Second Information Revolution, also referred to as the Fourth Revolution or Artificial Intelligence Revolution, goes well beyond the confines of the original Information Revolution.

We are currently on the verge of another momentous transformation of comparable proportions to the watershed marked by the Industrial Revolution. The full-fledged unleashing of the Artificial Intelligence Revolution represents another pivotal moment with potentially transformative forces on the scale of the original Industrial Revolution, which marked a clear before-and-after in the history of humankind and the planet. The Artificial Intelligence Revolution is the pivotal moment in which for the first time inorganic entities, that is computers, are becoming able to digest and create information and channel it into decision making. In so doing, computers have started competing and displacing the only entities able to do that before, humans, whose brainpower has been deciding all matters concerning their societies, Planet Earth, and beyond. Now, we may be reaching the point that the Artificial Intelligence Revolution will displace the human brains the way that the Industrial Revolution displaced the human and animal muscles.

The first concrete move in that direction was made back in 1956, when a brainstorming multidisciplinary workshop conducted in Dartmouth College concluded that human intelligence can be described so precisely that a machine can be made to simulate it.[64] Looking back at this early point of departure, stagnation, and setbacks during four decades makes clear that the Artificial Intelligence Revolution advanced as a gradualution (gradual revolution, see above, pp. 30–31). However, by the early twenty-first century the tremendous cumulative successes of the Information Revolution, including the growth of computing power, the huge amounts of ever-growing collected data, and better theoretical understanding had increasingly provided computers with the core of human cognitive functions of problem-solving and learning.[65] That is achieved by programming careful and precise instructions known as algorithms, with some algorithms being capable of learning from data, deploying new strategies to respond to data, and even to write other algorithms.[66]

This set of capacities has been under experimentation for more than two decades in a multiplicity of fields in which previously only humans partook. In cyberspace, artificial intelligence is now fully in charge of certain domains such as search engines, spam filtering, and targeting online advertisements. In the field of gaming, artificial intelligence has already been proving its superiority for a while. Back in 1997, Deep Blue, an IBM chess-playing computer, defeated Garry Kasparov, the world chess champion. A subsequent trend of computers and programs defeating world champions in multiple games unfolded. In 2011, another IBM computer, Watson, a question answering system, defeated Brad Rutter and Ken Jennings, the champions of a popular American television game show *Jeopardy!* based on general-knowledge quizzes. In 2016, the computer program AlphaGo defeated Lee Sedol, the world champion of Go, a strategy game even more complex than chess.[67] For more mundane but useful and consequential purposes the competition continues unfolding in multiple fields including transportation and telecommunications, medicine, science, jurisprudence, finance, marketing, and economics, agriculture, industry, human resources, education, government, military, media, and the arts; in short, in virtually all fields of human activity.

Each of the three previous technological revolutions had far-reaching social repercussions. The Industrial Revolution gave birth to the industrial urban workers and industrial supplier miners. That was the nascent proletariat, namely, a new social class that possessed only its own labor power and its offspring (proles, in Latin). That was the social class with nothing to lose but its chains. As social polarization widened and the contrasts between the technological advances in the means of production and their ownership regime in a few hands sharpened, this was the social class that would unite in a world revolution.[68] The Second Industrial Revolution, however, brought the kernels of mass consumption alongside mass production. In the course of a century (ca. 1870s–1970s), these kernels delivered a bountiful harvest. The grim conditions of the original proletariat, far from deteriorating as expected by the Communists, started to improve by the 1910s and prominently after 1945 through the trickle-down of wealth, technological improvements, and social policies continuously expanded by nation-states.

As economies around the world developed along their own timelines–for example, the North Atlantic economies as early as the 1910s, the Chinese economy since the 1980s, and the Nigerian economy in the

2000s—the proletarians gradually accumulated resources. They reached the point of having quite a lot to lose, to the point that owning more than their own labor power and offspring they ceased to be proletarians and became part of the widening middle class. This increasingly assertive and empowered middle class, however, was thoroughly shaken by the synergy of the Information Revolution that fostered a post-industrial economy: neoliberalism that scaled back or eliminated social safety net policies, and globalization that outsourced jobs offshore.

Hence, since the late 1970s throughout the Western world a new class was on the rise: the precariat, a working class whose working and living conditions became precarious. At the same time, on the receiving ends of the offshore outsourced jobs, such as China and India, a new transition from proletariat to middle classes started to emerge and consolidate. The emergence of the precariat in the developed world asymmetrically mirrors the ascent of the proletarians into middle class in parts of the developing world. In the developed world, the 1870s–1970s century of trickle-down effect was replaced by a trickle-up effect of wealth concentration since the 1980s, while technological improvements and economic globalization led to unemployment, underemployment, or intermittent employment. Moreover, social policies left the precariat without much state support and safety net but instead with higher taxes and flexible labor rules that deemed them dispensable.

By contrast, in those parts of the developing world such as China, India, and South East Asia, the concomitant rise of the proletariat to middle class in the globalization-driven emergent economies resembles the emergence of that class in the North Atlantic a century before the 1980s, but at a remarkably accelerated pace and without much of the support of a welfare state. In the meantime, in the advanced economies, the middle class was reduced to those with professional access to the post-industrial economy—those who performed in multiple fields including transportation and telecommunications, medicine, science, jurisprudence, finance, marketing, economics, agriculture, industry, human resources, education, government, military, media, and the arts; in short, those working in virtually all fields for which the Artificial Intelligence revolution is grooming computers! What will be then the far-reaching social repercussion of this major fourth technological revolution? The risk of mass unemployment? The generalization of the precariat condition?

There are, of course, additional social dynamics triggered by the new technologies of the industrial age. There are additional grim prospects too. The Industrial Revolution liberated humankind from one of its worst recurring calamities: the Malthusian trap. Named after the Scottish scholar who formulated the pattern, this trap pertaining to agrarian societies resulted from the discrepant pace of demographic and economic growth. Whereas human populations grew following geometrical sequences (i.e., following a common ratio, for example doubling in the sequence 3, 6, 12, 24, 48, 96, etc.), economies grew following arithmetic sequences (i.e., following a common difference, for example +3 resulting in the sequence 3, 6, 9, 12, 15, 18, etc.). With human populations growing ever-larger than the available resources, the Four Horsemen of the Apocalypse—pestilence, war, famine, and death—were periodically unleashed to even out the numerical imbalance. Under these conditions, the growth of the human population has been very gradual for millennia. So much so, that it took over 200,000 years for humans to reach the first billion individuals around 1800.

One of the hallmarks of the Industrial Revolution is the dismantling of the Malthusian trap. The constant growth of productivity brought by industrialization evened the pace between demography and economy. So much so, that the Malthusian trap did not recur even as demographic growth accelerated into unimaginable speed. In the wake of the Industrial Revolution, it took only one century and a quarter to double the first billion people: by 1927 there were already two billion people on the planet. As the Industrial Revolution was progressively and globally embraced, demographic growth accelerated further. 33 years down the line, by 1960, the third billion was estimated. Then, an additional billion people was added to the world population within intervals of 14 to 12 years, that is one additional billion people in 1974, 1987, 1999, 2012. The eight billion is expected for 2023.[69]

But the cumulative effects of the technological revolutions go even beyond dismantling the Malthusian trap and growing the world population by a factor of eight in less than two centuries. These technological revolutions also made these people so much wealthier! The estimates for per capita GDP (in 1990 U.S. dollars rounded to nearest 100) amount to $900 in 1870, $1,500 in 1913, $2,100 in 1950, $4,100 in 1973, $6,500 in 2003, and $7,800 in 2010. These rises in per capita GDP, compounded by the almost eightfold demographic growth, means that the world GDP (in 2011 international dollars rounded to nearest 100) has been growing from almost US$2 trillion by 1870 to almost US$90 trillion by 2010.[70]

And yet, around two centuries into these wonders of combined demographic and economic growth, we are daily reminded that there are no free meals. We are now receiving the cumulative bill in the form of climate change, global warming, environmental biodegradation, and geological impact. These are just four of the many horsemen of the Anthropocene, or Human Epoch—namely, the period in the history of Planet Earth in which the planet is significantly impacted by human activity.

Of course, humans have been affecting the planet from very early on, setting fires and bringing species to extinction as hunters, taking down forests to plow fields as agriculturalists. But it is with the four waves of technological revolutionary breakthroughs opened by the Industrial Revolution, sharply intensified since the second half of the twentieth century, that the fast and sustained economic and demographic growth has resulted in widespread pollution, radioactive fallout, plastic accumulation, deforestation, species invasions, and mass species extinction. All these impacts and others have opened a new geological era recorded in rock, triggering urgent concerns for the viability of life conditions on Earth in the near future.[71]

Hence, looking back from our current moment we can recognize new waves of well-known tides in international and domestic politics, economics, and societies. These include world hegemony being contested, global economic integration rescinding, political regimes moving yet again away from democracy, and economic concentration and social inequalities reaching new heights. And yet, at the same time, this current moment confronts us with unprecedented technological and environmental challenges. Back in the days of the Industrial Revolution when human societies were confronted with unprecedented challenges, new ways of thinking were articulated to tackle them. This is how the social sciences and the modern ideologies were born. Now in the face of the conflating old and new challenges it remains to be seen if the critical challenges we are now facing—and will face even more acutely in the future—will result in some forms of intellectual and ideological invigoration capable of tackling them.

Notes

1. Friedrich Katz, *The Life and Times of Pancho Villa* (Palo Alto, CA: Stanford University Press, 1998), 364. Lee Stacy, *Mexico and the United States: Volume 3* (Marshall Cavendish, 2002), 869.

2. Timothy J. Runyan and Jan M. Copes, *To Die Gallantly: The Battle of the Atlantic* (Boulder, CO: Westview Press, 1994), Chapter 7.
3. Robert C. Mikesh, *Japan's World War II Balloon Bomb Attacks on North America* (Washington, DC: Smithsonian Institution Press, 1973). Johnna Rizzo, "Japan's Secret WWII Weapon: Balloon Bombs," *National Geographic,* May 27, 2013, https://news.nationalgeographic.com/news/2013/05/130527-map-video-balloon-bomb-wwii-japanese-air-current-jet-stream/.
4. Matthew J. Morgan, *The Impact of 9/11 on Politics and War: The Day that Changed Everything?* (Palgrave Macmillan, 2009), 222.
5. Patrick Tyler, "A New Power in the Streets," *The New York Times,* February 17, 2003, https://www.nytimes.com/2003/02/17/world/threats-and-responses-news-analysis-a-new-power-in-the-streets.html.
6. "World View of US Role Goes From Bad to Worse," BBC World Service Poll, January 23, 2007, http://news.bbc.co.uk/2/shared/bsp/hi/pdfs/23_01_07_us_poll.pdf. "Most people 'want Iraq pull-out'," *BBC News,* September 7, 2007, http://news.bbc.co.uk/2/hi/middle_east/6981553.stm.
7. "Iraq War Illegal, Says Annan," *BBC News,* September 16, 2004, http://news.bbc.co.uk/2/hi/middle_east/3661134.stm. Ewen MacAskill and Julian Borger, "Iraq War Was Illegal and Breached UN Charter, Says Annan," *The Guardian,* September 15, 2004, https://www.theguardian.com/world/2004/sep/16/iraq.iraq.
8. "Body Count – Casualty Figures after 10 Years of the 'War on Terror' – Iraq Afghanistan Pakistan," archived April 30, 2015 at the Wayback Machine, by IPPNW, PGS and PSR, 1st international edition (March 2015). http://www.ippnw.de/commonFiles/pdfs/Frieden/Body_Count_first_international_edition_2015_final.pdf. Gabriela Motroc, "U.S. War on Terror Has Reportedly Killed 1.3 Million People in a Decade," *Australian National Review,* April 7, 2015. Archived from the original on May 5, 2015, https://web.archive.org/web/20150505004045/http://www.australiannationalreview.com/war-terror-reportedly-killed-13-million-people-decade/.
9. Neta Crawford, "War-related Death, Injury, and Displacement in Afghanistan and Pakistan 2001–2014," Costs of War Series, Brown University, May 22, 2015, https://watson.brown.edu/costsofwar/files/cow/imce/papers/2015/War%20Related%20Casu

alties%20Afghanistan%20and%20Pakistan%202001-2014%20FIN.
pdf.

10. Rod Nordland and Mujib Mashal, "U.S. and Taliban Edge Toward Deal to End America's Longest War," *The New York Times*, January 26, 2019, https://www.nytimes.com/2019/01/26/world/asia/afghanistan-taliban-peace-deal.html.

11. "New Study Estimates 151,000 Violent Iraqi Deaths Since 2003 Invasion," World Health Organization, January 9, 2008, https://www.who.int/mediacentre/news/releases/2008/pr02/en/.

12. Antonio Guterres, "High-Level Segment of the 66th session of the Executive Committee of the High Commissioner's Programme on the Afghan Refugee Situation," UNHCR, October 6, 2015, https://www.unhcr.org/en-us/admin/hcspeeches/5613bd406/high-level-segment-66th-session-executive-committee-high-commissioners.html.

13. "Global Policy Forum Report on Iraq: Displacement and Mortality in Iraq," *globalpolicy.org*, June 2007, https://www.globalpolicy.org/humanitarian-issues-in-iraq/consequences-of-the-war-and-occupation-of-iraq/35742.html.

14. "Estimated Cost to Each U.S. Taxpayer of Each of the Wars in Afghanistan, Iraq and Syria," https://comptroller.defense.gov/Portals/45/documents/Section1090RepSection1090Reports/Section_1090_FY17_NDAA_Cost_of_Wars_to_Per_Taxpayer-March_2019.pdf. Rod Nordland and Mujib Mashal, "U.S. and Taliban Edge Toward Deal to End America's Longest War," *The New York Times*, January 26, 2019, https://www.nytimes.com/2019/01/26/world/asia/afghanistan-taliban-peace-deal.html. Daniel Trotta, "Iraq War Costs U.S. More than $2 Trillion: Study," Reuters World News, March 14, 2013. https://www.reuters.com/article/us-iraq-war-anniversary-idUSBRE92D0PG20130314. Linda Bilmes and Joseph Stiglitz, *The Three Trillion Dollar War: The True Cost of the Iraq Conflict* (W. W. Norton & Company, 2008). Gordon Lubold, "U.S. Spent $5.6 Trillion on Wars in Middle East and Asia: Study," *The Wall Street Journal*, November 8, 2017, https://www.wsj.com/articles/study-estimates-war-costs-at-5-6-trillion-1510106400.

15. Toby Harnden, "Barack Obama Declares the 'War on Terror' Is Over," *The Telegraph*, May 27, 2010, https://www.telegraph.

co.uk/news/worldnews/barackobama/7772598/Barack-Obama-declares-the-War-on-Terror-is-over.html.

16. Thom Shanker, Michael Schmidt and Robert Worth, "In Baghdad, Panetta Leads Uneasy Moment of Closure," *The New York Times*, December 15, 2011, https://www.nytimes.com/2011/12/16/world/middleeast/panetta-in-baghdad-for-iraq-military-handover-ceremony.html.

17. Elise Labott, "Clinton to Syrian Opposition: Ousting al-Assad Is Only First Step in transition," *CNN,* December 6, 2011, https://www.cnn.com/2011/12/06/world/meast/clinton-syrian-opposition/index.html. Mark Landler, "U.S. Considers Resuming Nonlethal Aid to Syrian Opposition," *The New York Times,* January 9, 2014, https://www.nytimes.com/2014/01/10/world/middleeast/syria-aid-may-resume-despite-fears-over-where-it-will-go.html. Ian Black, "US Axes $500 m Scheme to Train Syrian Rebels, Says NYT," *The Guardian,* October 9, 2015, https://www.theguardian.com/world/2015/oct/09/us-to-axe-5-scheme-train-syrian-rebels-nyt.

18. "Obama: U.S. Underestimated Rise of Isis in Iraq and Syria," *CBS News*, September 28, 2014, https://www.cbsnews.com/news/obama-u-s-underestimated-rise-of-isis-in-iraq-and-syria/. Helene Cooper, Mark Landler and Alissa J. Rubin, "Obama Allows Limited Airstrikes on ISIS," *The New York Times*, August 7, 2014, https://www.nytimes.com/2014/08/08/world/middleeast/obama-weighs-military-strikes-to-aid-trapped-iraqis-officials-say.html?_r=0. Jane Timm, "Fact Check: Trump's Right, ISIS Did Lose Almost All Its Territory in Iraq and Syria," *NBC News,* January 30, 2018, https://www.nbcnews.com/card/fact-check-trump-s-right-isis-did-lose-almost-all-n843111.

19. Fawaz A. Gerges, *A History of ISIS* (Princeton, NJ: Princeton University Press, 2016), 21–22.

20. Julian Borger, Patrick Wintour and Kareem Shaheen, "US Military to Maintain Open-Ended Presence in Syria," *The Guardian*, January 17, 2018, https://www.theguardian.com/us-news/2018/jan/17/us-military-syria-isis-iran-assad-tillerson. Karen DeYoung, "Trump Agrees to an Indefinite Military Effort and New Diplomatic Push in Syria, U.S. Officials Say," *The Washington Post*, September 6, 2018, https://www.washingtonpost.com/world/national-security/in-a-shift-trump-approves-an-indefi

nite-military-and-diplomatic-effort-in-syria-us-officials-say/2018/
09/06/0351ab54-b20f-11e8-9a6a-565d92a3585d_story.html?
noredirect=on&utm_term=.64ca5d9e6fe9. Mark Landler, Helene
Cooper and Eric Schmitt, "Trump Withdraws U.S. Forces from
Syria, Declaring 'We Have Won Against ISIS'," *The New York
Times*, December 19, 2018, https://www.nytimes.com/2018/
12/19/us/politics/trump-syria-turkey-troop-withdrawal.html. W.
J. Hennigan, "The U.S. Will Withdraw from Syria. No One's Sure
What Comes Next," *Time*, December 19, 2018, https://time.
com/5484972/donald-trump-syria-withdrawal/. Julian Borger
and Martin Chulov, "Trump Shocks Allies and Advisers with Plan
to Pull US Troops out of Syria," *The Guardian*, December 20,
2018, https://www.theguardian.com/us-news/2018/dec/19/
us-troops-syria-withdrawal-trump.

21. Mark Kramer and Joshua R. Itzkowitz Shifrinson, "NATO
Enlargement—Was There a Promise?" *International Security*
42, no. 1 (2017): 186–192. https://doi.org/10.1162/ISEC_c_
00287. Joshua R. Itzkowitz Shifrinson, "Deal or No Deal? The
End of the Cold War and the U.S. Offer to Limit NATO Expansion," *International Security* 40, no. 4 (2016): 7–44. https://doi.
org/10.1162/ISEC_a_00236. Dave Majumdar, "Newly Declassified Documents: Gorbachev Told NATO Wouldn't Move
Past East German Border," *The National Interest*, December
12, 2017, https://nationalinterest.org/blog/the-buzz/newly-dec
lassified-documents-gorbachev-told-nato-wouldnt-23629.

22. Steven Erlanger and Steven Lee Myers, "NATO Allies Oppose
Bush on Georgia and Ukraine," *The New York Times*, April
3, 2008, https://web.archive.org/web/20190305061544/
https://www.nytimes.com/2008/04/03/world/europe/03n
ato.html?pagewanted=all. Denis Dyomkin, "Russia Says Georgia
War Stopped NATO Expansion," Reuters World News, November
21, 2011, https://in.reuters.com/article/idINIndia-606457201
11121.

23. Marc Champion and Andrew Osborn, "Smoldering Feud,
Then War Tensions at Obscure Border Led to Georgia-Russia
Clash," *The Wall Street Journal,* August 16, 2008, https://
www.wsj.com/articles/SB121884450978145997. Luke Harding,
"Georgia Calls on EU for Independent Inquiry into War," *The*

Guardian, November 19, 2008, https://www.theguardian.com/world/2008/nov/19/georgia-russia-eu-media-inquiry.

24. Roy Allison, "Russia Resurgent? Moscow's Campaign to 'Coerce Georgia to Peace'," *International Affairs* 84, no. 6 (2008): 1145–1171, http://www.chathamhouse.org.uk/files/12445_84_6allison.pdf. Asher Moses, "Georgian Websites Forced Offline in 'Cyber War'," *The Sydney Morning Herald*, August 12, 2008, https://www.smh.com.au/technology/georgian-websites-forced-offline-in-cyber-war-20080812-gdsqac.html. Andrew North, "Georgia Accuses Russia of Violating International Law over South Ossetia," *The Guardian,* July 14, 2015, https://www.theguardian.com/world/2015/jul/14/georgia-accuses-russia-of-violating-international-law-over-south-ossetia. European Parliament Resolution of 17 November 2011 Containing the European Parliament's Recommendations to the Council, the Commission and the EEAS on the Negotiations of the EU-Georgia Association Agreement (2011/2133(INI)). Line 11i. http://www.europarl.europa.eu/sides/getDoc.do?type=TA&language=EN&reference=P7-TA-2011-0514.

25. Steven Erlanger and Steven Lee Myers, "NATO Allies Oppose Bush on Georgia and Ukraine," *The New York Times*, April 3, 2008, https://www.nytimes.com/2008/04/03/world/europe/03nato.html.

26. T. Korotkyi and N. Hendel, "The Legal Status of the Donetsk and Luhansk "Peoples' Republics"," in *The Use of Force against Ukraine and International Law*, eds. S. Sayapin and E. Tsybulenko (The Hague: T.M.C. Asser Press, 2018), https://doi.org/10.1007/978-94-6265-222-4_7.

27. Robert Legvold, *Return to Cold War* (Cambridge: Polity, 2016). Stephen F. Cohen, "If America 'Won the Cold War,' Why Is There Now a 'Second Cold War with Russia'?" *The Nation*, February 14, 2018, https://www.thenation.com/article/if-america-won-the-cold-war-why-is-there-now-a-second-cold-war-with-russia/. Robert D. Crane, "Psychostrategic Warfare and a New U.S.-Russian Cold War," *The American Muslim* (Tam), February 12, 2015, http://theamericanmuslim.org/tam.php/features/articles/psychostrategic-warfare-and-a-new-u.s.-russian-cold-war. Alex Vatanka, "Russian Bombers in Iran and Tehran's Internal Power Struggle," *The National Interest*, August 16, 2016,

https://nationalinterest.org/feature/russian-bombers-iran-teh
rans-internal-power-struggle-17379.

28. U.S. Congress, House, "House Permanent Select Committee on
    Intelligence Report on Russian Active Measures: Majority Report,
    March 22, 2018—Final Report of the Republican Majority,"
    https://docs.house.gov/meetings/IG/IG00/20180322/108
    023/HRPT-115-1_1-p1-U3.pdf. U.S. Congress, House, "House
    Permanent Select Committee on Intelligence Report on Russian
    Active Measures: Minority Views, March 26, 2018—a 98-page
    Response by the Democratic Minority," https://docs.house.gov/
    meetings/IG/IG00/20180322/108023/HRPT-115-2.pdf.

29. Congressional Research Service, "U.S. Sanctions on Russia,"
    updated January 11, 2019, https://fas.org/sgp/crs/row/R45
    415.pdf.

30. Edward Wong, "China Hedges Over Whether South China Sea Is
    a 'Core Interest' Worth War," *The New York Times*, March 30,
    2011, https://www.nytimes.com/2011/03/31/world/asia/31b
    eijing.html.

31. Wade Shepard, "Why the China–Europe 'Silk Road' Rail Network
    Is Growing Fast," *Forbes*, January 28, 2016, https://www.forbes.
    com/sites/wadeshepard/2016/01/28/why-china-europe-silk-
    road-rail-transport-is-growing-fast/#7415b948659a. Salvatore
    Babones, "The New Eurasian Land Bridge Linking China and
    Europe Makes No Economic Sense, So Why Build It?" *Forbes*,
    December 28, 2017, https://www.forbes.com/sites/salvatorebab
    ones/2017/12/28/the-new-eurasian-land-bridge-linking-china-
    and-europe-makes-no-economic-sense-so-why-build-it/#7d3241
    545c9c.

32. World Bank, *Belt and Road Economics: Opportunities and Risks
    of Transport Corridors*, Advance Edition (Washington, DC: World
    Bank, 2019). License: Creative Commons Attribution CC BY 3.0
    IGO, https://openknowledge.worldbank.org/bitstream/handle/
    10986/31878/9781464813924.pdf.

33. "Defense Spending by Country (2020)," *GlobalFirePower.com*,
    https://www.globalfirepower.com/defense-spending-budget.asp.
    "The world's biggest defense budgets in 2019," *Army-
    technology.com*, June 13, 2019. https://www.army-technology.
    com/features/biggest-military-budgets-world/.

34. U.S. Federal Reserve, *U.S. Household Debt Relative to Disposable Income and GDP 1980–2011* (U.S. Federal Reserve, 2012). "The End of the Affair," *The Economist*, November 20, 2008. https://www.economist.com/united-states/2008/11/20/the-end-of-the-affair. Gwynn Guilford, "House Flippers Triggered the US Housing Market Crash, Not Poor Subprime Borrowers," *Quartz*, August 29, 2017, https://qz.com/1064061/house-flippers-tri ggered-the-us-housing-market-crash-not-poor-subprime-borrow ers-a-new-study-shows/. Stefania Albanesi, Giacomo De Giorgi and Jaromir Nosal, "Credit Growth and the Financial Crisis: A New Narrative," NBER Working Paper No. 23740 (August 2017). 10.3386/w23740.

35. Joe Nocera, "Lehman Had to Die So Global Finance Could Live," *The New York Times*, September 11, 2009, https://www.nytimes.com/2009/09/12/business/12nocera.html.

36. Eric Dash, "$5 Billion Said to Be Near for WaMu," *The New York Times*, April 7, 2008, https://www.nytimes.com/2008/04/07/business/07cnd-wamu.html?_r=1&oref=slogin.   Kimberley Amadeo, "Stock Market Crash of 2008," *The Balance*, August 22, 2019, https://www.thebalance.com/stock-market-crash-of-2008-3305535#targetText=The%20stock%20market%20crash%20of,rej ected%20the%20bank%20bailout%20bill. Mike Collins, "The Big Bank Bailout," *Forbes*, July 14, 2015, https://www.forbes.com/sites/mikecollins/2015/07/14/the-big-bank-bailout/#1f1ed8 9b2d83.

37. Aaron Smith, "Eurozone Unemployment Hits Record High," *CNN Business*, October 31, 2012, https://money.cnn.com/2012/10/31/news/economy/euro-unemployment/index.html. "Eurozone Unemployment at Record High in May," *CBS News,* July 1, 2013.

38. Floyd Norris, "United Panic," *The New York Times*, October 24, 2008, https://economix.blogs.nytimes.com//2008/10/24/united-panic. Monica Singhania and Jugal Anchalia, "Volatility in Asian Stock Markets and Global Financial Crisis," *Journal of Advances in Management Research* 10, no. 3 (2013): 333–351.

39. David Goldman, "Summary of U.S. Government Financial Commitments and Investments Related to the Crisis," *CNNMoney.com's Bailout Tracker,* https://money.cnn.com/news/storysupplement/economy/bailouttracker/index.html.

Collins, "The Big Bank Bailout." Michael J. Fleming, "Federal Reserve Liquidity Provision during the Financial Crisis of 2007–2009," Federal Reserve Bank of New York Staff Reports, No. 563, July 2012, https://www.newyorkfed.org/medialibrary/media/research/staff_reports/sr563.pdf.

40. Jon Swaine, "Bank Bailout: Alistair Darling Unveils £500billion Rescue Package," *The Telegraph,* October 8, 2008, https://www.telegraph.co.uk/finance/financialcrisis/3156711/Bank-bailout-Alistair-Darling-unveils-500billion-rescue-package.html.

41. Ken Bensinger, "Public isn't Buying Wall Street Bailout," *Los Angeles Times,* September 26, 2008, https://www.latimes.com/archives/la-xpm-2008-sep-26-fi-voxpop26-story.html.

42. David M. Herszenhorn, "House Approves Bailout on Second Try," *The New York Times,* October 3, 2008, https://www.nytimes.com/2008/10/04/business/economy/04bailout.html.

43. https://www.zillow.com/home-values/ Emmie Martin, "Here's How Much Housing Prices Have Skyrocketed over the Last 50 Years," *CNBS Make It,* June 23, 2017, https://www.cnbc.com/2017/06/23/how-much-housing-prices-have-risen-since-1940.html. Jacob Passy, "These Homes Are Still Worth Less Than They Were in 2007," *MarketWatch,* September 22, 2017, https://www.marketwatch.com/story/these-homes-are-still-worth-less-than-they-were-in-2007-2017-09-21#targetText=In%20August%2C%20the%20median%20national,April%20when%20it%20hit%20%24198%2C000. "Inflation Adjusted Housing Prices," *InflationData.com,* https://inflationdata.com/articles/inflation-adjusted-prices/inflation-adjusted-housing-prices/. "US Inflation Calculator," https://www.usinflationcalculator.com/.

44. "FRED Economic Data: Stock Market Capitalization to GDP for United States," Federal Reserve of St. Louis, https://fred.stlouisfed.org/series/DDDM01USA156NWDB?utm_source=series_page&utm_medium=related_content&utm_term=related_resources&utm_campaign=categories. "Stock Market Capitalization, Percent of GDP - Country Rankings," *TheGlobalEconomy.com,* https://www.theglobaleconomy.com/rankings/Stock_market_capitalization/.

45. "Commodity Prices: Cocoa Beans," Index Mundi, https://www.indexmundi.com/Commodities/?commodity=cocoa-beans&months=360.

46. J. B. Maverick, "How Big Is the Derivatives Market?" *Investopedia*, June 6, 2018, https://www.investopedia.com/ask/answers/052715/how-big-derivatives-market.asp#targetText=According%20to%20the%20most%20recent,significantly%20less%3A%20approximately%20%2412.7%20trillion. Kathrin Brandmeir, Michaela Grimm and Arne Holzhausen, *Allianz Global Wealth Report 2018* (Munich: Allianz SE, September 26, 2018). "GDP (current US$)," The World Bank, https://data.worldbank.org/indicator/ny.gdp.mktp.cd.

47. Jason Fang and Michael Walsh, "Made in China 2025: Beijing's Manufacturing Blueprint and Why the World Is Concerned," *ABC News*, April 28, 2018, https://www.abc.net.au/news/2018-04-29/why-is-made-in-china-2025-making-people-angry/9702374. Ana Swanson, "U.S. and China Expand Trade War as Beijing Matches Trump's Tariffs," *The New York Times*, June 15, 2018, https://www.nytimes.com/2018/06/15/us/politics/us-china-tariffs-trade.html. Lily Kuo, "'There Will Be conflict': US Has Underestimated Huawei, Says Founder," *The Guardian*, May 21, 2019, https://www.theguardian.com/technology/2019/may/21/there-will-be-conflict-huawei-founder-says-us-underestimates-companys-strength.

48. Mattathias Schwartz, "Pre-Occupied: The Origins and Future of Occupy Wall Street." *The New Yorker*, November 20, 2011, https://www.newyorker.com/magazine/2011/11/28/pre-occupied.

49. Lizzy Davies, "Occupy Movement: City-by-City Police Crackdowns So Far," *The Guardian*, November 15, 2011, https://www.theguardian.com/world/blog/2011/nov/15/occupy-movement-police-crackdowns?CMP=twt_gu. https://web.archive.org/web/20130514230107/http://www.occupytogether.org/.

50. Derek Thompson, "Occupy the World: The '99 Percent' Movement Goes Global", *The Atlantic,* October 15, 2011, https://www.theatlantic.com/business/archive/2011/10/occupy-the-world-the-99-percent-movement-goes-global/246757/. Karla Adam, "Occupy Wall Street Protests Go Global," *The Washington Post,* October 15, 2011, https://www.washingtonpost.com/world/europe/occupy-wall-street-protests-go-global/2011/10/15/gIQAp7kimL_story.html. "As 'Occupy' Protesters Promise New Strategies for 2012, Global Citizens Are in the Dark but

Sympathetic," *Ipsos*, January 20, 2012, https://www.ipsos.com/en-us/occupy-protesters-promise-new-strategies-2012-global-citizens-are-dark-sympathetic.

51. Megan Leonhardt, "The Lasting Effects of Occupy Wall Street, Five Years Later," *Money*, September 16, 2016, http://money.com/money/4495707/occupy-wall-street-anniversary-effects/.

52. Steve Ember, "Latin American Economic Crisis," In the News, *VOA Learning English*, August 9, 2002, https://learningenglish.voanews.com/a/a-23-a-2002-08-09-4-1-83109052/119706.html.

53. Jim Saxton, "Argentina's Economic Crisis: Causes and Cures," *Joint Economic Committee*. Washington, DC: United States Congress, June 2003.

54. "Argentina Memorandum of Economic Policies," International Monetary Fund, February 14, 2000. https://www.imf.org/external/np/loi/2000/arg/01/index.htm.

55. Clifford Krauss, "Argentina Scrambles for I.M.F. Loans," *The New York Times*, December 11, 2001, https://www.nytimes.com/2001/12/11/business/argentina-scrambles-for-imf-loans.html?pagewanted=print.

56. Bolivia: Evo Morales (2006–present), Chile: Michelle Bachelet (2006–2010; 2014–2018), Dominican Republic: Leonel Fernández (2004–2012), Ecuador: Rafael Correa (2007–2017), El Salvador: Mauricio Funes (2009–2014), Honduras: Manuel Zelaya (2006–2009), Nicaragua: Daniel Ortega (2007–present), Paraguay: Fernando Lugo (2008–2012), Uruguay: Tabaré Vázquez (2005–2010).

57. José Antonio Ocampo, "Commodity-Led Development in Latin America," *International Development Policy* 9, (2017): 51–76. https://journals.openedition.org/poldev/2354. Angus Deaton, "Commodity Prices and Growth in Africa," *Journal of Economic Perspectives* 13, no. 3 (1999): 23–40.

58. Mark Goldberg, "European Union Releases Facts and Figures for Migrant and Refugees Arrivals in 2018," *UN Dispatch*, December 11, 2018, https://www.undispatch.com/european-union-releases-facts-and-figures-for-migrant-and-refugees-arrivals-in-2018/.

59. Vergel O. Santos, "The Philippines Just Became More Authoritarian, Thanks to the People," *The New York Times*, May

24, 2019, https://www.nytimes.com/2019/05/24/opinion/phi lippines-duterte-election-senate.html.

60. Judy Dempseyjan, "Study Looks at Mortality in Post-Soviet Era," *The New York Times*, January 16, 2009, https://www.nyt imes.com/2009/01/16/world/europe/16europe.html. Andrei Shleifer and Daniel Treisman, *A Normal Country*, Harvard Institute of Economic Research Discussion, Paper Number 2019 (Cambridge, MA: Harvard University, 2003), 41.

61. Mingfu Liu, *The China Dream: Great Power Thinking and Strategic Posture in the Post-American Era* (CN Times Beijing Media Time United Publishing Company Limited, 2015). "What does Xi Jinping's China Dream mean?" *BBC News*, June 6, 2013.

62. Citizens United v. Federal Election Commission. Legal Information Institute. https://www.law.cornell.edu/supct/cert/08-205.

63. Alison Faupel et al., "Hate Crimes Are on the Rise. What Does It Take to Get State Governments to Respond?" *The Washington Post,* August 13, 2019, https://www.washingtonpost.com/pol itics/2019/08/13/hate-crimes-are-rise-what-does-it-take-get-state-governments-respond/. Bradley Sawyer and Cynthia Cox, "How Does Health Spending in the U.S. Compare to Other Countries?" *Peterson-KFF Health System Tracker*, December 7, 2018, https://www.healthsystemtracker.org/chart-collection/hea lth-spending-u-s-compare-countries/#item-start. Jasmine Kim, "Rate of Uninsured Americans Rises for the First Time Since Obamacare Took Effect in 2014," *CNBS*, September 10, 2019, https://www.cnbc.com/2019/09/10/rate-of-insured-americ ans-decreases-for-the-first-time-since-obamacare.html. "Overdose Death Rates," National Institute of Drug Abuse. Revised January 2019, https://www.drugabuse.gov/related-topics/trends-statis tics/overdose-death-rates. Grace Donnelly, "Here's Why Life Expectancy in the U.S. Dropped Again This Year," *Fortune*, February 9, 2018, https://fortune.com/2018/02/09/us-life-expectancy-dropped-again/. Anthony McGann, *Gerrymandering in America: The House of Representatives, the Supreme Court, and the Future of Popular Sovereignty* (Cambridge University Press, 2016). Nicholas Confessore, Sarah Cohen and Karen Yourish, "Buying Power: The Families Funding the 2016 Presidential Election," *The New York Times*, October 10, 2015, https://www.

nytimes.com/interactive/2015/10/11/us/politics/2016-presid
ential-election-super-pac-donors.html.

64. Stuart J. Russell and Peter Norvig, *Artificial Intelligence: A Modern Approach*, 3rd ed. (Upper Saddle River, NJ: Prentice Hall, 2009), 17.

65. Andreas Kaplan and Michael Haenlein, "Siri, Siri, in My Hand: Who's the Fairest in the Land? On the Interpretations, Illustrations, and Implications of Artificial Intelligence," *Business Horizons* 62, no.1 (2019): 15–25. 10.1016/j.bushor.2018.08.004.

66. Pedro Domingos, *The Master Algorithm: How the Quest for the Ultimate Learning Machine Will Remake Our World* (Basic Books, 2015).

67. Pamela McCorduck, *Machines Who Think*, 2nd ed. (Natick, MA: A. K. Peters, Ltd., 2004), 480–483. John Markoff, "Computer Wins on 'Jeopardy!': Trivial, It's Not," *The New York Times*, February 16, 2011, https://www.nytimes.com/2011/02/17/science/17jeopardy-watson.html. "Artificial Intelligence: Google's AlphaGo Beats Go Master Lee Se-dol,"*BBC News*, March 12, 2016, https://www.bbc.com/news/technology-35785875.

68. Marx and Engels, *The Communist Manifesto*.

69. Vaclav Smil, "Global Population: Milestones, Hopes, and Concerns," *Medicine & Global Survival* 5, no. 2 (1998): 105–108.

70. Hunt, Michael, The World Transformed, 436. Max Roser, "Economic Growth," *Our World in Data*, https://ourworldindata.org/economic-growth.

71. Erle C. Ellis, *Anthropocene: A Very Short Introduction* (Oxford: Oxford University Press, 2018). Anthropocene Working Group, International Commission on Stratigraphy, "Results of Binding Vote by AWG," Subcommission on Quaternary Stratigraphy, May 21, 2019, https://web.archive.org/web/20190605091924/http://quaternary.stratigraphy.org/working-groups/anthropocene/. Meera Subramanian, "Anthropocene Now: Influential Panel Votes to Recognize Earth's New Epoch," *Nature*, May 21, 2019, https://www.nature.com/articles/d41586-019-01641-5.

CHAPTER 8

The Big Picture: Overall Patterns Amidst Convoluted Developments

A Brief Recapitulation
of Convoluted Developments

There are many ways to tell every single history and *The Brief History of Now* is no exception. The point of departure (1851–1914) was the rise and consolidation of the British world hegemony enabled by the techno-logical, economic, social, and political transformations embodied in the synergy of the industrial and democratic revolutions. Together with the ideologies and policies of free trade and comparative advantage, a global economy was fully articulated with British culture—and Western Euro-pean more broadly—making inroads in the four corners of the world. In the second act (1914–1945), the contestation of the British world hegemony in the form of two world wars—with Communist Revolution that sent shockwaves inspiring or triggering anti-hegemonic party states around the world and a global economic depression in between—sank that hegemonic position at the same time that economic globalization imploded. A brave new world (1946–1973), a bi-polar one, emerged next with a new world hegemon, the United States. This new world hegemon was very different from the previous one because, among many other reasons, the United States world hegemony co-existed with a contending counter-hegemon. Amidst this confrontation, the nations of the world gained some wiggle room to experiment with developmental strategies aiming to converge with the advanced economies. These experiments,

© The Author(s), under exclusive license to Springer Nature Switzerland AG 2021
D. Olstein, *A Brief History of Now*,
https://doi.org/10.1007/978-3-030-82420-4_8

however, came to a halt when global convergence occurred (1973–2003). That global convergence, however, was not the intended one that sought an even economic development. That global convergence, instead, consisted on the deployment of the same governance style around the world. Neoliberalism, the ideology and practice espoused by both world hegemons, past and present, took root worldwide in tandem with a new major technological breakthrough. The Information Revolution, which was the crystallization of economic globalization as we know it, coincided with the demise of the Soviet Union, and the enthronement of the United States as the uncontested world hegemon. Yet, its privileged position was short-lived (2001–2020), and to a significant extent, because of failures of its own making. This has left the world in its current quagmire as we confront the critical challenges of a qualitatively different technological revolution and climate change.

These many developments moving in multiple, unexpected, convoluted, and untamed directions characterize the chaotic unfolding of history. And yet, for all this long-lasting and unstoppable commotion that *The Brief History of Now* has described, we have also tried to visualize the major trends that bring a visible order underneath the apparent chaos. That order was encapsulated by the image of two successive bell curves describing the trajectories of five crucial dimensions: world hegemony, economic globalization, political regimes, socioeconomic inequality, and technological breakthroughs. Hence, by now, not only have some of the key turns of the chaotic unfolding of history been grasped and digested, but also the evolution of these five variables has been presented. This has permitted us a closer look at the interplay between them in order to discern some ongoing recurrent patterns that indicate regularities and, hence, order.

The identification of such patterns can enhance our understanding of past trajectories, contextualize our particular moment in the present within a recognizable pattern, and envision future possible trajectories if these patterns were to continue unfolding in ways that they have undergone in the past. Patterns, however, have their limits as they experience transformations, reach dead ends, or are marginalized by more decisive emerging dynamics.

OVERALL PATTERNS: FIVEFOLD CORRESPONDENCES

The pairing of the trajectories of world hegemony and economic global-ization make for a clear-cut departing point in the exploration of interplay between five of the trajectories. A strong correspondence governs the interplay between these two. The days of British world hegemony (1851–1914) as well as the timespan of United States world hegemony since 1945 correspond with time periods in which the world economy became articulated and integrated. Similarly, by the time that United States world hegemony became uncontested in 1991, such economic integra-tion achieved global reach, larger volume, faster speed, and more intense effects. Conversely, during the time period in which the world hegemonic position remained vacant between 1914 and 1945, with Great Britain unable and the United States unwilling to fill in, global economic inte-gration went into decline, falling to its lowest levels in the wake of the 1929 Global Depression. Finally, in the present moment, the uncertain-ties about the future of the United States world hegemony and economic globalization seem to move hand in hand once again.

A similar sequence is observed by observing the co-evolution of world hegemony and technological breakthroughs. Among all other attributes—economic, political, and military power as well as ideological and cultural appeal—the world hegemon was the undisputed leader in technolog-ical innovation. That was clearly the case during the British emergence and consolidation as the world hegemon unfolding in tandem with the British technological lead. Its home-grown Industrial Revolution harnessed hydro-power and steam engine technology (e.g., Newcomen steam-powered pump for coal extraction, spinning jenny for spinning threads, power loom for weaving cloth), transportation (e.g., the locomo-tive and steamship), and communications (e.g., telegraph) to transform production beyond recognition. Conversely, the road toward the Big Brexit was paved by the British loss of leadership in technological inno-vation during the Second Industrial Revolution (1870–1920) fostered by electrification, chemical industry, and the mass production assembly line in which both Germany and the United States—two of the party spoilers—took the lead. The attrition and collapse of the British world hegemony between 1914 and 1945 fully correspond with the relegation of Great Britain from its previous role as the world's technological leader.

The United States had emerged as the world hegemon in 1945 in tandem with the unlocking of nuclear power. The Soviet Union, as the counter-hegemon, however, was able to catch up with this technology soon after and even to briefly surpass the world hegemon in some specific technological fields with its rocket technology and space exploration capabilities. These technological circumstances correspond to a firm contestation of the U.S. world hegemony. The United States was denied access to a significant portion of the world and was precluded from prevailing as the one and only role model for the nations of the world to follow in their paths toward the future.

However, it was precisely in the context of the competition produced by this momentary and specific Soviet technological preeminence that the world hegemon ended up fostering the Information Revolution. With this, the United States reasserted not only its technological leadership but its world hegemony, bringing it up to a whole new level by dismantling the bi-polar world of the Cold War and replaced it with a globalized one.

Now with the leading role of the United States in the "Industrial Revolution 4.0" or Artificial Intelligence Revolution, the expectation would be that, based on this long-lasting correspondence between technological leadership and world hegemony, this Fourth Industrial Revolution will carry U.S. world hegemony further. And yet, in contrast with the Information Revolution, which was decisively led by the United States alone, the Industrial Revolution 4.0 is being simultaneously, independently, and interdependently fostered within the European Union, China, and additional countries as well. That makes for a potentially different landscape of technological leadership and world hegemony. The uncertainty of the future with regard to the continuing correspondence between United States technological leadership and U.S. world hegemony has parallel uncertainties regarding the future of the U.S. world hegemony and economic globalization.

In the past, there have been clear correspondences between these two pairs—world hegemony and economic globalization, world hegemony and technological leadership. Unsurprisingly this also means that these three factors can be consistently aligned. During the British world hegemony, coincidental with its leadership of the major technological breakthroughs of the Industrial Revolution, a globalized economy had coalesced, expanded, and intensified. The loss of the technological leadership amidst the unfolding of the Second Industrial Revolution parallels the contestation of the British world hegemony by two emerging challengers: Germany, which tried to overtake that role by military means, and the United States, which ended up taking over the role in the wake of Germany's failure.

Throughout this contested phase of world hegemony, the global economy established in the nineteenth century was shaken to its core and the first wave of industrial globalization eventually subsided. The gradual rise of the second wave of globalization starting after the end of the Second World War corresponded with the assertion of the United States, already the leader in technology, as the new world hegemon. These three dimensions—the reach, volume, and speed of globalization, the presence of the world hegemon, and the continuous expansion of the technological frontiers—continued growing in sync. That was shown yet again with the technological breakthrough represented by the Information Revolution, the assertion of the United States as the world hegemon with unbounded global reach and sole role model pointing the direction toward the future, and the articulation of a full-fledged global economy on an unprecedented scale, speed, and intensity.

This triple correspondence can be extended to a fourth variable: socioeconomic inequality. Very simply put, the two phases of economic globalization under a world hegemon that corresponded with major technological breakthroughs also coincided with growing absolute socioeconomic inequalities within and between societies.

That clearly was the case between societies during the first wave of globalization under British hegemony. The widening gap resulting from the Industrial Revolution first in Great Britain, then Western Europe, and then the United States was depicted by the notions of the Great Divergence and the American Divergence (see above, pp. 52–59, 73–74). The widening gap within the industrializing societies consisted of the emergence of a new pyramidal society in the urban centers that was highly polarized between the owners of the growing industries and the growing masses of workers working in them.

Similarly, as the second wave of globalization under U.S. hegemony entered its unbounded phase following the replacement of the bi-polar world of the Cold World with that of contemporary globalization, a widening socioeconomic gap of inequalities between and within societies has been observed once again. This time the widening gap, referred to as the Great Bifurcation, was led by a new technological breakthrough, the Information Revolution, in tandem with a set of economic policies known as neoliberalism that recapitulated some of the same economic policies deployed during the first wave of globalization.

This Great Bifurcation took place for the most part both between and within societies. However, the surge of China during this period defies this overall trend. This country succeeded remarkably in narrowing its inequality gap with the most prosperous economies. This Chinese path is being emulated by the South East Asian countries that are growing their economies and, hence, closing the relative inequality gap with the developed economies. At the same time, however, China and South East Asia are no exception to the widening inequalities within societies as they actually represent extreme cases for this trend (see above, pp. xx).

It is worth emphasizing that the consistency of this clear quadruple correspondence between world hegemony and economic globalization, leadership in technological breakthroughs and socioeconomic inequalities is independently observed in three separate instances of the global past. First, during the period running between 1851 and 1914 as well as for a second time during the period from the 1970s up to the opening of the twenty-first century, the presence of a clear world hegemon corresponded with a globalizing economy, a major technological breakthrough, and widening inequality gaps within and between societies. Conversely, during the period in between these two phases (1914–1970s), a reversed quadruple correspondence is further evidence of the affinity between these four variables.

During this sandwiched period, world hegemony was contested, throughout the Big Brexit (1914–1945), or contained, throughout the Cold War. Under both circumstances, economic globalization was diminished in volume, intensity, and/or scope. The Big Brexit corresponds with the dismantling of the globalized economy of the first wave of globalization. During the days of the Cold War, the drives toward a global economy were limited and a new wave of globalization could not take-off in a full-fledged fashion. True, major technological breakthroughs occurred throughout this period, particularly in aviation, nuclear power, and rocket technology. And yet, the impact of those cutting-edge technologies, crucial for military might and space exploration, were not as transformative for economy and society as were the First and Second Industrial Revolutions before them and the Information Revolution after.

As for the unfolding of socioeconomic inequality between and within societies, this period was characterized as the Great Compression, namely, a period of narrowing socioeconomic gaps, domestically and internationally. This compression, tragically began during the Big Brexit as the thorough devastation self-inflicted by the European society, unintendedly closed the wide gap established during the Great Divergence. This same process of wealth and capital destruction accounts for the shrinking of domestic inequality within European societies.

And yet, beyond this negative path of equalization by sheer wealth and capital destruction in the wake of the First World War, the Global Depression, and most crucially the Second World War, a positive path toward equalization was proactively pursued. Throughout the world, different measures of capital, wealth, and/or income redistribution were established, from the most radical steps of eliminating private property in Communist regimes, throughout multiple forms of wealth (e.g., land distribution) and income (e.g., welfare state) redistribution. The period between 1914 and the mid-1970s, and more prominently since 1945, lacked an uncontested world hegemon, an economic tight globalization, and a productively transformative technological breakthrough. This was also the period that corresponded with the shrinking of socioeconomic gaps between and within societies.

When coming to interpret the quadruple correspondence by prioritizing one of the four variables over the others, linear models can be articulated. For example, in designating technological innovation as the leading variable, the availability of a pathbreaking technology can be seen as a precondition for the making of a world hegemon standing above all other states in economic, political, and military power, as well as cultural appeal. Similarly, the availability of such a technology can simultaneously be seen as a precondition or at least a facilitating condition to articulate the world economy into globalization, given its contributions to production, transportation, communication, and/or information. Finally, a technological breakthrough generates or accentuates the inequality gap between and within societies between those who have or do not have access to the new pathbreaking technologies. The contrast between industrialized and un-industrialized societies as well as the wealth and income gap between industrialists and workers illustrates this point for the second half of the nineteenth century. For the late twentieth century, the technology-inequality link is exemplified by the digital divide (see above, pp. 256–257).

Given the mighty transformative power of technology, it may be tempting to embrace such a series of linear processes ruled by technological innovation. However, such technological primacy does not preclude critical roles for the other variables. For instance, in addition to this technologically driven dynamic, the existence of a world hegemon able to stabilize the world order can be seen as a necessary precondition for opening up the world economy and subsequent articulation of economic globalization. Historically, both waves of economic globalization were preceded by the rise of a world hegemon. Conversely, the absence of a world hegemon coincided with the demise of the globalized economy. A globalized economy, in its turn, brings new opportunities to those who can benefit from economic openness and new potential damages that it can inflict on the rest. This globalization has historically amplified the levels of absolute socioeconomic inequalities within and between societies.

And yet such socioeconomic inequalities can be adopted not only as the destination of this linear process but actually as its very point of departure; because it is among the better-off societies in the world and institutions that the preconditions for technological breakthroughs abound: economic resources, cutting-edge knowledge, and hence investment in education, research, and development. And so, societies ranking at the top of the world division of wealth and power represent both plausible cradles for major technological breakthroughs and potential candidates for world hegemony.

That said, turning the table around from a linear technological interpretation into an equally linear one in which socioeconomic inequality is the departing point is less useful than visualizing the feedback loop at play between these four variables. Socioeconomic inequality, technological breakthroughs, world hegemony, and economic globalization have been swirling in tandem, synergizing with one another as the synchronicity of their corresponding trends has shown. Technological breakthrough, consolidation of a world hegemon, economic globalization, and growing inequalities had clearly spiraled up between 1851 and 1914 and since the 1980s. By contrast, this synergy was absent between 1914 and the 1970s (Diagram 8.1).

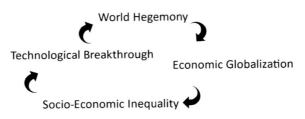

Diagram 8.1   Linear versus synergic model

Besides these synergies, every process unfolds according to its own dynamics. For instance, it is true that a technological breakthrough was a necessary condition for a world hegemon to reach its privileged position. And yet this is not how the ascent to world hegemony unfolded in either the British or the U.S. case. Ascent to world hegemony is a political process attained by political means, or more precisely by a defining showdown of force of global proportions, namely, a world war before the nuclear era, a cold war during it. Being fundamentally a political process, it is closely related to the trends in political regimes, the fifth variable, so far absent from the pattern analysis of correspondences.

By tracing the links between the rise of world hegemons and the trends of political regimes, a clear and consistent pattern can also be visualized. This pattern consists of the following sequence: An inconclusive imperial war triggers a revolution, which sparks both a reaction against it as well as its diffusion to other societies. Next, a conclusive imperial war follows in the wake of which the triumphant power becomes the world hegemon. And with the rise of the world hegemon, a new wave of democracy emerges. This six-stage pattern of ascendency to world hegemony and rise of democracy has played out three times (Diagram 8.2).

The first cycle started in 1756 with the outbreak of the Seven Years War. The second cycle was sparked by the First World War (1914–1918).

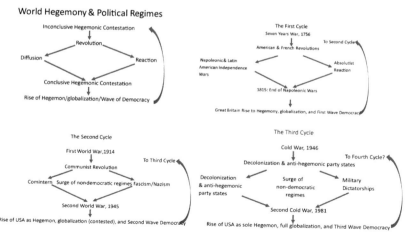

Diagram 8.2   Cycles of world hegemony & political regimes

Finally, the third cycle was triggered by the Cold War. The dire conditions suffered by the societies engaged in these conflicts resulted in the outbreak of a revolution in one or more of the societies involved. In this way, the Seven Years War is directly related to the onset of the American Revolution, whose participants refused to pay the bill for that war. The Seven Years War with the American Revolution in its wake, backed by France as a revanche against Britain, were also related to the unfolding of the French Revolution after the gathering of an assembly, the States General, in 1789 to discuss how to pay for those campaigns.

The second occurrence of the link "inconclusive imperial war – revolution" happened in the wake of more than three years of total war between July 1914 and the outbreak of the Communist Revolution in Russia in November 1917. The third instance unfolded amidst the Cold War as the massive second wave of anti-hegemonic party states emerged, decolonization unfolded, and multiple revolutions in the Global South took off. All these three revolutionary developments occurred rather simultaneously and in many cases, they overlapped. The sequence of "decolonization-revolution-rise of anti-hegemonic party states" as experienced in multiple societies exemplifies such overlaps.

Each of these revolutions in the wake of inconclusive imperial wars fostered one of the most radicalized ideologies of the time: republicanism and liberalism in the monarchic world of 1756, communism in the capitalist world of 1914, and multiple combinations of nationalism and socialism in the colonial world and Global South of 1947 onward. These three rounds of revolution and the fostering of their ideologies, on their turn, led to one of two reactions. The first of those was indeed, pure and simple, a reaction: a reactionary confrontation. That is, a forceful rejection of the new ideologies and a violent suppression of the constituencies that supported them. The monarchists, the absolutists, the conservatives, the loyalists (to the king) reacted against republicanism and liberalism. The nineteenth century provided an ample battleground for the confrontation between these ideologies. Fascism, Nazism, conservatism, and liberalism reacted against communism and its supporters during the second quarter of the twentieth century. Conservatism and liberalism, mostly in the form of military dictatorship and other forms of authoritarianism, reacted against anti-hegemonic party states mostly between 1955 and 1989.

The second possible reaction to revolutions was attempts to disseminate them. The first channel for such diffusion was ideological. Republicanism, liberalism, communism, and combinations of nationalism and socialism gained supporters beyond the boundaries of the states in which these revolutions happened. Supporters of these ideologies attempted to foster them in their own societies. This is what German Liberals did in 1848 and German Communists did in 1918, for example. This is what Nkrumah did in Africa for the first time (in Ghana, 1957) following in the footsteps of Nehru in India a decade earlier. Conversely, and sometimes in addition, the revolutionary state exported its revolution by moving beyond its boundaries. Napoleon invaded Europe presumably carrying the republican message, even if in practice he also had several monarchs established. The Soviet Union supported to different degrees the communist revolutionary attempts in Germany, Finland, and Bulgaria. Nasser supported the Yemen Arab Republic in its revolution and the Algerian FLN (National Liberation Front) in launching its struggle for independence.

Subsequently, the antagonist responses to the revolutions—still lingering because the imperial war was inconclusive—crystallized and fomented what was to become a conclusive imperial war. The French Revolution resulted in the Revolutionary and Napoleonic Wars in which France aimed to crash the absolutist dynasties while those reciprocated in kind. The Communist Revolution in Russia led to the establishment of the Comintern that aimed to export the revolution. These attempts nurtured the rise to power of fascism and Nazism. Shortly after, these two reactionary regimes launched the Second World War. The second wave of anti-hegemonic party states, inspired, backed, and/or rolled over by the Soviet Union was confronted in one country after the other by military coups backed by the United States. By 1980 the détente between the superpowers (1969–1980) was displaced by the launching of the Second Cold War.

Finally, each of these conclusive imperial wars crowned the rising mightier power as world hegemon. The Napoleonic Wars did that for Britain, which was clearly on the rise since the Seven Years War. The Second World War did that for the United States, which was clearly on the rise since the First World War. The Cold War managed to cast doubts on the U.S. hegemony but the Second Cold War assured that position. Each of these three cycles (1756–1914; 1914–1945; 1947–1991) ended in the ascent of a world hegemon and corresponded with each one of the three waves of democracy. Each of these three cycles was triggered by the explosion of the antagonism between the mightiest two powers (France and Great Britain; Great Britain and Germany; United States and USSR) into a naked struggle. Are there any such triggers on the horizon now?

Overall Patterns and Some of the Questions of the Present and Future

One cluster of urgent questions rooted in these patterns has to do with the present and future of world hegemony. By now, it seems that we have indeed opened a fourth cycle; we are amidst an inconclusive hegemonic contestation. The possession of nuclear weapons has made the Second World War the last world war, thus far. Hence, during the third cycle, both the inconclusive and conclusive hegemonic contestations took the form of "cold wars" instead of world wars. The current international situation, at the outset of this fourth cycle, can also be depicted as that of a renewed cold war, by now on a milder and smaller scale, in which regional proxy wars are being fought by Russia in the Ukraine and Syria, with the United States disengaging from these conflicts. Multiple revolutions—the second phase of the six stages pattern of ascendency to world hegemony and rise of democratic wave—were attempted during the Arab Spring. They resulted, for the most part, in different forms of failure: chaos in Libya, civil war in Syria and Yemen, restoration of authoritarianism in Egypt and Syria and most likely in Libya and Yemen as well. This reassertion of authoritarian regimes in reaction to these revolutionary attempts is, in turn, part of the broader surge of nondemocratic regimes and illiberal democracies since the 2010s. These preliminary developments of the fourth cycle are reminiscent of the sequences observed in the previous ones, although they are unfolding with a far milder intensity and are less consequential so far. At the same time, hegemonic contestation is taking the form of mounting economic tensions between the United States and China that exploded in the outbreak of a full-fledged trade war after 40 years of sustained collaboration beginning in 1979.

The United States had lost the clear economic leadership that set it apart from the rest of the world in 1945. The United States had also lost the clear political leadership that made it the undisputed world hegemon in 1990. Acknowledgment of these losses is part of what is behind the "Make America Great Again" mindset. The loss of U.S. economic competitiveness is currently being addressed with protectionist policies, in itself an acknowledgment of losing hegemonic ground; an undisputed world hegemon promotes free trade ("let us all compete and let us alone—the world hegemon—prevail") (see above, pp. 120–121) and renegotiation of trade deals. It is also subject to demands by its political and military allies (e.g., NATO, Japan, South Korea) to pay a bigger share of the military bill. From the ally's perspective, such demands may address an economic need, but they also reflect and deepen the loss of political leadership compounded by swift military withdrawals (Syria, Iraq, Afghanistan) that compromise the future of past allies. And yet, for all of these heavy losses, their unraveling, and the contestations coming from contenders, competitors, and disgruntled allies, the United States still is the world hegemon.

When it comes to contenders, Russia leads the list. Russia is a military and geostrategic mighty state, as it has been for more than two centuries, commanding the eastern third of Europe and the northern half of Asia. Whereas the maritime empires established by the Atlantic powers underwent decolonization, the Russian continental empire did not. The result: the largest country on Earth. The equivalent would be, say, Spain still holding to the Americas, from California to Tierra del Fuego. This mighty state's economy, however, depends heavily on its natural resources, of which it has plenty, perhaps as much as a third of the planetary total. Russia is fundamentally a gas and oil exporting economy with a large and top-notch arms industry. These are its strengths but also its limits.

The strengths of China go far beyond those of Russia with an economy that after growing at a yearly average rate of 10% for three decades has become the world's second largest. If there is one prominent feature about world hegemons past and present, it is that they have been in their turn the factory of the world. This is what China has become. However, Great Britain and the United States achieved that position during the industrial age whereas China is taking on this role in the post-industrial age, when the source of economic prowess and power lies somewhere else. Nevertheless, for more than a decade the Chinese economy, even though the major destination for industrial production outsourcing, has been also moving beyond the development of its industrial sector. One direction of growth has been into the financial sector, making investments all around the world. The other direction has been moving its industries up the technological ladder, reaching the very highest rungs of high-tech.

Still, the emphasis on China's rise and prospects as future world hegemon doesn't fully take into account the fundamental problems underneath the visible success. China's economic growth is slowing down. Since the 2010s annual GDP growth has been in single digits, declining to 6% in 2019. Most economies would be more than satisfied with such a rate of growth; but not necessarily the Chinese population, which has granted their tolerance of an authoritarian regime as long as the economic benefits continue to grow. Would a continuing and perhaps deepening slowdown in the economy alter the uncontested position of the Communist Party authoritarian regime?

At the margins of China, contention is visible in Hong Kong and noticeable in Xingjian, based on the thorough repression of the Uighur population. And even if the economy were to rise again, the ecological damage will continue deepening, causing disaffection with a regime whose economic success can't buy breathable air for its subjects. In short, the standard terms of the discussion on the future of world hegemony tend to emphasize the decline of the United States and the rise of China. A corrective call is in order: China has declined on its own.

A more formidable challenge to the U.S. world hegemony would be a strategic alliance between these two mighty states, Russia and China. This triangular relation played out potently in the previous rounds of hegemonic contestation. The triumph of the Communist Party in the Chinese Civil War (1949) was a major boost for the Soviet Union and a major preoccupation for the United States, which has since been even more deeply involved in East Asia. However, Nixon's visit to China in 1972 widened the wedge between the two Communist powers alienated since the Sino-Soviet Split that started evolving in 1956. By 1979, American diplomacy redrew the map of strategic alliances by snatching Communist China out of the Soviet sphere and into the hegemonic camp.

Right now, we are witnessing a process working the other way around, with Russia and China becoming ever closer as they both become more alienated from the United States. The consolidation of this alliance represents both a stronger challenge for the U.S. world hegemony and a reassurance for authoritarian regimes and parties around the world willing to cluster themselves around this mighty coalition. Such associates would be willing to embrace the authoritarian dream, the only one that this strategic partnership seems to provide: there is no such thing as the "Russian Dream," and the "China Dream" has been tailored for Chinese only.

It is amidst this process of an emerging strategic Russo-Chinese alliance that the European Union may have a major role to play. As a major consumer of Russian oil and gas exports, the EU can be a counterweight to the allure of embracing a strategic alliance with China. For that to happen, the EU needs to find ways to articulate a foreign policy that is unified from within and independent from the United States. And if that were to happen, counterbalancing Russia's attraction toward China could be just a sideshow. The EU, the largest world economy, a powerhouse of research and development forwardly looking into a post-fossil fuels economy could become a candidate for world hegemon; and if not world hegemon, then a fourth contender for world hegemony.

Such a scenario could transform the hegemonic world order into a genuine multi-polar one, with four major states simultaneously collaborating and competing in multiple and fluid changing configurations: China bouncing between its collaborations with Russia and the United States; Russia with China and the EU; and the United States and the EU with one another and with China. Such multilateral collaborations between the two bastions of authoritarianism and the two bastions of democracy are possible. Democracies have an ample history of close collaborations with authoritarian regimes throughout the last 170 years. Moreover, democracies have been eclipsed during the last decade.

Hence, another cluster of questions concerning the lasting patterns has to do with the present and future of democracy and dictatorship. Looking at the last 170 years panoramically to tackle questions about the evolution of political regimes shows very prominently the stellar development that democracy has undergone in gaining terrain from perennial authoritarianism. However, the historical trajectory also shows that the global rise of democracy, far from being a steadily rising straight line, has experienced major backlashes, throughout the 1920s to the 1940s, during the 1960s and 1970s, and now. Democratic regimes grew deep roots and gained permanent status only in societies atop the world pyramid of wealth and power: The North Atlantic nations and offspring states (e.g., Australia and New Zealand). For the rest of the world, it was either a recurring fluctuation between dictatorships and democratic periods (e.g., Latin American and African republics) or outright dictatorships (e.g., Russia, Central Asia, and China), with the remarkable exception of the world's largest democracy, India. It was only with Third Wave Democracy that this type of regime has become globally generalized. Many of the accomplishments of the First Wave of Democracy and most of those of the second were rolled back by undemocratic waves. Third Wave Democracy seems to be no different in this regard.

Moreover, even while Third Wave Democracy was formally blooming during the 1990s and 2000s there were very firm limits to the democratic nature of its democracies. First, democratic elections are mediated by lobbying and funding of elections. That allows big money to speak at high volumes through the power of advertisement to manipulate the electorate. Second, in the context of a tightly interdependent neoliberal global economy, the range of policymaking maneuverability by freely elected governments has been highly constrained. Currently, the compounding impacts of the internet, social media, "fake news," and the algorithms of the Artificial Intelligence Revolution that identify what makes each one of us tick present a refined venue to more effectively manipulate electoral results. The manipulation is conducted both by contending political parties within a democracy and by foreign states willing to meddle in the fate of other countries. Third Wave democracies are, then, currently facing a detrimental oscillation away from democracy, as in the past, but now compounded by the impact of these new technological tools that are further enhancing anti-democratic practices.

This preoccupation with the role of new technologies in the present and future of political life can be paired with similar concerns pertaining to economic and social life. This currently unfolding technological revolution is also depicted as being geared to deepen socioeconomic inequalities. In the most dystopian of scenarios, such inequalities are expected to reach qualitatively unprecedented levels that would make not just for a confrontation between social classes but between different species, one deriving from the new useless class, the other from the ruling oligarchies. Following the track of the interplay between technological innovation and inequality for 170 years shows, indeed, a close correspondence between revolutionary technological innovations and the widening of socioeconomic gaps.

That was the case with the Industrial Revolution, which consolidated a pyramidal social urban structure, and with the Information Revolution, which added a digital divide to mounting socioeconomic inequalities. And yet, the substantial innovations brought by the Second Industrial Revolution corresponded with a period in which socioeconomic gaps shrank. To some extent, that result was intrinsic to the specific types of technological innovations that led to mass production and hence required wealth redistribution to make mass consumption affordable and the business cycle successful. But the decrease in socioeconomic inequalities in tandem with a major wave of technological innovation was also the result of governmental policies decidedly targeting this goal. Hence, what this sequence of interplays between three major technological waves of innovations and the fluctuations in socioeconomic inequalities shows is that it is for political will to determine what sort of impact technological innovations will have on socioeconomic inequalities. As with all previous technological achievements, the resulting enhanced economies could further enthrone the owners of the means of production, setting them even more apart from the rest of society. Alternatively, the enhanced resources of the economies could be made to serve society at large.

Another source of socioeconomic inequality is economic globalization. A global business elite, a global middle class, and a global precariat have been emerging in tandem with the unfolding of globalization. A wide gulf divides these three global classes. Economic globalization is currently being confronted by a protectionist backlash with "America First" policies as its epicenter. The past 170-year trajectory shows that economic globalization comes and goes in sync with the decline of the world hegemon. At the present, just when the downward spiraling of retaliatory protectionist steps seemed to be reaching a truce if not an end, the outbreak of the COVID-19 epidemic, with its immediate and long-term economic repercussions poses an additional challenge. The cautionary tale emerging from the past regarding economic globalization is that efforts at international collaboration are needed to sustain it.

The previous period of economic de-globalization (1929–1970s) witnessed a significant narrowing of socioeconomic inequalities within and between societies, the so-called Great Compression. The context, however, was entirely different. Back then, inequality gaps closed due to the sheer devastation caused by two world wars; to deliberate attempts made throughout the Global South to industrialize and catch up; and last but not least to wealth and income redistributive policies embraced throughout the world. This time around, as economic globalization stalls socioeconomic inequalities continue widening. Fair trade rather than free trade would account for narrowing disparities between societies while redistributive policies are the proven way to do the same domestically.

The handling of globalization also poses major repercussions in confronting climate change. More global collaboration is required to confront this global problem. No single state or group of states can tackle it single-handedly. More globalization is also needed to spread the word about the major sources of contamination driving global warming, starting with the animal farming industry. Paradoxically, however, *less* globalization is also required. Consuming locally, as well as traveling less to reduce the carbon footprint of transportation, is mandatory. That is, consuming responsibly, by "refusing, reducing, and reusing," would also mean less globalization for the sake of reducing detrimental emissions.

At the present moment, contestation of U.S. world hegemony is synchronized with mounting challenges on both the globalized economy and on global democracy. From this *Brief History of Now*, we know that economic globalization can evaporate if world hegemony does; that also applies to the prominence of democratic regimes. However, from past patterns, we know that when this triple correspondence unfolds, socioeconomic inequalities shrink, which is not the case now, as those are actually continuing to grow. We also know that hegemonic decline is preceded by displacement in technological leadership, which the United States is not experiencing even if the technological competition is tightening as never before. Patterns can provide some guidance by their heuristic power, but patterns have their limits.

GLOBAL TRAJECTORIES CRYSTALIZED IN GLOBAL REGIMES

Limitations and all, the sequence of convoluted developments side by side with their underlying patterns of six major trajectories highlights two important conclusions about how world societies evolve across time and space. The most crucial developments that led us from 1851 to now—the surge of free trade and comparative advantage in the wake of the industrial and democratic revolutions; the First, Second, and Cold Wars; decolonization; the rise and demise of a communist counter-hegemonic sphere with worldwide repercussions in both instances; and global economic recessions (starting 1873 and 2008, respectively) and depressions—all of them had a global reach in real time. That is, all world societies were affected by these major developments simultaneously and subsequently, with more or less prominent lasting effects in every case. In other words, these globally outreaching developments made these last 170 years of history global in their spatial scope. The world's societies, for all their singularities and specificities, experienced a unifying shared history even if the impacts of the global developments affected them to different extents.

Moreover, world societies were not only making and being impacted by the same major developments simultaneously and subsequently but were also part and had been embarked in the same major trends presented in this *Brief History of Now*. As such, all world societies participated in the same overarching trajectory made by the convergence of these five trends for the last 170 years. All world societies were subject to the remarkable synchronicity in which the fivefold correspondence oscillated with its cadence of expansions and contractions of world hegemony and globalization, technological breakthrough, shifts in socioeconomic inequalities, and political regime cycles. Exposing the synchronicity of these global developments and patterns allows us to visualize that for the last 170 years world societies had been ruled by four major global regimes.

A global regime consists of a set of fundamental assumptions, prevailing worldwide, that determine the allocation of power in society, the geographical scope of economic activity, and the desirable model of society. These assumptions include: How is power distributed in society? What is the relevant unit for running the economy? What is the desirable model of society to be built?

One way to depict the distribution of power in society is by identifying how much of it is concentrated into each of the three major constituent sectors, or building blocks, that make up every modern society: a governmental set of institutions in charge of the political sphere; the owners of the means of production and services dominating the economic activity; and a civil society made of the vast bulk of the members of society organized into households, ruled by the governmental institutions, working for and consuming the products and services of the economy. Next, the geographical scope of economic activity is a matter of scale that defines the targeted units for that activity: Are the intended boundaries of economic activity overlapping with those of the empire or the nation-state, or are these boundaries dislodged such that economies can move beyond political boundaries? The fundamental choice is about protecting more, less, or not at all the economic activity within sovereign boundaries from the economic activity everywhere else; in short, protectionism or liberalism. Finally, two key instances for defining a desirable model of society are the degree of tolerance or intolerance for both socioeconomic inequality and cultural heterogeneity.

During the global trajectory described by the fivefold correspondence, major changes took place in the ways in which these fundamental assumptions were conceived and deployed. Defining who holds most social power—government, owners, or civil society; whether economic interactions should be flowing in a protectionist or liberal framework; and the degrees of tolerance for socioeconomic inequality and cultural hetero-geneity resulted in the constitution of four global regimes that have been ruling the fates of world societies. These global regimes are: imperial liberalism, statism, neoliberalism, and currently, still in the process of coalescing, ethno-religious-nationalistic demotarianism (Diagram 8.3).

Imperial liberalism, in place between 1851 and 1914, ruled over a world carved up between some ten empires (Chinese, Ottoman, Russian, German, Austro-Hungarian, French, Belgian, Spanish, Portuguese, American); their colonies (most of Africa, South and Southeast Asia), protectorates, and dependencies (e.g., New Zealand, Australia, Canada, Egypt, and Hong Kong); and independent states deeply embedded in the webs of informal empires (most prominently the oligarchic republics of Latin America). This global regime was highly hierarchical, with the imperial metropoles on top, the colonies at the bottom, and the protec-torates, dependencies, and the informally embedded independent states in between. In this liberal imperialist regime, social power was concentrated in the hands of empires, hierarchically arranged, with the British Empire atop. Given the ideologies and policies of free trade and comparative advantage that this world hegemon had espoused by 1851 and onward, the envisioned geographical scope of economic activity was global.

This aim was contested by the protectionist policies of the two other mightiest empires, the German and the American, as well as by a general-ized protectionist interlude in the wake of the Great Recession of 1873.

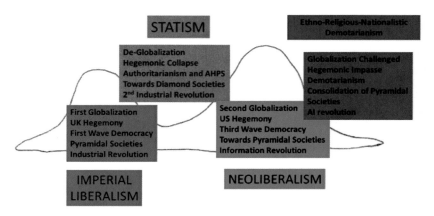

Diagram 8.3 Four global regimes, 1850–2020

Overall, however, during the second half of the nineteenth century and continuing up until the outbreak of the First World War, the world was mostly open for free trade. As for the desirable model of society, it was, like the world power structure itself, highly hierarchical with high tolerance for socioeconomic inequality and low tolerance for cultural heterogeneity. One of the self-assigned tasks of liberal imperialism was its civilizing mission to disseminate the superior culture of the empire domestically and abroad regardless of the resulting flagrant socioeconomic inequalities.

The outbreak of the First World War signaled the beginning of the end of the British world hegemony, economic globalization, and First Wave Democracy. By then, the Second Industrial Revolution was firmly consolidated and a new global regime, statism, was starting to emerge toward its global consolidation by the 1930s. It was fostered by the Communist Revolution in Russia and its repercussions, the Great Depression, and the Second World War. The demise of the statist global regime started in the mid-1970s and by the opening of the 1990s it was fully displaced.

More than any other global regime, statism assumed a wide variety of appearances in societies as deeply different from one another as Communist, fascist, and democratic with market economies. Yet, underneath these drastic differences, some fundamental commonalities existed in the primordial assumptions about the main locus of power, the type of insertion in the world economy, and the desirable model of society. For this second global regime, social power was concentrated in the hands of nation-states. This time period coincides with the progressive dismantlement of empires unfolding between 1918 onward, the independence of former colonies, protectorates, and dependencies, and the reassertion of national sovereignty and economic independence by already existing nation-states that had been caught in the webs of informal empires. Under this global regime, nation-states expanded the realms of action beyond the mere political sphere to intervene and shape economy and society as well. In so doing, nation-states regulated and controlled the interactions between their national economies and the wider world economy as well as the domestic activity. The exception to this trend was the new world hegemon—the United States—which progressively managed to make more and more inroads into the economies of its allies and client states, taming their protectionist policies and pushing for the adoption of freer trade. State interventionism was also to be found in the lack of tolerance for both socioeconomic inequalities and cultural heterogeneity.

The statist global regime led to the Great Compression and the "melting pot."

The global revolt of 1968 was followed by a string of regional developments that shocked the prevailing global regime, culminating in the 1989 global revolution. During this 30-year time period, the statist global regime was gradually dismantled and replaced by the neoliberal global regime that had fully crystallized by 1990. The world map at this point was carved into almost 200 independent states, most of them inherited from the age of the statist global regime. Although these nation-states remained in place, they lost much of their power to the owners of the means of production and services, which were for the most part corporations. The proactive role that the state had been adopting since the outbreak of the First World War in mobilizing and managing economy and society was replaced by a proactive dismantling of those state capacities: the economy was privatized and deregulated, public spending decreased and with that wealth and income redistribution sharply diminished. The vacuum left by the withdrawal of the state as the key container of social power was quickly filled by international institutions, regional trade blocks, and multinational corporations. Deregulation also meant the opening up of domestic economies to the global economy. Last but not least, the neoliberal global regime displayed high levels of tolerance for both socioeconomic inequality and cultural heterogeneity. This global regime promoted the socioeconomic Great Bifurcation and the cultural salad bowl.

To a large extent, the neoliberal global regime is still present. However, since the last global recession, the emergence of a new global regime started to become more visible, reaching prominence in the 2010s, and probably moving toward full coalescence into the 2020s. In this rising fourth global regime, ethno-religious-nationalistic demotarianism, the state is reasserting its presence as a locus of power through the interventionist role of the ruler—often a charismatic populist—and to differing extents the ruler's party. This is by no means a comeback of the interventionist states of the statist era. Now, the corporations retain and even enlarge their concentration of power. The interventions of the ruler under this new global regime are oriented toward, on the one hand, their perpetuation in power and, on the other hand, on tackling the grievances that the neoliberal regime imposed upon their constituencies. For those countries that defined the globalism of the previous regime as detrimental, the response is protectionism. For the constituencies punished by the growing socioeconomic inequality and/or disgruntled by cultural diversity, the response is a reactionary bigotry against the blooming salad bowl of the previous era and the assertion of new forms of the primordial ethno-religious-nationalistic identities that once were at the center of the melting pot. Socioeconomic inequality is rarely addressed by deploying redistributive policies reminiscent of the statist era (Diagram 8.4).

No two empires, colonies, or dependencies were like each other in the age of liberal imperialism. There was a world of difference between political regimes in the age of statism. The global implementation of neoliberalism was the most thorough, systematic, and homogeneous among the four global regimes, with its epicenter in the International Monetary Fund and the World Bank and with its unifying credo set in stone as the Washington Consensus. But even then, every country reshaped by neoliberalism had its singularities. Conversely, now as the multiple authoritarian regimes and illiberal democracies run their economies and societies, a degree of similarity clearly surfaces, even though it is also clear that each case has its peculiarities. So, there is clearly much to be said for each tree, and vast literatures are indeed devoted to that. However, there is still room to point toward the forests. Far from being mutually exclusive, inclusivity is the way to grasp the singularities of each tree and the general features of the forests.

By zooming out and identifying the most impactful developments worldwide, the recurring patterns underneath these four global regimes that have ruled over world societies for the last 170 years become visible. The proof of the pudding is in the eating: Take a world map. Pick one country. Ponder its trajectory. Doesn't it conform to the sequence of the four global regimes? Repeat the exercise as many times as you wish. Of course, multiple qualifications and nuances are required, with slight time adjustments for the beginning and end of each era. Certainly, further specifications will be mandatory. But overall, we can appreciate the extent to which time synchronicity had a global reach, making the trajectories presented in the *Brief History of Now* truly global. We were all embarked on these trajectories that has brought us to the present moment.

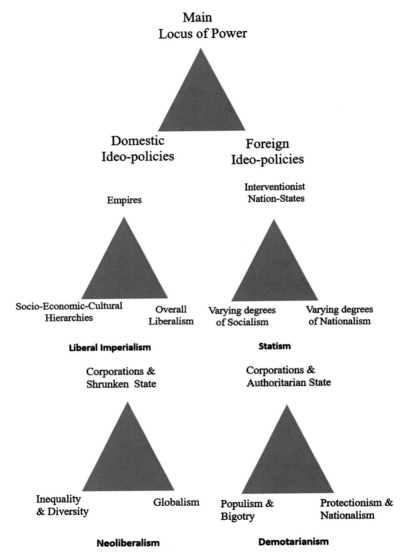

Diagram 8.4 The pillars of the four global regimes

Index

Made in the USA
Las Vegas, NV
28 June 2022